Prepare for Microsoft's tough simulation questions with the brand-new WinSim 2000 program!

✔ Use the simulators to guide you through real-world tasks step-by-step, or watch the movies to see the "invisible hand" perform the tasks for you.

Search through two complete books in PDF–MCSE: Windows 2000 Directory Services Adminstration Study Guide *and the* Dictionary of Networking!

✔ Access the entire *MCSE: Windows 2000 Directory Services Administration Study Guide*, complete with figures and tables, in electronic format.

✔ Search the *MCSE: Windows 2000 Directory Services Administration Study Guide* chapters to find information on any topic in seconds.

✔ Look up any networking term in the *Dictionary of Networking*.

SYBEX®

MCSE: Windows 2000 Directory Services Administration Study Guide
Exam 70-217: Objectives

OBJECTIVE	PAGE
Installing, Configuring, and Troubleshooting Active Directory	
Install, configure, and troubleshoot the components of Active Directory.	127, 134, 161, 206, 214, 234, 237, 247, 252, 257
• Install Active Directory.	127
• Create sites.	234
• Create subnets.	237
• Create site links.	247
• Create site link bridges.	247
• Create connection objects.	252
• Create global catalog servers.	214
• Move server objects between sites.	257
• Transfer operations master roles.	206
• Verify Active Directory installation.	134
• Implement an organizational unit (OU) structure.	161
Back up and restore Active Directory.	414, 426
• Perform an authoritative restore of Active Directory.	414, 426
• Recover from a system failure.	414, 426
Installing, Configuring, Managing, Monitoring, and Troubleshooting DNS for Active Directory	
Install, configure, and troubleshoot DNS for Active Directory.	69, 85, 90
• Integrate Active Directory DNS zones with non-Active Directory DNS zones.	69, 85, 90
• Configure zones for dynamic updates.	69, 85, 90
Manage, monitor, and troubleshoot DNS.	88, 98
• Manage replication of DNS data.	88, 98
Installing, Configuring, Managing, Monitoring, Optimizing, and Troubleshooting Change and Configuration Management	
Implement and troubleshoot Group Policy.	454, 466
• Create a Group Policy object (GPO).	454
• Link an existing GPO.	454
• Delegate administrative control of Group Policy.	466
• Modify Group Policy inheritance.	466
• Filter Group Policy settings by associating security groups to GPOs.	466
• Modify Group Policy.	454
Manage and troubleshoot user environments by using Group Policy.	454, 466
• Control user environments by using administrative templates.	454, 466
• Assign script policies to users and computers.	454, 466

SYBEX

NOTE Exam objectives are subject to change at any time without prior notice and at Microsoft's sole discretion. Please visit Microsoft's Training & Certification Web site (www.microsoft.com/Train_Cert) for the most current listing of exam objectives.

SYBEX

MCSE:
Windows 2000
Directory Services Administration
Study Guide

MCSE:
Windows® 2000
Directory Services Administration
Study Guide

Anil Desai

with James Chellis

San Francisco • Paris • Düsseldorf • Soest • London

SYBEX

Associate Publisher: Neil Edde
Contracts and Licensing Manager: Kristine O'Callaghan
Developmental Editors: Dann McDorman and Ben Tomkins
Editor: Julie Sakaue
Production Editor: Teresa Trego
Technical Editors: Michael Chacon and Donald Fuller
Book Designer: Bill Gibson
Graphic Illustrator: Tony Jonick
Electronic Publishing Specialist: Nila Nichols
Proofreader: Andrea Fox
Indexer: Ted Laux
CD Coordinator: Kara Eve Schwartz
CD Technician: Keith McNeil
Cover Designer: Archer Design
Cover Illustrator/Photographer: Natural Selection

Library of Congress Card Number: 00-105385

ISBN: 0-7821-2756-8

SYBEX and the SYBEX logo are trademarks of SYBEX Inc. in the USA and other countries.

The CD interface was created using Macromedia Director, ©1994, 1997-1999 Macromedia Inc. For more information on Macromedia and Macromedia Director, visit http://www.macromedia.com.

Internet screen shot(s) using Microsoft Internet Explorer 5.0 reprinted by permission from Microsoft Corporation.

Microsoft® Internet Explorer © 1996 Microsoft Corporation. All rights reserved. Microsoft, the Microsoft Internet Explorer logo, Windows, Windows NT, and the Windows logo are either registered trademarks or trademarks of Microsoft Corporation in the United States and/or other countries.

Use of the Microsoft Approved Study Guide logo on this product signifies that it has been independently reviewed and approved in compliance with the following standards:

- acceptable coverage of all content related to Microsoft exam number 70-217, entitled Implementing and Administering a Microsoft Windows 2000 Directory Services Infrastructure;
- sufficient performance-based exercises that relate closely to all required content; and
- technically accurate content, based on sampling of text.

SYBEX is an independent entity from Microsoft Corporation, and not affiliated with Microsoft Corporation in any manner. This publication may be used in assisting students to prepare for a Microsoft Certified Professional Exam. Neither Microsoft Corporation, its designated review company, nor SYBEX warrants that use of this publication will ensure passing the relevant exam. Microsoft is either a registered trademark or trademark of Microsoft Corporation in the United States and/or other countries.

TRADEMARKS: SYBEX has attempted throughout this book to distinguish proprietary trademarks from descriptive terms by following the capitalization style used by the manufacturer.

The author and publisher have made their best efforts to prepare this book, and the content is based upon final release software whenever possible. Portions of the manuscript may be based upon pre-release versions supplied by software manufacturer(s). The author and the publisher make no representation or warranties of any kind with regard to the completeness or accuracy of the contents herein and accept no liability of any kind including but not limited to performance, merchantability, fitness for any particular purpose, or any losses or damages of any kind caused or alleged to be caused directly or indirectly from this book.

Manufactured in the United States of America

10 9 8 7 6 5 4 3 2 1

SYBEX

To Our Valued Readers:

In recent years, Microsoft's MCSE program has established itself as the premier computer and networking industry certification. Nearly a quarter of a million IT professionals have attained MCSE status in the NT 4 track. Sybex is proud to have helped thousands of MCSE candidates prepare for their exams over these years, and we are excited about the opportunity to continue to provide people with the skills they'll need to succeed in the highly competitive IT industry.

For the Windows 2000 MCSE track, Microsoft has made it their mission to demand more of exam candidates. Exam developers have gone to great lengths to raise the bar in order to prevent a paper-certification syndrome, one in which individuals obtain a certification without a thorough understanding of the technology. Sybex welcomes this new philosophy as we have always advocated a comprehensive instructional approach to certification courseware. It has always been Sybex's mission to teach exam candidates how new technologies work in the real world, not to simply feed them answers to test questions. Sybex was founded on the premise of providing technical skills to IT professionals, and we have continued to build on that foundation, making significant improvements to our study guides based on feedback from readers, suggestions from instructors, and comments from industry leaders.

The depth and breadth of technical knowledge required to obtain Microsoft's new Windows 2000 MCSE is staggering. Sybex has assembled some of the most technically skilled instructors in the industry to write our study guides, and we're confident that our Windows 2000 MCSE study guides will meet and exceed the demanding standards both of Microsoft and you, the exam candidate.

Good luck in pursuit of your MCSE!

Neil Edde
Associate Publisher—Certification
Sybex, Inc.

SYBEX Inc. 1151 Marina Village Parkway, Alameda, CA 94501
Tel: 510/523-8233   Fax: 510/523-2373   HTTP://www.sybex.com

To Monica

Acknowledgments

As professionals in the IT industry, many of you have probably learned the value of teamwork. Therefore, it will probably come as no surprise to you that this book is the result of a lot of hard work from several people. In this brief section, I'll try to give credit where it's due.

During the last year, I've had the pleasure of working with many energetic, enthusiastic, and driven people at QuickArrow, Inc. At first, I was planning to acknowledge some of the people that I work with. But, it's much more appropriate to thank all of them. Just a few short months ago, I could have easily listed the names of everyone in the company on this page. We used to be a small team with big plans. Things have changed, and we're now a large team (with even bigger plans). The company has grown dramatically, without sacrificing focus and dedication. In particular, I'd like to thank Abdul Malik Yoosufani for his continued support, technical direction, and leadership of such a great company.

Next, I'd like to thank the many people at Sybex with whom I have worked on this project. Thanks to Neil Edde, Ben Tomkins, and Dann McDorman for their assistance in the writing process. And, as operating systems get more and more complex, it seems to become increasingly important to verify the accuracy of technical information. That's why technical input from Michael Chacon and Donald Fuller was so important. Special thanks must go to Julie Sakaue, the editor with whom I worked most closely throughout the duration of this project. She's planning to run a full marathon soon, but I'm sure that will be a walk in the park compared to her hard work on this project! Thanks also to James Chellis and Matthew Sheltz for their work on the WinSim tool and other content that you'll find on the accompanying CD-ROM. And finally, thanks to Teresa Trego for steering this project through the many twists and turns that it took before going to the printer and to Nila Nichols and Andrea Fox for making sure everything looked just right on the pages before you. I thank all of these people for making my job easier, and you can thank them for making this book a complete, accurate, and valuable resource for IT professionals.

Acknowledgements are difficult to write (at least for me), but the Dedication was an easy choice—my wife, Monica, has always been a great source of support and encouragement, despite the seemingly incessant clicking of my keyboard throughout the night and through long weekends of writing.

Finally, thanks to you—the reader—for using this book. I'm confident that the information you find here will be an excellent resource as you prepare to work with Windows 2000 in the real world. For most of you, I suspect that it will be a challenge. However, I trust that it will be a personally and professionally rewarding one.

If you have any questions or comments about the contents of the book, please feel free to e-mail me at `anil@austin.rr.com`. Good luck!

Contents at a Glance

Contents

Table of Exercises

Introduction

Microsoft's new Microsoft Certified Systems Engineer (MCSE) track for Windows 2000 is the premier certification for computer industry professionals. Covering the core technologies around which Microsoft's future will be built, the new MCSE certification is a powerful credential for career advancement.

This book has been developed, in cooperation with Microsoft Corporation, to give you the critical skills and knowledge you need to prepare for one of the core requirements of the new MCSE certification program, Implementing and Administering Windows 2000 Directory Services. You will find the information you need to acquire a solid understanding of how to setup and manage the Active Directory, to prepare for Exam 70-217: *Implementing and Administering a Microsoft Windows 2000 Directory Services Infrastructure*, and to progress toward MCSE certification.

Why Become Certified in Windows 2000?

As the computer network industry grows in both size and complexity, the need for *proven* ability is increasing. Companies rely on certifications to verify the skills of prospective employees and contractors.

Whether you are just getting started or are ready to move ahead in the computer industry, the knowledge, skills, and credentials you have are your most valuable assets. Microsoft has developed its Microsoft Certified Professional (MCP) program to give you credentials that verify your ability to work with Microsoft products effectively and professionally. The MCP credential for professionals who work with Microsoft Windows 2000 networks is the new MCSE certification.

Over the next few years, companies around the world will deploy millions of copies of Windows 2000 as the central operating system for their mission-critical networks. This will generate an enormous need for qualified consultants and personnel to design, deploy, and support Windows 2000 networks.

Windows 2000 is a huge product that requires professional skills of its administrators. Consider that Windows NT 4 has about 12 million lines of code, while Windows 2000 has more than 35 million! Much of this code is needed to deal with the wide range of functionality that Windows 2000 offers.

Windows 2000 actually consists of several different versions:

Windows 2000 Professional   The client edition of Windows 2000, which is comparable to Windows NT 4 Workstation, but also includes the best features of Windows 98 and many new features.

Windows 2000 Server/Windows 2000 Advanced Server   A server edition of Windows 2000 for small to mid-sized deployments. Advanced Server supports more memory and processors than Server does.

Windows 2000 Datacenter Server   A server edition of Windows 2000 for large, wide-scale deployments and computer clusters. Datacenter Server supports the most memory and processors of the three versions.

With such an expansive operating system, companies need to be certain that you are the right person for the job being offered. The MCSE is designed to help prove that you are.

As part of its promotion of Windows 2000, Microsoft has announced that MCSEs who have passed the Windows NT 4 core exams must upgrade their certifications to the new Windows 2000 track by December 31, 2001 to remain certified. The MCSE Study Guide series published by Sybex covers the full range of exams required for either obtaining or upgrading your certification. For more information, see the "Exam Requirements" section later in this Introduction.

Is This Book for You?

If you want to acquire a solid foundation in implementing and administering Windows 2000 Directory Services, this book is for you. You'll find clear explanations of the fundamental concepts you need to grasp.

If you want to become certified as an MCSE, this book is definitely for you. However, if you just want to attempt to pass the exam without really understanding Windows 2000, this book is *not* for you. This book is written for those who want to acquire hands-on skills and in-depth knowledge of Windows 2000.

If your goal is to prepare for the exam by learning how to use and manage the new operating system, this book is for you. It will help you to achieve the high level of professional competency you need to succeed in this field.

What Does This Book Cover?

This book contains detailed explanations, hands-on exercises, and review questions to test your knowledge.

Think of this book as your complete guide to implementing and administering Windows 2000 Directory Services. It begins by presenting an overview of the Active Directory. Next, you will learn how to perform important tasks, including:

- Creating a Windows 2000 Active Directory domain

- Installing and configuring objects within the Active Directory

- Monitoring and managing various aspects of the Active Directory

- Managing new features of the Active Directory, including security configuration, the use of Group Policies, DNS, and software deployment

- Working with the Active Directory in distributed network environments

- Troubleshooting various aspects of the Active Directory

Throughout the book, you will be guided through hands-on exercises, which give you practical experience for each exam objective. At the end of each chapter, you'll find a summary of the topics covered in the chapter, which also includes a list of the key terms used in that chapter. The key terms represent not only the terminology that you should recognize, but also the underlying concepts that you should understand to pass the exam. All of the key terms are defined in the glossary at the back of the study guide.

Finally, each chapter concludes with 20 review questions that test your knowledge of the information covered. You'll find an entire practice exam, with 50 additional questions, in Appendix A. Many more questions, as well as multimedia demonstrations of the hands-on exercises, are included on the CD that accompanies this book, as explained in the "What's on the CD?" section at the end of this Introduction.

The topics covered in this book map directly to Microsoft's official exam objectives. Each exam objective is covered completely.

How Do You Become an MCSE?

Attaining MCSE certification has always been a challenge. However, in the past, individuals could acquire detailed exam information—even most of the exam questions—from online "brain dumps" and third-party "cram" books or software products. For the new MCSE exams, this simply will not be the case.

To avoid the "paper-MCSE syndrome" (a devaluation of the MCSE certification because unqualified individuals manage to pass the exams), Microsoft has taken strong steps to protect the security and integrity of the new MCSE track. Prospective MSCEs will need to complete a course of study that provides not only detailed knowledge of a wide range of topics, but true skills derived from working with Windows 2000 and related software products.

In the new MCSE program, Microsoft is heavily emphasizing hands-on skills. Microsoft has stated that, "Nearly half of the core required exams' content demands that the candidate have troubleshooting skills acquired through hands-on experience and working knowledge."

Fortunately, if you are willing to dedicate time and effort with Windows 2000, you can prepare for the exams by using the proper tools. If you work through this book and the other books in this series, you should successfully meet the exam requirements.

This book is a part of a complete series of Sybex MCSE Study Guides, published by Sybex, that covers the five core Windows 2000 requirements as well as the new Design electives you need to complete your MCSE track. Titles include:

- MCSE: Windows 2000 Professional Study Guide

- MCSE: Windows 2000 Server Study Guide

- MCSE: Windows 2000 Network Infrastructure Administration Study Guide

- MCSE: Windows 2000 Network Security Design Study Guide

- MCSE: Windows 2000 Network Infrastructure Design Study Guide

- MCSE: Windows 2000 Directory Services Design Study Guide

There are also study guides available from Sybex on additional MCSE electives.

Exam Requirements

Successful candidates must pass a minimum set of exams that measure technical proficiency and expertise:

- Candidates for MCSE certification must pass seven exams, including four core operating system exams, one design exam, and two electives.

- Candidates who have already passed three Windows NT 4 exams (70-067, 70-068, and 70-073) may opt to take an "accelerated" exam plus one core design exam and two electives.

If you do not pass the accelerated exam after one attempt, you must pass the five core requirements and two electives.

The following table shows the exams a new certification candidate must pass.

All of these exams are required

Exam #	Title	Requirement Met
70-216	Implementing and Administering a Microsoft® Windows® 2000 Network Infrastructure	Core (Operating System)
70-210	Installing, Configuring, and Administering Microsoft® Windows® 2000 Professional	Core (Operating System)
70-215	Installing, Configuring, and Administering Microsoft® Windows® 2000 Server	Core (Operating System)
70-217	Implementing and Administering a Microsoft® Windows® 2000 Directory Services Infrastructure	Core (Operating System)

One of these exams is required

Exam #	Title	Requirement Met
70-219	Designing a Microsoft® Windows® 2000 Directory Services Infrastructure	Core (Design)
70-220	Designing Security for a Microsoft® Windows® 2000 Network	Core (Design)
70-221	Designing a Microsoft® Windows® 2000 Network Infrastructure	Core (Design)

Two of these exams are required

Exam #	Title	Requirement Met
70-219	Designing a Microsoft® Windows® 2000 Directory Services Infrastructure	Elective
70-220	Designing Security for a Microsoft® Windows® 2000 Network	Elective
70-221	Designing a Microsoft® Windows® 2000 Network Infrastructure	Elective
Any current MCSE elective	Exams cover topics such as Exchange Server, SQL Server, Systems Management Server, Internet Explorer Administrators Kit, and Proxy Server (new exams are added regularly)	Elective

For a more detailed description of the Microsoft certification programs, including a list of current MCSE electives, check Microsoft's Training and Certification Web site at www.microsoft.com/train_cert.

The Implementing and Administering Windows 2000 Directory Services Exam

The Implementing and Administering Windows 2000 Directory Services exam covers concepts and skills related to installing, configuring, and managing the Active Directory. It emphasizes the following areas related to working with Windows 2000 Directory Services:

- Concepts related to the Windows 2000 Directory Services

- Preparing your network environment for Windows 2000 Directory Services

- Installing the Active Directory

- Configuring and managing features of the Active Directory

- Monitoring and optimizing the Active Directory

- Managing the Active Directory in distributed network environments

- Managing Active Directory environments through the use of security features, Group Policy settings, and software deployment tools

- Troubleshooting problems with the Active Directory

This exam can be quite specific regarding setting up and administering Windows 2000 Directory Services requirements and operational settings, and it can be particular about how administrative tasks are performed in the operating system. It also focuses on fundamental concepts that are related to the way an Active Directory environment is implemented. Careful study of this book, along with hands-on experience, will help you to prepare for this exam.

Microsoft provides exam objectives to give you a very general overview of possible areas of coverage of the Microsoft exams. For your convenience, we have added in-text objectives listings at the points in the text where specific Microsoft exam objectives are covered. However, exam objectives are subject to change at any time without prior notice and at Microsoft's sole discretion. Please visit Microsoft's Training and Certification Web site (www.microsoft .com/Train_Cert) for the most current exam objectives listing.

Types of Exam Questions

In the previous tracks, the formats of the MCSE exams were fairly straight-forward, consisting almost entirely of multiple-choice questions appearing in a few different sets. Prior to taking an exam, you knew how many questions you would see and what type of questions would appear. If you had purchased the right third-party exam preparation products, you could even be quite familiar with the pool of questions you might be asked. As mentioned earlier, all of this is changing.

In an effort to both refine the testing process and protect the quality of its certifications, Microsoft has introduced adaptive testing, as well as some new exam elements. You will not know in advance which type of format you will see on your exam. These innovations make the exams more challenging, and they make it much more difficult for someone to pass an exam after simply "cramming" for it.

Microsoft will be accomplishing its goal of protecting the exams by regularly adding and removing exam questions, limiting the number of questions that any individual sees in a beta exam, limiting the number of questions delivered to an individual by using adaptive testing, and adding new exam elements.

Exam questions may be in multiple-choice, select-and-place, simulation, or case study-based formats. You may also find yourself taking an adaptive format exam. Let's take a look at the exam question types and adaptive testing, so you can be prepared for all of the possibilities.

Multiple-Choice Questions

Multiple-choice questions include two main types of questions. One is a straightforward type that presents a question, followed by several possible answers, of which one or more is correct.

The other type of multiple-choice question is more complex. This type presents a set of desired results along with a proposed solution. You must then decide which results would be achieved by the proposed solution.

You will see many multiple-choice questions in this study guide and on the accompanying CD, as well as on your exam.

Select-and-Place Questions

Select-and-place exam questions involve graphical elements that you must manipulate in order to successfully answer a question. For example, a question could present a diagram of a computer network, as shown below.

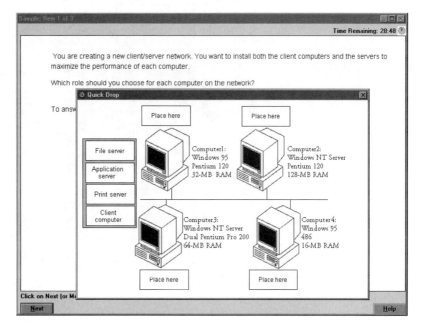

The diagram shows several computers next to boxes that contain the text "Place here." The labels represent different computer roles on a network, such as print server and file server. Based on information given for each computer, you are asked to drag and drop each label to the correct box. You need to place *all* of the labels correctly. No credit is given if you correctly label only some of the boxes.

Simulations

Simulations are the kinds of questions that most closely represent and test the actual skills you use while working with Microsoft software interfaces. These types of exam questions include a mock interface on which you must perform certain actions according to a given scenario. The simulated interfaces look nearly identical to what you see in the actual product, as shown in the example below.

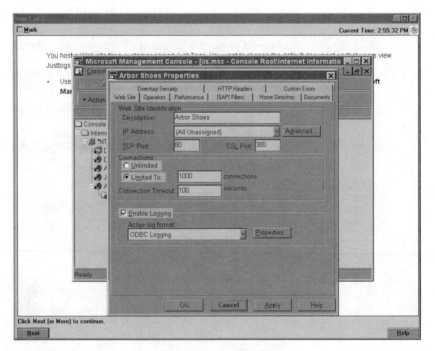

Simulations are by far the most complex element introduced into Microsoft exams to date. Because of the number of possible errors that can be made on simulations, it is worthwhile to consider the following recommendations from Microsoft:

- Do not change any simulation settings that don't pertain to the solution directly.

- Assume that the default settings are used when related information has not been provided.

- Make sure that your entries are spelled correctly.

- Close all of the simulation application windows after completing the set of tasks in the simulation.

The best way to prepare for the simulation questions is to spend time working with the graphical interface of the product on which you will be tested.

 We recommend that you study with the Edge Test WinSim 2000 product, which is included on the CD that accompanies this study guide. By completing the exercises in this study guide and working with the WinSim 2000 software, you can greatly improve your level of preparation for simulation questions.

Case Study-Based Questions

Case study-based questions first appeared in the Microsoft Certified Solution Developer program (Microsoft's certification program for software programmers). Case study-based questions present a scenario with a range of requirements. Based on the information provided, you need to answer a series of multiple-choice and ranking questions. The interface for case study-based questions has a number of tabs that each contains information about the scenario. At present, this type of question appears only in the Design exams.

Adaptive Exam Format

Microsoft presents many of its exams in an *adaptive* format. This format is radically different from the conventional format previously used for Microsoft certification exams. Conventional tests are static, containing a fixed number of questions. Adaptive tests change, or "adapt," depending on your answers to the questions presented.

The number of questions presented in your adaptive test will depend on how long it takes the exam to ascertain your level of ability (according to the statistical measurements on which the exam questions are ranked). To determine a test-taker's level of ability, the exam presents questions in increasing or decreasing order of difficulty.

Unlike the previous test format, the adaptive format will *not* allow you to go back to see a question again. The exam only goes forward. Once you enter your answer, that's it—you cannot change it. Be very careful before entering your answer. There is no time limit for each individual question (only for the exam as a whole). Your exam may be shortened by correct answers (or lengthened by incorrect answers), so there is no advantage to rushing through questions.

HOW ADAPTIVE EXAMS DETERMINE ABILITY LEVELS

As an example of how adaptive testing works, suppose that you know three people who are taking the exam: Herman, Sally, and Rashad. Herman doesn't know much about the subject, Sally is moderately informed, and Rashad is an expert.

Herman answers his first question incorrectly, so the exam presents him with a second, easier question. He misses that, so the exam gives him a few more easy questions, all of which he misses. Shortly thereafter, the exam ends, and he receives his failure report.

Sally answers her first question correctly, so the exam gives her a more difficult question, which she answers correctly. She then receives an even more difficult question, which she answers incorrectly. Next, the exam gives her a somewhat easier question, as it tries to gauge her level of understanding. After numerous questions of varying levels of difficulty, Sally's exam ends, perhaps with a passing score, perhaps not. Her exam included far more questions than were in Herman's exam, because her level of understanding needed to be more carefully tested to determine whether or not it was at a passing level.

When Rashad takes his exam, he answers his first question correctly, so he is given a more difficult question, which he also answers correctly. Next, the exam presents an even more difficult question, which he also answers correctly. He then is given a few more very difficult questions, all of which he answers correctly. Shortly thereafter, his exam ends. He passes. His exam was short, about as long as Herman's test.

BENEFITS OF ADAPTIVE TESTING

Microsoft has begun moving to adaptive testing for several reasons:

- It saves time by focusing only on the questions needed to determine a test-taker's abilities. An exam that might take an hour and a half in the conventional format could be completed in less than half that time when presented in adaptive format. The number of questions in an adaptive exam may be far fewer than the number required by a conventional exam.

- It protects the integrity of the exams. By exposing a fewer number of questions at any one time, it makes it more difficult for individuals to collect the questions in the exam pools with the intent of facilitating exam "cramming."

- It saves Microsoft and/or the test-delivery company money by reducing the amount of time it takes to deliver a test.

We recommend that you try the Edge Test Adaptive Exam, which is included on the CD that accompanies this study guide.

Exam Question Development

Microsoft follows an exam-development process consisting of eight mandatory phases. The process takes an average of seven months and involves more than 150 specific steps. The MCP exam development consists of the following phases:

Phase 1: Job Analysis   Phase 1 is an analysis of all the tasks that make up a specific job function, based on tasks performed by people who are currently performing that job function. This phase also identifies the knowledge, skills, and abilities that relate specifically to the performance area to be certified.

Phase 2: Objective Domain Definition   The results of the job analysis provide the framework used to develop objectives. The development of objectives involves translating the job-function tasks into a comprehensive set of more specific and measurable knowledge, skills, and abilities. The resulting list of objectives—the *objective domain*—is the basis for the development of both the certification exams and the training materials.

Phase 3: Blueprint Survey   The final objective domain is transformed into a blueprint survey in which contributors are asked to rate each objective. These contributors may be past MCP candidates, appropriately skilled exam development volunteers, or Microsoft employees. Based on the contributors' input, the objectives are prioritized and weighted. The actual exam items are written according to the prioritized objectives. Contributors are queried about how they spend their time on the job. If a contributor doesn't spend an adequate amount of time actually performing the specified job function, his or her data is eliminated from the analysis. The blueprint survey phase helps determine which objectives to measure, as well as the appropriate number and types of items to include on the exam.

Phase 4: Item Development   A pool of items is developed to measure the blueprinted objective domain. The number and types of items to be written are based on the results of the blueprint survey.

Phase 5: Alpha Review and Item Revision   During this phase, a panel of technical and job-function experts reviews each item for technical accuracy, then answers each item, reaching a consensus on all technical issues. Once the items have been verified as technically accurate, they are edited to ensure that they are expressed in the clearest language possible.

Phase 6: Beta Exam   The reviewed and edited items are collected into beta exams. Based on the responses of all beta participants, Microsoft performs a statistical analysis to verify the validity of the exam items and to determine which items will be used in the certification exam. Once the analysis has been completed, the items are distributed into multiple parallel forms, or *versions*, of the final certification exam.

Phase 7: Item Selection and Cut-Score Setting   The results of the beta exams are analyzed to determine which items should be included in the certification exam based on many factors, including item difficulty and relevance. During this phase, a panel of job-function experts determines the *cut score* (minimum passing score) for the exams. The cut score differs from exam to exam because it is based on an item-by-item determination of the percentage of candidates who answered the item correctly and who would be expected to answer the item correctly.

Phase 8: Live Exam   As the final phase, the exams are given to candidates. MCP exams are administered by Sylvan Prometric and Virtual University Enterprises (VUE).

Microsoft will regularly add and remove questions from the exams. This is called *item seeding*. It is part of the effort to make it more difficult for individuals to merely memorize exam questions passed along by previous test-takers.

Tips for Taking the Implementing and Administering Windows 2000 Directory Services Exam

Here are some general tips for taking the exam successfully:

- Arrive early at the exam center, so you can relax and review your study materials. During your final review, you can look over tables and lists of exam-related information.

- Read the questions carefully. Don't be tempted to jump to an early conclusion. Make sure you know *exactly* what the question is asking.

- Answer all questions. Remember that the adaptive format will *not* allow you to return to a question. Be very careful before entering your answer. Because your exam may be shortened by correct answers (and lengthened by incorrect answers), there is no advantage to rushing through questions.

- On simulations, do not change settings that are not directly related to the question. Also, assume default settings if the question does not specify or imply which settings are used.

- Use a process of elimination to get rid of the obviously incorrect answers first on questions that you're not sure about. This method will improve your odds of selecting the correct answer if you need to make an educated guess.

Exam Registration

You may take the exams at any of more than 1,000 Authorized Prometric Testing Centers (APTCs) and VUE Testing Centers around the world. For the location of a testing center near you, call Sylvan Prometric at 800-755-EXAM (755-3926), or call VUE at 888-837-8616. Outside the United States and Canada, contact your local Sylvan Prometric or VUE registration center.

You should determine the number of the exam you want to take, and then register with the Sylvan Prometric or VUE registration center nearest to you. At this point, you will be asked for advance payment for the exam. The exams are $100 each. Exams must be taken within one year of payment. You can schedule exams up to six weeks in advance or as late as one working day prior to the date of the exam. You can cancel or reschedule your exam if you contact the center at least two working days prior to the exam. Same-day registration is available in some locations, subject to space availability. Where same-day registration is available, you must register a minimum of two hours before test time.

You may also register for your exams online at www.sylvanprometric.com or www.vue.com.

When you schedule the exam, you will be provided with instructions regarding appointment and cancellation procedures, ID requirements, and information about the testing center location. In addition, you will receive a registration and payment confirmation letter from Sylvan Prometric or VUE.

Microsoft requires certification candidates to accept the terms of a Non-Disclosure Agreement before taking certification exams.

What's on the CD?

With this new book in our best-selling MCSE study guide series, we are including quite an array of training resources. On the CD are numerous simulations, practice exams, and flashcards to help you study for the exam. Also included are the entire contents of the study guide. These resources are described in the following sections.

The Sybex Ebook for Implementing and Administering Windows 2000 Directory Services

Many people like the convenience of being able to carry their whole study guide on a CD. They also like being able to search the text to find specific information quickly and easily. For these reasons, we have included the entire contents of this study guide on a CD, in PDF format. We've also included Adobe Acrobat Reader, which provides the interface for the contents, as well as the search capabilities.

Sybex WinSim 2000

We developed WinSim 2000 to allow you to experience the multimedia and interactive operation of working with the Active Directory. The WinSim 2000 product provides both audio/video files and hands-on experience with key features of the tools you can use in Windows 2000 to administer the Active Directory. Built around the exercises in this study guide, WinSim 2000 can give you the knowledge and hands-on skills that are invaluable for understanding Windows 2000 (and passing the exam). A sample screen from WinSim 2000 is shown below.

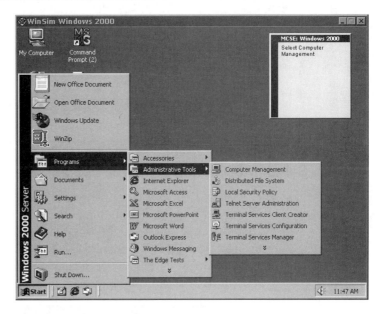

The Sybex MCSE Edge Tests

The Edge Tests are a collection of multiple-choice questions that can help you prepare for your exam. There are three sets of questions:

- Bonus questions specially prepared for this edition of the study guide, including 50 questions that appear only on the CD

- An adaptive test simulator that will give the feel for how adaptive testing works

- All of the questions from the study guide presented in a test engine for your review

A sample screen from the Sybex MCSE Edge Tests is shown below.

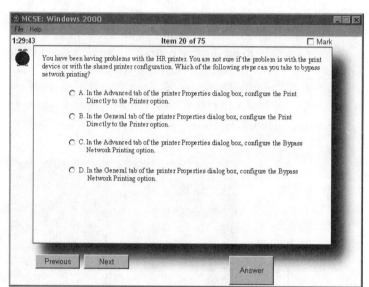

Sybex MCSE Flashcards for PCs and Palm Devices

The "flashcard" style of exam question offers an effective way to quickly and efficiently test your understanding of the fundamental concepts covered in the Implementing and Administering Windows 2000 Directory Services exam. The Sybex MCSE Flashcards set consists of 150 questions presented in a special engine developed specifically for this study guide series. The Sybex MCSE Flashcards interface is shown below.

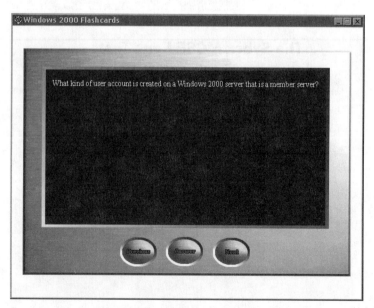

Because of the high demand for a product that will run on Palm devices, we have also developed, in conjunction with Land-J Technologies, a version of the flashcard questions that you can take with you on your Palm OS PDA (including the PalmPilot and Handspring's Visor).

How Do You Use This Book?

This book can provide a solid foundation for the serious effort of preparing for the Implementing and Administering Windows 2000 Directory Services exam. To best benefit from this book, you may wish to use the following study method:

1. Study each chapter carefully. Do your best to fully understand the information.

2. Complete all hands-on exercises in the chapter, referring back to the text as necessary so that you understand each step you take. If you do not have access to a lab environment in which you can complete the exercises, install and work with the exercises available in the Win-Sim 2000 software included with this study guide.

3. Answer the review questions at the end of each chapter. If you would prefer to answer the questions in a timed and graded format, install the Edge Tests from the CD that accompanies this book and answer the chapter questions there instead of in the book.

4. Note which questions you did not understand and study the corresponding sections of the book again.

5. Make sure you complete the entire book.

6. Before taking the exam, go through the training resources included on the CD that accompanies this book. Try the adaptive version that is included with the Sybex MCSE Edge Test. Review and sharpen your knowledge with the MCSE Flashcards.

In order to complete the exercises in this book, your hardware should meet the minimum hardware requirements for installing Windows 2000 Server as a domain controller. These requirements are described in Chapter 3, "Installing and Configuring the Active Directory."

To learn all of the material covered in this book, you will need to study regularly and with discipline. Try to set aside the same time every day to study and select a comfortable and quiet place in which to do it. If you work hard, you will be surprised at how quickly you learn this material. Good luck!

Contacts and Resources

To find out more about Microsoft Education and Certification materials and programs, to register with Sylvan Prometric or VUE, or to get other useful information, check the following resources.

Microsoft Certification Development Team
www.microsoft.com/Train_Cert/mcp/examinfo/certsd.htm

Contact the Microsoft Certification Development Team through their Web site to volunteer for one or more exam development phases or to report a problem with an exam. Address written correspondence to:

Certification Development Team
Microsoft Education and Certification
One Microsoft Way
Redmond, WA 98052

Microsoft TechNet Technical Information Network
www.microsoft.com/technet/subscription/about.htm
(800) 344-2121

Use this Web site or number to contact support professionals and system administrators. Outside the United States and Canada, contact your local Microsoft subsidiary for information.

Microsoft Training and Certification Home Page
www.microsoft.com/train_cert

This Web site provides information about the MCP program and exams. You can also order the latest Microsoft Roadmap to Education and Certification.

Palm Pilot Training Product Development: Land-J
www.land-j.com
(407) 359-2217

Land-J Technologies is a consulting and programming business currently specializing in application development for the 3Com PalmPilot Personal Digital Assistant. Land-J developed the Palm version of the Edge Tests, which is included on the CD that accompanies this study guide.

Sylvan Prometric
www.sylvanprometric.com
(800) 755-EXAM

Contact Sylvan Prometric to register to take an MCP exam at any of more than 800 Sylvan Prometric Testing Centers around the world.

Virtual University Enterprises (VUE)
www.vue.com
(888) 837-8616

Contact the VUE registration center to register to take an MCP exam at one of the VUE Testing Centers.

Assessment Test

1. Which of the following operations is *not* supported by the Active Directory?

   A. Assigning applications to users

   B. Assigning applications to computers

   C. Publishing applications to users

   D. Publishing applications to computers

   E. None of the above

2. Which of the following single master operations apply to the entire forest?

   A. Schema Master

   B. Domain Naming Master

   C. Relative ID Master

   D. Infrastructure Master

   E. Both A and B

3. Which of the following is *not* a valid Active Directory object?

   A. User

   B. Group

   C. Organizational units

   D. Computer

   E. None of the above

4. Which of the following pieces of information should you have before beginning the Active Directory Installation Wizard?

A. Active Directory domain name

B. Administrator password for the local computer

C. NetBIOS name for the server

D. DNS configuration information

E. All of the above

5. Which of the following is *not* considered a security principal?

A. Users

B. Security groups

C. Distribution groups

D. Computers

E. None of the above

6. All of the following types of network computers can be used with RIS *except*:

A. A laptop with a PCMCIA network card

B. A laptop attached to a docking station

C. A desktop computer with a PXE Boot ROM-enabled network adapter

D. A desktop computer with a PCI network adapter

E. None of the above

7. True or False? A single DNS server can perform as a primary server, a master server, and a caching-only server at the same time.

8. Which of the following are valid roles for Windows 2000 Server computers?

   A. Stand-alone server

   B. Member server

   C. Domain controller

   D. All of the above

9. Trust relationships *cannot* be configured as which of the following?

   A. One-way and transitive

   B. Two-way and transitive

   C. One-way and nontransitive

   D. Two-way and nontransitive

   E. None of the above

10. Which of the following should play the *least* significant role in planning an OU structure?

    A. Network infrastructure

    B. Domain organization

    C. Delegation of permissions

    D. Group Policy settings

11. Which of the following file extensions is used primarily for backwards compatibility with non-Windows Installer setup programs?

    A. .MSI

    B. .MST

    C. .ZAP

    D. .AAS

    E. None of the above

12. How can the Windows NT 4 file and printer resources be made available from within the Active Directory?

   A. A systems administrator can right-click the resource and select Publish.

   B. A systems administrator can create Printer and Shared Folder objects that point to these resources.

   C. The Active Directory Domains and Trusts tool can be used to make resources available.

   D. Only Windows 2000 resources can be accessed from within the Active Directory.

13. An Active Directory environment consists of three domains. What is the maximum number of sites that can be created for this environment?

   A. 2

   B. 3

   C. 9

   D. None of the above

14. Which of the following statements regarding auditing and the Active Directory is false?

   A. Auditing prevents users from attempting to guess passwords.

   B. Systems administrators should regularly review audit logs for suspicious activity.

   C. Auditing information can be generated when users view specific information within the Active Directory.

   D. Auditing information can be generated when users modify specific information within the Active Directory.

   E. All of the above.

15. A systems administrator wants to allow a group of users to add Computer accounts to only a specific OU. What is the easiest way to grant only the required permissions?

   A. Delegate control of a User account.

   B. Delegate control at the domain level.

   C. Delegate control of an OU.

   D. Delegate control of a Computer account.

   E. None of the above.

16. A GPO at the domain level sets a certain option to Disabled, while a GPO at the OU level sets the same option to Enabled. All other settings are left at their default. Which setting will be effective for objects within the OU?

   A. Enabled

   B. Disabled

   C. No effect

   D. None of the above

17. The process by which a higher-level security authority assigns permissions to other administrators is known as:

   A. Inheritance

   B. Delegation

   C. Assignment

   D. None of the above

18. What is the minimum amount of information needed to create a Shared Folder Active Directory object?

A. The name of the share

B. The name of the server

C. The name of the server and the name of the share

D. The name of the server, the server's IP address, and the name of the share

19. Which of the following is *not* a benefit of using the Active Directory?

A. Hierarchical object structure

B. Fault-tolerant architecture

C. Ability to configure centralized and distributed administration

D. Flexible replication

E. None of the above

20. A systems administrator plans to deploy 50 computers using RIS. There are two RIS servers on the network. They want to assign half of the client computers to receive images from one RIS server and the other half to receive images from the other RIS server. How can they accomplish this?

A. Divide the computers into two different OUs, and use GPOs to specify to which server each client will be directed.

B. Use the Delegation of Control Wizard to assign permissions to half of the computers.

C. Prestage the computers, and assign half of the computers to each RIS server.

D. Nothing—the default behavior of RIS will ensure that load balancing occurs.

E. None of the above—the first RIS server to respond will provide the image files.

21. Which of the following features of DNS can be used to improve performance?

  A. Caching-only servers

  B. DNS forwarding

  C. Secondary servers

  D. Zone delegation

  E. All of the above

22. Which of the following tools can be used to create GPO links to the Active Directory?

  A. Active Directory Users and Computers

  B. Active Directory Domains and Trusts

  C. Active Directory Sites and Services

  D. Both A and C

23. Which of the following tools can be used to automate the creation and management of User accounts?

  A. LDIFDE

  B. ADSI

  C. CSVDE

  D. WSH

  E. All of the above

24. A systems administrator suspects that the amount of RAM in a domain controller is insufficient and that an upgrade is required. Which of the following System Monitor counters would provide the most useful information regarding the upgrade?

   A. Network Segment ➢ % Utilization

   B. Memory ➢ Page faults/sec

   C. Processor ➢ % Utilization

   D. System ➢ Processes

   E. All of the above would be equally useful

25. Which of the following tools are considered security principals?

   A. User accounts and groups

   B. User accounts, groups, and OUs

   C. Groups and OUs

   D. None of the above

26. Which of the following single master roles does *not* apply to each domain within an Active Directory forest?

   A. PDC Emulator Master

   B. RID Master

   C. Infrastructure Master

   D. None of the above

27. Which of the following types of server configurations *cannot* be used within a single DNS zone?

   A. A single primary server with no secondary servers

   B. Multiple primary servers

   C. A single primary server with a single secondary server

   D. A single primary server with multiple secondary servers

   E. A single primary server and multiple caching-only servers

28. A GPO at the domain level sets a certain option to Disabled, while a GPO at the OU level sets the same option to Enabled. No other GPOs have been created. Which option can a systems administrator use to ensure that the effective policy for objects within the OU is Enabled?

   A. Block Policy Inheritance on the OU

   B. Block Policy Inheritance on the site

   C. Set No Override on the OU

   D. Set No Override on the site

   E. None of the above

29. Which of the following is *not* a type of backup operation that is supported by the Windows 2000 Backup utility?

   A. Normal

   B. Daily

   C. Weekly

   D. Differential

   E. All of the above

30. Which of the following is generally *not* true regarding the domain controllers within a site?

   A. They are generally connected by a high-speed network.

   B. They may reside on different subnets.

   C. They are generally connected by reliable connections.

   D. They may be domain controllers for different domains.

   E. None of the above.

31. Which of the following types of servers contain a copy of the Active Directory?

   A. Member server

   B. Stand-alone server

   C. Domain controller

   D. All of the above

32. When running in native mode, which of the following Group scope changes *cannot* be performed?

   A. Universal ➢ Global

   B. Domain Local ➢ Universal

   C. Global ➢ Universal

   D. None of the above

33. Which of the following protocols may be used for intrasite replication?

   A. RPC

   B. IP

   C. SMTP

   D. NNTP

   E. All of the above

34. Which of the following is *not* a benefit of Windows 2000's DNS?

   A. Dynamic updates

   B. Integration with WINS

   C. Integration with DHCP

   D. Integration with Active Directory

   E. None of the above

Answers to Assessment Test

1. **D.** Applications cannot be published to computers. See Chapter 11 for more information.

2. **E.** There can be only one Domain Naming Master and one Schema Master per Active Directory forest. The remaining roles apply at the domain level. See Chapter 5 for more information.

3. **E.** All of the choices are valid types of Active Directory objects and can be created and managed using the Active Directory Users and Computers tool. See Chapter 7 for more information.

4. **E.** Before beginning the installation of a domain controller, you should have all of the information listed. See Chapter 3 for more information.

5. **C.** Permissions and Security settings cannot be made on Distribution groups. Distribution groups are used only for the purpose of sending e-mail. See Chapter 8 for more information.

6. **A.** Windows 2000 RIS does not support the use of PCMCIA or PC Card network adapters. All of the other configurations are supported (although specific drivers from third-party manufacturers may be required). See Chapter 12 for more information.

7. **True.** A single DNS server can serve multiple roles, as long as they are for different DNS zones. See Chapter 2 for more information.

8. **D.** Based on the business needs of an organization, a Windows 2000 Server computer can be configured in any of the above roles. See Chapter 1 for more information.

9. **E.** All of the trust configurations listed are possible. See Chapter 5 for more information.

10. A. In general, you can accommodate your network infrastructure through the use of Active Directory sites. All of the other options should play a significant role when designing your OU structure. See Chapter 4 for more information.

11. C. Initialization (.ZAP) files are used primarily to point to older programs that do not use the Windows Installer. See Chapter 11 for more information.

12. B. Printer and Shared Folder objects within the Active Directory can point to Windows NT 4 file and printer resources, as well as Windows 2000 resources. See Chapter 7 for more information.

13. D. The number of sites in an Active Directory environment is independent of the domain organization. An environment that consists of three domains may have one or more sites, based on the physical network setup. See Chapter 6 for more information.

14. A. The purpose of auditing is to monitor and record actions taken by users. Auditing will not prevent users from attempting to guess passwords (although it might discourage them from trying, if they are aware it is enabled). See Chapter 8 for more information.

15. E. In order to allow this permission at the OU level, the systems administrator must create a Group Policy Object with the appropriate settings and link it to the OU. See Chapter 12 for more information.

16. A. Assuming that the default settings are left in place, the Group Policy setting at the OU level will take effect. See Chapter 10 for more information.

17. B. Delegation is the process by which administrators can assign permissions on the objects within an OU. See Chapter 4 for more information.

18. C. The name of the server and the name of the share make up the UNC information required to create a Shared Folder object. See Chapter 7 for more information.

19. E. All of the options listed are benefits of using the Active Directory. See Chapter 1 for more information.

20. C. One of the primary advantages of using prestaging is that systems administrators can distribute the load of installations between multiple RIS servers. See Chapter 12 for more information.

21. E. One of the major design goals for DNS was support for scalability. All of the features listed can be used to increase the performance of DNS. See Chapter 2 for more information.

22. D. Both the Active Directory Users and Computers tool and the Active Directory Sites and Services tool can be used to create GPO links to the Active Directory. See Chapter 10 for more information.

23. E. All of the above tools and scripting languages can be used to automate common administrative tasks, such as the creation and management of user accounts. See Chapter 7 for more information.

24. B. A page fault occurs when the operating system must retrieve information from disk instead of from RAM. If the number of page faults per second is high, then it is likely that the server would benefit from a RAM upgrade. See Chapter 9 for more information.

25. A. User accounts and groups are used for setting security permissions, while OUs are used for creating the organizational structure within the Active Directory. See Chapter 4 for more information.

26. D. All of the roles listed are configured for each domain within the Active Directory forest. See Chapter 5 for more information.

27. B. DNS does not allow for the use of more than one primary server per zone. See Chapter 2 for more information.

28. A. By blocking policy inheritance on the OU, you can be sure that other settings defined at higher levels do not change the settings at the OU level. However, this will only work if the No Override option is not set at the site level. See Chapter 10 for more information.

29. C. The Windows 2000 Backup utility does not include an operation for weekly backups. Weekly backups can be performed, however, by using the scheduling functionality of the Backup utility. See Chapter 9 for more information.

30. E. All of the descriptions listed are characteristics that are common to domain controllers within a single site. See Chapter 6 for more information.

31. C. Only Windows 2000 Server computers configured as domain controllers contain a copy of the Active Directory database. See Chapter 3 for more information.

32. A. The scope of Universal groups cannot be changed. See Chapter 8 for more information.

33. A. Remote Procedure Calls (RPCs) are used for intrasite replication. See Chapter 6 for more information.

34. E. All of the above are features and benefits of Windows 2000's DNS service. See Chapter 2 for more information.

Chapter

1

Overview of the Active Directory

Managing *users*, *computers*, applications, and network devices can seem like a never-ending process. However, it's for this very reason that many of us (as systems administrators) have jobs in the first place! Nevertheless, there's a great need for organization, especially when it comes to some of the most fundamental yet tedious tasks we perform every day. That's where the concept of directory services comes in.

To truly appreciate the value of a directory service, let's first look at a real-world example of a situation without organization. Suppose we're trying to find an old friend from college. The first step we would take would probably be to look for their name in the local phone book. If we couldn't find it there, we might try searching in the phone books of a few other cities or on the Internet. If none of those methods were successful, we'd probably resort to calling friends who might have kept in touch with others.

As you can see, this is not an exact science! We could search forever without finding our old friend's telephone number. Part of the problem is due to the lack of a single central repository of phone number information. Without knowing where the information is stored, perseverance and luck are one's strongest tools. Clearly, this is a problem. Yet, it's the way a lot of networks are managed in the real world. That is, information is scattered throughout the organization, and finding what you need may take several phone calls and database searches.

If you've heard about the *Active Directory*, there's a good chance that you already have an idea of its purpose. Microsoft's Active Directory technology is designed to store information about all of the objects within your network environment, including hardware, software, network devices, and users. Furthermore, it is designed to increase capabilities while it decreases administration through the use of a hierarchical structure that mirrors a business's logical organization. In other words, it forms the universal "phone book" we so badly need in the network world!

You've probably also heard that a great deal of planning and training is required to properly implement the Active Directory's many features. We're not talking about a few new administrative tools or check boxes here! In order to reap the true benefits of this new technology, you must be willing to invest the time and effort to get it right. And, you'll need buy-in from the entire organization. From end users to executive management, the success of your directory services implementation will be based on input from the entire business. All of these statements about the Active Directory are true.

There's no excuse for poor planning when it comes to the Active Directory. If you're not sure how to configure the directory services for your environment, you'll probably benefit very little from its implementation. In fact, you could make your network more difficult to manage if you improperly implement Windows 2000. It's not a "one size fits all" type of feature. Once you have a good idea for the logical organization of your business and technical environment, however, you will have made much progress toward successfully installing and configuring the Active Directory. That's where the content of this book—and the Microsoft exam for which it will prepare you—come in.

It's a difficult task to cover the various aspects of Windows 2000's most important feature—the Active Directory—even in a whole book. As we briefly mentioned in the Introduction, Microsoft's main goal in *Exam 70-217: Implementing and Administering a Microsoft Windows 2000 Directory Services Infrastructure* is to test your ability to *implement* the various features of the Active Directory. The problem is that it doesn't make much sense to begin implementing the Active Directory until you understand the terms, concepts, and goals behind Active Directory and this big change in the network operating system.

Planning an entire directory services architecture that conforms to your business and technical requirements is beyond the scope of this book. The topic is considerably complex and requires a thorough understanding of all the ramifications for your organization. You must take into account, for example, business concerns, the geographic organization of your company, and its technical infrastructure. In fact, it's such an important topic that Microsoft has decided to test those concepts under a separate exam: *Exam 70-219: Designing a Microsoft Windows 2000 Directory Services Infrastructure*. You can study for that exam using another Sybex book, *MCSE: Windows 2000 Directory Services Design Study Guide*. It would be difficult to overemphasize the importance of planning for Windows 2000 and the Active Directory.

Planning, however, is just one part of the process. Once you have determined exactly *what* your Active Directory should look like, it's time to find out *how* to implement it. And that's what we'll cover throughout this book. Specifically, we'll talk about the various methods for implementing the tools and features of Windows 2000 based on your company's business and technical requirements. Despite the underlying complexity of the Active Directory and all of its features, Microsoft has gone to great lengths to ensure that implementation and management of the Active Directory are intuitive and straightforward, for no technology is useful if no one can figure out how to use it.

In this chapter, we'll take a look at some of the many benefits of using a directory services system and, specifically, Microsoft's Active Directory. We'll cover basic information regarding the various concepts related to Microsoft's Active Directory. The emphasis will be on addressing why the entire idea of directory services came about and how it can be used to improve operations in your environment. We'll then move on to looking at the various logical objects created in the Active Directory and the ways in which you can configure them to work with your network environment. Finally, we'll cover the details related to mapping your organization's physical network infrastructure to the directory services architecture. The goal is to describe the framework on which the Active Directory is based.

With that goal in mind, let's get started!

No specific exam objectives are covered in this chapter, but a basic understanding of how the Active Directory is structured and why it was created are essential for performing well on the exam. If you've had little previous exposure to the Active Directory, or if you want to know how Active Directory is different from NT's domain model, you should definitely read this chapter! Also, be sure to see Appendix B, "Planning the Active Directory," for more information on designing a directory services environment.

The World Before Active Directory

The title of this section hints of a time long past. However, the overwhelming majority of networks today run without any single unified directory service. Almost all companies—from small businesses to global enterprises—store information in various disconnected systems. For example, a company might record data about its employees in a human resources database while network accounts reside on a Windows NT 4 domain controller. Other information—such as security settings for applications—reside within various other systems. And, there's always the classic: paper-based forms. The main reason for this disparity is that no single flexible data storage mechanism was available. But, implementing and managing many separate systems is a huge challenge for most organizations. Before we look at some potential solutions, let's examine the problem further.

The Benefits of Windows NT 4

Microsoft designed the Windows 2000 operating system platform to succeed its highly successful Windows NT 4 Workstation and Server products. It's therefore important to understand the basics of Windows NT before diving into the new features that are available with the Active Directory, a completely new technology introduced with Windows 2000.

The goal of using a network operating system (NOS) is to bring security, organization, and accessibility to information throughout a company's network. In contrast to a peer-to-peer network, properly configured file and print servers allow users and systems administrators to make the most of their resources.

For many years, the realm of network and systems management was one that was controlled by administrators who often worked with cryptic command-line interfaces. That is, only specialists normally managed information systems. Newer network operating systems such as Novell NetWare and Windows NT started bringing ease of administration into the network computing world so that network administration no longer needed to be a task delegated to only a few individuals. For example, by bringing the intuitive graphical user interface (GUI) to the world of systems and network administration, Windows NT 4 opened up the doors to simplifying management while still providing the types of security required by most businesses. With these tools, managers and nontechnical staff could perform basic systems management functions.

Windows NT Server and Workstation computers offered many benefits, including reliability, scalability, performance, and flexibility. In many cases, companies saw Windows NT 4 as a much more cost-effective solution than their existing client-server solutions. Other benefits of Windows NT included its compatibility with a large installed base of current software products. Application developers could, with a minimal amount of effort, develop programs that would run properly on various Windows-based platforms.

The purpose of this introduction is to provide an overview of the functionality of Windows NT 4. For more details about the product, see www.microsoft.com/ntserver.

A major design goal for the Windows NT 4 operating system was to provide for a secure yet flexible network infrastructure. A few years ago, few technical and business professionals would have imagined that personal computers would make inroads into corporate server rooms and data centers. For many reasons, including cost-efficiency and price-performance ratios, they have done just that. With these characteristics in mind, we have set the stage for discussing the model used by Windows NT to organize users and secure resources and some of its shortcomings.

The Domain Model in Windows NT 4

The Windows NT 4 platform has met many of the challenges of the network world. However, like any technical solution, it has its limitations. First and foremost, questions regarding the scalability of its rudimentary directory services prevented some potential inroads into corporate data centers. Windows NT uses the concept of a domain to organize users and secure resources. A Windows NT domain is essentially a centralized database of security information that allows for the management of network resources.

Domains are implemented through the use of Windows NT Server computers that function as *domain controllers*. Every domain has exactly one Primary Domain Controller (PDC) and may have one or more Backup Domain Controllers (BDCs). All network security accounts are stored within a central database on the PDC. To improve performance and reliability in distributed environments, this database is replicated to BDCs. Although BDCs can help distribute the load of network logon requests and updates, there can be only one master copy of the accounts database. This primary copy resides on the PDC, and all user and security account changes must be recorded by this machine and transmitted to all other domain controllers. Figure 1.1 provides an example of such a topology.

FIGURE 1.1 A Windows NT 4 domain topology using PDCs and BDCs

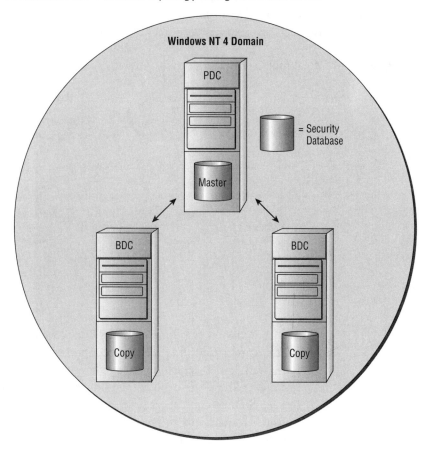

In order to meet some of these design issues, several different Windows NT domain models have been used. Figure 1.2 provides an example of a multiple-master domain topology. In this scenario, user accounts are stored

on one or more master domains. The servers in these domains are responsible primarily for managing network accounts. BDCs for these user domains are stored in various locations throughout the organization. Network files, printers, databases, and other resources are placed in resource domains with their own PDC and BDCs. These domains may be created and managed as needed by the organization itself and are often administered separately. In order for resources to be made available to users, each of the resource domains must trust the master domain(s). The overall process places all users from the master domains into global *groups*. These global groups are then granted access to network resources in the resource domains.

FIGURE 1.2   A multiple-master domain topology

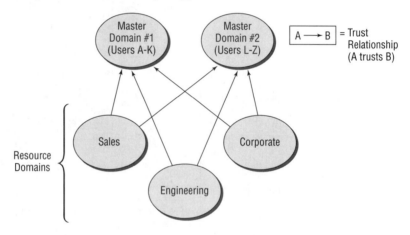

The Windows NT domain model works well for small- to medium-sized organizations. It is able to accommodate several thousands of users fairly well, and a single domain can handle a reasonable number of resources. Above these guidelines, however, the network traffic required to keep domain controllers synchronized and the number of trust relationships to manage can present a challenge to network and systems administrators. As the numbers of users grow, it can get much more difficult for the domains to accommodate large numbers of changes and network logon requests.

The Limitations of Windows NT 4

The Windows NT 4 domain model has several limitations that hinder its scalability to larger and more complex environments. We already alluded to one earlier—it can't accommodate the number of users supported by large organizations. Although multiple domains can be set up to ease administration and network constraint issues, administering these domains quickly becomes quite complicated and management-intensive. For example, trust relationships between the domains can quickly grow out of control if not managed properly, and providing adequate bandwidth for keeping network accounts synchronized can be a costly burden on the network.

Domains, themselves, are flat entities used to organize and administer security information. They do not take into account the structure of businesses and cannot be organized in a hierarchical fashion (using subdomains for administrative purposes). Therefore, systems administrators are forced to place users into groups. As groups cannot be nested (that is, have subgroups), it is not uncommon for many organizations to manage hundreds of groups within each domain. Setting permissions on resources (such as file and print services) can become an extremely tedious and error-prone process.

As far as security is concerned, administration is often delegated to one or more users of the IT department. These individuals have complete control over the domain controllers and resources within the domain itself. This poses several potential problems—both business and technical. As the distribution of administrator rights is extremely important, it would be best to assign permissions to certain areas of the business. However, the options available in the Windows NT operating system were either difficult to implement or did not provide enough flexibility. All of this leads to a less-than-optimal configuration. For example, security policies are often set to allow users far more permissions than they need to complete their jobs.

If you have worked with Windows NT 4 domains in a medium- to large-sized environment, you are probably familiar with many of the issues related to the domain model. Nevertheless, Windows NT 4 provides an excellent solution for many businesses and offers security, flexibility, and network management features unmatched by many of its competitors. As with almost any technical solution, however, there are areas in which improvements can be made.

Now that we've gone over the basics of Windows NT 4 and its directory structure, let's move on and examine how Windows 2000's Active Directory addresses some of these challenges.

The Benefits of the Active Directory

Most businesses have created an organizational structure in an attempt to better manage their environments. For example, companies often divide themselves into departments (such as Sales, Marketing, and Engineering), and individuals fill roles within these departments (such as managers and staff). The goal is to add constructs that help coordinate the various functions required for the success of the organization as a whole.

The Information Technology (IT) department in these companies is responsible for maintaining the security of the company's information. In modern businesses, this involves planning for, implementing, and managing various network resources. Servers, workstations, and routers are common tools that are used to connect users with the information they need to do their jobs. In all but the smallest environments, the effort required to manage each of these technological resources can be great.

That's where Windows 2000 and Microsoft's Active Directory come in. In its most basic definition, a directory is a repository that records information and makes it available to users. The overall design goal for the Active Directory was to create a single centralized repository of information that securely manages a company's resources. User account management, security, and applications are just a few of these areas. The Active Directory is a data store that allows administrators to manage various types of information within a single distributed database, thus solving one of the problems we stated earlier. This is no small task, but there are many features of this directory services technology that allow it to meet the needs of organizations of any size. Specifically, the Active Directory's features include the following:

Hierarchical Organization   In sharp contrast to the flat structure of the Windows NT 4 domain model, the Active Directory is based on a hierarchical layout. Through the use of various organizational components, a company can create a network management infrastructure that mirrors its business organization. So, if a company has 10 major divisions, each of which has several departments, the directory services model can reflect this structure through the use of various objects within the directory. This structure can efficiently accommodate the physical and logical aspects of information resources such as databases, users, and computers. In addition to the hierarchical organization of objects within the Active Directory, the integration of network naming services with the Domain Name System (*DNS*) provides for the hierarchical naming and location of resources throughout the company and on the public Internet.

Extensible Schema   One of the foremost concerns with any type of database is the difficulty encountered when trying to accommodate all types of information in one storage repository. That's why the Active Directory has been designed with extensibility (i.e., the ability to add to and change the schema) in mind. In this case, extensibility means the ability to expand the directory schema. The *schema* is the actual structure of the database in terms of data types and location of the attributes. This is important because it allows applications to will know where particular pieces of information reside. You cannot delete any portion of the schema, even the pieces that you may add. The information stored within the structure of the Active Directory can be expanded and customized through the use of various tools. One such tool is the Active Directory Services Interface (ADSI), which is available to Windows developers. ADSI provides objects and interfaces that can be accessed from within common programming languages such as Visual Basic, Visual C++, and Active Server Pages (ASP). This feature allows the Active Directory to adapt to special applications and to store additional information as needed. It also allows all of the various areas within an organization (or even between them) to share data easily based on the structure of the Active Directory.

Centralized Data Storage   All of the information within the Active Directory resides within a single, yet distributed, data repository. This allows users and systems administrators to easily access the information they need from wherever they may be within the company. The benefits of the centralized data storage include reduced administration requirements, less duplication, greater availability, and increased organization of data.

Replication   If server performance and reliability were not concerns, it might make sense to store the entire Active Directory on a single server. In the real world, however, accessibility and cost constraints require the database to be replicated throughout the network. Active Directory provides for this functionality. Through the use of replication technology, the data store can be distributed between many different servers in a network environment. The ability to define sites allows systems and network administrators to limit the amount of traffic between remote sites while still ensuring adequate performance and usability. Reliable data synchronization allows for multimaster replication—that is, all domain controllers can update information stored within the Active Directory and can ensure its consistency at the same time.

Ease of Administration   In order to accommodate various business models, the Active Directory can be configured for centralized or decentralized administration. This gives network and systems administrators the ability to delegate authority and responsibilities throughout the organization while still maintaining security. Furthermore, the tools and utilities used to add, remove, and modify Active Directory objects are available from all Windows 2000 domain controllers. They allow for making companywide changes with just a few mouse clicks.

Network Security   Through the use of a single logon and various authentication and encryption mechanisms, the Active Directory can facilitate security throughout an entire enterprise. Through the process of *delegation*, higher-level security authorities can grant permissions to other administrators. For ease of administration, objects in the Active Directory tree inherit permissions from their parent objects. Application developers can take advantage of many of these features to ensure that users are identified uniquely and securely. Network administrators can create and update permissions as needed from within a single repository, thereby reducing chances of inaccurate or outdated configuration.

Client Configuration Management   One of the biggest struggles for systems administrators comes with maintaining a network of heterogeneous systems and applications. A fairly simple failure—such as a hard disk crash—can cause hours of work in reconfiguring and restoring a workstation or server. Hours of work can also be generated when users are forced to move between computers and they need to have all of their applications reinstalled and the necessary system settings updated. Many IT organizations have found that these types of operations can consume a great deal of IT staffers' time and resources. New technologies integrated with the Active Directory allow for greatly enhanced control and administration of these types of network issues. The overall benefit is decreased downtime, a better end user experience, and reduced administration.

Scalability and Performance   Large organizations often have many users and large quantities of information to manage. The Active Directory was designed with scalability in mind. Not only does it allow for storing up to millions of objects within a single domain, it also provides methods for distributing the necessary information between servers and locations. These features relieve much of the burden of designing a directory services infrastructure based on technical instead of business factors.

Searching Functionality   One of the most important benefits of having all of your network resources stored in a single repository is the ability to perform accurate searches. Users often see network operating systems as extremely complicated because of the naming and location of resources. But it shouldn't be that complicated. For example, if we need to find a printer, we should not need to know the name of the domain or print server for that object. Using the Active Directory, users can quickly find information about other users or resources, such as printers and servers, through an intuitive querying interface.

We'll cover the technical aspects of how Windows 2000 addresses all of the above within the technical chapters of this book. For now, keep in mind the various challenges that the Active Directory was designed to address. The scope of this chapter is limited to introducing only the technical concepts on which the Active Directory is based. In order to better understand this topic, let's now discuss the various areas that make up the logical and physical structure of the Active Directory.

Active Directory's Logical Structure

Database professionals often use the term schema to describe the structure of data. A schema usually defines the types of information that can be stored within a certain repository and special rules on how the information is to be organized. Within a relational database or Microsoft Excel spreadsheet, for example, we might define tables with columns and rows.

Similarly, the Active Directory schema specifies the types of information that are stored within a directory. By default, the schema supports information regarding user names, passwords, and permissions information. The schema itself also describes the structure of the information stored within the Active Directory data store. The Active Directory data store, in turn, resides on one or more domain controllers that are deployed throughout the enterprise. In this section, we'll take a look at the various concepts that are used to specify how the Active Directory is logically organized.

Components and Mechanisms of the Active Directory

In order to maintain the types of information required to support an entire organization, the Active Directory must provide for many different types of functionality. These include the following:

Data Store   When you envision the Active Directory from a physical point of view, you probably imagine a set of files stored on the hard disk that contain all of the objects within it. The term *data store* is used to refer to the actual structure that contains the information stored within the Active Directory. The data store is implemented as just that—a set of files that reside within the file system of a domain controller. This is the fundamental structure of the Active Directory.

The data store itself has a structure that describes the types of information it can contain. Within the data store, data about objects is recorded and made available to users. For example, configuration information about the domain topology, including trust relationships (which we'll cover later in this chapter), are contained within the Active Directory. Similarly, information about users, groups, and computers that are part of the domain are also recorded.

Schema   The Active Directory schema consists of rules on the types of information that can be stored within the directory. The schema is made up of two types of objects: attributes and classes. *Attributes* define a single granular piece of information stored within the Active Directory. First Name and Last Name, for example, are considered attributes, which may contain the values of Bob and Smith. *Classes* are objects that are defined as collections of attributes. For example, a class called Employee could include the First Name and Last Name attributes.

It is important to understand that classes and attributes are defined independently and that any number of classes can use the same attributes. For example, if we create an attribute called Nickname, this value could conceivably be used to describe a User class and a Computer class. By default, Microsoft has included several different schema objects. In order to support custom data, however, applications developers can extend the schema by creating their own classes and attributes. As we'll see in Chapter 5, "Installing and Managing Trees and Forests," the entire schema is replicated to all of the domain controllers within the environment to ensure data consistency between them.

The overall result of the schema is a centralized data store that can contain information about many different types of objects—including users, groups, computers, network devices, applications, and more.

Global Catalog   The *Global Catalog* is a database that contains all of the information pertaining to objects within all domains in the Active Directory environment. One of the potential problems with working in a multi–domain environment is that users in one domain may want to find objects stored in another domain, but they may not have any additional information about those objects.

The purpose of the Global Catalog is to index information stored in the Active Directory so that it can be more quickly and easily searched. In order to store and replicate all of this information, the Global Catalog can be distributed to servers within the network environment. That is, network and systems administrators must specify which servers within the Active Directory environment should contain copies of the Global Catalog. This decision is usually made based on technical considerations (such as network links) and organizational considerations (such as the number of users at each remote site). You can think of the Global Catalog as a universal phone book. Such an object would be quite large and bulky, but also very useful. Your goal (as a systems administrator) would be to find a balance between maintaining copies of the phone book and making potential users of the book travel long distances to use it.

This distribution of Global Catalog information allows for increased performance during companywide resource searches and can prevent excessive traffic across network links. Since the Global Catalog includes information about objects stored in all domains within the Active Directory environment, its management and location should be an important concern for network and systems administrators.

Searching Mechanisms   The best-designed data repository in the world is useless if users can't access the information stored within it. The Active Directory includes a search engine that can be queried by users to find information about objects stored within it. For example, if a member of the Human Resources department is looking for a color printer, they can easily query the Active Directory to find the one located closest to them. Best of all, the query tools are already built into Windows 2000 operating systems and are only a few mouse clicks away.

Replication   Although it is theoretically possible to create a directory service that involves only one central computer, there are several problems with this configuration. First, all of the data is stored on one machine. This server would be responsible for processing all of the logon requests and search queries associated with the objects that it contained. Although this scenario might work well for a small network, it would create a tremendous load on servers in larger environments. Furthermore, clients that are located on remote networks would experience slower response times due to the pace of network traffic. Another drawback is that the entire directory would be stored in only one location. If this server became unavailable (due to a failed power supply, for example), network authentication and other vital processes could not be carried out. To solve these problems, the Active Directory has been designed with a replication engine. The purpose of *replication* is to distribute the data stored within the directory throughout the organization for increased availability, performance, and data protection. Systems administrators can tune replication to occur based on their physical network infrastructure and other constraints.

Each of these components must work together to ensure that the Active Directory remains accessible to all of the users that require it and to maintain the accuracy and consistency of its information. Now that we've seen the logical structure and features of the Active Directory, let's move on to looking at organizational concepts.

An Overview of Active Directory Domains

In Windows 2000 Active Directory, a domain is a logical security boundary that allows for the creation, administration, and management of related resources. You can think of a domain as a logical division, such as a neighborhood within a city. Although each neighborhood is part of a larger group of neighborhoods (the city), it may carry on many of its functions independently of the others. For example, resources such as tennis courts and swimming pools may be made available only to members of the neighborhood, while resources such as electricity and water supplies would probably be shared between neighborhoods. So, think of a domain as a grouping of objects that utilizes resources exclusive to its domain, but keep in mind that those resources can also be shared *between* domains.

Although the names and fundamental features are the same, Active Directory domains vary greatly from those in Windows NT. As we mentioned earlier, an Active Directory domain can store many more objects than a Windows NT domain. Furthermore, Active Directory domains can be combined together into *forests* and *trees* to form hierarchical structures. This is in contrast to Windows NT domains, which treat all domains as peers of each other (that is, they are all on equal footing and cannot be organized into trees and forests). Before going into the details, let's discuss the concept of domains.

Within most business organizations, network and systems administration duties are delegated to certain individuals and departments. For example, a company might have a centralized IT department that is responsible for all implementation, support, and maintenance of network resources throughout the organization. In another example, network support may be largely decentralized—that is, each department, business unit, or office may have it's own IT support staff. Both of these models may work well for a company, but implementing such a structure through directory services requires the use of logical objects.

Domains are comprised of a collection of computers and resources that share a common security database. An Active Directory domain contains a logical partition of users, groups, and other objects within the environment. Objects within a domain share several characteristics, including the following:

Group Policy and Security Permissions   Security for all of the objects within a domain can be administered based on one set of policies. Thus, a domain administrator can make changes to any of the settings within the domain. These settings can apply to all of the users, computers, and objects within the domain. For more granular security settings, however, permissions can be granted on specific objects, thereby distributing administration responsibilities and increasing security. Domains are configured as a single security entity. Objects, permissions, and other settings within a domain do not automatically apply to other domains.

Hierarchical Object Naming   All of the objects within an Active Directory container share a common namespace. When domains are combined together, however, the namespace is hierarchical. For example, a user in one department might have an object name called `janedoe@engineering.microsoft.com` while a user in another department might have one called `johndoe@sales.microsoft.com`. The first part of the name is determined by the name of the object within the domain (in these examples, the user name). The suffix is determined by the organization of the domains. The hierarchical naming system allows each object within the Active Directory to have a unique name. For more information on naming Active Directory objects, see Appendix B, "Planning the Active Directory."

Hierarchical Properties   Containers called *organizational units* (described later) can be created within a domain. These units are used for creating a logical grouping of objects within the Active Directory. The specific user settings and permissions that are assigned to these objects can be inherited by lower-level objects. For example, if we have an organizational unit for the North America division within our company, we can set user permissions on this object. All of the objects within the North America object (such as the Sales, Marketing, and Engineering departments) would automatically inherit these settings. This makes administration easier, but inheritance is an important concept to remember when implementing and administering security since it results in the implicit assignment of permissions. The proper use of hierarchical properties allows systems administrators to avoid inconsistent security policies (such as a minimum password length of six characters in one object and a minimum password length of eight characters in another).

Trust Relationships   In order to facilitate the sharing of information between domains, trust relationships are automatically created between them. Additionally, the administrator can break and establish trust relationships based on business requirements. A trust relationship allows two domains to share security information and objects, but does not automatically assign permissions to these objects. This allows users that are contained within one domain to be granted access to resources in other domains. To make administrating trust relationships easier, Microsoft has made transitive two-way *trusts* the default relationship between domains. As shown in Figure 1.3, if Domain A trusts Domain B and Domain B trusts Domain C, Domain A implicitly trusts Domain C.

FIGURE 1.3   Transitive two-way trust relationships

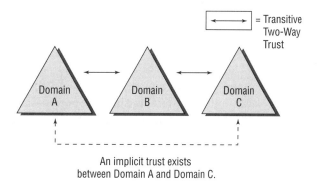

An implicit trust exists between Domain A and Domain C.

 Generally, triangles are used to represent Active Directory domains (thereby indicating their hierarchical structure), and circles are used to represent flat domains (such as those in Windows NT domains).

Overall, the purpose of domains is to ease administration while providing for a common security and resource database.

Using Multiple Domains

Although the flexibility and power afforded by the use of an Active Directory domain will meet the needs of many organizations, there are reasons for which companies might want to implement more than one domain. We'll cover these planning issues in Appendix B, "Planning the Active Directory." For now, however, it is important to know that domains can be combined together into domain trees.

Domain trees are hierarchical collections of domains that are designed to meet the organizational needs of a business (see Figure 1.4). Trees are defined by the use of a contiguous namespace. For example, the following domains are all considered part of the same tree:

- `microsoft.com`

- `sales.microsoft.com`

- `research.microsoft.com`

- `us.sales.microsoft.com`

Notice that all of these domains are part of the `microsoft.com` domain. Domains within trees still maintain separate security and resource databases, but can be administered together through the use of trust relationships. By default, trust relationships are automatically established between parent and child domains within a tree.

FIGURE 1.4 A domain tree

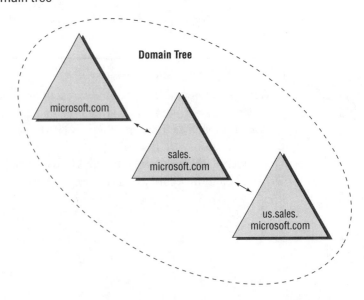

Although single companies will often want to configure domains to fit within a single namespace, noncontiguous namespaces may be used for several reasons. We'll look at several of these reasons in Chapter 5, "Installing and Managing Trees and Forests." When domain trees are combined together into noncontiguous groupings, they are known as forests (see Figure 1.5). Forests often contain multiple noncontiguous namespaces consisting of domains that are kept separate for technical or political reasons. Just as trust relationships are created between domains within a tree, trust relationships are also created between trees within a forest so resources can be shared between them.

FIGURE 1.5 An Active Directory forest

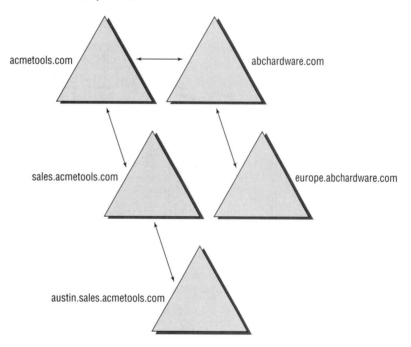

Physically, domains are implemented and managed by the use of domain controllers. We'll cover this topic later in this chapter.

Creating a Domain Structure with Organizational Units

As we mentioned earlier, one of the fundamental limitations of the Windows NT 4 domain organization is that it consists of a flat structure. All users and groups are stored as part of a single namespace. Real-world organizations, however, often require further organization within domains. For example, we may have three thousand users in one domain. Some of these should be grouped together in an Engineering group. Within the Engineering group, we might also want to further subdivide users into other groups (for example, Development and Testing). The Active Directory supports this kind of hierarchy. Figure 1.6 provides a depiction of the differences between the structure of a Windows NT 4 domain and that of an Active Directory domain.

FIGURE 1.6   Windows NT 4 vs. Active Directory domains

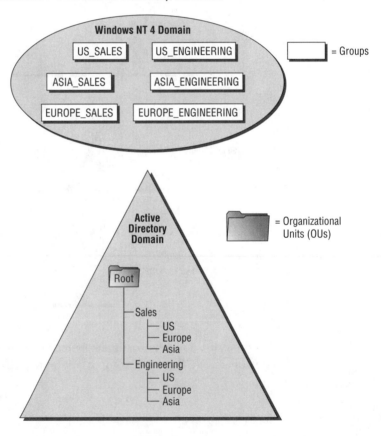

The fundamental unit of organization within an Active Directory domain is the organizational unit (OU). OUs are container objects that can be hierarchically arranged within a domain. Figure 1.7 provides an example of a typical OU setup. OUs can contain other objects such as users, groups, computers, and even other OUs. The proper planning and usage of OUs are important because they are generally the objects to which security permissions and Group Policies are assigned. A well-designed OU structure can greatly ease the administration of Active Directory objects.

OUs can be organized based on various criteria. For example, we might choose to implement an OU organization based on the geographic distribution of our company's business units.

FIGURE 1.7 Two different OU hierarchy models

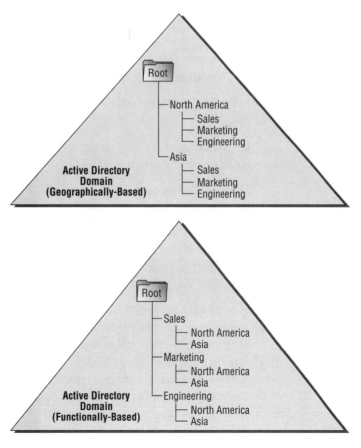

We'll look at various planning issues for OUs in Appendix B, "Planning the Active Directory."

Active Directory Object Names

A fundamental feature of a directory service is that each object within the directory should contain its own unique name. For example, our organization may have two different users named John Smith (who may or may not be in different departments or locations within the company). There should be some unique way for us to distinguish these users (and their corresponding user objects).

Generally, this unique identifier is called the *distinguished name*. Within the Active Directory, each object can be uniquely identified using a long name that specifies the full path to the object. Following is an example of a distinguished name:

```
/O=Internet/DC=Com/DC=MyCompany/DC=Sales
➡/CN=Managers/CN=John Smith
```

In the above name, we have specified the following several different types of objects:

Organization (O)   The company or root-level domain. In this case, the root-level is the Internet.

Domain Component (DC)   A portion of the hierarchical path. DCs are used for organizing objects within the directory service. The DCs specify that the user object is located within the `sales.mycompany.com` domain.

Common Name (CN)   Specifies the names of objects in the directory. In this example, the user John Smith is contained within the Managers container.

When used together, the components of the distinguished name uniquely identify where the user object is stored. Instead of specifying the full distinguished name, we might also choose to use a *relative distinguished name*. This name specifies only part of the path above and is relative to another object. For example, if our current context is already the Managers group within the `sales.mycompany.com` domain, we could simply specify the user as `CN=John Smith`.

Note that if we change the structure of the domain, the distinguished name of this object would also change. A change might happen if we rename one of the containers in the path or move the user object itself. This type of naming system allows for flexibility and the ability to easily identify the potentially millions of objects that might exist in the Active Directory.

User, Computer, and Group Objects

The real objects that you will want to control and manage with the Active Directory are the users, computers, and groups within your network environment. These are the types of objects that allow for the most granular level of control over permissions and allow you to configure your network to meet business needs.

User accounts are used to enforce the security within the network environment. These accounts define the login information and passwords that are used to receive permissions to network objects. *Computer objects* allow systems administrators to configure the functions that can be performed on client machines throughout the environment. Both user accounts and computer objects enable security to be maintained at a granular level.

Although security can be enforced by placing permissions directly on user and computer objects, it is much more convenient to combine users into *groups*. For example, if there are three users who will require similar permissions within the Accounting department, we could place all of them in one group. If users are removed or added to the department, we could easily make changes to the group without having to make any further changes to security permissions. Figure 1.8 shows how groups can be used to easily administer permissions.

FIGURE 1.8   Using groups to administer security

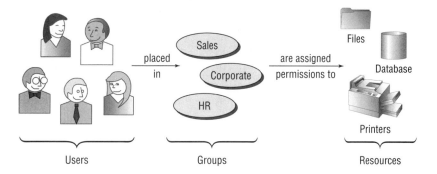

There are two main types of groups within the Active Directory: security groups and distribution groups. *Security groups* are used for the administration of permissions. All members of a security group will receive the same security settings. *Distribution groups*, on the other hand, are used only for sending e-mail and other messages to several different users at once. They do not involve the maintenance of security permissions but can be helpful in handling multiple users.

Overall, the proper use of groups assists greatly in implementing and managing security and permissions within the Active Directory.

Active Directory's Physical Structure

So far, we have focused our attention on the logical units that make up the Active Directory. That is, the ideas presented so far are designed to bring organization to the structure of the network. What we haven't discussed is exactly *how* domains, trees, forests, and the Active Directory itself are created and managed. In this section, we'll see how various servers and network devices can be used to implement and manage the components of the Active Directory.

Server Roles within the Active Directory

The Active Directory data store is stored on one or more computers within an organization's network environment. All editions of the Windows 2000 Server platform are able to participate in Active Directory domains under the following roles:

Domain Controllers   The heart of the Active Directory's functionality resides on domain controllers. These machines are responsible for maintaining the Active Directory data store, including all of its objects, and for providing security for the entire domain. Although an Active Directory configuration may involve only one domain controller, it is much more likely that organizations will have more servers in order to increase performance and establish fault-tolerance. All of the information that resides within the Active Directory is synchronized between the domain controllers, and most changes can be made at any of these servers. This functionality is referred to as multimaster replication and is the basis through which Active Directory information is distributed throughout an organization.

Member Servers   Often, you will want to have servers that function as part of the domain but are not responsible for containing Active Directory information or authenticating users. Common examples include file/print servers and Web servers. A Windows 2000 Server computer that is a *member* of a domain but is not a domain controller itself is referred to as a *member server*. By using member servers, systems administrators can take advantage of the centralized security database of the Active Directory without dedicating server processing and storage resources to maintaining the directory information.

Stand-Alone Servers   It is possible to run Windows 2000 Server computers in a workgroup environment that does not include Active Directory functionality at all. These machines are known as *stand-alone servers*. They maintain their own security database and are administered independently of other servers, as no centralized security database exists. Stand-alone servers might be used for functions such as public Web servers or in situations in which only a few users require resources from a machine and the administrative overhead for managing security separately on various machines is acceptable.

A major benefit in the Windows 2000 Server operating system is the ability to easily promote and demote domain controllers after the operating system has been installed. Unlike the situation with Windows NT 4, reinstallation of the entire operating system is no longer required to change the role of a server. Furthermore, by properly promoting and demoting domain controllers, you can effectively move them between domains, trees, and forests.

In addition to the various types of server roles that the Windows 2000 Server platform can take on within the Active Directory domains, the Active Directory requires systems administrators to assign specific functionalities to other servers. In discussing replication, certain servers might be referred to as masters. Masters contain copies of a database and generally allow both read and write operations. Some types of replication may allow multiple masters to exist, while others specify that only a single master is allowed. Certain tasks within the Active Directory work well using multimaster replication. For example, the ability to update information at one or more of the domain controllers can speed up response times while still maintaining data integrity through replication. Other functions, however, better lend themselves to being defined centrally. These operations are referred to as single-master operations because the function only supports modification on a single machine in the environment. These machines are referred to as Flexible Single Master Operation (FSMO) servers. Some of these are unique within a domain, and others are unique within the tree or forest. The changes made on these machines are then propagated to other domain controllers, as necessary. The various roles for FSMO servers within the Active Directory include the following:

Schema Master   As we mentioned earlier, one of the benefits of the Active Directory schema is that it can be modified. All changes to the schema, however, are propagated to all domain controllers within the forest. In order for the information to stay synchronized and consistent, it is necessary for one machine within the entire tree or forest to be designated as the Schema Master. All changes to the schema must be made on this machine. By default the first domain controller installed in the tree or forest is the Schema Master.

Domain Naming Master   When creating, adding, or removing domains, it is necessary for one machine in the tree or forest to serve as a central authority for the Active Directory configuration. The Domain Naming Master ensures that all of the information within the Active Directory forest is kept consistent and is responsible for registering new domains.

Within each Active Directory domain, the following roles can be assigned to domain controllers:

Relative ID Master   A fundamental requirement of any directory service is that each object must have a unique identifier. All users, groups, computers, and other objects within the Active Directory, for example, are identified by a unique value. The Relative ID (RID) Master is responsible for creating all of these identifiers within each domain and for ensuring that objects have unique IDs between domains by working with RID Masters in other domains.

Primary Domain Controller (PDC) Emulator   In order to support Windows NT, Windows 2000 Server must have the ability to serve as a Windows NT PDC. Microsoft has made a conscious decision to allow networks to work in a mixed-mode of Windows NT domains and Active Directory domains in order to facilitate the migration process (and encourage more people to buy Windows 2000!). As long as there are computers in the environment running Windows NT 4, the PDC Emulator will allow for the transmission of security information between domain controllers. This provides for backwards compatibility while an organization moves to Windows 2000 and the Active Directory.

Infrastructure Master   Managing group memberships is an important role fulfilled manually by systems administrators. In a potentially distributed Active Directory environment, though, it is important to make sure that group and user memberships stay synchronized throughout the network. In order to understand how information might become inconsistent, let's look at an example using two domain controllers named DC1 and DC2. Suppose we make a change to a user's settings on DC1. At the same time, suppose another systems administrator makes a change to the same user account but on DC2. There must be some way to determine which change takes precedence over the other. More importantly, all domain controllers should be made aware of these changes so that the Active Directory database information remains consistent. The role of the Infrastructure Master is to ensure consistency between users and their group memberships as changes, additions, and deletions are made.

If there is more than one domain controller in the domain, the Global Catalog should not reside on the same server as the Infrastructure Master. This would prevent it from seeing any changes to the data and would result in replication not occurring between the various domain controllers.

It is important to note that the above assignments are *roles* and that a single machine may perform multiple roles. For example, in an environment in which only a single domain controller exists, that server will assume all of the above roles by default. On the other hand, if multiple servers are present, these functions can be distributed between them for business and technical reasons. By properly assigning roles to the servers in your environment, you'll be able to ensure that single-master operations are carried out securely and efficiently.

Accessing the Active Directory through LDAP

In order to insert, update, and query information from within the Active Directory, Microsoft has chosen to employ the worldwide Internet Engineering Task Force (IETF) standard protocol called the Lightweight Directory Access Protocol (*LDAP*). LDAP is designed to allow for the transfer of information between domain controllers and to allow users to query information about objects within the directory.

As LDAP is a standard, it also facilitates interoperability between other directory services. Furthermore, communications can be programmed using objects such as the Active Directory Services Interface (ADSI). For data transport, LDAP can be used over TCP/IP, thus making it an excellent choice for communicating over the Internet, as well as private TCP/IP-based networks.

Managing Replication with Sites

A common mistake made in planning the Active Directory is to base its structure on the technical constraints of a business instead of on business practices. For instance, a systems administrator might recommend that a separate domain be placed at each of a company's three remote sites. The rationale for this decision is understandable—the goal is to reduce network traffic between potentially slow and costly remote links. However, the multidomain structure may not make sense for organizations that have a centralized IT department and require common security settings for each of the three locations.

In order to allow the Active Directory to be based on business and political decisions while still accommodating network infrastructure issues, Windows 2000 supports the concept of *sites*. Active Directory sites are designed to define the physical layout of a company's network by taking into account multiple subnets, remote access links, and other network factors. When performing vital functions between domain controllers, for example, you might want to limit bandwidth usage across a slow link. However, within your Local Area Network (LAN) environment, you will want replication to occur as quickly as possible to keep machines synchronized.

Sites are usually defined as locations in which network access is quick and inexpensive. Windows 2000 uses sites to determine when and how information should be replicated between domain controllers and other machines within the environment. Figure 1.9 provides an example of how a distributed company might choose to implement sites.

FIGURE 1.9   A typical site configuration

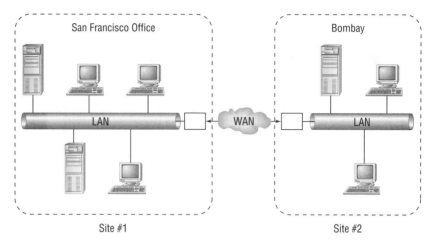

It is important to understand the distinction between logical and physical components of the Active Directory. When planning your objects and domains, you will want to take into account the business requirements of your organization. This will create the logical structure of the directory. In planning for the implementation of the Active Directory, however, you must take into account your network infrastructure—the physical aspects. Sites provide a great way to isolate these two requirements.

Active Directory Names and DNS

The Domain Name System (DNS) is a distributed database built upon an Internet standard that is used to resolve friendly, hierarchical names to TCP/IP network addresses. Systems administrators who have to remember many server IP addresses will easily recall the need for DNS—it can be quite a difficult and error-prone process to remember all of these numbers. For example, if we have a server on the Internet with an IP address of

24.133.155.7, we may want to give it a friendly name, such as `sales` `.mycompany.com`. Instead of typing the IP address every time we need to access the resource, we could specify the fully-qualified name of the machine and leave it to the DNS servers on the Internet to resolve the address.

Understanding TCP/IP is vital to understanding the use of almost any modern network operating system. If you're planning to deploy a Windows 2000 environment, be sure you take the time to learn the details of working with TCP/IP.

The Windows 2000 Active Directory relies on DNS for finding DCs and naming and accessing Active Directory objects. Windows 2000 includes a DNS server service that can be used for automatically updating records that store machine name to IP address mappings. DNS offers many advantages. First, it is the primary name resolution method used on the Internet. Therefore, it has widespread support in all modern operating systems and works well between various operating system platforms.

Second, DNS is designed with fault-tolerance and distributed databases in mind. If a single DNS server does not have the information required to fulfill a request for information, it automatically queries another DNS server for this information. Systems administrators are only responsible for maintaining the DNS entries for their own machines. Through the use of efficient caching, the load of performing worldwide queries on large networks can be minimized.

The various technical details related to DNS are well beyond the scope of this section, but we will cover them later in Chapter 2, "Integrating DNS with the Active Directory."

Summary

In this chapter, we took a high-level overview of the concepts related to the Active Directory. We started with an introduction to why you might want to implement this new technology in your environment and then zoomed in on the logical and physical components. If you're new to the terms and concepts related to directory services, you'll probably find yourself referring back to this chapter to reinforce key ideas. Rest assured, the information presented here will reinforce the technical content presented in later chapters and will help you to understand how it all fits together.

Now that we have a basic understanding of the design goals and components of the Windows 2000 Active Directory, let's move on to look at how you can deploy this new technology in your own environment.

Key Terms

Before you take the exam, be sure you're familiar with the following terms:

Active Directory

computers

distinguished name

DNS

domain controllers

domains

forests

Global Catalog

groups

LDAP

member server

organizational units

replication

schema

sites

trees

trusts

users

Review Questions

1. Which of the following is not a feature of the Active Directory?

   A. The use of LDAP for transferring information

   B. Reliance on DNS for name resolution

   C. A flat domain namespace

   D. The ability to extend the schema

2. Domains provide which of the following functions?

   A. Creating security boundaries to protect resources and ease of administration

   B. Easing the administration of users, groups, computers, and other objects

   C. Providing a central database of network objects

   D. All of the above

3. Which of the following types of servers contain copies of the Active Directory database?

   A. Member servers

   B. Domain controllers

   C. Stand-alone servers

   D. None of the above

4. Which of the following objects are used for creating the logical structure within Active Directory domains?

   A. Users

   B. Sites

   C. Organizational units (OUs)

   D. Trees

   E. None of the above

5. Which of the following is *false* regarding the naming of Active Directory objects?

    A. Active Directory relies on DNS for name resolution.

    B. Two objects can have the same relative name.

    C. Two objects can have the same distinguished name.

    D. All objects within a domain are based on the name of the domain.

6. Which of the following are *true* regarding Active Directory trust relationships?

    A. Trusts are transitive.

    B. By default, trusts are two-way relationships.

    C. Trusts are used to allow the authentication of users between domains.

    D. All of the above.

7. Which of the following protocols is used to query Active Directory information?

    A. LDAP

    B. NetBEUI

    C. NetBIOS

    D. IPX/SPX

8. Which of the following is not true regarding the Windows NT domain namespace?

    A. Windows NT domains have a hierarchical namespace.

    B. Windows NT domains allow thousands of users.

    C. Windows NT domains can be implemented as master domains.

    D. Windows NT domains can be implemented as resource domains.

    E. All of the above.

9. Which of the following is a possible role for a Windows 2000 Server?

   A. Member server

   B. Primary Domain Controller

   C. Backup Domain Controller

   D. Stand-alone server

   E. Both A and D

10. Which of the following statements is *true* regarding domain controllers?

    A. All Active Directory domain controllers are automatically configured as Windows NT domain controllers.

    B. Windows NT domain controllers can host a copy of the Active Directory database.

    C. Windows 2000 domain controllers can be configured to provide the functionality of Windows NT domain controllers.

    D. None of the above.

11. Which of the following is not a characteristic of DNS?

    A. Built-in redundancy

    B. Reliance on proprietary technologies

    C. Scalability

    D. Distributed databases

12. An organization uses 12 Active Directory domains in a single forest. How many Schema Masters must this environment have?

    A. 0

    B. 1

    C. 12

    D. More than 12

    E. None of the above

13. An organization has three remote offices and one large central one. How many sites should this environment contain?

A. 0

B. 1

C. 3

D. 4

E. Not enough information

14. Which of the following features of the Active Directory allows information between domain controllers to remain synchronized?

A. Replication

B. The Global Catalog

C. The schema

D. None of the above

15. Which of the following components of the Active Directory allows for fast searching of objects in *all* domains?

A. Data store

B. Global Catalog

C. Schema

D. None of the above

Answers to Review Questions

1. C. The Active Directory uses a hierarchical namespace for managing objects.

2. D. Each of these options are features of domains and are reasons for their usefulness.

3. B. Only domain controllers contain a copy of the Active Directory database. Member servers rely on the Active Directory but do not contain a copy of the database, and stand-alone servers do not participate in the Active Directory at all.

4. C. OUs are used for creating a hierarchical structure within a domain. Users are objects within the directory, sites are used for physical planning, and trees are relationships between domains.

5. C. The distinguished name of each object in the Active Directory must be unique, but the relative names may be the same. For example, we might have a user object named Jane Doe in two different containers.

6. D. Trusts are designed for facilitating the sharing of information and have all of the above features.

7. A. LDAP is the IETF standard protocol for accessing information from directory services. It is also the standard used by the Active Directory.

8. A. The Windows NT namespace is a flat model.

9. E. Primary Domain Controllers and Backup Domain Controllers are only used in Windows NT domains.

10. C. Through the use of the PDC Emulator functionality, Windows 2000 domain controllers can provide services for Windows NT domains.

11. B. DNS is a worldwide standard that is widely supported in all modern operating systems.

12. B. Only one Schema Master is allowed in an Active Directory environment, regardless of the number of domains.

13. E. The site topology is completely independent from domain architecture—a domain can span many sites, and many domains can be part of the same site. The fact that the organization has four locations does not necessarily mean that it should use a specific number of sites. Rather, this determination should be made based on physical network characteristics.

14. A. Replication ensures that information remains synchronized between domain controllers.

15. B. The Global Catalog contains information about multiple domains. The other options are features of the Active Directory but are not designed for fast searching across multiple domains.

Chapter 2

Integrating DNS with the Active Directory

MICROSOFT EXAM OBJECTIVES COVERED IN THIS CHAPTER:

✓ **Install, configure, and troubleshoot DNS for Active Directory.**

- Integrate Active Directory DNS zones with non-Active Directory DNS zones.

- Configure zones for dynamic updates.

✓ **Manage, monitor, and troubleshoot DNS.**

- Manage replication of DNS data.

In the previous chapter, we looked at the things you need to consider before you implement the Active Directory in your own environment. In this chapter on the *Domain Name System* (DNS), we'll look at the technical details of implementing the Active Directory and DNS.

Understanding DNS is vital to the deployment of the Active Directory and is a prerequisite for installing and configuring domain controllers (which we'll cover in more detail in Chapter 3, "Installing and Configuring the Active Directory"). A common mistake made by systems administrators is underestimating the importance and complexity of DNS. The Active Directory, itself, relies on DNS in order to find clients, servers, and network services that are available throughout your environment. Clients rely on DNS in order to find the file, print, and other resources they require to get their jobs done. Fully understanding DNS is not an easy task, especially for those who have limited experience with *Transmission Control Protocol/Internet Protocol (TCP/IP)*. However, the understanding and proper implementation of DNS is vital to the use of Active Directory.

DNS Overview

DNS is a TCP/IP standard that is designed to resolve Internet Protocol (IP) addresses to host names. One of the inherent complexities of working in networked environments involves working with various protocols and network addresses. Thanks largely to the tremendous rise in popularity of the Internet, however, most environments have transitioned to the use of TCP/IP as their primary networking protocol, and Microsoft is no exception when it comes to support for TCP/IP. All current versions of Microsoft operating systems support it, as do almost all other modern operating systems. Since the introduction of Windows NT 4, TCP/IP has been the default protocol installed.

TCP/IP is actually a collection of different technologies that allow computers to function together on a single network. Some of the major advantages of the protocol include widespread support for hardware, software, and network devices, reliance on a system of standards, and scalability.

TCP/IP is not the simplest protocol to understand, however. As it was designed to support large heterogeneous networks, there are many issues involved with TCP/IP addressing, the use of subnets, routing, and name resolution. It is beyond the scope of this chapter to fully describe the intricacies of working with TCP/IP. However, we will cover the information required to understand DNS as it relates to Windows 2000 and the Active Directory.

TCP/IP and DNS are based on a series of standards ratified by the Internet Engineering Task Force (IETF), a global standards organization. The job of this committee is to consider submissions for new features to the TCP/IP protocol and other related communications methods. Standards that are approved by the IETF are covered in Requests for Comments (RFCs). If you are looking for in-depth technical information on various Internet protocols and standards, see www.ietf.org.

An IP address is simply a number used to uniquely identify a computer on a TCP/IP network. The address takes the form of four octets (eight binary bits) each of which is represented by a decimal number between 0 and 255. Decimal points logically separate each of the decimally represented numbers. For example, all of the following are valid IP addresses:

- 128.45.23.17

- 230.212.43.100

- 10.1.1.1

Believe it or not the dotted decimal notated representation was created to make it easier for humans to deal with IP addresses. Obviously, this idea did not go far enough, hence the development of the other abstraction layer of using names to represent the dotted decimal notation. For example 11000000 10101000 00000001 00010101 maps to 192.168.1.21, which maps to `server1.company.org`, which is how the address is usually presented to the user or application. First, ASCII flat files, called HOSTS files, were used, but as the number of entries grew, this became unwieldy with manual updates required. This was the impetus for the development of DNS.

When dealing with large networks, it is vital for users and network administrators alike to be able to locate the resources they require with a minimal amount of searching. From a user's standpoint, they don't care about the actual physical or logical network address of the machine. They just want to be able to connect to it using a simple name. From a network administrator's standpoint, however, each machine must have its own logical address that makes it part of the network on which it resides. Therefore, some method for resolving a machine's logical name to an IP address is required. DNS was created to do just that.

DNS is based on an Internet standard defined by the IETF. It is a hierarchical naming system that contains a distributed database of name-to-IP address mappings. A DNS name is much friendlier and easier to remember than an IP address. For example, every time you enter a URL (such as `www.microsoft.com`), your computer makes a query to a DNS server that resolves it to an IP address. From then on, all communications between your computer and Microsoft's Web server take place using the IP address. The beauty of the system is that it's all transparent to users. The scalability and reliability of DNS can easily be seen by its widespread use on the Internet.

From a network and systems administration standpoint, however, things are considerably more complex. The Active Directory itself is designed to use DNS to locate servers and clients. Microsoft has included a DNS server service with the Windows 2000 operating system. As we'll see, Microsoft has also included many advanced features (some of which are not yet part of the IETF-approved standard DNS) in order to reduce the complexity of maintaining DNS databases.

If you're new to DNS, the following sections will provide a lot of useful information on how DNS works. If you're a seasoned DNS veteran, you should still read about Windows 2000's DNS, which includes several additional features and enhancements that will be covered thoroughly in this chapter. We'll begin this chapter by looking at how DNS works. Then, we'll move on to look at how Microsoft's implementation of DNS can be used for name resolution. Finally, we'll look at the integration between the Active Directory and DNS.

DNS Namespace

If the world could run on only one flat network, things might be easier. We wouldn't need subnets, routers, and switches to isolate connections from each other. In the real world, however, technological and other limitations force network and systems administrators to create and adhere to their own specific set of names and network addresses. Furthermore, hierarchical names are extremely useful and necessary when participating in a worldwide network such as the Internet. For example, if I have a computer called Workstation 1, there must be some way to distinguish it from another computer with the same name at a different company. Similar to the way the Active Directory uses hierarchical names for objects, DNS allows for the use of a virtually unlimited number of machines. In this section, we'll look at how these friendly names are structured.

The Anatomy of a DNS Name

We already mentioned that DNS is designed to resolve network addresses with friendly names. DNS names take the form of a series of alphanumeric strings separated by decimal points. Together, the various portions of a DNS name form what is called the *DNS namespace,* and each address within it is unique. All of the following examples are valid DNS names:

- `microsoft.com`
- `www.microsoft.com`
- `sales.microsoft.com`
- `engineering.microsoft.com`

The leftmost portion of the name is called the *host name* and refers to the actual name of a machine. The remaining portions are part of the domain name and uniquely specify the network on which the host resides. The full name is referred to as the *Fully-Qualified Domain Name* (FQDN). For example, the host name might be engineering, whereas the FQDN is `engineering.microsoft.com`.

There are several features and limitations to note about a DNS name:

The name is hierarchical. The domains listed at the right-most side of the address are higher-level domains. As you move left, each portion zooms in on the actual host. In other words, as you read from left to right, you are moving from the specific host name to its various containers.

The name is case-insensitive. Although DNS names are sometimes printed in mixed-case for clarity, the case of the characters has no relevance.

Each FQDN on a given network must be unique. No two machines on the same network may have the same FQDN. This requirement ensures that each machine can be uniquely identified.

Only certain characters are allowed. Each portion of the DNS name may include only standard English characters, decimal numbers, and dashes.

There are maximum lengths for addresses. A DNS address can have a maximum length of 255 characters, and each name within the full name can have up to 63 characters.

Figure 2.1 shows an example of a valid hierarchical domain name.

FIGURE 2.1 A sample DNS namespace

Now that we know the structure of a DNS name, let's move on to look at how the name is actually composed in the real world.

The Root

In order to be able to resolve friendly names with IP addresses, we must have some starting point. All DNS names originate from one address known as the root. This address typically does not have a name and is represented in the DNS as a ".". Until recently there were only nine root DNS servers in the world.

After the last Internet brownout, this number was increased and their administration policies were modified. Registered in the root servers are the standard top-level domains with which most people are familiar.

Many organizations worldwide require domain names to be resolved starting at the root. That is the purpose of the top-level domains. On the Internet, there are several established top-level domains. Table 2.1 provides a list of the common North American top-level domains. Each domain space is reserved for a particular type of user, also shown in the table.

TABLE 2.1   North American Top-Level Domain Names

Top-Level Domain	Typical Users
.com	Commercial organizations
.edu	Educational institutions
.gov	U.S. governmental organizations
.int	International organizations
.mil	U.S. military organizations
.net	Large network providers (such as Internet Service Providers)
.org	Nonprofit organizations

In addition to these top-level domain names, there are many country codes for top-level domains throughout the world. Each is managed by its own authority. For example, a DNS name that is based in the United Kingdom may have a domain name of `mycompany.co.uk`. If you require a foreign domain name registration, you should inquire with the country's name service provider.

In order for an organization's own domain name to be resolved on the Internet, it must request that a second-level domain name be added to the global top-level DNS servers. Several registrars can perform this function worldwide.

For more information on registering a domain name for your own organization, see www.internic.net. There, you will find a list of common registrars available worldwide. There is a nominal charge for each domain name you register.

The name that is registered on the Internet is known as a second-level domain name. Company1.com, for example, would be considered a second-level domain name. Within an organization, however, all of the domain names would be subdomains of this one. Figure 2.2 provides an example of how the various levels of DNS domain names form a hierarchy.

FIGURE 2.2 A DNS name hierarchy

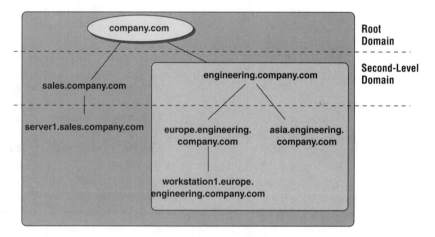

A major consideration of DNS namespace configuration is whether or not you want to trust public Internet Service Providers (ISPs) for name resolution. If not, the alternative is to host your own domain name (which can consist of any top-level domain name you choose), but your servers cannot be made directly accessible on the Internet. For example, I might choose to use the names sales.mycompany and engineering.mycompany. Although these are perfectly valid DNS names for internal use, Internet users will not be able to access them. On the other hand, I could trust public Internet authorities and use names such as sales.mycompany.com and engineering.mycompany.com (as long as I am the registered owner of the mycompany.com domain name). In this last scenario, you would need to rely on the DNS servers managed by your ISP (Internet Service Provider) for external name resolution.

Parent and Child Names

Once an organization has registered its own domain name, it must list that name on a DNS server. This might be a server controlled by the organization itself, or it might be one controlled by a third party such as an ISP that hosts the name. In either case, systems and network administrators can start adding names to their DNS servers using this top-level domain name.

If, for example, I have three computers that I want to make available on the Internet, I would first need to register a second-level domain name, such as mycompany.com. I could then choose to add my own domain names, such as the following:

- www.mycompany.com

- mail.mycompany.com

- computer1.northamerica.sales.mycompany.com

Each of these domain names must be listed on the DNS server as a *resource record (RR)*. The records themselves consist of a domain name to IP address mapping. When users try to access one of these machines (through a Web browser, for example), the name will be resolved with the appropriate TCP/IP address.

DNS servers themselves are responsible for carrying out various functions related to name resolution. One of its functions is related to fulfilling DNS name mapping requests. If a DNS server has information about the specific host name specified in the request, it simply returns the appropriate information to the client that made the request. If, however, the DNS server does not have information about the specific host name, it must obtain that information from another DNS server. In this case, a process called name resolution is required. In order to resolve names of which it has no knowledge, DNS servers query other DNS servers for that information. As a result, you can see how a worldwide network of names can be formed. Later in this chapter, we'll see the various steps required to ensure that DNS servers are communicating worldwide.

Planning a DNS Structure

It is extremely important for your organization to choose intuitive and consistent names when planning its DNS infrastructure. These are the names that users throughout the world will use to access your resources. The *root domain* name is especially important since it will be a part of the FQDN of all the machines on your network. For example, many users are accustomed to accessing a company's main Web servers via the host name www, and they may find it difficult to access your main Web servers if you use another host name. In this section, we'll look at several issues related to selecting internal and external DNS names.

Selecting a DNS Root Name

The first step in establishing a DNS structure for your organization involves selecting a top-level domain name. The most common choice for a top-level domain is .COM (for commercial companies). Usually, you would then want to reserve a second-level domain name based on the name of your company. Currently, however, due to the large number of registered domains, it may be difficult to reserve that name. In any case, you should inquire with the Internet Network Information Center (InterNIC) at www.internic.net to find a usable domain name. A good name would be one that is easy to remember and that people will quickly associate with your company. If your company has a long name or its name consists of multiple words, you might want to abbreviate it. For example, users might find ComputerTechnologies-Inc.com difficult to type, whereas CompTech.com is much simpler. Some common guidelines for choosing a suitable name include the following:

- Choose a name that is similar to the name of your company.

- Use a name that will not usually change. Department or product names, for example, might change over time, whereas company names will remain relatively static.

- Ensure that you have the approval of your company's management before registering and using a name.

- Consult with your company's legal department (or a legal service) to ensure that the domain name is not currently being used and that a trademark on the name is not currently held by another company.

Once you have found a name, the process to register it is quite simple and can be carried out entirely online. To start the registration process, connect to `rs.internic.net` and follow the links for registering a new domain name. You will need to choose from among several official registrars and then follow the instructions provided.

During the rise in popularity of the World Wide Web, many people rushed to reserve domain names based, for example, on the names of popular companies. These people (sometimes affectionately referred to as cyber-squatters) planned to sell the domain names to the companies that owned the copyright for the name. Today, however, organizations are in place to prevent trademarked names from being used by third parties as domain names. To inquire into the process of regaining a domain name to which you may have rights, see `rs.internic.net`.

In order for your computers to be accessible via the Internet, you will need to have a worldwide-registered domain name. As part of the name registration process, you will be required to provide technical information about the DNS server(s) that will host your domain name. If you have your own DNS servers, you can simply provide their IP addresses. Otherwise, you can receive this service from many commercial ISPs (for a fee). Figure 2.3 shows how DNS names are resolved with company domain names.

FIGURE 2.3 How root domain requests are resolved

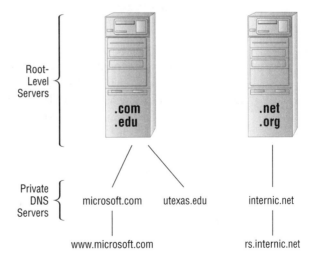

Choosing Internal and External Names

So far, we have been talking about choosing an Internet root domain name. This external name is designed to make computers accessible publicly on the Internet. You will also need to choose a domain name for your internal network. The internal domain name may be the same as the external one, or it may be different. When you're managing internal names, you can choose any name that meets your own standards. You should, however, ensure that any external domain name you use has been properly registered with the Internet name authorities. Figure 2.4 provides an example of how different internal and external DNS names can be used.

FIGURE 2.4 Using different internal and external DNS names

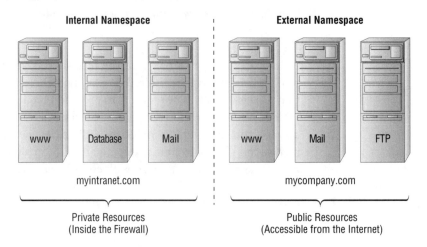

There are several pros and cons to consider when deciding whether or not to use the same domain name for internal and external resources. The advantages of using the same name include consistency between internal and external resources. This means that users will be able to use the same e-mail address for internal and external communications. However, having the same name will require taking great care in naming resources and configuring DNS servers. A small mistake in the naming, for instance, may result in an internal server being made available on the public Internet. Similarly, users must be told which resources are only available from the internal network and which machines are accessible from the public Internet.

If you choose separate internal and external names, you will be able to easily determine which resources are publicly accessible and which ones are restricted to your private network. This also simplifies routing and DNS settings. However, this method requires that you reserve two domain names (which are getting more and more difficult to find!) and that users have two different e-mail addresses (one for internal e-mail and one for e-mail sent by users that are located outside of the private network (such as Internet users).

You should base your decision regarding whether to use separate or identical internal and external namespaces on your organization's business and technical requirements.

Overview of DNS Zones

DNS servers work together to resolve hierarchical names. If they already have information about a name, they simply fulfill the query for the client; otherwise, they query other DNS servers for the appropriate information. The system works well as it distributes the authority of separate parts of the DNS structure to specific servers. A DNS *zone* is a portion of the DNS namespace over which a specific DNS server has authority. In this section, we'll see how the concept of zones is used to ensure accurate name resolution on the Internet.

Purpose and Function of DNS Zones

In order to ensure that naming remains accurate in a distributed network environment, one DNS server must be designated as the master database for a specific set of addresses. It is on this server that updates to host-name–to–IP-address mappings can be updated. Whenever a DNS server is unable to resolve a specific DNS name, it simply queries other servers that can provide the information. Zones are necessary because many different DNS servers could otherwise be caching the same information. If changes are made, this information could become outdated. Therefore, one central DNS server must assume the role of the ultimate authority for a specific subset of domain names.

There is an important distinction to make between DNS zones and Active Directory domains. Although both use hierarchical names and require name resolution, DNS zones do not map directly to DNS domains.

As shown in Figure 2.5, a zone may be an entire domain or represent only part of one.

FIGURE 2.5 The relationship between DNS domains and zones

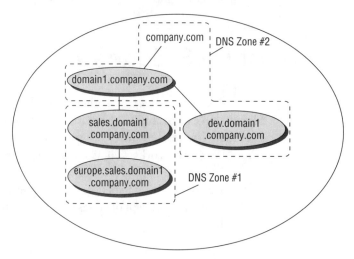

With this information in mind, let's take a more detailed look at the actual process of DNS name resolution.

DNS Name Resolution

When using the Internet, DNS queries are extremely common. For example, every time you click a link to visit a Web site, a DNS query must be made. In the simplest scenario, the client computer requests a DNS address from its designated DNS server. The DNS server has information about the IP address for the specified host name, it returns that information to the client, and the client then uses the IP address to initiate communications with the host. This process is shown in Figure 2.6.

FIGURE 2.6   A simple DNS name resolution process

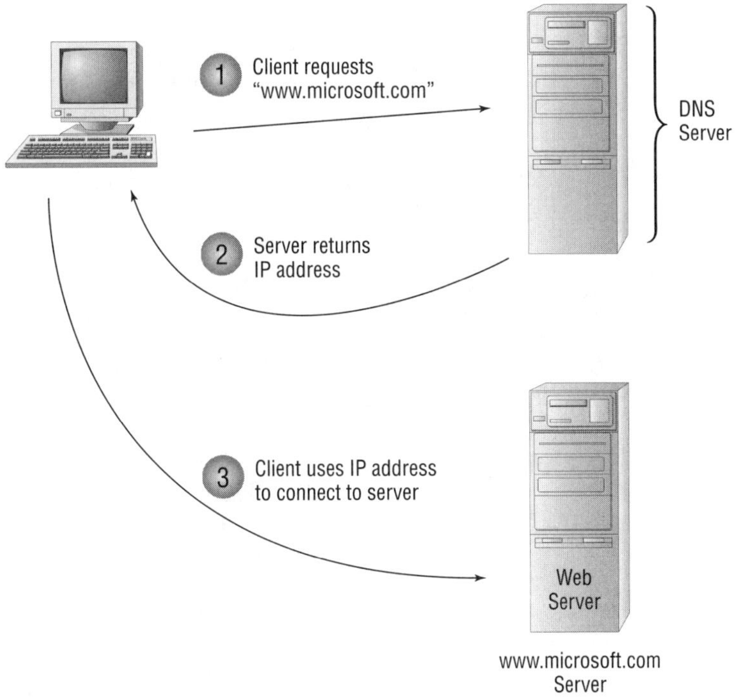

What happens, though, if the DNS server does not contain information about the specific host requested? In this case, the DNS server itself initiates a query to another DNS server, which thereby assumes responsibility for ultimately resolving the name. If the second DNS server is unable to fulfill the request, it, in turn, queries another. This process is known as *recursion*. In the process of recursion, one DNS server will contact another, which will then contact another until one of the servers is able to resolve the host name. The name resolution process will usually begin with a query to the top-level DNS servers and continue downward through the domain hierarchy until the resource is reached. If, at this point, the name still cannot be resolved, an error is returned to the client. Figure 2.7 illustrates the process of recursion. Usually, DNS servers include information about the root- and top-level DNS servers. This information is entered in during the initial configuration of the server.

FIGURE 2.7   DNS name resolution through recursion

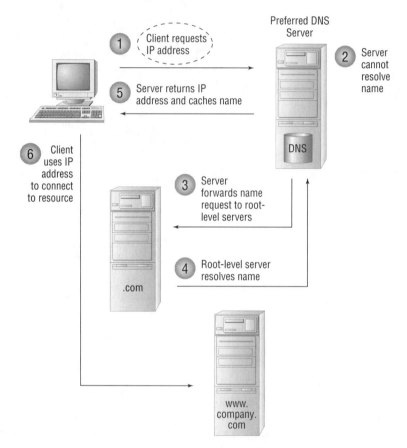

Because recursion is such an important process, let's look at an example. Suppose I want to connect to the DNS name `Computer1.sales.somecompany.com`. The following steps will occur to make this happen:

1. The client requests information from its preferred DNS server.

2. The preferred DNS server is unable to find a resource record for this information in its own cache and must therefore query another server. The DNS server first queries a root server and then sends a query to the top-level domain server and requests information about the server that has authority over the `somecompany.com` domain.

3. Once the information is obtained, the preferred DNS server then queries the `somecompany.com` DNS server for information about the computer1 host name within the sales domain.

4. The client's preferred DNS server then returns the IP address of the host name to the client. It can then use the IP address to communicate with the host. The preferred DNS server may choose to cache a copy of the resource record information just in case additional requests for the domain name are made.

A client may also be configured to query multiple DNS servers for names. This process is known as *iteration*. Iteration is normally used when a client queries DNS servers, but instructs them not to use recursion. Alternatively, systems administrators may configure DNS servers, themselves, not to perform recursion. For example, we may configure all DNS servers to forward resolution requests to one DNS server on our network. This will direct all DNS traffic through this one server, thereby reducing network traffic and allowing us to secure DNS requests.

In the iteration process, the DNS server fulfills a request if it is able to do so based on the information in its own database. If it cannot, it will either return an error or will point the client to another DNS server that may be able to resolve the name. Iteration requires the client to remain responsible for ultimately resolving the name request.

Usually, the client is configured with multiple DNS servers that are utilized according to a certain search order. This is useful, for example, if different DNS servers are required to resolve intranet and Internet names. For example, a client may use one DNS server to resolve names for a specific department within the organization and another DNS server to resolve names of public Web sites. This method places the burden of finding the right name server on the client. In certain configurations, though, you may want to reduce network traffic with DNS *forwarding*, which allows you to specify exactly which DNS servers will be used for resolving names. For example, if you have multiple DNS servers located on a fast network (such as a LAN), you may want each of them to request DNS information from only a few specific DNS servers that can then gain information from other DNS servers on the network. Figure 2.8 provides an example of how DNS forwarding can be used.

FIGURE 2.8   Using DNS forwarding to reduce network traffic

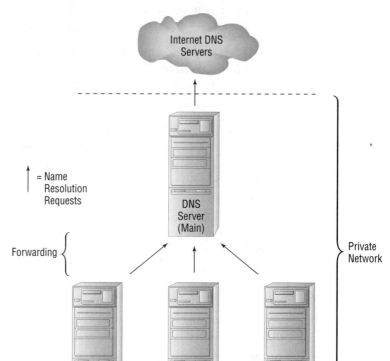

Another feature of DNS servers is their ability to cache information. As you can imagine, going through the recursion process each time a DNS query is initiated can place a significant load on servers worldwide. In order to limit some of this traffic, DNS servers usually save information about mapped domain names in their own local database. If future requests are made for the same host and domain names, this cached information is usually used. To ensure that the cached information is reasonably up-to-date, a Time to Live (TTL) value is attached to each cached DNS record. Typical TTL values range from three to seven days. Once this time limit is exceeded, the cached value is no longer used, and the next request for the information will result in going through the entire recursion process again.

Since DNS names are updated on a pull basis, it can take time for some DNS servers to update their databases. If you are required to make changes to a DNS entry, be sure to allow sufficient time for all of the name servers on the Internet to be updated. Usually, this should take only a few days, but, in some cases, it may take more than a week.

Although the most common DNS functions involve the mapping of DNS names to IP addresses, certain applications might require the opposite functionality—the resolution of an IP address to a DNS name. This is handled through a *reverse lookup zone* in the DNS server. Reverse lookup zones start with a special Internet authority address and allow the DNS server to resolve queries for specific TCP/IP addresses. As we'll see later in this chapter, reverse lookup zones are configured similarly to standard *forward lookup zones*.

In order to determine from which DNS server specific information can be found, zones must be used. Let's now examine the process of establishing authority for specific DNS zones.

Delegating Authority in DNS Zones

Every DNS server can be configured to be responsible for one or more DNS domains. The DNS server is then known as the authoritative source of address information for that zone. Generally, if you are using only a single DNS domain, you will have only one zone. Remember that there can be a many-to-many relationship between domains (which are used to create a logical naming structure) and zones (which refer primarily to the physical structure of a DNS implementation).

When you add subdomains, however, you have two options. You can allow the original DNS server to continue functioning as the authority for the *parent and child domains*. Or, you can choose to create another DNS zone and give a different server authority over it. The process of giving authority for specific domains to other DNS servers is known as *delegation*. Figure 2.9 shows how delegation can be configured.

The main reasons for using delegation are performance and administration. Using multiple DNS servers in a large network can help distribute the load involved in resolving names. It can also help in administering security by allowing only certain types of records to be modified by specified systems administrators.

DNS Server Roles

One of the potential problems with configuring specific DNS servers as authorities for their own domains is fault tolerance. What happens if an authoritative server becomes unavailable? Normally, none of the names for the resources in that zone could be resolved to network addresses. This could be a potentially serious problem for networks of any size. For example, if the primary server for the `sales.mycompany.com` zone becomes unavailable (and there are no secondary servers in that zone), users will not be able to find resources such as `server1.sales.mycompany.com` or `workstation1.sales.mycompany.com`. In order to prevent the potential network problems of a single failed server, the DNS specification allows for supporting multiple servers per zone.

To maintain a distributed and hierarchical naming system, DNS servers can assume several different roles at once. In this section, we'll look at the various roles that DNS servers can assume within a zone. In later sections of this chapter, we'll see how Windows 2000 Server computers can assume these roles.

Primary Server

Each DNS zone must have one *primary DNS server*. The primary server is responsible for maintaining all of the records for the DNS zone and contains the primary copy of the DNS database. Additionally, all updates of records occur on the primary server. You will want to create and add primary servers whenever you create a new DNS domain. When creating child domains, however, you may want to use the primary server from the parent domain.

Secondary Server

A *secondary DNS server* contains a database of all of the same information as the primary name server and can be used to resolve DNS requests. The main purpose of a secondary server is to provide for fault tolerance. That is, in case the primary server becomes unavailable, name resolution can still occur using the secondary server. Therefore, it is a good general practice to ensure that each zone has at least one secondary server to protect against failures.

Secondary DNS servers can also increase performance by offloading some of the traffic that would otherwise go to the primary server. Secondary servers are also often located within each location of an organization that has high-speed network access. This prevents DNS queries from having to run across slow WAN connections. For example, if there are two remote offices within the `mycompany.com` organization, we may want to place a secondary DNS server in each remote office. This way, when clients require name resolution, they will contact the nearest server for this IP address information, thus preventing unnecessary WAN traffic.

Although it is a good idea to have secondary servers, having too many of them can cause increases in network traffic due to replication. Therefore, you should always weigh the benefits and drawbacks and properly plan for secondary servers.

Master Server

Master DNS servers are used in the replication of DNS data between primary and secondary servers. Usually, the primary server also serves as the master server, but these tasks can be separated for performance reasons. The master server is responsible for propagating any changes to the DNS database to all secondary servers within a particular zone.

Caching-Only Server

Caching-only DNS servers serve the same function as primary DNS servers in that they assist clients in resolving DNS names to network addresses. The only difference is that caching-only servers are not authoritative for any DNS zones, and they don't contain copies of the zone files. They only contain mappings as a result of resolved queries and in fact will lose all of their mapping information when the server is shut down. Therefore, they are installed only for performance reasons. A caching-only DNS server may be used at sites that have slow connectivity to DNS servers at other sites.

Zone Transfers

Similar to the situation with domain controllers and the Active Directory, it is important to ensure that DNS zone information is consistent between the primary and secondary servers. The process used to keep the servers synchronized is known as a *zone transfer*. When a secondary DNS server is configured for a zone, it first performs a zone transfer during which it obtains a copy of the primary server's address database. This process is known as an all-zone transfer (AXFR).

In order to ensure that information is kept up-to-date after the initial synchronization, incremental zone transfers (IXFRs) are used. Through this process, the changes in the DNS zone databases are communicated between primary and secondary servers. IXFRs use a system of serial numbers to determine which records are new or updated. This system ensures that the newest DNS record is always used, even if changes were made on more than one server.

Not all DNS servers support IXFRs. Windows NT 4's DNS services and earlier implementations of other DNS services require a full zone transfer of the entire database in order to update their records. This can sometimes cause significant network traffic. As with any software implementation, you should always verify the types of functionality supported before deploying it.

Zone transfers may occur in response to the following different events:

- The zone refresh interval has been exceeded.

- A master server notifies a secondary server of a zone change.

- A secondary DNS server service is started for the zone.

- A DNS zone transfer is manually initiated (by a systems administrator) at the secondary server.

An important factor regarding zone transfers is that secondary servers always initiate them. This type of replication is commonly known as a pull operation. Normally, a zone transfer request is made when a refresh interval is reached on the secondary server. The request is sent to a *master server*, which then sends any changes to the secondary server. Usually the primary server is also configured as a master server, but this can be changed for performance reasons.

One of the problems with pull replication is that the information stored on secondary servers can sometimes be out-of-date. For example, suppose an IXFR occurs today, but the refresh interval is set to three days. If I make a change on the primary DNS server, this change will not be reflected on the secondary server for at least several days. One potential way to circumvent this problem is to set a very low refresh interval (such as a few hours). However, this can cause a lot of unnecessary network traffic and increased processing overhead.

In order to solve the problems related to keeping resource records up-to-date, a feature known as DNS notify was developed. This method employs push replication to inform secondary servers whenever a change is made. When secondary servers receive the DNS notify message, they immediately initiate an IXFR request. Figure 2.10 shows how DNS notify is used to keep secondary servers up-to-date. This method ensures that compatible DNS servers are updated immediately whenever changes are made.

FIGURE 2.10 Using DNS notify to update secondary servers

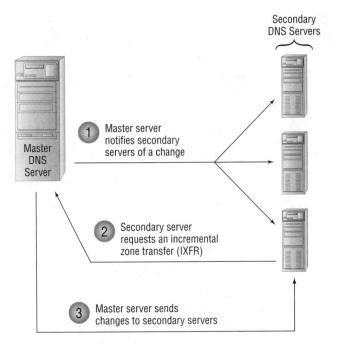

Managing DNS Resource Records

So far, we have looked at various ways in which DNS servers remain synchronized with each other. Now, it's time to look at the actual types of information stored within the DNS database. Table 2.2 provides a list of the types of records that are used within the DNS database. Each of these records is important for ensuring that the proper type of resource is made available. For example, if a client is attempting to send e-mail, the DNS server should respond with the IP address corresponding to the Mail Exchanger (MX) record of the domain.

TABLE 2.2   DNS Resource Record Types

Resource Record Type	Meaning	Notes
A	Address	Used to map host names to IP addresses; multiple A records may be used to map to a single IP address
CNAME	Canonical Name	Used as an alias or a nickname for a host (in addition to the A record)
MX	Mail Exchanger	Specifies the Simple Mail Transfer Protocol (SMTP) e-mail server address for the domain
NS	Name Server	Specifies the IP address of DNS servers for the domain
PTR	Pointer	Used for reverse lookup operations
RP	Responsible Person	Specifies information about the individual that is responsible for maintaining the DNS information
SOA	Start of Authority	Specifies the authoritative server for a zone
SRV	Service	Specifies server services available on a host; used by the Active Directory to identify domain controllers; the standard for SRV records has not yet been finalized

Additionally, certain conventions are often used on the Internet. For example, the host names mail, www, ftp, and news are usually reserved for e-mail, World Wide Web, file transfer protocol, and USENET news servers, respectively.

Now that you have a good understanding of the purpose and methods of DNS, let's move on to looking at how Microsoft's DNS service operates.

Planning for Microsoft DNS

So far, we've presented a lot of information regarding DNS concepts. By covering the DNS namespace and how DNS servers interact with each other, you should have a good understanding of the name resolution infrastructure required by the Active Directory. If you are still unclear on some of the concepts related to planning a DNS structure for an organization, be sure to review the information presented earlier in this chapter.

One of the major benefits of using Microsoft DNS is the ability to manage and replicate the DNS database as a part of the Active Directory. This allows for automating much of the administration of the DNS service while still keeping information up-to-date.

With respect to your DNS environment, you'll want to plan for the use of various DNS servers. As we mentioned earlier in this chapter, there are several possible roles for DNS servers, including primary, secondary, master, and caching-only servers. With respect to the Active Directory, DNS services are absolutely vital. Without the proper functioning of DNS, Active Directory clients and servers will not be able to locate each other, and network services will be severely impacted.

Let's look at how DNS zones and servers can be planned for use with the Active Directory.

Planning DNS Zones

The first step in planning for DNS server deployment is to determine the size and layout of your DNS zones. In the simplest configurations, there will be a single Active Directory domain and a single DNS zone. This configuration usually meets the needs of single-domain environments.

When multiple domains are considered, you generally need to make some choices when planning for DNS. In some environments, you might choose to use only a single zone that spans over all of the domains. In other cases, you might want to break zones apart for administrative and performance reasons.

The DNS zone configuration you choose is largely independent of the Active Directory configuration. That is, for any given Active Directory configuration, you could use any setup of zones, as long as all names can be properly resolved. With that said, make no mistake—the proper functioning of DNS zones is critical to the functionality of the Active Directory.

Planning Server Roles

So far in this section, we've talked about the logical layout of DNS zones in relation to Active Directory domains. Now, it's time to look at how DNS servers should optimally be configured for various environments.

First and foremost, DNS servers are extremely important in the Active Directory environment. In order to provide for fault tolerance for DNS servers, you should ensure that each DNS zone you configure consists of one primary DNS server and at least one secondary server. If the primary DNS computer fails, the secondary server can still carry out name resolution operations, and most operations will continue normally. This is, however, a temporary solution since you will need to restore or replace the primary DNS server in order to make updates to the DNS zone information.

Generally, you will want to make the primary DNS server the master server for the zone. If it is necessary for performance reasons, however, you can choose to use a separate machine for DNS services.

Caching-only servers are generally used when you want to make DNS information available for multiple computers that do not have a fast or reliable connection to the main network. Because they do not have any authority over specific zones, the decision to use caching-only servers is generally based on the physical network layout.

Figure 2.11 shows a representative DNS server configuration for an Active Directory domain.

FIGURE 2.11 Arranging servers for the Active Directory

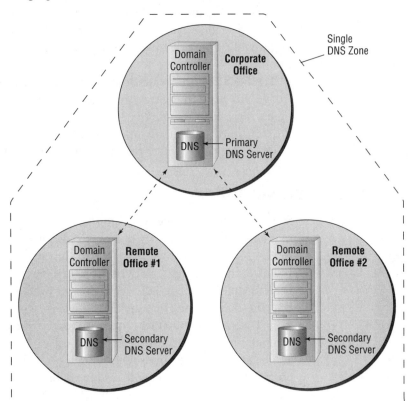

Installing and Configuring a DNS Server

Microsoft has made the technical steps involved in installing the DNS service extremely simple. This, however, is not an excuse for not thoroughly understanding and planning for a DNS configuration. In this section, we'll cover the actual steps required to install and configure a DNS server for use with Microsoft's Active Directory.

**Microsoft
Exam
Objective**

Install, configure, and troubleshoot DNS for Active Directory.

- Integrate Active Directory DNS zones with non-Active Directory DNS zones.

- Configure zones for dynamic updates.

See "Managing DNS Interoperability," a section later in this chapter, for coverage of the "Integrate Active Directory DNS zones with non-Active Directory DNS zones" subobjective and "Configuring Zones for Automatic Updates," another section later in this chapter, for coverage of the "Configure zones for dynamic updates" subobjective.

Exercise 2.1 walks you through the steps required to install the DNS service.

EXERCISE 2.1

Installing the DNS Service

This exercise will walk you through the steps required to install the DNS service.

1. Click Start ➤ Settings ➤ Control Panel, and then double-click the Add/Remove Programs icon.

2. Select Add/Remove Windows Components.

3. Click the Components button to access a list of services and options available for installation on Windows 2000.

4. In the Windows 2000 Components Wizard, select Networking Services, and then click Details.

EXERCISE 2.1 *(continued)*

5. Place a check mark next to the option titled Domain Name System (DNS).

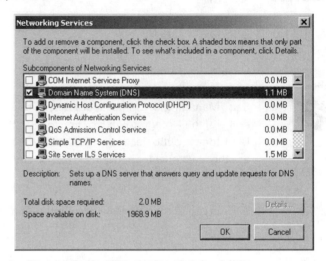

6. Click OK to accept your choice, then click Next to continue with the Wizard.

Once you have installed the DNS service, you are ready to begin configuring the server for the Active Directory.

Adding DNS Zones

Once you have installed the DNS service, you'll need to configure DNS for your specific environment. The most important aspect of configuring the DNS properly is planning. Based on the information presented in the previous sections, you should be aware of how you plan to configure DNS zones for your Active Directory environment.

The technical implementation process is quite easy, thanks to the Configure DNS Server Wizard. Exercise 2.2 walks you through the process used to configure DNS zones.

EXERCISE 2.2

Using the Configure DNS Server Wizard

In this exercise, you will configure basic DNS zones, including a standard primary forward lookup zone. This exercise assumes that you have already installed the DNS service and that no configuration options have been set.

1. Open the DNS snap-in in the Administrative Tools program group.

2. In the DNS administrative tool, right-click the name of your local server and select Configure the Server…. The introduction page will inform you that the Configure DNS Server Wizard will help you configure DNS zones for this server. Click Next to begin the process.

3. Create a forward lookup zone by choosing Yes, Create a Forward Lookup Zone, then click Next.

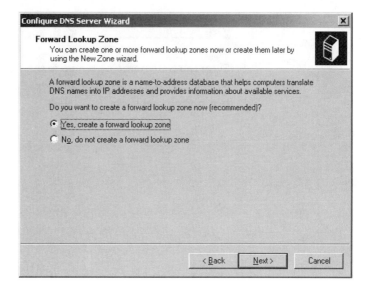

EXERCISE 2.2 *(continued)*

4. Select the type of DNS zone you want to create. The available options include Active Directory-integrated (only available if Active Directory is installed), Standard Primary, and Standard Secondary. Select Standard Primary, and click Next.

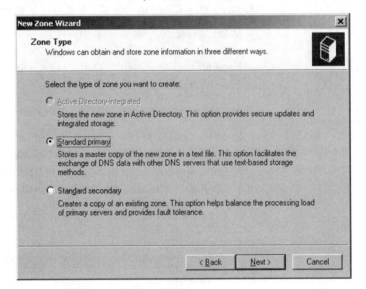

5. Enter the zone name by typing in the name of the DNS zone for which you want to record addresses. For example, you might type **test.mycompany.com**. Click Next.

6. Once you have determined the name for the DNS domain, you can choose either to create a new local DNS file or to use an existing DNS file. DNS zone files are standard text files that contain mappings of IP addresses to DNS names. Usually, zone files are named as the name of the domain followed by a .DNS suffix (for example, test.mycompany.com.dns). These files must be stored in the system32/dns subdirectory of your Windows 2000 system root. Leave the default option, and click Next.

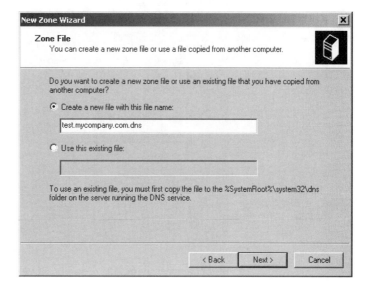

7. Although reverse lookup zones are not required for basic DNS functionality and are, therefore, optional, you will probably want to create one. Reverse lookup zones are used to map IP addresses to DNS names and are required for the proper operation of some TCP/IP applications. Select Yes, Create a Reverse Lookup Zone, and click Next.

8. Choose the reverse lookup zone type. The options are similar to those for the forward lookup zone. Select Standard Primary, and click Next.

9. Specify the reverse lookup zone. In order for reverse lookups to work properly, you must specify the network to which the zone applies. You can specify the value using a network ID or the name of the reverse lookup zone. The value you enter will be based on the subnet(s) for which this DNS server will provide reverse lookup information. Enter **169** for the Network ID, and click Next to continue.

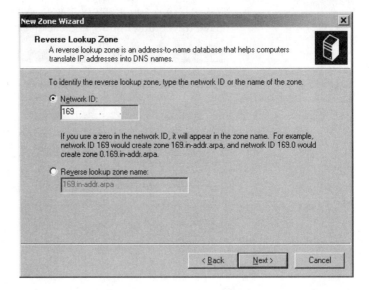

10. Select a reverse lookup zone file. Reverse lookup zone files are created and managed similarly to forward lookup zone files. Choose the default option, and click Next.

11. To finalize the settings made by the Wizard, click Next. The Wizard will automatically create the forward and reverse lookup zones based on the information you specified.

If your network environment will require this DNS server to manage multiple zones, you can run the Configure DNS Server Wizard again. Alternatively, if you are comfortable with the options available, you can right-click the name of your server and select New Zone.

Configuring DNS Zone Properties

Once you have properly configured forward and reverse lookup zones for your DNS server, you can make additional configuration settings for each zone by right-clicking its name within the DNS administrative tool and selecting Properties. The following tabs and settings are available for forward lookup zones:

General   The General tab allows you to set various options for the forward lookup zone. Using this tab (see Figure 2.12), you can pause the DNS service. When the service is paused, it continues to run, but clients cannot complete name resolution requests from this machine. The second option is to change the type of the zone. Choices include primary, secondary, and Active Directory-integrated (available only if the Active Directory is installed). You can also specify the name of the DNS zone file. Allowing dynamic updates is extremely useful for reducing the management and administration headaches associated with creating resource records. Finally, you can specify aging and scavenging properties for this zone.

FIGURE 2.12   Setting zone properties with the General tab

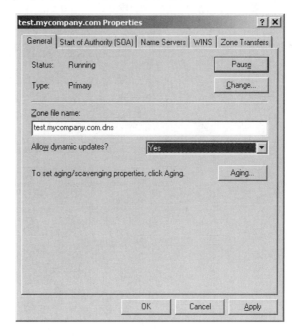

Start of Authority (SOA) The SOA tab allows you to specify information regarding the authority of the DNS server (see Figure 2.13). The Serial Number text box is used to determine whether a zone transfer is needed to keep any secondary servers up-to-date. For example, if a secondary server has a serial number of 7, but the SOA serial number is set to 6, the secondary server will request a zone transfer. The Primary Server text box allows you to designate the primary DNS server for the zone. The Responsible Person text box allows you to specify contact information for the systems administrator of the DNS server. The Refresh Interval text box and drop-down menu are used to specify how often a secondary zone should verify its information. Lower times ensure greater accuracy but can cause increased network traffic. The Retry Interval text box and drop-down menu are used to specify how often zone transfers will be requested. The Expires After text box and drop-down menu allow you to specify how long secondary DNS servers must try to request updated information before resource records expire. The Minimum (default) TTL text box is used to specify how long a resource record will be considered current. If you are working in an environment where many changes are expected, a lower TTL value can help in maintaining the accuracy of information.

FIGURE 2.13 Setting zone properties with the SOA tab

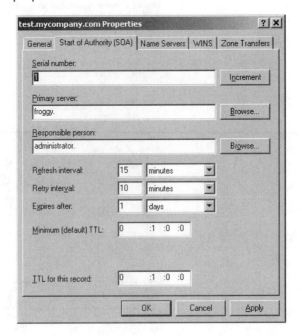

Name Servers The Name Servers tab shows a list of DNS servers for the specified domain. You can add specific DNS servers based on the configuration of your network. Generally, the list of name servers will include the primary name server and any secondary name servers for that zone.

WINS This tab allows you to set options for allowing Windows Internet Naming Service (WINS) lookups to resolve DNS names. WINS and DNS issues are covered later in this chapter.

Zone Transfers Using the options on this tab, you can select which servers will be allowed to serve as a secondary server for the forward lookup zones specified in the properties for the zone. The default option allows any server to request a zone transfer, but you can restrict this by specifying specific IP addresses or allowing only the name servers listed on the Name Servers tab to request transfers. Setting restrictions on zone transfers can increase security by preventing unauthorized users from copying the entire DNS database.

The ability to set each of these options gives systems administrators the power to control DNS operations and resource record settings for their environment.

Configuring DNS Server Options

DNS record databases would tend to become disorganized and filled with outdated information if processes that periodically removed unused records were not present. The process of removing inactive or outdated entries in the DNS database is known as scavenging. Systems administrators use scavenging to configure DNS records to require refreshing based on a certain time setting. When the DNS record has not been refreshed for a certain amount of time, the next DNS query forces the record to be updated. By default, the DNS server is not configured to perform this process at all.

To implement scavenging in the DNS snap-in, you should right-click the name of the server or DNS zone for which you want the settings to apply and choose Set Aging/Scavenging. For example, if you right-click the server name and choose this option, the aging and scavenging settings you specify will apply to all of the DNS zones managed by that server. As shown in Figure 2.14, you can specify two different options:

No-Refresh Interval This allows you to specify the *minimum* amount of time that must elapse before a DNS record is refreshed. Higher values can reduce network traffic but may cause outdated information to be returned to clients.

Refresh Interval This allows you to specify the amount of time between when the no-refresh interval expires and when the resource record information may be refreshed. Lower values can provide for greater accuracy in information but may increase network traffic.

FIGURE 2.14 Setting aging and scavenging options

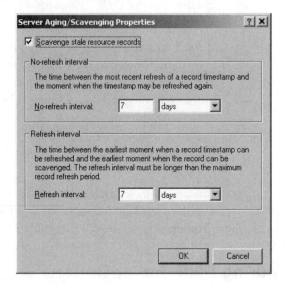

There are also several other DNS server options that can be set to maximize performance functionality in your network environment. To access the properties of the DNS server using the DNS snap-in, right-click the name of the server and choose Properties. The following options will be available:

Interfaces On servers that are enabled with multiple network adapters, you might want to provide DNS services on only one of the interfaces. The default option is to allow DNS requests on all interfaces, but you can limit operations to specific adapters by clicking the Only the Following IP Addresses option (see Figure 2.15).

FIGURE 2.15   Selecting DNS server interfaces

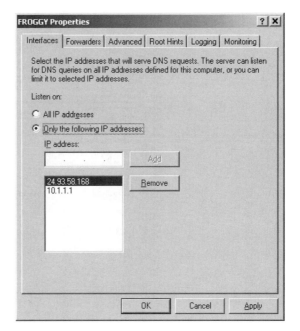

Forwarders   DNS forwarding can be configured to relay all DNS requests that cannot be resolved by this server to one or more specific machines. To configure forwarders, check the box and specify the IP address of one or more DNS servers. If you check the Do Not Use Recursion option, name resolution will occur only through the configured forwarders.

Advanced   The DNS service has several advanced options (see Figure 2.16). For example, you can disable DNS recursion for the entire server by checking the appropriate box. We'll cover specific options as they pertain to the Active Directory later in this chapter.

Root Hints   In order to resolve domain names on the Internet, the local DNS server must know the identities of the worldwide root servers. By default, the Microsoft DNS server is configured with several valid root IP addresses (see Figure 2.17). Additionally, you can add or modify the root hints as needed, but you should only do this if you are sure of the configuration information.

FIGURE 2.16 Advanced DNS server configuration options

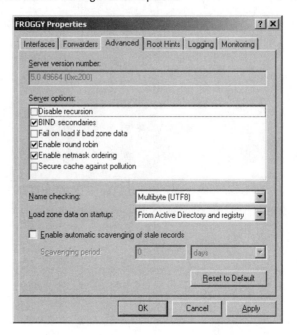

FIGURE 2.17 Viewing default DNS server root hints

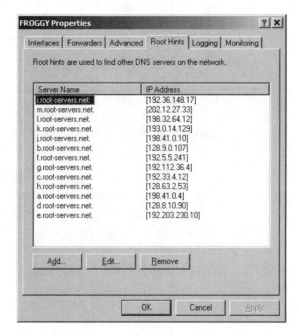

Logging   Logging various DNS operations can be useful for monitoring and troubleshooting the DNS service. You can select various different events to monitor using the properties on this tab. We'll cover more details on logging later in this chapter.

Monitoring   The Monitoring tab is useful for performing a quick check to ensure that the DNS service is operating properly. Using this tab, you will be able to perform a simple query as well as a recursive request. If both operations are successful, you can be reasonably sure that the DNS server is functioning properly.

Once you are satisfied with the DNS server settings, it's time to look at how resource records can be configured.

Creating DNS Resource Records

The main functionality of a DNS server is based on the various resource records present within it. During the Active Directory installation process, you have the option of automatically configuring the DNS server for use with Active Directory. We'll cover the details of this process in Chapter 3, "Installing and Configuring the Active Directory." If you choose to create the default records, the resource records listed in Table 2.3 will automatically be created. Each of these records is of the type SRV (Service). The Domain and DomainTree specifiers will be based on the DNS domain name for the local domain controller, and the Site specifier will be based on your site configuration.

TABLE 2.3   Default Active Directory DNS Resource Records

Resource Record	Purpose
_ldap._tcp.*Domain*	Enumerates the domain controllers for a given domain
_ldap._tcp.*Site*.sites.*Domain*	Allows clients to find domain controllers within a specific site

TABLE 2.3 Default Active Directory DNS Resource Records *(continued)*

Resource Record	Purpose
_ldap._tcp.pdc.ms-dcs.*Domain*	Provides the address of the server acting as the Windows NT Primary Domain Controller (PDC) for the domain
_ldap._tcp.pdc.ms-dcs.*DomainTree*	Enumerates the Global Catalog servers within a domain
_ldap._tcp.S*ite*.gc.ms-dcs .*DomainTree*	Allows a client to find a Global Catalog server based on site configuration
_ldap._tcp.*GUID*.domains .ms-dcs.*DomainTree*	Used by computers to locate machines based on the Global Unique Identifier (GUID)
_ldap._tcp.writable.ms-dcs.*Domain*	Enumerates the domain controller(s) that hold(s) modifiable copies of the Active Directory
_ldap._tcp.*site*.sites.writable .ms-dcs.*Domain*	Enumerates domain controller(s) based on sites

In addition to the default DNS records, you will likely want to create new ones to identify specific servers and clients on your network. Exercise 2.3 provides a walk-through of the creation of a DNS MX record. Although different resource record types require different pieces of information, the process is similar for other types of records.

EXERCISE 2.3

Creating a DNS Mail Exchanger (MX) Record

In this exercise, you will specify a new DNS MX record. This exercise assumes that you have installed the DNS service and have configured at least one forward lookup zone.

1. Open the DNS snap-in in the Administrative Tools program group.

2. Expand the forward lookup zones folder for the local server.

3. Right-click the name of a zone and select New Mail Exchanger.

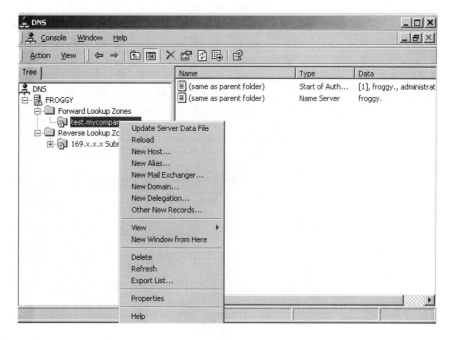

4. Specify the MX options. You'll need to configure several options for the MX record. The options are as follows:

   - Host or Domain: You will need to type the name of the host that will serve as the mail server for this domain. This is the machine to which clients will connect in order to send e-mail messages using SMTP. Usually, this will be a standard DNS name (such as "mail"), but it can also be left blank if you want the entire domain name itself to be used for mail services. Note that the name must be part of the current domain.

- Mail Server: Here, you will be able to specify the actual DNS name of the mail server. This must be a machine name that has a corresponding Address (A) record already configured. You can either type the name or click Browse to find the specific record within any available DNS server on your network.

- Mail Server Priority: DNS supports the assignment of more than one MX record per domain. In order to specify the order in which the various mail servers will be used, a systems administrator can specify priorities for each server. The priority value must be an integer between 0 and 65,535 (inclusive). The lower the number, the higher the priority will be (0 specifies the highest priority). For example, if you have three MX records in the same domain, clients will prefer to use the lowest number mail server priority first. If this server is unavailable or busy, they can then contact the other mail servers.

5. When you are ready to create the record, click OK. This will add the MX record to the forward lookup zone specified in Step 3.

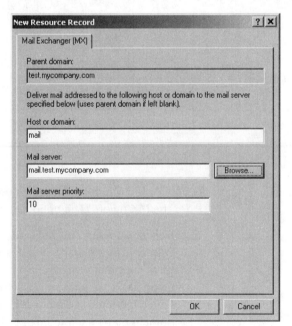

Although you can manually specify DNS server records, this process can become quite tedious. In Chapter 3, "Installing and Configuring the Active Directory," we'll look at how DNS services can be configured for the Active Directory.

Managing DNS Servers

Once your DNS server is installed and configured properly, you will need to manage various settings. In the previous section, we looked at the various options and features available within the DNS service. In this section, we'll focus on some specific operations that are required for working with the Active Directory. The exercises should be helpful in learning your way around the various operations.

Configuring Zones for Automatic Updates

By allowing automatic updates to DNS zones, you will be able to dramatically reduce the administrative burden of managing resource records. Exercise 2.4 shows how to enable this option.

Microsoft ✓ *Exam* *Objective*

Install, configure, and troubleshoot DNS for Active Directory.

- Integrate Active Directory DNS zones with non-Active Directory DNS zones.

- Configure zones for dynamic updates.

See "Managing DNS Interoperability," a section that appears later in this chapter, for coverage of the "Integrate Active Directory DNS zones with non-Active Directory DNS zones" subobjective.

EXERCISE 2.4

Allowing Automatic Updates

This exercise assumes that you have properly installed and configured the DNS service and have configured at least one forward lookup zone.

1. Open the DNS snap-in in the Administrative Tools program group.

2. Expand the forward lookup zones folder under the name of the current server.

3. Right-click the name of a zone, and select Properties.

4. Change the Allow Dynamic Updates option to Yes.

5. Click OK to accept and commit the setting.

Creating Zone Delegations

When you configure a DNS server as a primary server for a zone, that server is responsible for performing name resolution for all of the resources within that zone. In some cases, you might want to delegate authority for a portion of the zone to another DNS server. Exercise 2.5 shows how this can be done.

EXERCISE 2.5

Creating a Zone Delegation

This exercise will delegate authority for a DNS zone to another DNS server. This exercise assumes that you have already created at least one DNS zone. Additionally, this server must be the primary DNS server for at least one zone.

1. Open the DNS administrative tool and expand the branch for the local server.

2. Right-click the name of a zone for which the machine is the primary server, and select New Delegation.

3. This will open the New Delegation Wizard. Click Next.

EXERCISE 2.5 *(continued)*

4. Enter the name of the delegated domain. The delegated domain must be a subdomain of the domain you selected in step 2. For example, if the domain name is `activedirectory.test`, the subdomain might be `domain2`. This will make the fully-qualified domain name `domain2.activedirectory.test`. Click Next.

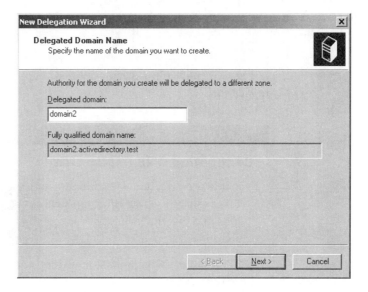

5. Specify the name server(s) to which you want to delegate authority for the domain. To add servers to the list, click Add. You will be able to browse a list of available name servers or specify one by name or IP address. You can also click Edit to change the properties for servers you have already added to the delegation list.

6. Click Next to accept the setting, and then click Finish to create the new delegation.

Managing DNS Replication

Managing DNS replication is an important concern. If optimal settings are not chosen, you might encounter too much replication traffic. Alternatively, you might have the opposite problem—updates are not occurring frequently enough. Earlier in this chapter, we looked at ways to configure the DNS Notify properties within a zone. In this section, we'll see what is required to enable DNS replication.

Microsoft ✓ ***Exam*** ***Objective***	**Manage, monitor, and troubleshoot DNS.** · Manage replication of DNS data.

Exercise 2.6 walks through the steps required to configure DNS replication.

EXERCISE 2.6

Configuring DNS Replication

In this exercise, you will configure various DNS replication options. This exercise assumes that you have already created at least one DNS zone and that the local server is the primary DNS server for at least one zone.

1. Open the DNS administrative tool, and expand the branch for the local server.

2. Right-click the name of a zone for which this machine is the primary server, and select Properties.

3. Select the Zone Transfers tab.

4. Place a check mark in the Allow Zone Transfers box.

5. Choose whether you want to allow zone transfers from any server (the default setting), only servers specified on the Name Servers tab, or specific DNS servers based on their IP addresses. It is recommended that you choose one of the latter two options as these provide greater security.

6. Click the Notify button. Place a check mark in the Automatically Notify box. You can choose to automatically notify the servers listed on the Name Servers tab, or you can specify DNS servers by IP addresses. Each of these servers will be notified automatically whenever a change to the DNS database is made.

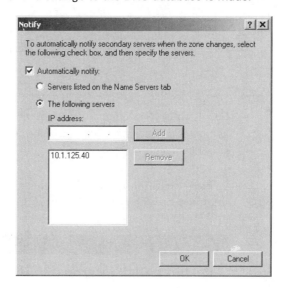

7. Click OK twice to save the settings.

Managing DNS Interoperability

In a pure Windows 2000 environment, you would probably choose to use only Microsoft's DNS service. However, in the real world (and especially in larger environments), you might require the DNS service to interact with other implementations of DNS. A common Unix implementation of DNS is known as the Berkeley Internet Name Domain (BIND) service. Active Directory mandates the use of SRV records and optionally supports DNS dynamic updates. The minimum version of BIND that supports both is version 8.2.1. When using a BIND server as the DNS server for Active Directory, it must be running version 8.2.1 or greater. Before you can configure various DNS server settings for interoperability, you must know which features are supported by the non-Microsoft DNS system you are using.

Microsoft Exam Objective

Install, configure, and troubleshoot DNS for Active Directory.

- Integrate Active Directory DNS zones with non-Active Directory DNS zones.

- Configure zones for dynamic updates.

See "Configuring Zones for Automatic Updates," a section that appears earlier in this chapter, for coverage of the "Configure zones for dynamic updates" subobjective.

Exercise 2.7 shows you how to set up a Windows 2000 DNS server to interoperate with non-Windows 2000 DNS servers.

EXERCISE 2.7

Enabling DNS Interoperability

This exercise assumes that you have properly installed and configured the DNS service and have configured at least one forward lookup zone. It also assumes that you know the various features supported by the types of DNS servers in your environment.

1. Open the DNS snap-in in the Administrative Tools program group.

2. Right-click the name of the local server, and click Properties.

3. Click the Advanced tab. You will see a list of the various settings that can be enabled and disabled. Place a check mark next to a feature to enable it, or remove the check mark to disable it. For more information about the various options, click the Question Mark icon, then click the option.

4. Click OK to save the changes.

Interoperation with WINS and DHCP

Earlier in this chapter, we saw some of the benefits of Microsoft's implementation of DNS. We mentioned integration with other services such as *WINS* and Dynamic Host Configuration Protocol (*DHCP*). In this section, we'll drill down into the details of how these two services work and how they can further reduce administration headaches by integrating with Microsoft's DNS.

Overview of DHCP

As we mentioned in the beginning of this chapter, TCP/IP requires a considerable amount of manual configuration. Some of the information that might be required by a TCP/IP client in a Windows environment may include the following pieces of information:

- TCP/IP address
- Subnet mask
- Default gateway
- DNS servers
- DNS domain name
- WINS servers

Additionally, other TCP/IP services must be set. For example, if the network is using the Network Time Protocol (NTP), information on the timeserver address should also be transmitted. It's easy to see how maintaining this information even on small networks can be quite troublesome. For much larger ones, the technical and management issues associated with assigning appropriate information can be overwhelming. DHCP was designed to ease some of these problems. DHCP works by automatically assigning TCP/IP address information to client computers when they are first connected to the network. The general process works as follows:

- A client computer is initialized on the network. During the boot up process, a broadcast is sent requesting information from a DHCP server.

- If a DHCP server is present, it receives the request and generates an IP address from its database of valid assignments. It sends an offer of TCP/IP information to the client that requested it.

- The client receives the packet and sends an acknowledgement to the DHCP server that it will accept the offer.

- The DHCP server sends an acknowledgement to the client, which then configures its IP stack. The DHCP server prevents the address from being used again from its database as long as it is assigned to the client.

Figure 2.18 provides an example of the DHCP process.

FIGURE 2.18 Obtaining a DHCP lease

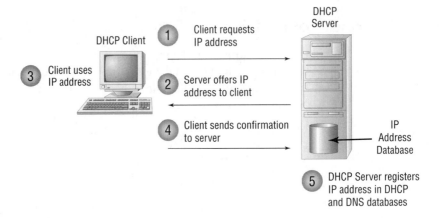

If more than one DHCP server is present on the network, the client would simply take the IP address from the first one to respond. Since IP addresses are a limited resource on most networks, DHCP servers generally assign a lease duration to each IP address they assign to clients. The typical lease duration is approximately three to five days for networks with mobile workstations like laptops and longer for a more static environment. Clients are required to renew their IP address lease within this time frame, or the IP address will be retired and made available for other clients.

The pool of TCP/IP addresses that are available for assignment to clients is called the DHCP scope. A scope consists of a range of IP addresses and a subnet mask. Additionally, scope options can be used to specify other TCP/IP parameters, such as the default gateway, DNS servers, and WINS servers. Figure 2.19 shows the Server Options dialog box within the DHCP administrative tool.

FIGURE 2.19 Setting DHCP server options

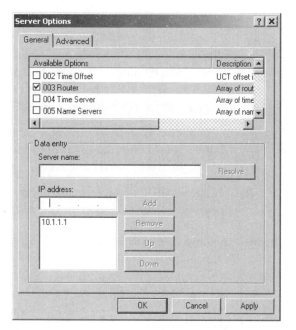

To provide for fault tolerance of DHCP services, a common practice is to place more than one DHCP server on the same network. However, in order to prevent any problems with duplicate IP address assignments, the DHCP servers are configured with non-overlapping scopes.

Integrating DHCP and DNS

It doesn't take much imagination to see how DHCP information can be used to populate a DNS database. The DHCP service already records all of the IP address assignments within its own database. In order to reduce manual administration of DNS entries for client computers, Windows 2000's DNS implementation can automatically create Address (A) records for hosts based on DHCP information. When Windows 2000 dynamic updates are enabled, the client updates the A record and the DHCP server updates the client's PTR record. However, the method in which DHCP information is transmitted to the DNS server varies based on the client. There are two different modes of DHCP/DNS integration based on the client type:

For Windows 2000 Clients   Windows 2000 DHCP clients have the ability to automatically send updates to a dynamic DNS server as soon as they receive an IP address. This method places the task of registering the new address on the client. It also allows the client to specify whether or not the update of the DNS database should occur at all.

For Earlier Clients   The DHCP client code for Windows 95/98 and Windows NT 4 computers does not support dynamic DNS updates. Therefore, the DHCP server itself must update the DNS A and PTR records.

Figure 2.20 illustrates the two different methods of Dynamic DHCP/DNS updates based on the different client types.

FIGURE 2.20   Dynamic DHCP/DNS updates

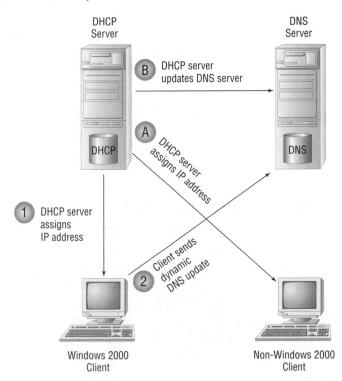

Implementing dynamic updates of DNS using information from DHCP can be done by opening the DHCP administrative tool. By right-clicking the name of the server and choosing Properties, you will have the option to select the DNS tab (see Figure 2.21).

FIGURE 2.21 Setting DNS options using the DHCP administrative tool

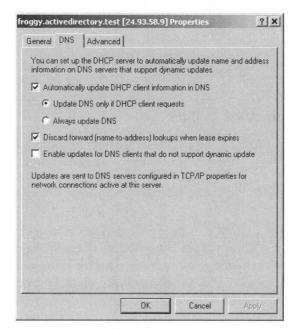

The options on this tab include the following:

Automatically Update DHCP Client Information in DNS This option allows you to enable dynamic DNS updates from the client. This selection applies only to Windows 2000 clients. Systems administrators can choose between two options:

- The client can decide whether or not the update is made.

- DNS is always updated.

Discard Forward (Name-to-Address) Lookups when Lease Expires When this option is checked, DNS entries for clients are automatically removed if a lease is not renewed in time. This is a useful option as it will ensure that outdated entries no longer exist in the DNS database.

Enable Updates for DNS Clients That Do Not Support Dynamic Update If you are using Windows NT 4, Windows 95, or Windows 98 DHCP clients and want dynamic updates of DNS, you should choose this option. When it is set, the DHCP server will be responsible for updating the DNS database whenever a new IP address is assigned.

By using the DHCP/DNS integration features of Windows 2000, you can automate what can be a very tedious process—managing client host name address mappings.

Overview of WINS

Although TCP/IP has been the default base protocol since Windows NT 4, the NetBIOS protocol is heavily relied upon by versions of Windows before Windows 2000. The Windows Internet Naming Service (WINS) was designed to allow clients using the NetBIOS over TCP/IP protocols to resolve host names to network addresses. One of the major benefits of using WINS is that it is largely self-configuring and manages itself. That is, names are added automatically to the WINS database as the server learns the addresses of clients. This facilitates browsing on the network. However, WINS has several limitations in larger environments. First, the performance of WINS can begin to degrade when many clients are registered in its database. Second, the replication functionality of the WINS database is not as robust as that of other methods (such as DNS).

With Windows 2000 and the Active Directory, Microsoft has eliminated the need for WINS altogether. However, most networks will still require the use of WINS for down-level clients (including Windows NT 4, Windows 95, and Windows 98 computers). Therefore, Windows 2000 includes an improved version of WINS. To make it easier to manage two different name resolution methods (WINS and DNS), Windows 2000 supports automatic querying of WINS records if a host name is not found within a DNS server's database. This process, called a WINS referral, occurs on the server side and requires no special configuration on the client.

Integrating WINS and DNS

To enable the automatic update process, right-click the name of a forward lookup zone using the DNS administrative tool and select Properties. Click the WINS tab to set the dynamic update options (see Figure 2.22).

FIGURE 2.22 Setting WINS updates

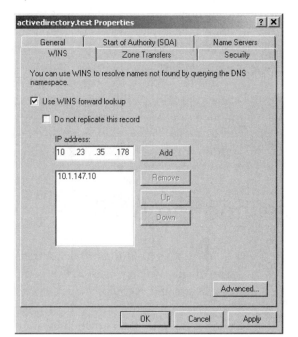

The available options include the following:

Use WINS Forward Lookup   Checking this box instructs the DNS server to query one or more WINS servers if it is unable to fulfill a host name request. The DNS server adds a new record type—the WINS record—to its own database.

Do Not Replicate This Record   This option prevents the WINS record from being sent as part of a zone transfer request. Therefore, the WINS records are not sent to other secondary DNS servers in the domain. You should enable this option if you are using non-Windows 2000 DNS servers on your network as those servers will not support the WINS record type and might cause errors.

IP Address   Here, you can specify the IP address(es) of the server(s) to be contacted for name resolution. If a lookup in the DNS database fails, these servers will be queried for the host name information. Note that the order of the IP addresses matters. That is, WINS server addresses higher in the list will be contacted before those lower on the list. You can re-sort the numbers using the Up and Down buttons.

Once the preceding options are configured, the DNS server will automatically query the specified WINS servers for host names if it is unable to resolve the request within its own database. This allows both WINS and DNS clients to perform name resolution accurately while reducing administrative burdens.

In addition to WINS forward lookups, Windows 2000 DNS servers are able to perform WINS reverse lookups. The configuration options are similar and can be set by right-clicking the name of a reverse lookup zone in the DNS administrative tool and then clicking Properties. The WINS-R tab allows you to set the WINS-R lookup information.

Troubleshooting DNS

Name resolution problems are extremely common when working with distributed networks. If, for example, we are unable to connect to a specific host name, it could be due to various reasons. First, the host itself may be unavailable. This could occur if a server has gone down or if a client computer is not online. In other cases, we may be receiving an incorrect IP address from a DNS server. Usually, the most common symptom of a DNS configuration problem is the ability to connect to a host using its IP address, but not its host name. In this section, we'll look at some ways in which you can troubleshoot client and server DNS problems.

Microsoft
✓ *Exam*
Objective

Manage, monitor, and troubleshoot DNS.

- Manage replication of DNS data.

See "Managing DNS Replication," an earlier section of this chapter, for coverage of the "Manage replication of DNS data" subobjective.

Troubleshooting Clients

The most common client-side problem related to DNS is incorrect TCP/IP configuration. For example, if the DNS server values are incorrect or the default gateway is set incorrectly, clients may not be able to contact their DNS server. Consequently, they will be unable to connect to other computers using DNS names.

One of the fundamental troubleshooting steps in diagnosing network problems is to determine whether the problem is occurring on the client side or is the fault of the server side. The most common way to determine this is by testing if other clients are having the same problem. If, on the one hand, a whole subnet is having problems resolving DNS names, it is much more likely that a server or network device is unavailable or improperly configured. On the other hand, if only one or a few clients are having problems, then it is likely that the clients are misconfigured.

In this section, we'll look at ways to diagnose and troubleshoot client-side DNS configuration problems.

Using IPCONFIG

Many times, an error in client configuration can cause computers to be unable to resolve DNS names. The common symptom is that the client computer can connect to a machine if it is using the machine's IP address, but cannot connect if it is using the DNS name. The first step in troubleshooting such problems is to verify the proper TCP/IP configuration on the client. This can easily be done using the following command in Windows NT 4, Windows 98, or Windows 2000 (note that in Windows 95, you must use the WINIPCFG command):

```
IPCONFIG /ALL |More
```

This command will list the TCP/IP configuration information for each of the client's network adapters (as shown in Figure 2.23).

FIGURE 2.23 Viewing TCP/IP configuration information using IPCONFIG

```
H:\WINNT\System32\cmd.exe                                              _ □ x
H:\>ipconfig /all |more

Windows 2000 IP Configuration

        Host Name . . . . . . . . . . . . . : froggy
        Primary DNS Suffix . . . . . . . : ActiveDirectory.test
        Node Type . . . . . . . . . . . . : Broadcast
        IP Routing Enabled. . . . . . . . : Yes
        WINS Proxy Enabled. . . . . . . . : No
        DNS Suffix Search List. . . . . . : ActiveDirectory.test
                                            austin.rr.com

Ethernet adapter RoadRunner:

        Connection-specific DNS Suffix  . : austin.rr.com
        Description . . . . . . . . . . . : 3Com EtherLink III Bus-Master PCI Et
hernet Adapter
        Physical Address. . . . . . . . . : 00-A0-24-6B-26-14
        DHCP Enabled. . . . . . . . . . . : Yes
        Autoconfiguration Enabled . . . . : Yes
        IP Address. . . . . . . . . . . . : 24.93.58.9
        Subnet Mask . . . . . . . . . . . : 255.255.255.0
        Default Gateway . . . . . . . . . : 24.93.58.1
        DHCP Server . . . . . . . . . . . : 24.93.35.64
        DNS Servers . . . . . . . . . . . : 24.93.35.64
                                            24.93.35.65
        Lease Obtained. . . . . . . . . . : Saturday, January 08, 2000 7:51:16 A
M
        Lease Expires . . . . . . . . . . : Sunday, January 09, 2000 7:51:16 AM
Ethernet adapter LAN (Osborne):
-- More --
```

The command-line parameters and output of the IPCONFIG utility are slightly different in various Microsoft operation systems. To get a listing of the exact syntax, just type **IPCONFIG /?**.

If the client computer is using DHCP, you can use the IPCONFIG / RELEASE command to release the current TCP/IP information. Then, you can issue the IPCONFIG /RENEW command to obtain a new IP address lease from a DHCP server.

Windows 95/98 clients include a graphical utility for viewing the same information provided by IPCONFIG. The easiest way to access the utility is to click Start ➢ Run, and then type **winipcfg**.

The Windows 2000 version of IPCONFIG also supports several new command-line switches in addition to those already described. These options are shown in Table 2.4.

TABLE 2.4 Windows 2000 IPCONFIG Command-Line Switches

Switch	Function
/flushdns	Clears all of the entries in the local DNS cache; useful if names are being resolved to incorrect IP addresses
/registerdns	Renews all current DHCP leases and updates DNS server information
/displaydns	Shows the contents of the current local DNS resolver cache
/showclassid	Shows the current DHCP class ID; used when different types of machines require specific DHCP information (for example, a different class might be used for servers and workstations)
/setclassid	Allows the current DHCP class ID to be changed

Using PING

After verifying the client configuration, a good second step when troubleshooting a DNS client problem is to ensure that the server is accessible on the network. The PING command provides a simple way to do this. You can use PING by simply typing **PING** and then an IP address or host name at the command line.

When troubleshooting DNS problems, you should first start by PINGing a machine's TCP/IP address. For example, the command PING 172.16.25.33 should return a response from a server. If no response is received, either the server is down, or there is a problem with the network connectivity (such as a failed router). If, however, a response is received, you should attempt to PING a computer using it's machine name. An example is PING server1.mycompany.com. If this test fails (but using PING with an IP address works), then you have a problem with your name resolution services.

Using NSLOOKUP

Sometimes, it is useful to find information about the name servers on the network. The NSLOOKUP command is designed to do just that. A basic test is to run the command with no arguments. This will display the IP address of the current DNS server for this client. For NSLOOKUP to work properly, a PTR record must exist in the server's database.

The NSLOOKUP command is only available on Windows NT 4 and Windows 2000 machines. Windows 95/98 computers do not include the command.

The NSLOOKUP command supports many other functions for determining name resolution paths and testing recursion. For further information, type **HELP** at the NSLOOKUP command prompt. A sample of this display is shown in Figure 2.24.

FIGURE 2.24 Viewing NSLOOKUP commands

```
H:\WINNT\System32\cmd.exe - nslookup                                    _ □ X
> ?
Commands:   (identifiers are shown in uppercase, [] means optional)
NAME            - print info about the host/domain NAME using default server
NAME1 NAME2     - as above, but use NAME2 as server
help or ?       - print info on common commands
set OPTION      - set an option
    all                 - print options, current server and host
    [no]debug           - print debugging information
    [no]d2              - print exhaustive debugging information
    [no]defname         - append domain name to each query
    [no]recurse         - ask for recursive answer to query
    [no]search          - use domain search list
    [no]vc              - always use a virtual circuit
    domain=NAME         - set default domain name to NAME
    srchlist=N1[/N2/.../N6] - set domain to N1 and search list to N1,N2, etc.
    root=NAME           - set root server to NAME
    retry=X             - set number of retries to X
    timeout=X           - set initial time-out interval to X seconds
    type=X              - set query type (ex. A,ANY,CNAME,MX,NS,PTR,SOA,SRV)
    querytype=X         - same as type
    class=X             - set query class (ex. IN (Internet), ANY)
    [no]msxfr           - use MS fast zone transfer
    ixfrver=X           - current version to use in IXFR transfer request
server NAME     - set default server to NAME, using current default server
lserver NAME    - set default server to NAME, using initial server
finger [USER]   - finger the optional NAME at the current default host
root            - set current default server to the root
ls [opt] DOMAIN [> FILE] - list addresses in DOMAIN (optional: output to FILE)
    -a          - list canonical names and aliases
    -d          - list all records
    -t TYPE     - list records of the given type (e.g. A,CNAME,MX,NS,PTR etc.)
view FILE       - sort an 'ls' output file and view it with pg
exit            - exit the program
> _
```

Exercise 2.8 provides an example of how NSLOOKUP can be used to verify the DNS server settings on the local machine.

EXERCISE 2.8

Using NSLOOKUP to Verify DNS Configuration

In this exercise, the NSLOOKUP command will be used to verify the proper operation of the DNS server on the local machine. This exercise assumes that you have already installed and configured DNS.

1. Open a command prompt by clicking Start ➤ Programs ➤ Accessories ➤ Command Prompt. Alternatively, you can click Start ➤ Run and type **cmd**.

2. At the command prompt, type **NSLOOKUP** and press Enter. This will run the NSLOOKUP command and present you with a > prompt. This prompt indicates that NSLOOKUP is awaiting a command.

3. To activate the local DNS server, type **Server 127.0.0.1**.

4. Type **set type = SRV** to filter resource records to only SRV types, and press Enter. If the command is successful, you will receive another > prompt.

5. To verify a resource record, simply type its FQDN. For example, if our domain name is activedirectory.test, we would type **_ldap._tcp.activedirectory.test**. You should receive information about the host name that is mapped as a domain controller for this domain.

6. If you want to test other resources, simply type the names of the resources. You should receive valid responses. Table 2.3 provided a list of the default resource records that should be present.

7. When you are finished using NSLOOKUP, type **exit** and then press Enter. This will return you to the command prompt. To close the command prompt, type **exit** again and hit Enter.

Unfortunately, the NSLOOKUP command is not as user-friendly as it could be. It requires you to learn several different commands and use them in a specific syntax. Nevertheless, NSLOOKUP is an invaluable tool for troubleshooting DNS configuration issues.

Troubleshooting DNS Servers

The symptoms related to DNS server problems generally include the inability to perform accurate name resolution. Provided that the DNS server has been installed, some troubleshooting steps to take include the following:

Verify that the DNS service has started.   By using the DNS administrative tool, you can quickly determine the status of the DNS server.

Check the Event Viewer.   Especially if you are having intermittent problems with the DNS server or the service has stopped unexpectedly, you can find more information in the Windows NT Event Log.

Verify that the DNS server is accessible to clients.   A simple check for network connectivity between clients and the DNS server can eliminate a lot of potential problems. Browsing the network and connecting to clients or using the PING command is the easiest way to do this. Note, however, that if name resolution is not occurring properly, you may not be able to connect to clients.

Verify operations with NSLOOKUP.   The NSLOOKUP command provides several very powerful options for testing recursion, WINS lookups, and other features of Microsoft's DNS.

Verify the DNS configuration.   If the DNS server is providing inaccurate or outdated results, you may need to manually change the server settings or retire individual records. If outdated records are truly the problem, it is likely that users are able to get to many other machines (on the LAN or the Internet) but cannot connect to one or more specific computers.

Additionally, if you're using implementations other than Microsoft DNS, you should consult with the documentation that accompanies that product. Although DNS is an Internet standard, various DNS server software applications function quite differently from one another.

Monitoring DNS Servers

It's always a good idea to know how your network services are performing at any given moment. Monitoring performance allows you to adequately determine the load on current servers, evaluate resource usage, and plan for any necessary upgrades. After you install the DNS service, you will be able to select the DNS object in the Windows 2000 System Monitor. This object contains many different counters that are related to monitoring DNS server performance and usage.

Using the System Monitor, you can generate statistics on the following types of events:

- AXFR requests (all-zone transfer requests)

- IXFR requests (incremental zone transfer requests)

- DNS server memory usage

- Dynamic updates

- DNS Notify events

- Recursive queries

- TCP and UDP statistics

- WINS statistics

- Zone transfer issues

All of this information can be analyzed easily using the Chart, Histogram, or Report views of the System Monitor. Additionally, you can use the Alerts function to automatically notify you (or other systems administrators) whenever certain performance statistic thresholds are exceeded. For example, if the total number of recursive queries is very high, you might want to be notified so you can examine the situation. Finally, information from Performance logs and Alerts can be stored to a log data file.

The System Monitor application in Windows 2000 is an extremely powerful and useful tool for managing and troubleshooting systems. You should become familiar with its various functions to ensure that system services are operating properly. For more information on using Windows 2000 Performance Monitor, see Chapter 9, "Active Directory Optimization and Reliability."

Summary

In this chapter, we looked at a very powerful but complicated prerequisite to installing the Active Directory. DNS was designed to be a robust, scalable, and high-performance system for resolving friendly names to TCP/IP host addresses. We started by taking an overview of the basics of DNS and how DNS names are generated. We then looked at the many features available in Microsoft's version of DNS and focused on how to install, configure, and manage the necessary services.

Understanding DNS is extremely important for using the Active Directory, so if you aren't yet comfortable with the concepts described in this chapter, be sure to review them before going on.

Key Terms

Following are some of the key terms related to DNS that you should understand before taking the exam:

Caching-only DNS servers

DHCP

DNS namespace

forward lookup zones

forwarding

iteration

master DNS servers

parent and child domains

primary DNS server

recursion

resource record (RR)

reverse lookup zone

root domain

secondary DNS server

Transmission Control Protocol/Internet Protocol (TCP/IP)

WINS

zone

zone transfer

Review Questions

1. Which of the following tools can be used to troubleshoot DNS problems?

    A. IPCONFIG

    B. NSLOOKUP

    C. PING

    D. All of the above

2. Which of the following domain names does not share a contiguous namespace with the others?

    A. sales.mycompany.com

    B. marketing.mycompany.com

    C. workstation1.organization.com

    D. workstation1.mycompany.com

    E. All of the above are in the same namespace

3. The failure of which of the following commands indicates a possible DNS misconfiguration?

    A. PING 127.0.0.1

    B. PING localhost

    C. PING server1.mycompany.com

    D. None of the above

4. Which of the following is used to automatically assign TCP/IP information to clients?

    A. WINS

    B. DNS

    C. DHCP

    D. RRAS

5. When a secondary server requests an update from a master server, the transmission of information is known as a:

   A. Zone transfer

   B. Forwarding

   C. Recursion

   D. Iteration

6. Which of the following methods can be used to inform secondary DNS servers that changes have occurred in the master DNS database?

   A. Zone transfer

   B. Forwarding

   C. Recursion

   D. Iteration

   E. DNS Notify

7. Clients are ultimately responsible for resolving TCP/IP addresses in the process known as:

   A. Recursion

   B. Iteration

   C. Zone transfers

   D. Dynamic DNS updates

8. In the process of *recursion*, which machine is ultimately responsible for resolving TCP/IP addresses?

   A. The DNS Server

   B. The client

   C. Both A and B

9. Which of the following is *not* a valid type of resource record (RR)?

A. SRV

B. PTR

C. A

D. MX

E. PDC

10. When using which of the following types of clients is the DHCP server responsible for dynamically updating the DNS database?

A. Windows 95

B. Windows 98

C. Windows NT 4

D. Windows 2000

E. All of the above

11. Which of the following types of DNS servers do not serve as an authority over any DNS zone and is used strictly for performance reasons?

A. Master server

B. Caching-only server

C. Primary server

D. Secondary server

12. The process through which authority for a portion of a DNS zone is assigned to another DNS server is known as:

A. Zone transfer

B. Forwarding

C. Delegation

D. Promotion

13. Which of the following types of resource records (RRs) is relied upon by the Active Directory to find domain controllers?

A. SRV

B. PTR

C. A

D. MX

E. None of the above

14. Which of the following tools can be used to monitor the DNS server?

A. Event Viewer

B. System Monitor

C. DNS administrative tool

D. All of the above

15. Which of the following represents the host name portion of the address `server1.asia.mycompany.com`?

A. `asia.mycompany.com`

B. `.com`

C. `server1`

D. `server1.asia.mycompany`

16. The process through which one or more DNS servers use a specified DNS server for all recursive lookups is known as:

A. Recursion

B. Iteration

C. DNS Notify

D. Forwarding

17. Which of the following resource records (RRs) indicates the domain(s) for which a DNS server is an authority?

A. SRV

B. PTR

C. SOA

D. MX

18. Which of the following name resolution methods is provided primarily for backwards compatibility with previous versions of Windows?

A. DNS

B. DHCP

C. WINS

D. IPX/SPX

19. Which of the following accurately describes which servers *must* be running the DNS service?

A. All domain controllers

B. At least one server in the environment

C. At least one domain controller per Active Directory site

D. None of the above

20. Which of the following types of DNS servers provides for fault tolerance?

A. Caching-only server

B. Secondary server

C. Primary server

D. Master server

Answers to Review Questions

1. D. All of the tools listed here are helpful for resolving TCP/IP connectivity and name resolution issues.

2. C. The `organization.com` namespace is not part of the mycompany .com namespace.

3. C. If DNS is not configured properly, resolving the name of a server will fail. Option A uses an IP address (which is not dependent on DNS), and option B uses a special alias for the localhost.

4. C. The Dynamic Host Configuration Protocol (DHCP) automatically assigns TCP/IP address information to clients.

5. A. Zone transfers are the process by which information is transmitted between master and secondary DNS servers.

6. E. DNS Notify can be used with compatible DNS servers to inform them of changes to the DNS master database. If changes have occurred, the secondary servers can then request a zone transfer.

7. B. In the process of iteration, a DNS server will return its best guess about a domain name, but the client will be responsible for ultimately resolving the name.

8. A. In recursion, the client instructs its DNS server to continue querying other DNS servers until the DNS server that first received the recursive query can return a response to the client.

9. E. All of the other options are standard DNS RRs.

10. D. When using Windows 2000, the *client* can be responsible for sending dynamic updates to DNS. The legacy clients do not have DNS update capability so the updates are handled with W2K DHCP.

11. B. All of the other server types contain information about specific DNS zones.

12. C. Delegation is used to break zones apart into smaller units for performance or manageability.

13. A. SRV records are used by the Active Directory and client computers to find domain controllers for a specific domain.

14. D. All of the above can be used to view performance or operational information about the DNS service.

15. C. The host name is always the leftmost portion of a DNS name.

16. D. Forwarding can be used to route all recursive DNS requests through specific DNS servers. This is often used to reduce network traffic across slow links.

17. C. The Start of Authority (SOA) record indicates that a server is considered an authority for a specific domain.

18. C. Windows 2000's support for WINS is primarily included for backwards compatibility.

19. D. Although DNS is required for the proper operation of the Active Directory, DNS is not required on all domain controllers. While DNS is required to locate a DC it does not have to be running on a W2K server.

20. B. Secondary DNS servers contain copies of the zone database and can be used to perform name resolution should the primary server become unavailable.

Chapter 3

Installing and Configuring the Active Directory

MICROSOFT EXAM OBJECTIVES COVERED IN THIS CHAPTER:

✓ **Install, configure, and troubleshoot the components of Active Directory.**

- Install Active Directory.
- Create sites.
- Create subnets.
- Create site links.
- Create site link bridges.
- Create connection objects.
- Create global catalog servers.
- Move server objects between sites.
- Transfer operations master roles.
- Verify Active Directory installation.
- Implement an organizational unit (OU) structure.

In previous chapters, we looked at the various factors you need to take into account when planning for the Active Directory. Then, we moved on to understand the Domain Name System (DNS) and how it works with the Active Directory. The time you spend understanding these concepts is very important, as the success of your Active Directory implementation will depend on them. If you plan to work through the exercises presented in this chapter, be sure that you have either already installed DNS or have at least planned for doing so as part of the process.

With the basic information out of the way, it's time to start looking at exactly how the Active Directory can be implemented. This chapter will walk you through the steps required to prepare for and implement the Active Directory using Windows 2000 domain controllers.

This chapter covers material related to the Active Directory and its installation, for the "Install, configure, and troubleshoot the components of Active Directory" objective. See Chapter 4, "Creating and Managing Organizational Units," for coverage on implementing an OU structure; Chapter 5, "Installing and Managing Trees and Forests," for material on creating Global Catalog servers and transferring operations master roles; and Chapter 6, "Configuring Sites and Managing Replication," for coverage on creating sites, subnets, site links, site link bridges, and connection objects, as well as on moving server objects between sites.

Preparing for Active Directory Installation

All too often, systems and network administrators implement hardware and software without first taking the time to evaluate the prerequisites. For example, purchasing and installing a tape backup solution will not be possible without first ensuring that the appropriate network connectivity and attachment interface are available on servers. Installation and configuration of the Active Directory is no exception.

The physical components that form the basis of the Active Directory are Windows 2000 domain controllers. Before you begin installing domain controllers to set up your Active Directory environment, you should ensure that you are properly prepared to do so. In this section, we'll examine some of the prerequisites and types of information you'll need to successfully install the Active Directory.

The technical information and exercises in this chapter are based on the assumption that you will be using Microsoft's implementation of DNS (unless otherwise noted). If you are using other types of DNS servers in your environment, you may not be able to take advantage of all the features mentioned in this chapter.

Install DNS

In Chapter 2, "Integrating DNS with the Active Directory," we described how the Active Directory depends on DNS for name resolution. Therefore, it should come as no surprise that the proper installation and configuration of DNS must be completed before installing an Active Directory domain. If it is not already installed on the system, you can install the DNS service by using the Add/Remove programs icon in the Control Panel. DNS will be used for performing name resolution to other domain controllers or resources on your network (if any).

Technically, if you haven't yet installed DNS, you will be prompted to do so as part of the configuration of a domain controller. In some cases, this provides an easy way to configure DNS with the appropriate options for the Active Directory. It's not the right choice for every environment, however. Unless you are setting up the Active Directory in a test environment or on a network that doesn't yet have DNS services, it can be easier to test and verify DNS configuration before starting the Active Directory installation.

Although the presence of DNS servers on your network is a requirement, you are not forced to use Microsoft's DNS service. If other DNS servers are available on the network, you may choose to use those servers when installing the Active Directory. Note, however, that if you're using other implementations of DNS servers (such as Unix or Windows NT 4), you will not be able to take advantage of all of the features of Windows 2000's DNS and its integration with the Active Directory. In addition you will be required to enter the proper SRV records manually as most current DNS servers do not support dynamic updates.

For more details on planning for, installing, and configuring DNS, see Chapter 2, "Integrating DNS with the Active Directory."

Verify the DNS Configuration

Once DNS has been installed, you should ensure that it has been configured to allow updates. This option allows the Active Directory to automatically add, modify, and remove resource records (RRs) to the DNS database whenever changes are made in the Active Directory. The Allow Updates option is extremely useful, as it reduces the chances for error in manual data entry and greatly reduces the effort required for administration.

You should also verify the proper creation of DNS forward and reverse lookup zones. These zones will be used for resolving names to network addresses and are extremely important for the successful setup of the Active Directory.

For more information on configuring the Allow Updates option and configuring forward and reverse lookup zones for DNS, see Chapter 2, "Integrating DNS with the Active Directory."

Verify the File System

The file system used by an operating system is an important concern for many reasons. First, the file system can provide the ultimate level of security for all of the information stored on the server itself. Second, the file system is responsible for managing and tracking all of this data. Furthermore, certain features are available only on certain file systems. These features include support for encryption, remote file access, remote storage, disk redundancy, and disk quotas.

The Windows 2000 platform allows the use of multiple different file systems, including:

- *File Allocation Table (FAT) file system*
- File Allocation Table 32 (FAT32) file system
- *Windows NT File System (NTFS)*
- Windows NT File System 5 (NTFS 5)

The fundamental difference between FAT and NTFS partitions is that NTFS allows for file-system–level security. Support for FAT and FAT32 are mainly included in Windows 2000 for backwards compatibility. Specifically, these file systems are required in order to accommodate multiple boot partitions. For example, if we wanted to configure a single computer to boot into Windows 98 and Windows 2000, we would need to have at least one FAT or FAT32 partition. Although this is a good solution for situations such as training labs and test environments, you should strongly consider using only NTFS partitions on production server machines.

Windows 2000 uses an updated version of the NTFS file system called NTFS 5. There are many other benefits to using the NTFS 5 file system, including support for the following functionality:

Disk Quotas   In order to restrict the amount of disk space used by users on the network, systems administrators can establish disk quotas. By default, Windows 2000 supports disk quota restrictions on a volume level. That is, we could restrict the amount of storage space used by a specific user on a single disk volume. Third-party solutions that allow more granular quota settings are also available.

File System Encryption   One of the fundamental problems with network operating systems is that systems administrators are often given full permissions to view all files and data stored on hard disks. In some cases, this is necessary. For example, in order to perform backup, recovery, and disk management functions, at least one user must have all permissions. Windows 2000 and NTFS 5 address these issues by allowing for file system encryption. Encryption essentially scrambles all of the data stored within files before they are written to the disk. When an authorized user requests the files, they are transparently decrypted and provided. The use of encryption prevents the usability of data in case it is stolen or intercepted by an unauthorized user.

Dynamic Volumes   Protecting against disk failures is an important concern for production servers. Although earlier versions of Windows NT supported various levels of Redundant Array of Independent Disks (RAID) technology, there were shortcomings with software-based solution. Perhaps the most significant was the requirement of server reboots in order to change RAID configurations. Some configuration changes could not be made without a complete reinstallation of the operating system. With the support for dynamic volumes in Windows 2000, systems administrators can change RAID and other disk configuration settings without requiring a reboot or reinstallation of the server. The end result is greater protection for data, increased scalability, and increased uptime.

Mounted Drives   With the use of mounted drives, systems administrators can map a local disk drive to an NTFS 5 directory name. This is useful for organizing disk space on servers and increasing manageability. By using mounted drives, I could mount the C:\Users directory to an actual physical disk. If that disk became full, I could copy all of the files to another, larger drive without requiring any changes to the directory path name or reconfiguration of applications.

Remote Storage   When it comes to disk space, it seems like you can never get enough of it! Systems administrators often notice that as soon as more space is added, the next upgrade must be planned. Moving infrequently used files to tape is one way to recover disk space. However, backing up and restoring these files could be quite difficult and time consuming. Systems administrators can use the Remote Storage features supported by NTFS 5 to automatically off-load seldom-used data to tape or other devices. The files remain available to users. Should they request an archived file, Windows 2000 can automatically restore the file from a remote storage device and make it available. Using remote storage frees up systems administrators' time and allows them to focus on more important tasks (such as installing the Active Directory!).

Although these reasons probably compel most systems administrators to use the NTFS 5 file system, there are reasons that prove its use is mandatory.

The most important reason is that the Active Directory data store must reside on an NTFS 5 partition. Therefore, before you begin the installation process for Active Directory, you should ensure that you have at least one NTFS partition available. Also, be sure you have a reasonable amount of disk space available (1GB). As the size of the Active Directory data store will grow as you add objects to it, be sure you have adequate space for the future.

Exercise 3.1 shows how you can use the administrative tools to view and modify disk configuration.

Before you make any disk configuration changes, be sure you completely understand their potential effects. Changing partition sizes and adding and removing partitions can result in a total loss of all information on one or more partitions.

EXERCISE 3.1

Viewing Disk Configuration

1. Open the Computer Management icon in the Administrative Tools program group.

2. Under the Storage branch, click Disk Management.

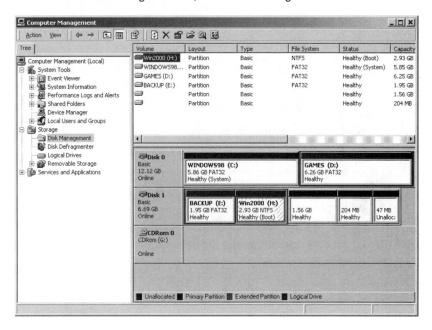

EXERCISE 3.1 *(continued)*

3. The Disk Management program will show you the logical and physical disks that are currently configured on your system. Note that information about the size of each partition is also displayed. By using the View menu, you can choose various depictions of the physical and logical drives in your system.

4. (Optional) To modify partition settings, you can right-click any of the disks or partitions and choose from the available options.

Windows 2000 allows the conversion of existing FAT or FAT32 partitions to NTFS. However, this is a one-way process. You cannot convert an NTFS partition to any other file system without losing data. If this conversion is required, the recommended process is to back up all existing data, delete and reformat the partition, and then restore the data. Needless to say, it's a time-consuming process!

If you want to convert an existing partition from FAT or FAT32 to NTFS, you'll need to use the CONVERT command-line utility. For example, the following command will convert the C: partition from FAT to FAT32:

```
CONVERT c: /fs:ntfs
```

Only the Windows NT and Windows 2000 operating systems can read and write to and from NTFS partitions. Therefore, if you are using other operating systems on the same computer, be sure you fully understand the effects of converting the file system.

If the partition you are trying to convert contains any system files or the Windows 2000 virtual memory page file, a command-line message will inform you that the conversion will take place during the next reboot of the machine. When the computer is rebooted, the conversion process will begin. After the partition is converted to NTFS, the computer will automatically reboot again, and you will be able to continue using the system.

Verify Network Connectivity

Although a Windows 2000 Server computer can exist on a network by itself (or without a network card at all), you will not be harnessing much of the potential of the operating system without network connectivity. As the fundamental purpose of a network operating system is to provide resources to users, you must verify network connectivity.

Before you begin to install the Active Directory, you should perform several checks of your current configuration to ensure that the server is configured properly on the network. Some general tests include:

Network Adapter   At least one network adapter should be installed and properly configured on your server. A quick way to verify that a network adapter is properly installed is to use the Computer Management administrative tool. Under the Network Adapters branch, you should have at least one network adapter listed. If not, you can use the Add/Remove Hardware icon in the Control Panel to configure hardware.

TCP/IP Protocol   The TCP/IP protocol should be installed, configured, and enabled on any necessary network adapters. The server should also be given a valid IP address and subnet mask. Optionally, you may need to configure a default gateway, DNS servers, WINS servers, and other network settings. If you are using the Dynamic Host Configuration Protocol (DHCP), be sure that the assigned information is correct. In general, it is a good idea to use a static IP address for servers because IP address changes can cause network connectivity problems if not handled properly.

Understanding TCP/IP is essential to the use of Windows 2000 and the Active Directory. See *MCSE: Windows 2000 Network Infrastructure Administration Study Guide* (Sybex, 2000) to learn more about TCP\IP.

Internet Access   If the server should have access to the Internet, you should verify that it is able to connect to external Web servers and other machines outside the LAN. If the server is unable to connect, you might have a problem with the TCP/IP configuration.

LAN Access   The server should be able to view other servers and workstations on the network. You can quickly verify this type of connectivity by using the My Network Places icon on the desktop. If other machines are not visible, ensure that the network and TCP/IP configuration is correct for your environment.

Client Access   Network client computers should be able to connect to your server and view any shared resources. A simple way to test connectivity is to create a share and test if other machines are able to see files and folders within it. If clients cannot access the machine, ensure that both the client and server are configured properly.

WAN Access   If you're working in a distributed environment, you should ensure that you have access to any remote sites or users that will need to connect to this machine. Usually, this is a simple test that can be performed by a network administrator.

In some cases, verifying network access can be quite simple. You might have some internal and external network resources with which to test. In other cases, it might be more complicated. There are several tools and techniques you can use to verify that your network configuration is correct. These include:

Using the IPCONFIG Utility   By typing the command IPCONFIG/ALL at the command prompt, you can view information about the TCP/IP settings of a computer. Figure 3.1 shows the types of information you'll receive.

FIGURE   3.1   Viewing TCP/IP information with IPCONFIG

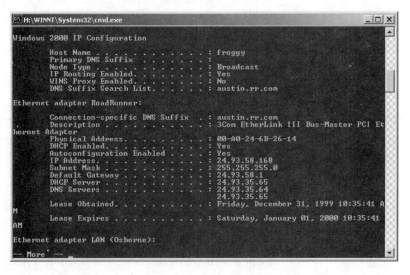

Using the PING Utility   The PING command was designed to test connectivity to other computers. You can use PING by simply typing PING and then an IP address or host name at the command line. The following are some steps for testing connectivity using the PING command.

PING Other Computers on the Same Subnet   You should start by PINGing a known active IP address on the network to check for a response. If one is received, then you have connectivity to the network. Next, check if you can PING another machine using its host name. If this works, then local name resolution works properly.

PING Other Computers on Different Subnets   In order to ensure that routing is set up properly, you should attempt to PING computers that are local on other subnets (if any exist) on your network. If this test fails, try PINGing the default gateway. Any errors will indicate a problem in the network configuration or a problem with a router.

Some firewalls, routers, or servers on your network or on the Internet might prevent you from receiving a successful response from a PING command. This is usually done for security reasons, as malicious users might attempt to disrupt network traffic using excessive PINGs. Just because you do not receive a response, do not assume that the service is not available. Instead, try to verify connectivity in other ways. For example TRACERT can be used to demonstrate connectivity beyond your subnet even if ICMP responses are ignored by the other routers. The path to an ultimate destination will show success even if it does not display the actual names and addresses, since the display of a second router implies connectivity.

Browsing the Network   To ensure that you have access to other computers on the network, be sure that they can be viewed using the Network Neighborhood icon. This will verify that your name resolution parameters are set up correctly and that other computers are accessible. Also, try connecting to resources (such as file shares or printers) on other machines.

Browsing the Internet   You can quickly verify whether your server has access to the Internet by visiting a known Web site such as www.microsoft.com. This will ensure that you have access outside of your network. If you do not have access to the Web, you might need to verify your proxy server settings (if applicable) and your DNS server settings.

By performing these simple tests, you can ensure that you have a properly configured network connection and that other network resources are available.

Determine the Domain Controller Mode

When you are installing a Windows 2000 domain controller, you must determine if you will be supporting a *mixed-mode Active Directory* or *native-mode Active Directory*. The decision should be quite simple.

Mixed mode is the default option when installing a domain controller. It is designed for allowing backwards compatibility with Windows NT 4 and earlier domain models. If you will need to support Windows NT domain controllers in your environment, you should choose mixed mode. However, as long as you are using mixed mode, certain Active Directory features (such as universal and nested groups) will be unavailable.

If your environment does not require support for Windows NT domains, then you can choose to implement the domain controller in native mode. Native mode allows the full functionality of the Active Directory for all domain controllers, but it does not allow for backwards compatibility. We'll cover specific differences in later chapters.

Plan the Domain Structure

Once you have verified the technical configuration of your server for the Active Directory, it's time to verify the Active Directory configuration for your organization. Since the content of this chapter focuses on the installation of the first domain in your environment, you really only need to know the following information prior to beginning setup:

- The DNS name of the domain

- The NetBIOS name of the server (used by previous versions of Windows to access server resources)

- Whether the domain will operate in mixed mode or native mode

- Whether or not other DNS servers are available on the network

However, if you will be installing additional domain controllers in your environment or will be attaching to an existing Active Directory structure, you should also have the following information:

- If this domain controller will join an existing domain, the name of that domain. You will also either require a password for an Enterprise Administrator or have someone with those permissions create a domain account before promotion.

- Whether the new domain will join an existing tree and, if so, the name of the tree it will join.

- The name of a forest to which this domain will connect (if applicable).

For more information on planning domain structure, review the information in Chapter 1, "Overview of the Active Directory." We'll cover the details of working in multidomain Active Directory environments (including the creation of new trees and participating in an existing forest) in Chapter 5, "Installing and Managing Trees and Forests."

Installing the Active Directory

Installation of the Active Directory is an easy and straightforward process as long as you have performed adequate planning and have made the necessary decisions beforehand. In this chapter, we'll look at the actual steps required to install the first domain controller in a given environment.

Microsoft *Exam* *Objective*	**Install, configure, and troubleshoot the components of Active Directory.** - Install Active Directory.

With previous versions of Windows NT Server, you had to determine the role of your server as it relates to the domain controller or member server during installation. Choices included making the machine a Primary Domain

Controller (PDC), a Backup Domain Controller (BDC), or a member server. This was an extremely important decision because ,even though a BDC can be promoted to a PDC, any changes to the server's role between a domain controller and a member server required a complete reinstallation of the operating system.

Instead of forcing you to choose whether or not the machine will participate as a domain controller during setup, Windows 2000 allows you to promote servers after installation. Therefore, at the end of the setup process, all Windows 2000 Server computers are configured as either member servers (if they are joined to a domain) or stand-alone servers (if they are part of a workgroup). The process of converting a member server to a domain controller is known as *promotion*. Through the use of a simple and intuitive Wizard, systems administrators can quickly configure servers to be domain controllers after installation.

In this chapter, we'll cover the steps required to use the *Active Directory Installation Wizard (DCPROMO)*. This tool is designed for use after a server has been installed in the environment. As part of the promotion process, the server will create or receive information related to the Active Directory configuration.

Promoting a Domain Controller

The first step in installing the Active Directory is to configure a domain controller. The first domain controller in an environment will serve as the starting point for the forest, trees, domains, and the Flexible Single Master Operation (FSMO) roles. Exercise 3.2 shows the steps required to promote an existing Windows 2000 Server to a domain controller.

EXERCISE 3.2

Promoting a Domain Controller

In this exercise, we will install the first domain controller in the Active Directory environment. In order to complete the steps in this exercise, you must have already installed and configured a Windows 2000 Server computer and a DNS server that supports SRV records.

1. To start the Active Directory Installation Wizard, open the Configure Your Server applet in the Administrative Tools program group.
   Click the Active Directory option. At the bottom of the page, click
   the Start the Active Directory Wizard hyperlink. Alternatively, you
   can click Start ➢ Run and type **dcpromo**.

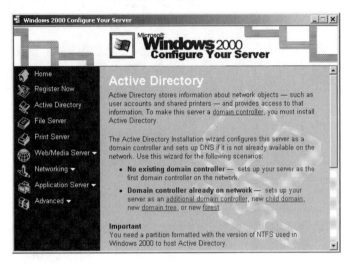

2. Click Next on the first page of the Wizard to begin the process.

3. The first option you will need to specify is the type of domain controller this server will be. To choose the domain controller type, select
   Domain Controller for a New Domain and click Next. Note the warning that proceeding will delete all local accounts on this machine.

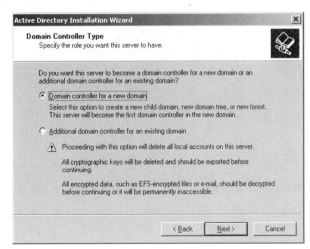

EXERCISE 3.2 *(continued)*

4. You will need to specify whether you want to create a new domain tree or make the new domain part of an existing tree. Since this will be the first domain in the Active Directory environment, choose Create a New Domain Tree and click Next.

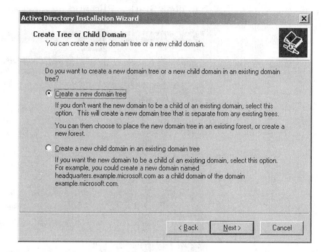

5. Choose whether the new domain tree will be part of an existing forest or a new one that you will create. Since this will be the first tree in the forest, select Create a New Forest of Domain Trees and click Next.

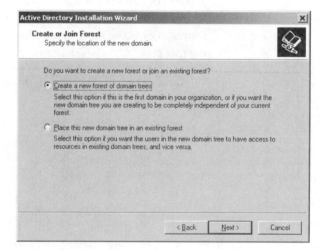

6. Specify a name for the new domain by typing in the full name of the DNS domain. For example, you can type **test.mycompany.com**. If you are not working in a test environment, be sure that you have chosen a root domain name that is consistent for your organization, and doesn't overlap with others. Click Next.

7. In order to preserve backwards compatibility with earlier versions of Windows, you must provide a NetBIOS computer name. A NetBIOS name can be up to 15 characters. Although special characters are supported, you should limit yourself to the English alphabet characters and Arabic numbers. Type in the NetBIOS name for this machine and click Next.

8. In the Database and Log Locations dialog box, you should specify the file system locations for the Active Directory database and log file. Microsoft recommends that these files reside on separate physical devices in order to improve performance and to provide for recoverability. The default file system location is in a directory called NTDS located within the system root. However, you can choose any folder located on a FAT, FAT32, or NTFS partition. Click Next.

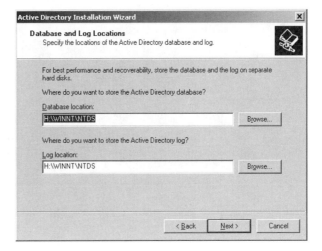

9. You will need to select a shared system volume location. The system volume folder will be used to store domain information that will be replicated to all of the other domain controllers in the domain. This folder must be stored on an NTFS 5 partition. The default location is in a directory called SYSVOL within the system root, but you can change this path based on your server configuration. Click Next.

10. As part of the promotion process, Windows 2000 will need you to set permissions on user and group objects. In this step, you can choose to select permissions that are compatible with previous versions of Windows. This is a good choice if you're running in a mixed environment. If you are sure you will not be supporting non-Windows 2000 machines, however, you should choose Permissions Compatible Only with Windows 2000 Servers. Although this option will not allow compatibility with previous operating systems, it will implement stronger security settings. Once you have made the appropriate selection, click Next.

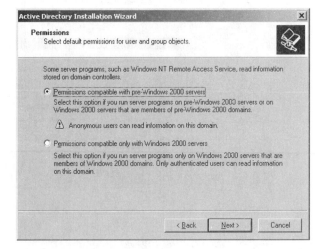

11. You will need to provide a Directory Services Restore Mode Administrator password that can be used to restore the Active Directory in the event of the loss or corruption of the Active Directory. Note that this password is not required to correspond with passwords set for any other Windows 2000 account. Type the password, confirm it, and then click Next.

12. Based on the installation options you've selected, the Active Directory Installation Wizard will present a summary of your choices. It is a good idea to copy and paste this information into a text file for later reference. Verify the options, and then click Next to begin the Active Directory installation process. When the necessary operations are complete, the Wizard will prompt you to click Finish.

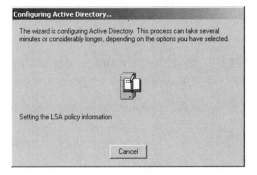

Once the Active Directory has been installed, you will be prompted to reboot the system. Following the reboot, you will be able to access the administrative tools that are related to the configuration and management of the Active Directory.

Implementing Additional Domain Controllers

The Active Directory Installation Wizard has been designed to make the process of promoting servers to domain controllers as easy as possible. With this tool, you can easily promote servers to domain controllers and demote them (that is, convert domain controllers back to member servers or stand-alone servers) without reinstalling the operating system.

The Wizard allows you to choose whether or not the domain will participate in an existing forest or tree. This allows systems administrators to easily specify the options necessary to create new domains and complete the promotion process. Later, in Chapter 5, "Installing and Managing Trees and Forests," you'll see how to install additional domain controllers in your environment.

Verifying the Active Directory Installation

Once the Active Directory has been configured, you'll want to verify that it is properly installed. There are several good ways to verify the proper installation and configuration of the Active Directory. In this section, we'll look at methods for verifying the proper installation and configuration of the Active Directory.

Microsoft ✓ *Exam* *Objective*	**Install, configure, and troubleshoot the components of Active Directory.** • Verify Active Directory installation.

Using Event Viewer

The first (and perhaps most informative) way to verify the operations of the Active Directory is to query information stored in the Windows 2000 event log. This can be done through the Windows 2000 Event Viewer. Exercise 3.3 walks you through this procedure. Entries seen with the Event Viewer include errors, warnings, and informational messages.

EXERCISE 3.3

Viewing the Active Directory Event Log

In order to complete the steps in this exercise, the local machine must be configured as a domain controller.

1. Open the Event Viewer snap-in from the Administrative Tools program group.

2. In the left pane, select Directory Service.

3. In the right pane, notice that you can sort information by clicking column headings. For example, you can click on the Source column to sort by the service or process that reported the event.

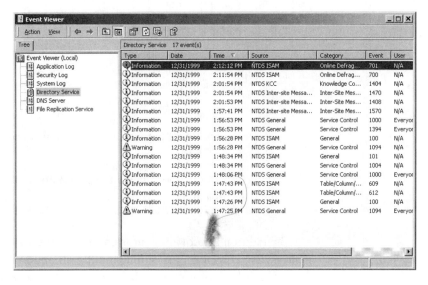

4. Double-click an event in the list to see the details for that item. Note that you can click the Copy button to copy the event information to the Clipboard. You can then paste the data into a document for later reference. Also, you can move between items using the Up and Down arrows. Click OK when you are done viewing an event.

5. You can filter specific events by right-clicking the Directory Service item in the left pane and selecting the Filter tab. Note that filtering does not remove entries from the event logs—it only restricts their display.

EXERCISE 3.3 *(continued)*

6. To verify the Active Directory installation, look for an event with information similar to the following:

   - Event Type: Information

   - Event Source: NTDS General

   - Event Category: Service Control

   - Event ID: 1000

   - Date: 12/31/1999

   - Time: 1:56:53 PM

   - User: Everyone

   - Computer: DC1

   - Description: Microsoft Directory startup complete, version 5.00.2160.1

7. When you're done viewing information in the Event Viewer, close the application.

In addition to providing information about the status of events related to the Active Directory, you should make it a habit to routinely visit the Event Viewer to find information about other system services and applications.

Using the Active Directory Administrative Tools

Following the promotion of a server to a domain controller, you will see various tools added to the Administrative Tools program group (see Figure 3.2). These include:

Active Directory Domains and Trusts   This tool is used to view and change information related to the various domains in an Active Directory environment. We'll cover this tool in more detail in Chapter 5, "Installing and Managing Trees and Forests."

Active Directory Sites and Services   This tool is used for creating and managing Active Directory sites and services to map to an organization's physical network infrastructure. We'll cover sites and services in detail in Chapter 6, "Configuring Sites and Managing Replication."

Active Directory Users and Computers   User and computer management is fundamental for an Active Directory environment. The Active Directory Users and Computers tool allows you to set machine- and user-specific settings across the domain.

FIGURE 3.2   Some of the many Windows 2000 Administrative Tools

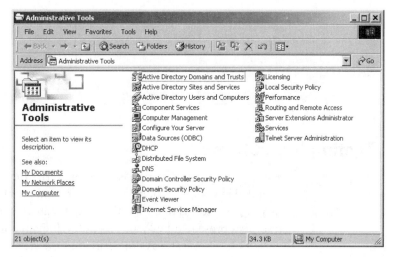

A good way to ensure that the Active Directory is functioning properly and accessible is to run the Active Directory Users and Computers tool. When you open the tool, you should see a configuration similar to that shown in Figure 3.3. Specifically, you should ensure that the name of the domain you created appears in the list. You should also click the Domain Controllers folder and ensure that the name of your local server appears in the right-hand pane. If your configuration passes these two checks, the Active Directory is present and configured.

FIGURE 3.3 Viewing Active Directory information

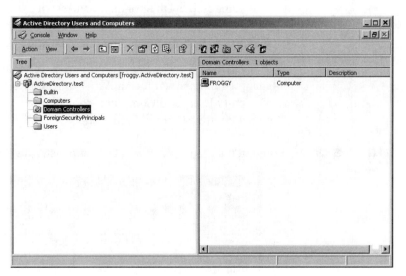

Testing from Clients

The best test of any solution is to simply verify that it works the way you had intended in your environment. When it comes to the use of the Active Directory, a good test is to ensure that clients can view and access the various resources presented by Windows 2000 domain controllers. In this section, we'll look at several ways to verify that the Active Directory is functioning properly.

Verifying Client Connectivity

Perhaps the most relevant way to test the Active Directory is by testing operations from clients. Using previous versions of Windows (such as Windows NT 4 or Windows 95/98), you should be able to see your server on the network. Earlier versions of Windows-based clients will recognize the NetBIOS name of the domain controller. Windows 2000 computers should also be able to see resources in the domain, and users can browse for resources using the My Network Places icon.

If you are unable to see the recently promoted server on the network, it is likely due to a network configuration error. If only one or a few clients are unable to see the machine, the problem is probably related to client-side configuration. Ensure that client computers have the appropriate TCP/IP configuration (including DNS server settings) and that they can see other computers on the network.

If, however, the new domain controller is unavailable from any of the other client computers, you should verify the proper startup of the Active Directory using the methods mentioned earlier in this chapter. If the Active Directory has been started, ensure that the DNS settings are correct. Finally, test network connectivity between the server and the clients by accessing the My Network Places icon.

Joining a Domain

If the Active Directory has been properly configured, clients and other servers should be able to join the domain. Exercise 3.4 provides an example of how you can join another computer to the domain.

EXERCISE 3.4

Joining a Computer to an Active Directory Domain

In order to complete this exercise, you must have already installed and properly configured at least one Active Directory domain controller and a DNS server that supports SRV records in your environment. In addition to the domain controller, you will need at least one other Windows 2000 computer. This computer may be an installation of Windows 2000 Professional or an installation of Windows 2000 Server that is not configured as a domain controller.

1. On the desktop of the computer that is to be joined to the new domain, right-click the My Computer icon and click Properties. Alternatively, you can right-click My Network Places, and choose Properties. From the Advanced menu, choose Advanced Settings.

2. Select the Network Identification tab. You will see the current name of the local computer as well as information on the workgroup or domain to which it belongs.

3. Click Properties to change the settings for this computer.

EXERCISE 3.4 *(continued)*

4. If you want to change the name of the computer, you can make the change here. This is useful if your domain has a specific naming convention for client computers. Otherwise, continue to the next step.

5. In the Member Of section, choose the Domain option. Type the name of the Active Directory domain that this computer should join. Click OK.

6. When prompted for the username and password of an account that has permissions to join computers to the domain, enter the information for an administrator of the domain. Click OK to commit the changes. If joining the domain was successful, you will see a dialog box welcoming you to the new domain.

7. You will be notified that you must reboot the computer before the changes take place. Select Yes when prompted to reboot.

Once clients are able to successfully join the domain, they should be able to view Active Directory resources using the My Network Places icon. This test validates the proper functioning of the Active Directory and ensures that you have connectivity with client computers.

Configuring DNS Integration with Active Directory

In Chapter 2, "Integrating DNS with the Active Directory," we looked at the details of the DNS service. We also covered many ways in which the Windows 2000 DNS service can be integrated to work with the Active Directory. There are many benefits to integrating the Active Directory and DNS services.

First, replication can be configured and managed along with other Active Directory components. Second, much of the maintenance of DNS resource records can be automated through the use of dynamic updates. Additionally, you will be able to set specific security options on the various properties of the DNS service. Exercise 3.5 shows the steps that you can take to ensure that these integration features are enabled.

If you instructed the Active Directory Installation Wizard to automatically configure DNS, many of the settings mentioned in this section may already be enabled. However, you should verify the configuration and be familiar with how the options can be set manually.

EXERCISE 3.5

Configuring DNS Integration with Active Directory

Before you begin this exercise, ensure that the local machine is configured as an Active Directory domain controller and that DNS services have been properly configured. In this exercise, we'll look at the various DNS functions that are specific to interoperability with the Active Directory.

1. Open the DNS snap-in from the Administrative Tools program group.

2. Right-click the icon for the local DNS Server, and select Properties. Click the Security tab. Notice that you can now specify which users and groups have access to modify the configuration of the DNS Server. Make any necessary changes, and click OK.

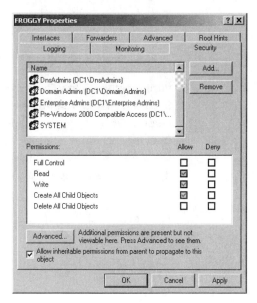

3. Expand the local server branch and the forward lookup zones folder.

4. Right-click the name of the Active Directory domain you created, and select Properties.

5. On the General tab, verify that the DNS server type is set to Active Directory-Integrated and that the message Data Is Stored in Active Directory is displayed. If this option is not currently selected, you can change it by clicking the Change button next to Type.

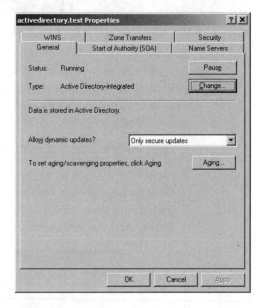

6. Verify that the Allow Dynamic Updates? option is set to Only Secure Updates. This will ensure that all updates to the DNS resource records database are made through authenticated Active Directory accounts and processes. The other options are Yes (to allow both secure and nonsecure dynamic updates) and No (to disallow dynamic updates).

7. Also, notice that you can define the security permissions at the zone level by clicking the Security tab. Make any necessary changes, and click OK.

Of course, all of the standard options related to configuring DNS are still available. For more information on configuring DNS, refer to Chapter 2, "Integrating DNS with the Active Directory."

Summary

In this chapter, we started by looking at the prerequisites for installing a Windows 2000 domain controller. This included technical considerations (such as verifying the file system and verifying DNS configuration), as well as domain planning issues (such as the name for the root domain). Based on this information, we used the Active Directory Installation Wizard to create the first domain controller in an Active Directory environment. Finally, we verified the configuration of the Active Directory by performing several tests of its functionality.

We limited the scope of this chapter to examining the issues related to installing and configuring the first domain in an Active Directory environment. In later chapters, we'll look at how more complex configurations can be created and managed.

With the installation and configuration of the Active Directory out of the way, it's time to move on to looking at how to establish the organizational unit structure *within* the domain.

Key Terms

Following are some key terms related to the installation and configuration of the Active Directory:

Active Directory Installation Wizard (DCPROMO)

File Allocation Table (FAT) file system

mixed-mode Active Directory

native-mode Active Directory

promotion

Windows NT File System (NTFS)

Review Questions

1. Which of the following file systems is supported by Windows 2000 and allows for file-level security?

   A. FAT

   B. FAT32

   C. HPFS

   D. NTFS

2. For security, it is recommended that which of the following file systems be used for all partitions on a domain controller?

   A. FAT

   B. FAT32

   C. HPFS

   D. NTFS

3. Which of the following tools can be used to verify that the Active Directory has been started?

   A. PING

   B. IPCONFIG

   C. NSLOOKUP

   D. Event Viewer

4. Which of the following commands can be used to view the TCP/IP configuration of the local machine?

   A. IPCONFIG

   B. NSLOOKUP

   C. PING

   D. TRACERT

5. At any given time, a domain controller may be a member of how many domains?

    A. 0

    B. 1

    C. 2

    D. Any number of domains

6. Which of the following administrative tools is only available if the local machine is a domain controller?

    A. DNS

    B. DHCP

    C. Active Directory Users and Computers

    D. Computer Management

7. In order to support Windows NT domain controllers in an Active Directory domain, which of the following modes must be used?

    A. Native mode

    B. Mixed mode

    C. Low-security mode

    D. Backwards-compatibility mode

    E. None of the above

8. The process of converting a Windows 2000 Server computer to a domain controller is known as:

    A. Advertising

    B. Reinstallation

    C. Promotion

    D. Conversion

9. DNS server services can be configured using which of the following tools?

   A. The DNS administrative tool

   B. Computer Management

   C. Network Properties

   D. None of the above

10. A domain controller can also run which of the following services?

    A. DNS

    B. DHCP

    C. Routing and Remote Access

    D. WINS

    E. All of the above

11. The NTFS 5 feature that limits the amount of disk space occupied by users is:

    A. Quotas

    B. Encryption

    C. Dynamic disks

    D. Remote storage

12. Which of the following NTFS features provides support for RAID?

    A. Fixed disks

    B. Dynamic disks

    C. FAT partitions

    D. FAT 32 partitions

    E. Both C and D

13. Which of the following commands is used to convert a FAT/FAT32 partition to NTFS?

  A. FILESYS

  B. CONVERTFS

  C. CONVERT

  D. None of the above

14. Which of the following file system conversion operations is supported in Windows 2000?

  A. FAT/FAT32 to NTFS

  B. NTFS to FAT/FAT32

  C. Both of the above

  D. None of the above

15. Which of the following desktop icons can be used to view other computers on the network?

  A. My Computer

  B. My Network Places

  C. Internet Explorer

  D. Briefcase

16. Which of the following types of computers can join a domain?

  A. Windows 2000 Professional (member of a workgroup)

  B. Windows 2000 Professional (member of a domain)

  C. Windows 2000 Server (member server)

  D. Windows 2000 Server (stand-alone server)

  E. All of the above

17. Which of the following operations is not supported by the Active Directory Installation Wizard?

   A. Promoting a server to a domain controller

   B. Demoting a domain controller to a server

   C. Moving servers between domains

   D. None of the above

18. Windows 2000 requires the use of which of the following protocols in order to support the Active Directory?

   A. DHCP

   B. TCP/IP

   C. NetBEUI

   D. IPX/SPX

19. Which of the following tools can be used to test connectivity between TCP/IP computers?

   A. PING

   B. Computer Management

   C. DNS

   D. DHCP

20. Which of the following domain names might be used by an organization for its initial Active Directory domain?

   A. mycompany.com

   B. test.mycompany.com

   C. mycompany.org

   D. activedirectory.test

   E. All of the above

Answers to Review Questions

1. D. File-system security is only available when using NTFS.

2. D. NTFS is recommended because it provides for file-level security. This is especially important on domain controllers since they contain sensitive security-related data. Support for FAT and FAT32 are provided primarily for backwards compatibility.

3. D. The Event Viewer provides information about various events related to the startup of the Active Directory.

4. A. Running IPCONFIG from the command line will display the current TCP/IP settings for the local computer.

5. B. A domain controller can contain Active Directory information for only one domain.

6. C. All of the other administrative tools are available for use whether or not the server is a domain controller.

7. B. In order to support Windows NT domain controllers, mixed-mode domains must be used.

8. C. Promotion is the process of creating a new domain controller.

9. A. The DNS administrative tool is designed to configure settings for the DNS server service. DNS zone files can also be manually edited using a standard text file editor.

10. E. Making a server a domain controller still allows the use of all of the same functionality allowed to member and stand-alone servers.

11. A. Quotas allow systems administrators to place restrictions on the amount of disk space used on NTFS volumes.

12. B. Only dynamic disks can be configured for RAID in Windows 2000.

13. C. The CONVERT command can be used to convert a FAT/FAT32 file system to NTFS.

14. A. FAT/FAT32 partitions can be converted to NTFS using the CONVERT command-line utility. NTFS partitions cannot be converted to FAT/FAT32 partitions without reformatting and re-creating the partition.

15. B. My Network Places is used to view other computers and Active Directory resources located on the network.

16. E. All of the above configurations can be joined to a domain.

17. C. The only way to move a domain controller between domains is to demote it from its current domain and then promote it into another domain.

18. B. The use of TCP/IP is required to support the Active Directory.

19. A. The PING tool is commonly used to verify connectivity between networked computers.

20. E. All of the domain names listed may be used. Although it is recommended, a standard domain name is not required for installing the Active Directory.

Chapter

4

Creating and Managing Organizational Units

MICROSOFT EXAM OBJECTIVES COVERED IN THIS CHAPTER:

✓ **Install, configure, and troubleshoot the components of Active Directory.**

- Install Active Directory.
- Create sites.
- Create subnets.
- Create site links.
- Create site link bridges.
- Create connection objects.
- Create global catalog servers.
- Move server objects between sites.
- Transfer operations master roles.
- Verify Active Directory installation.
- Implement an organizational unit (OU) structure.

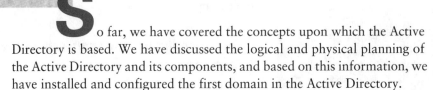

So far, we have covered the concepts upon which the Active Directory is based. We have discussed the logical and physical planning of the Active Directory and its components, and based on this information, we have installed and configured the first domain in the Active Directory.

In order to perform the exercises included in this chapter, you must have already installed the Active Directory. If you are still unsure about the steps and concepts associated with implementing an Active Directory domain, you should review the previous chapters before moving on. If you are working in a real-world environment, you've probably already seen how all of the planning steps mentioned in earlier chapters come into play.

In this chapter, we will begin to look at the structure of the various components *within* a domain. Specifically, we'll see how an organization's business structure can be mirrored within the Active Directory through the use of *organizational units (OUs)*.

Because the concepts related to OUs are quite simple, some systems administrators may underestimate their importance. Make no mistake — one of the fundamental components of a successful Active Directory installation is the proper design and deployment of OUs. With that in mind, let's look at the various steps required to plan for the use of OUs then, based on this information, walk through the steps required to implement and modify an OU structure.

This chapter covers material related to the implementation of an OU structure for the "Install, configure, and troubleshoot the components of Active Directory" objective. See Chapter 3, "Installing and Configuring the Active Directory," for material on the Active Directory and its installation; Chapter 5, "Installing and Managing Trees and Forests," for material on creating Global Catalog servers and transferring operations master roles; and Chapter 6, "Configuring Sites and Managing Replication," for coverage on creating sites, subnets, site links, site link bridges, and connection objects, as well as on moving server objects between sites.

An Overview of OUs

Before we begin to look at how OUs can be used within an Active Directory domain, we should first take a look at what OUs are and how they can be used to organize an Active Directory structure.

First and foremost, the purpose of OUs is to logically group Active Directory objects, just as their name implies. They serve as containers within which other Active Directory objects can be created. OUs do not form part of the DNS namespace. They are used solely to create organization within a domain.

OUs can contain the following types of Active Directory objects:

User Objects   User objects are the fundamental security principals used in an Active Directory environment. A User object includes a username, a password, group membership information, and many customizable fields that can be used to describe the user (e.g., fields for a street address, a telephone number, and other contact information).

Group Objects   Group objects are logical collections of users that are used primarily for assigning security permissions to resources. When managing users, the recommended practice is to place users into groups and then assign permissions to the group. This allows for flexible management and prevents systems administrators from having to set permissions for individual users.

Computer Objects   Computer objects represent workstations that are part of the Active Directory domain. Every computer within a domain shares the same security database, including user and group information. Computer objects are useful for managing security permissions and enforcing *Group Policy* restrictions.

Shared Folders   One of the fundamental functions of servers is to make resources available to users. Often, shared folders are used to give logical names to specific collections of files. For example, systems administrators might create shared folders for common applications, user data, and shared public files. Shared folders can be created and managed within the Active Directory.

Other Organizational Units   Perhaps the most useful feature of OUs is that they can contain *other* OUs. This allows systems administrators to hierarchically group resources and other objects in accordance with business practices. The OU structure is extremely flexible and, as we will see later in this chapter, can easily be rearranged to reflect business reorganizations.

Each of these types of objects has its own purpose within the organization of Active Directory domains. We'll look at the specifics of User, Computer, Group, and Shared Folder objects in later chapters. For now, let's focus on the purpose and benefits of using OUs.

The Purpose of OUs

The main purpose of OUs is to organize the objects within the Active Directory. Before diving into the details of OUs, however, it is very important to understand how OUs, users, and groups interact. Perhaps the most important concept to understand is that OUs are simply containers that are used for logically grouping various objects. They are not, however, groups in the classical sense. That is, they do not contain users, groups, or computers and are not used per se for assigning security permissions. Another way of stating this is that the User accounts, Computer accounts, and Group accounts that are contained in OUs are considered *security principals* while OUs themselves are not.

It is important to understand that OUs do not take the place of standard user and group permissions (a topic we'll cover in Chapter 8, "Active Directory Security"). A good general practice is to assign users to groups and then place the groups within OUs. This enhances the benefits of setting security permissions and of using the OU hierarchy for making settings. Figure 4.1 illustrates this concept.

FIGURE 4.1 Using Users, Groups, and OUs

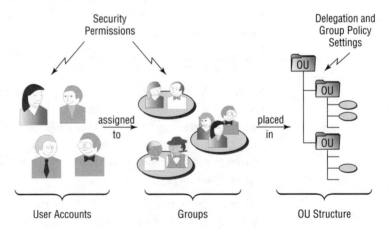

An organizational unit contains objects only from within the domain in which it resides. As we'll see later in this chapter, the OU is the finest level of granularity used for setting Group Policies and other administrative settings.

Benefits of OUs

There are many benefits to using OUs throughout your network environment. These include:

- OUs are the smallest unit to which you can assign permissions.
- The OU structure can be easily changed, and OU structure is more flexible than domain structure.
- The OU structure can support many different levels of hierarchy.
- OU settings can be inherited by child objects.
- You can set Group Policy settings on OUs.
- Administration of OUs and the objects within them can be easily delegated to the appropriate users and groups.

Now that we have a good idea of why you should use OUs, let's look at some general practices for planning the OU structure.

Planning the OU Structure

One of the key benefits of the Active Directory is the way in which it can bring organization to complex network environments. Before you can begin to implement OUs in various configurations, you must plan a structure that is compatible with business and technical needs. In this section, we'll look at several factors to consider when planning for the structure of OUs.

Logical Grouping of Resources

The fundamental purpose of using OUs is to hierarchically group resources that exist within the Active Directory. Fortunately, hierarchical groups are quite intuitive and widely used in most businesses. For example, a typical manufacturing business might divide its various operations into different departments. Examples include:

- Sales
- Marketing
- Engineering
- Research and Development
- Support
- Information Technology (IT)

Each of these departments usually has its own goals and missions. In order to make the business competitive, individuals within each of the departments will be assigned to various roles. Some types of roles might include:

- Managers
- Clerical Staff
- Technical Staff
- Planners

Each of these roles usually entails specific job responsibilities. For example, managers should be responsible for providing direction to general staff members. Note that the very nature of these roles suggests that employees may fill many different positions. That is, you might be a manager in one department and a member of the technical staff in another. In the modern workplace, such a situation is quite common.

So, how does all of this information help in planning for the use of OUs? First and foremost, the structure of OUs within a given network environment should map well to the needs of the business. This includes the political and logical structure of the organization, as well as its technical needs. Figure 4.2 provides an example of how a business organization might be mapped to the OU structure within an Active Directory domain.

FIGURE 4.2 Mapping a business organization to an OU structure

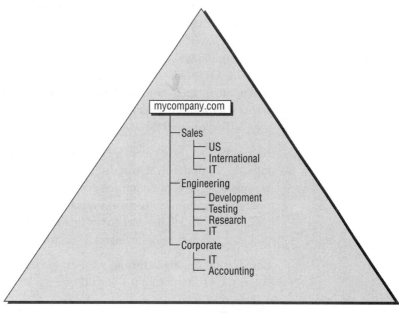

mycompany.com Domain

What's in a name? When it comes to designing the Active Directory, the answer is a lot! When naming OUs for your organization, you should keep several considerations and limitations in mind:

Keep it simple. The purpose of OUs is to make administration and usage of resources simple. Therefore, it's always a good idea to keep the names of your objects simple and descriptive. Sometimes, finding a balance between these two goals can be a challenge. For example, although a printer name like "The LaserJet located near Bob's Cube" might seem descriptive, it is certainly difficult to type. Imagine the naming changes that might be required if Bob moves (or leaves the company)!

Pay attention to limitations. The maximum length for the name of an OU is 65 characters. In most cases, this should be adequate for describing OUs. Remember that the name of an OU object does not have to uniquely describe it because the OU will generally be referenced as part of the overall hierarchy. For example, you can choose to create an IT OU within two different parent OUs. Even though the OUs have the same name, users and administrators will be able to distinguish them based on their complete path name.

Pay attention to the hierarchical consistency. The fundamental basis of an OU structure is adherence to a hierarchy. From a design standpoint, this means that you cannot have two OUs with the same name at the same level. However, you can have OUs with the same name at different levels. For example, we could create a Corporate OU within both the North America OU and the South America OU. This is because the fully qualified name includes information about the hierarchy. When an administrator tries to access resources in the Corporate OU, they must specify *which* Corporate OU they mean.

If, for example, you create a North America OU, the Canada OU should logically fit under it. If you decide that you want to separate them into completely different containers, then other names might be more appropriate. For example, North America could be changed to U.S. Users and administrators will depend on the hierarchy of OUs within the domain, so make sure that it remains logically consistent.

Based on these considerations, you should have a good idea of how to best organize the OU structure for your domain.

Understanding OU Inheritance

When OUs are rearranged within the structure of the Active Directory, several settings may be changed. Systems administrators must pay careful attention to changes in security permissions and other configuration options when moving and reorganizing OUs. By default, OUs will inherit the permissions of their new parent container when they are moved. Note that by using the built-in tools provided with Windows 2000 and the Active Directory, you can only move or copy OUs within the same domain.

If you need to move an entire OU structure between domains, you can use the MOVETREE command available in the Windows 2000 Resource Kit.

Delegation of Administrative Control

We already mentioned that OUs are the smallest component within a domain to which permissions and Group Policy can be assigned. Now, let's look specifically at how administrative control is set on OUs.

The idea of *delegation* involves a higher security authority that can give permissions to another. As a real-world example, assume that you are the director of IT for a large organization. Instead of doing all of the work yourself (which would result in a very long work day!), you would probably assign roles and responsibilities to other individuals. For example, you might make one systems administrator responsible for all operations within the Sales domain and another responsible for the Engineering domain. Similarly, you could assign the permissions for managing all printers and print queues within the organization to one individual while allowing another to manage all security permissions for users and groups.

In this way, the various roles and responsibilities of the IT staff can be distributed throughout the organization. Businesses generally have a division of labor to handle all of the tasks involved in keeping the company's networks humming along. Network operating systems, however, often make it difficult to assign just the right permissions. Sometimes, the complexity is necessary to ensure that only the right permissions are assigned. A good general rule of thumb is to provide users and administrators the minimum permissions they require to do their jobs. This ensures that accidental, malicious, and otherwise unwanted changes do not occur.

In the world of the Active Directory, the process of delegation is used to define the permissions for administrators of OUs. When considering implementing delegation, there are two main concerns to keep in mind:

Parent-Child Relationships The OU hierarchy you create will be very important when considering the maintainability of security permissions. As we've already mentioned, OUs can exist in a parent-child relationship. When it comes to the delegation of permissions, this is extremely important. You can choose to allow child containers to automatically inherit the permissions set on parent containers. For example, if the North America division of your organization contains 12 other OUs, you could delegate permissions to all of them by placing security permissions on the North America division. This feature can greatly ease administration, especially in larger organizations, but it is also a reminder of the importance of properly planning the OU structure within a domain.

You can only delegate control at the OU level and not at the object level within the OU.

Inheritance Settings   Now that we've seen how parent-child relation-ships can be useful for administration, we should consider the actual pro-cess of inheriting permissions. Logically, the process is known as *inheritance*. When permissions are set on a parent container, all of the child objects are configured to inherit the same permissions. This behav-ior can be overridden, however, if business rules do not lend themselves well to inheritance.

Application of Group Policy

One of the strengths of Windows operating systems is that they offer users a great deal of power and flexibility. From installing new software to adding device drivers, users can be given the ability to make many changes to their workstation configurations. This level of flexibility is also a potential prob-lem. Inexperienced users might inadvertently change settings, causing problems that can require many hours to fix.

In many cases (and especially in business environments), users will only require a subset of the complete functionality provided by the operating sys-tem. In the past, however, the difficulty associated with implementing and managing security and policy settings has led to lax security policies. Some of the reasons for this are technical—it can be very tedious and difficult to implement and manage security restrictions. Other problems have been political—users and management might feel that they should have full per-missions on their local machines, despite the potential problems this might cause.

One of the major design goals for the Windows 2000 platform (and spe-cifically, the Active Directory) was manageability. Although the broad range of features and functionality provided by the operating system can be help-ful, being able to lock down types of functionality is very important.

That's where the idea of Group Policies comes in. Simply defined, Group Policies are collections of permissions that can be applied to objects within the Active Directory. Specifically, Group Policy settings are assigned at the Site, Domain, and OU level and can apply to User accounts, Computer accounts, and groups. Examples of settings that a systems administrator can make using Group Policies include:

- Restricting access to the Start menu
- Disallowing the use of the Control Panel
- Limiting choices for display and desktop settings

We'll further cover the technical issues related to Group Policies in Chapter 10, "Managing Group Policy." In the following section, let's focus on how to plan OUs for the efficient use of policy settings.

Creating OUs

Now that we have looked at several different ways in which OUs can be used to bring organization to the objects within the Active Directory, it's time to look at how OUs can be created and managed. In this section, we'll look at ways to create OUs.

Microsoft
Exam
Objective

Install, configure, and troubleshoot the components of Active Directory.

- Implement an organizational unit (OU) structure.

Through the use of the Active Directory Users and Computers administrative tool, you can quickly and easily add, move, and change OUs. This graphical tool makes it easy to visualize and create the various levels of hierarchy required within an organization.

Figure 4.3 shows a geographically-based OU structure that might be used by a multinational company. Note that the organization is based in North America and has a corporate office located there. In general, all of the other offices are much smaller that those located in North America.

Also, it's important to note that this OU structure could have been designed in several different ways. For example, we could have chosen to group all of the offices located in the United States within a U.S. OU. However, due to the size of the offices, we choose to place these objects at the same level as the Canada and Mexico OUs. This prevents an unnecessarily deep OU hierarchy while still logically grouping the offices.

FIGURE 4.3 A geographically-based OU structure

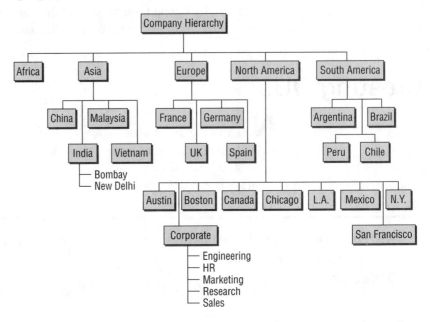

Exercise 4.1 walks you through the process of creating several OUs for a multinational business. We strongly recommend that you carry out this exercise since we'll be using this OU structure in later exercises within this chapter.

Creating OUs and other Active Directory objects can be a tedious process, especially for large organizations. A good way to speed up the process is to use keyboard shortcuts for creating objects instead of using the mouse. If your keyboard has a right-click key, be sure to use it. Also, learn the shortcuts for the context-sensitive menus. For example, the *n* key automatically chooses the *New* selection and the *o* key will specify that you want to create an OU.

EXERCISE 4.1

Creating an OU Structure

In this exercise, we'll create an OU structure for a multinational company. In order to complete this exercise, you must have first installed and configured at least one domain and have permissions to administer the domain.

EXERCISE 4.1 *(continued)*

1. Open the Active Directory Users and Computers administrative tool.

2. Right-click the name of the local domain, and choose New ➢ Organizational Unit. You will see the dialog box shown in the following graphic. Notice that this box shows you the current context within which the OU will be created. In this case, we're creating a top-level OU, so the full path is simply the name of the domain.

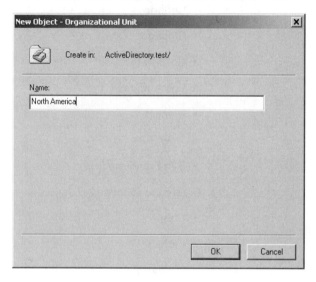

3. Type in **North America** for the name of the first OU. Click OK to create this object.

4. Now, create the following top-level OUs by right-clicking the name of the domain and choosing New ➢ Organizational Unit:

   - Africa

   - Asia

   - Europe

   - South America

5. Note that the order in which OUs are created is not important. In this exercise, we are simply using a method that emphasizes the hierarchical relationship.

6. Now, create the following second-level OUs within the North America OU by right-clicking the North America OU and selecting New ➤ Organizational Unit:

   - Austin
   - Boston
   - Canada
   - Chicago
   - Corporate
   - Los Angeles
   - Mexico
   - New York
   - San Francisco

7. Create the following OUs under the Asia OU:

   - China
   - India
   - Malaysia
   - Vietnam

8. Create the following OUs under the Europe OU:

   - France
   - Germany
   - Spain
   - UK

9. Create the following OUs under the South America OU:

   - Argentina
   - Brazil
   - Chile
   - Peru

EXERCISE 4.1 *(continued)*

10. Finally, it's time to create some third-level OUs. Right-click the India OU within the Asia OU, and select New ➤ Organizational Unit. Create the following OUs within this container:

   - Bombay

   - New Delhi

11. Within the North America Corporate OU, create the following OUs:

   - Engineering

   - HR

   - Marketing

   - Research

   - Sales

12. When you have completed the creation of the OUs, you should have a structure that looks similar to the one in the following graphic.

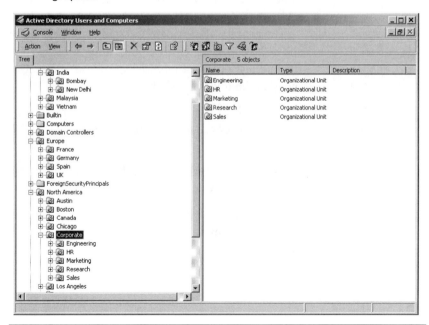

Once you have created a logical OU structure, it's time to look at the various operations that are required to manage OUs.

Managing OUs

Managing network environments would be challenging enough if things rarely changed. However, in the real world, business units, departments, and employee roles change frequently. As business and technical needs change, so should the structure of the Active Directory.

Fortunately, changing the structure of OUs within a domain is a relatively simple process. In this section, we'll look at ways to delegate control of OUs and make other changes.

Moving, Deleting, and Renaming OUs

When you delete an OU, the various objects contained within it are deleted along with the OU itself. There are several reasons that you might need to delete OUs. First, changes in the business structure (such as a consolidation of departments) may make a specific OU obsolete. Or, you might choose to make changes to better reflect the changing needs of a business.

The process of moving OUs is an extremely simple one. Exercise 4.2 shows how you can easily change and reorganize OUs to reflect changes in the business organization. The specific scenario covered in this exercise includes the following changes:

- The Research and Engineering departments have been combined together to form a department known as Research and Development (RD).

- The Sales department has been moved from the Corporate office to the New York office.

- The Marketing department has been moved from the Corporate office to the Chicago office.

EXERCISE 4.2

Modifying OU Structure

This exercise assumes that you have already completed the steps in the previous exercise within this chapter. In this exercise, we will make changes to the OUs as described in the text.

1. Open the Active Directory Users and Computers administrative tool.

2. To delete an OU, right-click the Engineering OU (located within North America ➢ Corporate) and click Delete. When prompted for confirmation, click Yes. Note that if this OU contained objects, all of the objects within the OU would have been automatically deleted as well.

3. Now, to rename an OU, right-click the Research OU and select Rename. Type RD to change the name of the OU and press Enter.

4. To move the Sales OU, right-click the Sales OU and select Move. In the Move dialog box, expand the North America branch and click the New York OU. Click OK to move the OU.

5. To move the Marketing OU, right-click the Marketing OU and select Move. In the Move dialog box, expand the North America branch and click the Chicago OU. Click OK to move the OU.

6. When you are finished, you should see an OU structure similar to the one shown in the following screen shot. Close the Active Directory Users and Computers administrative tool.

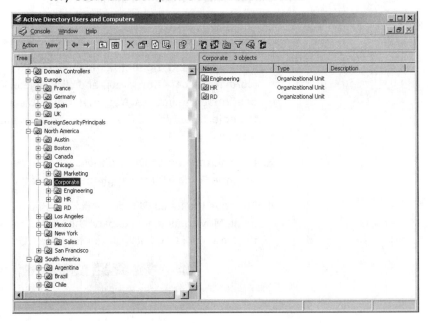

Administering Properties of OUs

Although OUs are primarily created for the purpose of organization within the Active Directory environment, they have several settings that can be modified. To modify the properties of an OU using the Active Directory Users and Computers administrative tool, you can right-click the name of any OU and select Properties. In the example shown in Figure 4.4, the Corporate Properties dialog box will appear, and you will then see the options on the General tab.

FIGURE 4.4 Viewing OU general properties

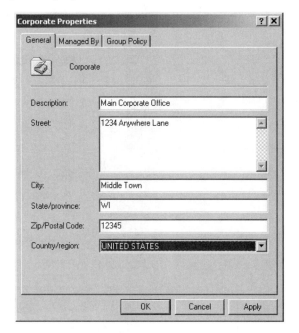

In any organization, it's useful to know who is responsible for the management of an OU. This information can be set on the Managed By tab (see Figure 4.5). The information specified on this tab is very convenient, as it will automatically pull the contact information from a user record. You should consider always having a contact for each OU within your organization so users and other systems administrators will know whom to contact should the need for any changes arise.

Additionally, you can set Group Policy settings for the OU on the Group Policy tab. We'll cover this topic later in Chapter 10, "Managing Group Policy." We'll also look at several ways to manage all types of objects within the Active Directory in Chapter 7, "Administering the Active Directory."

FIGURE 4.5 Setting OU Managed By properties

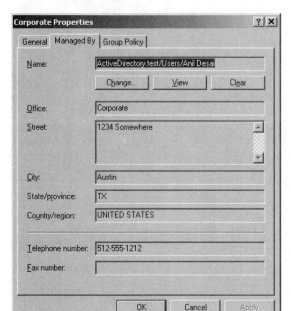

Delegating Control of OUs

In simple environments, one or a few systems administrators may be responsible for managing all of the settings within the Active Directory. For example, a single systems administrator could be responsible for managing all users within all OUs in the environment. In larger organizations, however, roles and responsibilities may be divided among many different individuals. A typical situation is one in which a systems administrator is responsible for objects within only a few OUs in an Active Directory domain. Or, one systems administrator may be responsible for managing User and Group objects while another is responsible for managing file and print services.

Fortunately, the Active Directory Users and Computers tool provides a quick and easy method for ensuring that specific users receive only the permissions that they require. In Exercise 4.3, we will use the *Delegation of Control Wizard* to assign permissions to individuals.

EXERCISE 4.3

Using the Delegation of Control Wizard

In this exercise, we will use the Delegation of Control Wizard to assign permissions to specific users within the Active Directory. In order to successfully complete these steps, you must first have created the objects in the previous exercises of this chapter.

1. Open the Active Directory Users and Computers administrative tool.

2. Right-click the Corporate OU (within the North America OU) and select Delegate Control. This will start the Delegation of Control Wizard. Click Next to begin making security settings.

3. In the Select Users, Computers, or Groups dialog box, select the account for the Built-In Account Operators Group and click Add. Click OK to accept this item, then click Next to continue.

4. In the Tasks to Delegate window, select Delegate the Following Common Tasks and place a check mark next to the following items:

   - Create, Delete, and Manage user accounts

   - Reset Passwords on User Accounts

   - Read All User Information

   - Create, Delete, and Manage Groups

   - Modify the Membership of a Group

5. Click Next to continue.

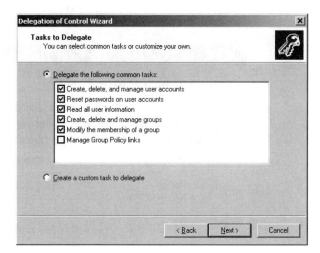

EXERCISE 4.3 *(continued)*

6. The Completing the Delegation of Control Wizard dialog box will provide a summary of the operations you have selected. To implement the changes, click Finish.

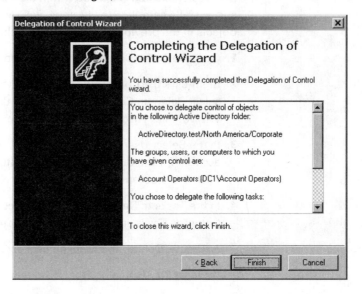

Although the common tasks available through the Wizard will be sufficient for many delegation operations, there might be cases in which you want more control. For example, you might want to give particular systems administrator permissions to modify only Computer objects. Exercise 4.4 uses the Delegation of Control Wizard to assign more granular permissions.

EXERCISE 4.4

Delegating Custom Tasks

In this exercise, we will use the Delegation of Control Wizard to delegate custom tasks to specific users within the Active Directory. In order to successfully complete these steps, you must first have created the objects in the previous exercises of this chapter.

1. Open the Active Directory Users and Computers administrative tool.

2. Right-click the Corporate OU (within the North America OU) and select Delegate Control. This will start the Delegation of Control Wizard. Click Next to begin making security settings.

3. In the Select Users, Computers, or Groups dialog box, select the account for the Built-In Server Operators Group and click Add. Click OK to accept this item, then click Next to continue.

4. Select Create a Custom Task to Delegate, and click Next to continue.

5. In the Active Directory Object Type dialog box, choose Only the Following Objects in the Folder, and place a check mark next to the following items:

- Computer Objects

- Contact Objects

- Group Objects

- Organizational Unit Objects

- Printer Objects

- User Objects

6. Click Next to continue.

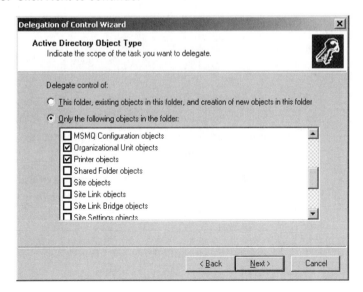

7. In the Permissions dialog box, place a check mark next to only the General option. Note that if the various objects within your Active Directory schema had property-specific settings, you would see those options here. Place a check mark next to the following items:

   • Create All Child Objects

   • Read All Properties

   • Write All Properties

8. Click Next to continue.

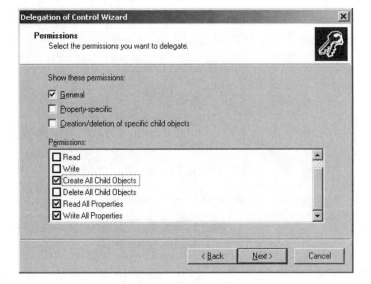

9. This will give the members of the Server Operators group the ability to create new objects within the Corporate OU and the permissions to read and write all properties for these objects. Click Next to continue.

10. The Completing the Delegation of Control Wizard dialog box will provide a summary of the operations you have selected. To implement the changes, click Finish.

In addition to the basic types of security options we set in the exercise, you can create custom tasks and place permissions on specific types of objects within a container. We'll cover security permissions in greater detail in Chapter 8, "Active Directory Security."

Troubleshooting OUs

In general, the use of OUs will be a straightforward and relatively painless process. With adequate planning, you'll be able to implement an intuitive and useful structure for OU objects.

The most common problems with OU configuration are related to the OU structure. When troubleshooting OUs, you should pay careful attention to the following factors:

Inheritance   By default, Group Policy and other settings are transferred automatically from parent OUs to child OUs and objects. This is an important point to consider. Even if a specific OU is not given a set of permissions, objects within that OU might still get them from parent objects.

Delegation of Administration   If the wrong User accounts or groups are allowed to perform specific tasks on OUs, you might be violating your company's security policy. Be sure to verify the delegations you have made at each OU level.

Organizational Issues   Sometimes, business practices may not easily map to the structure of the Active Directory. A few misplaced OUs, User accounts, Computer accounts, or groups can make administration difficult or inaccurate. In many cases, it might be beneficial to rearrange the OU structure to accommodate any changes in the business organization. In others, it might make more sense to change business processes.

If you make it a practice to regularly consider each of these issues when troubleshooting problems with OUs, you will be much less likely to make errors in the Active Directory configuration.

Summary

In this chapter, we looked at one of the most important objects within an Active Directory domain: organizational units (OUs). We began by looking at several factors to consider when designing an OU structure. Based on this information, we created a sample OU structure for a geographically organized business. We also saw that reorganizing OUs can be a simple and painless process. Finally, we used the Delegation of Control Wizard to set administrative permissions to the objects within an OU.

Through the use of OUs, organizations can quickly and easily group their resources in a hierarchical manner that is logical and consistent with the company's own organization. As we'll see in later chapters, the OUs offer an excellent way to manage Group Policy and administrative functions.

Key Terms

Before you take the exam, you should be familiar with the following terms and concepts:

- delegation
- Delegation of Control Wizard
- Group Policy
- inheritance
- organizational units (OUs)
- security principals

Review Questions

1. Which of the following is not a true characteristic of OUs?

   A. OUs can contain other Active Directory objects.

   B. OUs are security principals.

   C. OUs can contain other OUs.

   D. OUs can be arranged in a hierarchy.

2. The primary administrative tool used to manage OUs is:

   A. Active Directory Domains and Trusts

   B. Active Directory Users and Computers

   C. Active Directory Sites and Services

   D. Computer Management

3. Which of the following Active Directory components plays a role in the DNS namespace?

   A. Domains

   B. Organizational units (OUs)

   C. Groups

   D. Users

   E. All of the above

4. Which of the following characteristics of OUs specifies that settings can flow from parent objects to child objects?

   A. Inheritance

   B. Group Policy

   C. Delegation

   D. None of the above

5. Which of the following operations cannot be performed in a single operation?

   A. Moving an OU

   B. Renaming an OU

   C. Deleting an OU

   D. Copying an OU

6. An administrator can specify the contact information for an OU by using which of the following tabs in the properties of an OU?

   A. Contact Information

   B. General

   C. Managed By

   D. Advanced

   E. None of the above

7. A good reason to change the OU structure is:

   A. A user leaves the company

   B. An IT administrator leaves the company

   C. The business is reorganized

   D. None of the above

8. Which of the following operations is allowed when using the Active Directory Users and Computers tool?

   A. Moving OUs between domains

   B. Copying OUs between domains

   C. Merging OUs between domains

   D. None of the above

9. Which of the following is a common task presented in the Delegation of Control Wizard?

   A. Reset passwords on user accounts

   B. Manage Group Policy links

   C. Modify the membership of a group

   D. Create, delete and manage groups

   E. All of the above

10. Which of the following statements is *false* regarding the naming of OUs?

   A. No two OUs within the same domain can have the same name.

   B. No two domains can contain OUs with the same name.

   C. Both of the above are false.

11. Which of the following is *not* considered to be a security principal?

   A. User accounts

   B. Groups

   C. Computer accounts

   D. Organizational units (OUs)

12. Which of the following operations can be used to move OUs within an Active Directory domain?

   A. Dragging and dropping the OU to a new location

   B. Right-clicking the OU, and selecting Move

   C. Renaming the OU with the fully qualified path to the new location

   D. None of the above (OUs cannot be moved)

13. The maximum length for the name of an OU is:

   A. 16 characters

   B. 22 characters

   C. 65 characters

   D. 128 characters

   E. Unlimited

14. The General property tab for an OU includes which of the following information?

   A. The name of the OU

   B. Replication status information about the OU

   C. The number of objects within the OU

   D. All of the above

15. Which of the following OU settings allows systems administrators to restrict actions that can be performed by users and computers?

   A. Group Policy

   B. OU Registry settings

   C. Security permissions

   D. Auditing

   E. All of the above

16. A user is having trouble accessing an object contained within an OU and wants to know who should be contacted. Which of the following tabs might provide the appropriate information?

   A. General

   B. Security

   C. Managed By

   D. Properties

   E. None of the above

17. Which of the following statements regarding domain and OU structure best describes the flexibility of these Active Directory objects?

    A. In general, OU structure is more flexible than domain structure.

    B. In general, domain structure is more flexible than OU structure.

18. The process of inheritance states which of the following behaviors?

    A. Child OUs may inherit security and other settings from parent OUs.

    B. OUs can be copied across domains.

    C. OUs can be copied across forests.

    D. OUs can be created in Windows NT domains.

    E. None of the above

19. A systems administrator wants to allow another user permissions to reset passwords for all users within a specific OU. They can do this by:

    A. Creating a special administration account within the OU

    B. Moving the user's login account into the OU

    C. Moving the user's login account to an OU that contains the OU

    D. Using the Delegation of Control Wizard to assign the necessary permissions

    E. None of the above

20. In general, the OU structure of an organization should be based on all of the following except:

    A. Physical network topology

    B. Business organizational requirements

    C. System administration requirements

    D. None of the above

Answers to Review Questions

1. B. While the objects within OUs may be security principals, resource permissions are not assigned to OUs themselves.

2. B. The graphical interface of the Active Directory Users and Computers tool allows systems administrators to easily create, manage, and organize OUs.

3. A. Domains form the basis of the DNS namespace in an Active Directory environment. OUs do not form part of the DNS namespace, as do domains. OUs are used primarily for organization *within* a domain.

4. A. Inheritance is the process by which permissions placed on parent OUs affect child OUs.

5. D. The Active Directory Users and Computers tool does not allow for automatically copying an OU.

6. C. The Managed By tab allows placing information about an individual that is responsible for the management of that OU, along with their contact information.

7. C. A business reorganization is a good reason to change the OU structure. The other types of changes listed can be managed easily through the use of the Active Directory Users and Computers tool and the Delegation of Control Wizard rather than through modifications to the OU structure, a more drastic measure than would be necessary.

8. D. None of the operations listed are directly supported. The Active Directory Users and Computers tool only allows moving OUs within the same domain.

9. E. All of the options listed are common tasks presented in the Delegation of Control Wizard.

10. C. OU naming is hierarchical and must be unique only within the same parent container. Two or more OUs within a domain may have the same name, as long as they are not located within the same parent OU.

11. D. Security permissions can be assigned directly to User accounts, groups, and Computer accounts, but not directly to OUs.

12. B. The Active Directory Users and Computers tool allows you to move OUs by right-clicking the OU and selecting Move.

13. C. The name of an OU can be up to 65 characters.

14. A. The General tab of the OU properties lists the name of the OU.

15. A. Group Policies are designed to restrict the actions that can be carried out by users and computers within an OU.

16. C. The Managed By tab is used to specify the individual who is responsible for managing the objects within an OU.

17. A. OUs can be easily moved and renamed without requiring the promotion of domain controllers and network changes. This makes OU structure much more flexible.

18. A. One of the administrative benefits of using OUs is that permissions and other settings can be inherited by child OUs.

19. D. The Delegation of Control Wizard is designed to allow administrators to set up permissions on specific Active Directory objects.

20. A. OUs are created to reflect a company's logical organization. Other Active Directory features can be used to accommodate the network topology.

Chapter

5

Installing and Managing Trees and Forests

MICROSOFT EXAM OBJECTIVES COVERED IN THIS CHAPTER:

✓ **Install, configure, and troubleshoot the components of Active Directory.**

- Install Active Directory.
- Create sites.
- Create subnets.
- Create site links.
- Create site link bridges.
- Create connection objects.
- Create global catalog servers.
- Move server objects between sites.
- Transfer operations master roles.
- Verify Active Directory installation.
- Implement an organizational unit (OU) structure.

So far, we have focused on the steps required to plan for the Active Directory and to implement the first Active Directory domain. Although we did briefly cover the concepts related to multidomain Active Directory structures, the focus was on a single domain and the objects within it. Many businesses will find that the use of a single domain will provide an adequate solution to meet their business needs. Through the use of *trees* and *forests*, however, organizations can use multiple domains to better organize their environments.

In this chapter, we'll begin by covering some reasons to create more than one Active Directory domain. Then, we'll move on to looking at the exact processes involved creating a domain tree and joining multiple trees together into a domain forest.

NOTE This chapter covers material related to the "Create global catalog servers" and "Transfer operations master roles" subobjectives. See Chapter 3, "Installing and Configuring the Active Directory," for material on the Active Directory and its installation; Chapter 4, "Creating and Managing Organizational Units," for coverage on implementing an OU structure; and Chapter 6, "Configuring Sites and Managing Replication," for coverage on creating sites, subnets, site links, site link bridges, and connection objects, as well as on moving server objects between sites.

Reasons for Creating Multiple Domains

Before we look at the steps required to create multiple domains, we should cover the reasons why an organization might want to create them. In general, you should always try to reflect your organization's structure within a single domain. Through the use of organizational units (OUs) and other objects, you can usually create an accurate and efficient structure within one domain, and creating and managing a single domain is usually much simpler than managing a more complex environment. With that said, let's look at some real benefits and reasons for creating multiple domains.

Benefits of Multiple Domains

There are several reasons why you might need to implement multiple domains. These reasons include such considerations as:

Scalability   Although Microsoft has designed the Active Directory to accommodate millions of objects, this number may not be practical for your current environment. Supporting many thousands of users within a single domain will place higher disk space, CPU (Central Processing Unit), and network burdens on your *domain controllers*. Determining the scalability of the Active Directory is something you will have to test within your own environment.

Reducing Replication Traffic   All the domain controllers of a domain must keep an up-to-date copy of the entire Active Directory database. For small- to medium-sized domains, this is not generally a problem. Windows 2000 and the Active Directory data store manage all of the details of transferring data behind the scenes. Other business and technical limitations might, however, affect Active Directory's ability to perform adequate replication. For example, if you have two sites that are connected by a very slow network link (or no link at all), replication will not be practical. In this case, you will probably want to create separate domains to isolate replication traffic.

It is important to realize that the presence of slow network links alone is *not* a good reason to break an organization into multiple domains. Through the use of the Active Directory site configuration, replication traffic can be managed independently of the domain architecture. We'll cover these topics in detail in Chapter 6, "Configuring Sites and Managing Replication."

Political and Organizational Reasons   There are several business reasons that might justify the creation of multiple domains. One of the organizational reasons to use multiple domains is to avoid potential problems associated with the Domain Administrator account. At least one user will need to have permissions at this level. If your organization is unable or unwilling to place this level of trust with all business units, then multiple domains may be the best answer. Since each domain maintains its own security database, you will be able to keep permissions and resources isolated. Through the use of trusts, however, you will still be able to share resources.

Keep in mind that some types of organizational and political issues might require the use of multiple domains while others do not. If you are considering creating multiple domains for purely political reasons (e.g., so that an IT or business manager can retain control over certain resources), this decision might require some further thinking.

Many Levels of Hierarchy   Larger organizations tend to have more complex business structures. Even if the structure itself is not complicated, it is likely that a company that has many departments will have several levels within its structure. As we saw in Chapter 4, "Creating and Managing Organizational Units," OUs can accommodate many of these issues. If, however, you find that many levels of OUs will be required to manage resources (or if there are large numbers of objects within each OU), it might make sense to create additional domains. Each domain would contain its own OU hierarchy and serve as the root of a new set of objects.

Varying Security Policies   All of the objects within the domain share many characteristics in common. One of these characteristics is security policy. A domain is designed to be a single security entity. Settings such as usernames and password restrictions apply to all objects within the domain. If your organization requires separate security policies for different groups of users, you should consider creating multiple domains.

Migrating from Windows NT   Ideally, organizations should store all resources and user information within a single domain. In fact, Microsoft recommends that you try to consolidate multiple domains. In some cases, though, this might not be practical, and the use of multiple domains will be required. If, for instance, you're migrating from an existing multidomain structure, you will have several choices to make. For more information on planning domain structures, see Appendix B, "Planning the Active Directory."

Decentralized Administration   There are two main models of administration that are in common use: a centralized administration model and a decentralized administration model. In the centralized administration model, a single IT organization is responsible for managing all of the users, computers, and security permissions for the entire organization. In the decentralized administration model, each department or business unit might have its own IT department. In both cases, the needs of the administration model can play a significant role in the decision to use multiple domains.

Consider, for example, a multinational company that has a separate IT department for offices in each country. Each IT department is responsible for supporting only the users and computers within its own region. Since the administration model is largely decentralized, the creation of a separate domain for each of these major business units might make sense from a security and maintenance standpoint.

Multiple DNS or Domain Names   Although it might at first sound like a trivial reason to create additional domains, the use of multiple DNS or domain names requires the creation of multiple domains. Each domain can have only one Fully-Qualified Domain Name. For example, if I require some of my users to be placed within the `sales.mycompany.com` namespace and others to be placed in the `engineering.mycompany.com` namespace, multiple domains will be required. If the domain names are noncontiguous, you will need to create multiple domain trees (a topic we'll cover later in this chapter).

Drawbacks of Multiple Domains

Although many of these reasons for having multiple domains are compelling, there are also reasons *not* to break an organizational structure into multiple domains. Many of these are related to maintenance and administration.

Administrative Inconsistency   One of the fundamental responsibilities of most systems administrators is implementing and managing security. When you are implementing Group Policy and security settings in multiple domains, you must be careful to ensure that the settings are consistent. As we mentioned in the previous section, security policies can be different between domains. If this is what is intended, then it is not a problem. If, however, the organization wishes to make the same settings apply to all users, then similar security settings will be required in each domain.

More Difficult Management of Resources Server, user, and computer management can become a considerable challenge when managing multiple domains since there are many more administrative units required. In general, you will need to manage all user, group, and computer settings separately for the objects within each domain. The hierarchical structure provided by OUs, on the other hand, provides a much simpler and easier way to manage permissions.

Decreased Flexibility The creation of a domain involves the *promotion* of a domain controller to the new domain. Although the process is quite simple, it is much more difficult to rearrange the domain topology within an Active Directory environment than it is to simply reorganize OUs. When planning domains, you should ensure that the domain structure will not change often.

Now that we have examined the pros and cons related to the creation of multiple domains, let's see how trees and forests can be created.

Creating Domain Trees and Forests

Now that we've covered some important reasons for using multiple domains in a single network environment, it's time to look at how multidomain structures can be created. The fundamental structures that we'll be discussing are domain trees and domain forests.

An important fact to remember is that regardless of the number of domains you have in your environment, you always have a tree and a forest. This might come as a surprise to those of you who generally think of domain trees and forests as Active Directory environments that consist of multiple domains. However, when you install the first domain in an Active Directory environment, that domain automatically creates a new forest and a new tree. Of course, there are no other domains that form the tree or forest.

A domain tree is created from multiple domains that share a contiguous namespace. That is, all of the domains within a tree are linked together by a common root domain. For example, all of the following domains make up a single contiguous namespace (and can therefore be combined together to form a single domain tree):

- `sales.company.com`
- `it.company.com`

- company.com

- northamerica.sales.company.com

In some cases, you may want to combine Active Directory domains that do not share a contiguous namespace. In other words, you want to merge two or more trees together. Such a structure is known as a forest. The following domains do not share a contiguous namespace:

- sales.company1.com

- sales.company2.com

- company3.com

In order to manage the relationship between these domains, you would need to create three separate domain trees (one for each of the domains), and then combine them into a forest.

If you're unfamiliar with the use of multiple domains, you might be wondering "Why bother to join domains together into a tree or forest?" Well, that's a good question. The main reason to combine domains together is to allow for the sharing of resources. We'll look at how this is done through the use of trust relationships later in this chapter.

All of the domains within a single Active Directory forest have several features in common. Specifically, they share the following features:

Schema   The schema is the Active Directory structure that defines how the information within the data store will be structured. In order for the information stored on various domain controllers to remain compatible, all of the domain controllers within the entire Active Directory environment must share the same schema. For example, if I added a field for an employee's benefits plan number, all domain controllers throughout the environment would need to recognize this information before information could be shared between them.

Global Catalog   One of the problems associated with working in large network environments is that sharing information across multiple domains can be costly in terms of network and server resources. We already mentioned how the Active Directory schema allows for a standardized set of information to be stored. However, one potential problem with this is realized when users try to search for resources across many domains.

To illustrate this point, consider the question, "Where are all of the color printers in the company?" Clearly, a search throughout all of the domains is intended. So how should this be handled? One possible solution would be to send the query to one domain controller in each domain and then have each respond back with the necessary information. Although this could be done, it would create a large amount of network traffic and generate huge loads on each domain controller. Add in the fact that the nearest domain controller might be thousands of miles (and network hops) away, and you have a network nightmare!

Fortunately, the Active Directory has a better solution: the Global Catalog (GC). The GC serves as a repository for information about a subset of all of the objects within *all* Active Directory domains within a forest. Systems administrators can determine what types of information should be added to the defaults in the GC. Generally, the decision is to store commonly used information, such as a list of all of the printers, users, groups, and computers. Specific domain controllers can be configured to carry a copy of the GC. Now, going back to the question of where all the color printers in the company can be found, all that needs to be done is to contact the nearest GC server. It doesn't take much imagination to see how this could save a lot of time and computing resources!

Configuration Information   There are some roles and functions that must be managed for the entire forest. When dealing with multiple domains, this means that you must configure certain domain controllers to perform functions for the entire Active Directory environment. We'll look at some specifics later in this chapter.

The main purpose of allowing multiple domains to exist together is to provide for the sharing of information and other resources. Now that we've covered the basics of domain trees and forests, let's look at how domains are actually created.

The Promotion Process

A domain tree is created when a new domain is added as the child of an existing domain. This relationship is established during the promotion of a Windows 2000 server to a domain controller. Although the underlying relationships can be quite complicated in larger organizations, the *Active Directory Installation Wizard* makes it easy to create forests and trees.

Through the use of the Active Directory Installation Wizard, you can quickly and easily create new domains by promoting a Windows 2000 stand-alone server or a member server to a domain controller. When you install a new domain controller, you can choose to make it part of an existing domain, or you can choose to make it the first domain controller in a new domain. In any event, domains are created through the promotion of a server to a domain controller. In the following sections and exercises, we'll look at the exact steps required to create a domain tree and a domain forest when you promote a server to a domain controller.

The promotion process involves many steps and decisions. We covered the details in Chapter 3, "Installing and Configuring the Active Directory." If you are unfamiliar with the process and ramifications related to promoting a server to a domain controller, it will be helpful to review that chapter before continuing.

Creating a Domain Tree

To create a new domain tree, you will need to promote a Windows 2000 Server computer to a domain controller. In so doing, you'll have the option of making this domain controller the first machine in a new domain that is a child of an existing one. The result will be a new domain tree that contains two domains—a parent domain and a child domain.

Before you can create a new child domain, you will need the following information:

- The name of the parent domain
- The name of the child domain (the one you are planning to install)
- The file system locations for the Active Directory database, logs, and shared system volume
- DNS configuration information
- The NetBIOS name for the new server
- A domain administrator username and password

Exercise 5.1 walks you through the process of creating a new child domain using the Active Directory Installation Wizard.

EXERCISE 5.1

Creating a New Subdomain

In this exercise, we will create a domain tree by adding a new domain as a subdomain of an existing domain. This exercise assumes that you have already created the parent domain.

1. Open the Configure Your Server tool from the Administrative Tools program group. In the left navigation bar, click Active Directory, then click Start to start the Active Directory Installation Wizard. Alternatively, click Start ➤ Run, and type **dcpromo**. Click Next to begin the Wizard.

2. On the Domain Controller Type page, select Domain Controller for a New Domain. Click Next.

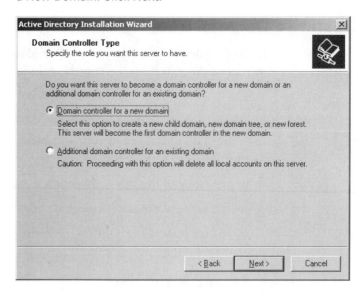

3. On the Create Tree or Child Domain page, choose Create a New
Child Domain in an Existing Domain Tree. Click Next.

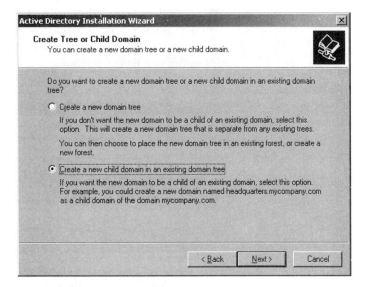

4. On the Network Credentials page, enter the username and password for the domain administrator of the domain you wish to join.
You will also need to specify the full name of the domain you want to
join. After you have entered the appropriate information, click Next.

5. If the information you entered was correct, you will see the Child Domain Installation page. Here, you will be able to confirm the name of the parent domain and then enter the domain name for the child domain. If you want to make a change, you can click the Browse button and search for a domain. The Complete DNS Name of New Domain field will show you the fully distinguished domain name for the domain you are creating. Click Next to continue.

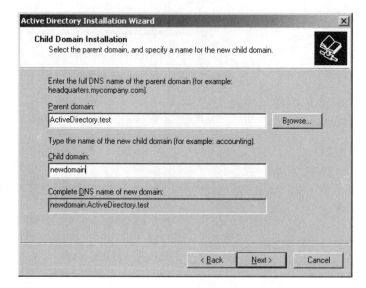

6. Next, you'll be prompted for the NetBIOS name for this domain controller. This is the name that will be used by previous versions of Windows to identify this machine. Choose a name that is up to 15 characters in length and includes only alphanumeric characters. Click Next to continue.

7. Now, it's time to specify the database and log locations. These settings will specify where the Active Directory database will reside on the local machine. As we mentioned previously, it is a good practice to place the log files on a separate physical hard disk as this will increase performance. Enter the path for a local directory, and click Next.

8. On the Shared System Volume page, specify the folder in which the Active Directory public files will reside. This directory must reside on an NTFS 5 partition. Choose the path, and then click Next.

9. If you have not yet installed and configured the DNS service, or if there is an error in the configuration, the Active Directory Installation Wizard will prompt you regarding whether or not the DNS service on the local machine should be configured automatically. Since the Active Directory and client computers will rely on DNS information for finding objects, you will generally want the Wizard to automatically configure DNS. Click Next to continue.

10. On the Permissions page, select whether or not you want to use permissions that are compatible with Windows NT domains. If you will be supporting any Windows NT Server computers or have existing Windows NT domains, you should choose Permissions Compatible with Pre-Windows 2000 Servers. Otherwise, choose Permissions Compatible Only with Windows 2000 Servers. Click Next.

11. In order to be able to recover this server in the event of a loss of Active Directory information, you will need to provide a Directory Services Restore Mode Administrator Password. This password will allow you to use the built-in recovery features of Windows 2000 in the event that the Active Directory database is lost or corrupted. Enter a password, confirm it, and then click Next.

12. On the Summary page, you will be given a brief listing of all the choices you made in the previous steps. Click Next to continue on.

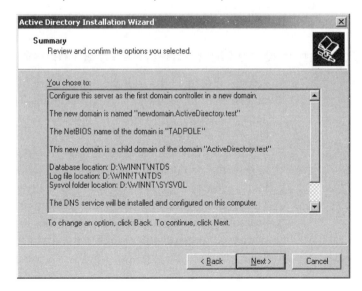

13. The Active Directory Installation Wizard will automatically begin performing the steps required to create a new domain in your environment. It's a good idea to copy this information and paste it into a text document for future reference, if needed. Note that you can press Cancel if you want to abort this process. When the process has completed, you will be prompted to reboot the system.

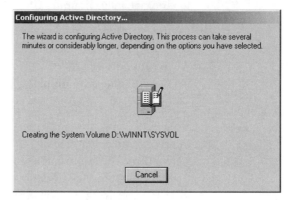

Following a reboot of the system, the local server will from then on be the first domain controller in a new domain. This domain will also be a sub–domain of an existing one. Congratulations, you have created a new domain tree!

Joining a New Domain Tree to a Forest

A forest is formed through the joining of two or more domains that do not share a contiguous namespace. For example, I could join the `organization1.com` and `organization2.com` domains together to create a single Active Directory environment.

Any two independent domains can be joined together to create a forest, as long as the two domains have non-contiguous namespaces. (If the name–spaces were contiguous, you would actually need to create a domain tree.) The process of creating a new tree to form or add to a forest is as simple as promoting a server to a domain controller for a new domain that does *not* share a namespace with an existing Active Directory domain.

In Exercise 5.2, you will use the Active Directory Installation Wizard to create a new domain tree to add to a forest. In order to add a new domain to an existing forest, you must already have at least one other domain. This domain will serve as the root domain for the entire forest. It is important to keep in mind that the entire forest structure will be destroyed if the original root domain is ever entirely removed. Therefore, it is highly recommended that you have at least two domain controllers in the Active Directory root domain. This will provide additional protection for the entire forest in case one of the domain controllers fails.

EXERCISE 5.2

Creating a New Domain Tree in the Forest

In this exercise, we will create a new domain tree by adding a new domain as a subdomain of an existing one. In order to complete this exercise, you must have already installed another domain controller that serves as the root domain for a forest.

1. Open the Configure Your Server tool from the Administrative Tools program group. In the left navigation bar, click Active Directory, then click Start to start the Active Directory Installation Wizard. Alternatively, click Start ➤ Run, and type **dcpromo**. Click Next to begin the Wizard.

2. On the Domain Controller Type page, select Domain Controller for a New Domain. Click Next.

3. On the Create Tree or Child Domain page, choose Create a New Domain Tree. Click Next.

EXERCISE 5.2 *(continued)*

4. You'll be given the option of either creating a new forest or joining an existing domain forest. Select Place This New Domain Tree in an Existing Forest, and click Next.

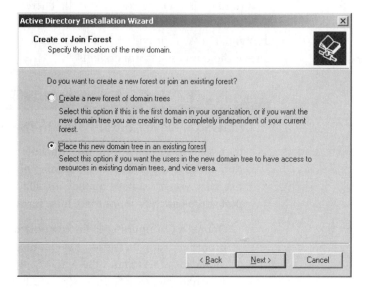

5. On the Network Credentials page, enter the username and password for a user account that has permissions to administer the domain you wish to join. You will also need to specify the full name of the domain you want to join. After you have entered the appropriate information, click Next.

6. In the New Domain Tree box, you will need to specify the full name of the new domain you wish to create. Note that this domain may not share a contiguous namespace with any other existing domain. Once you have entered the appropriate information, click Next.

7. You'll be prompted for the NetBIOS name of the domain controller. This is the name that will be used by previous versions of Windows to identify this machine. Choose a name that is up to 15 characters in length and includes only alphanumeric characters. Click Next to continue.

8. You'll need to specify the database and log locations. These settings will specify where the Active Directory database will reside on the local machine. Enter the path for a local directory, and click Next.

9. On the Shared System Volume page, specify the folder in which the Active Directory public files will reside. This directory must reside on an NTFS 5 partition. Choose the path, and then click Next.

10. If you have not yet configured the DNS service, you will be prompted to do so. Since the Active Directory and client computers will rely on DNS information for finding objects, you will generally want the Wizard to automatically configure DNS. Click Next to continue.

11. On the Permissions page, select whether or not you want to use permissions that are compatible with Windows NT domains. If you will be supporting any Windows NT Server computers or have existing Windows NT domains, you should choose Permissions Compatible with Pre-Windows 2000 Servers. Otherwise, choose Permissions Compatible Only with Windows 2000 Servers. Click Next.

12. In order to be able to recover this server in the event of a loss of Active Directory information, you will need to provide a Directory Services Restore Mode Administrator Password. This password will allow you to use the built-in recovery features of Windows 2000 in the event that the Active Directory database is lost or corrupted. Enter a password, confirm it, and then click Next.

13. On the Summary page, you will be given a brief listing of all of the choices you made in the previous steps. Click Next to continue.

EXERCISE 5.2 *(continued)*

14. The Active Directory Installation Wizard will automatically begin performing the steps required to create a new domain tree in an existing forest based on the information you provided. Note that you can press Cancel if you want to abort this process. When the setup is complete, you will be prompted to reboot the system.

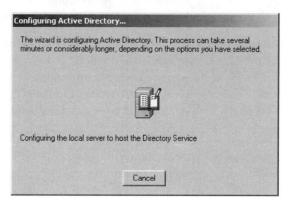

Adding Domain Controllers

In addition to the operations we've already performed, you can use the Active Directory Installation Wizard to create additional domain controllers for any of your domains. There are two main reasons to create additional domain controllers:

Fault Tolerance and Reliability In organizations that rely upon their network directory services infrastructures, the Active Directory is necessary for providing security and resources for all users. For this reason, downtime and data loss are very costly. Through the use of multiple domain controllers, you can ensure that if one of the servers goes down, another one will be available to perform the necessary tasks. Additionally, data loss (perhaps from the failure of a hard disk) will not result in the loss or unavailability of network security information, since you can easily recover the Active Directory information from the remaining domain controller.

Performance The burden of processing login requests and serving as a repository for security permissions and other information can be great, especially in larger businesses. By using multiple domain controllers, you can distribute this load across multiple computers. Additionally, the use of strategically placed domain controllers can greatly increase the response times for common network operations such as authentication and browsing for resources.

It is recommended that you always have at least two domain controllers per domain. For many organizations, this will provide a good balance between the cost of servers and the level of reliability and performance. For larger or more distributed organizations, however, additional domain controllers will greatly improve performance. We'll cover these issues in detail in Chapter 6, "Configuring Sites and Managing Replication."

Demoting a Domain Controller

In addition to being able to promote member servers to domain controllers, the Active Directory Installation Wizard can do the exact opposite—demote domain controllers.

You might choose to demote a domain controller for a couple of reasons. First, if you have determined that the role of a server should change (for example, from a domain controller to a Web server), you can easily demote it to effectuate this change. Another reason to demote a domain controller is if you wish to move the machine between domains. Since there is no way to do this in a single process, you will need to first demote the existing domain controller to remove it from the current domain. Then, you can promote it into a new domain. The end result is that the server is now a domain controller for a different domain.

To demote a domain controller, simply access the Active Directory Installation Wizard. The Wizard will automatically notice that the local server is a domain controller. You will be prompted to decide whether or not you really want to remove this machine from the current domain (see Figure 5.1). Note that if the local server is a Global Catalog server, you will be warned that at least one copy of the Global Catalog must remain available in order to perform logon authentication.

FIGURE 5.1   Demoting a domain controller using the Active Directory Installation Wizard

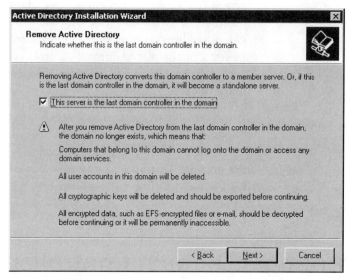

In order for a domain to continue to exist, there must be at least one remaining domain controller in that domain. As noted in the dialog box in Figure 5.1, there are some very important considerations to take into account if you are removing the last domain controller from the domain. Since all of the security accounts and information will be lost, you should ensure that the following steps are taken before removing a domain's last domain controller:

Computers no longer log on to this domain.   Ensure that computers that were once a member of this domain have changed domains. If computers are still attempting to log on to this domain, they will not be able to use any of the security features of the domain. This includes any security permissions or logon accounts. Users will, however, still be able to log on to the computer using cached authenticated information.

No user accounts are needed.   All of the user accounts that resided within the domain (and all of the resources and permissions associated with them) will be lost when the domain is destroyed. Therefore, if you have already set up usernames and passwords, you will need to transfer these accounts to another domain; otherwise, you will lose all of this information.

All encrypted data is unencrypted.   The security information (including User, Computer, and Group objects) stored within the Active Directory domain database is required to access any encrypted information. Once the domain fails to exist, the security information stored within it will no longer be available, and any encrypted information stored in the file system will become permanently inaccessible. So, unencrypt encrypted data before beginning the demotion process to ensure accessibility to this information afterwards. For example, if you have encrypted files or folders that reside on NTFS volumes, you should choose to decrypt them before continuing with the demotion process.

Back up all cryptographic keys.   If you are using cryptographic keys for the purpose of authentication and data security, you should export the key information before demoting the last domain controller in a domain. As this information is stored in the Active Directory database, any resources locked with these keys will become inaccessible once the database is lost as a result of the demotion process.

Removing a domain from your environment is not an operation that should be taken lightly. Before you plan to remove a domain, make a list of all the resources dependent on the domain and the reasons why the domain was originally created. If you are sure your organization no longer requires the domain, then you can safely continue. If not, think again!

By now, you've probably noticed a running theme—a lot of information will go away when you demote the last domain controller in a domain. The Active Directory Installation Wizard makes performing potentially disastrous decisions very easy. Be sure that you understand these effects before demoting the last domain controller for a given domain.

By default, at the end of the demotion process, the server will be joined as a member server to the domain for which it was previously a domain controller.

Managing Multiple Domains

You can easily manage most of the operations that must occur *between* domains by using the Active Directory Domains and Trusts administrative tool.

If, on the other hand, you want to configure settings *within* a domain, you should use the Active Directory Users and Computers tool. In this section, we'll look at ways to perform two common domain management functions with the tools just mentioned: managing *single master operations* and managing trusts.

Managing Single Master Operations

For the most part, the Active Directory functions in what is known as multi–master replication. That is, every domain controller within the environment contains a copy of the Active Directory data store that is both readable and writable. This works well for most types of information. For example, if we want to modify the password of a user, we can easily do this on *any* of the domain controllers within a domain. The change will then be automatically propagated to the other domain controllers.

Microsoft ✓ *Exam* *Objective*

Install, configure, and troubleshoot the components of Active Directory.

- Transfer operations master roles.

There are, however, some functions that are not managed in a multimaster fashion. These operations are known as FSMOs or flexible single master operations. Single master operations must be performed on specially designated machines within the Active Directory forest. There are five main single master functions: two that apply to an entire Active Directory forest and three that apply to each domain.

Within an Active Directory forest, the following two single master operations apply to the entire forest:

Schema Master Earlier, we mentioned the fact that all of the domain controllers within a single Active Directory environment share the same schema. This is necessary to ensure the consistency of information. Developers and systems administrators can, however, modify the Active Directory schema by adding custom information. An example might be adding a field to employee information that specifies a user's favorite color.

When these types of changes are required, they must be performed on the domain controller that serves as the *Schema Master* for the environment. The Schema Master is then responsible for propagating all of the changes to all of the other domain controllers within the forest.

Domain Naming Master   The purpose of the *Domain Naming Master* is to keep track of all the domains within an Active Directory forest. This domain controller is accessed whenever new domains are added to a tree or forest.

Within each domain, at least one domain controller must fulfill each of the following roles:

Relative ID (RID) Master   It is extremely important that every object within the Active Directory be assigned a unique identifier so that they are distinguishable from other objects. For example, if you have two OUs named IT that reside in different domains, there must be some way to easily distinguish the two objects. Furthermore, if you delete one of the IT OUs and then later re-create it, the system must be able to determine that it is not the same object as the other IT OU. The unique identifier for each object is made up of a domain identifier and a relative identifier. RIDs are always unique within an Active Directory domain and are used for managing security information and authenticating users. The *Relative ID (RID) Master* is responsible for creating these values within a domain whenever new Active Directory objects are created.

PDC Emulator Master   Within a domain, the *Primary Domain Controller (PDC) Emulator* is responsible for maintaining backwards compatibility with Windows NT domain controllers. When running in mixed-mode domains, the PDC Emulator is able to process authentication requests and serve as a PDC with Windows NT Backup Domain Controllers (BDCs).

When running in native-mode domains (which do not support the use of pre-Windows 2000 domain controllers), the PDC Emulator Master serves as the default domain controller to process authentication requests if another domain controller is unable to do so. The PDC Emulator Master will also receive preferential treatment whenever domain security changes are made.

Infrastructure Master Whenever a user is added to or removed from a group, all of the other domain controllers should be made aware of this change. The role of the domain controller that acts as an *Infrastructure Master* is to ensure that group membership information stays synchronized within an Active Directory domain.

Now that we are familiar with the different types of single master operations, Exercise 5.3 shows how these roles can be assigned to servers within the Active Directory environment.

EXERCISE 5.3

Assigning Single Master Operations

In this exercise, we will assign single master operations roles to various domain controllers within the environment. In order to complete the steps in this exercise, you will require only one Active Directory domain controller.

1. Open the Active Directory Domains and Trusts administrative tool.

2. Right-click Active Directory Domains and Trusts, and choose Operations Master.

3. In the Change Operations Master dialog box, note that you can change the operations master by clicking the Change button. If you want to move this assignment to another computer, you will first need to connect to that computer and then make the change. Click Cancel to continue without making any changes. Close the Active Directory Domains and Trusts administrative tool.

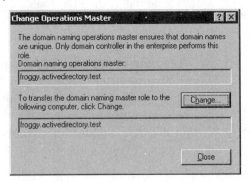

4. Open the Active Directory Users and Computers administrative tool.

5. Right-click the name of a domain and select Operations Master. This will bring up the RID tab of the Operations Master dialog box. Notice that you can change the computer that is assigned to the role. In order to change the role, you will first need to connect to the appropriate domain controller. Notice also that there are similar tabs for the PDC and Infrastructure roles. Click Cancel to continue without making any changes.

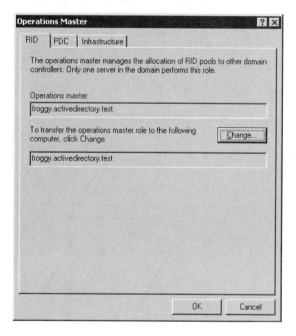

6. Click Cancel to exit the Operations Master dialog box without making any changes.

7. When finished, close the Active Directory Users and Computers tool.

Note that two different tools are used to manage single master operations. The Active Directory Domains and Trusts snap-in is used to configure forest-wide roles, while the Active Directory Users and Computers snap-in is used to administer roles within a domain. Although this might not seem intuitive at first, it can be helpful when remembering which roles apply to domains and which apply to the whole forest.

Managing Trusts

When it comes to creating Active Directory domains, the relationships must be based on trusts. OK, so this may be a weak attempt at humor. But, trust relationships facilitate the sharing of security information and network resources between domains. As we already mentioned, standard transitive two-way trusts are automatically created between the domains in a tree and between each of the trees in a forest. Figure 5.2 shows an example of the default trust relationships in an Active Directory forest.

FIGURE 5.2 Default trusts in an Active Directory forest

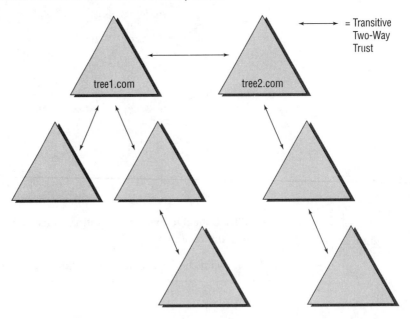

When configuring trusts, there are two main characteristics you'll need to consider. These characteristics are as follows:

Transitive Trusts   By default, Active Directory trusts are *transitive trusts*. The simplest way to understand transitive relationships is through an analogy like the following: If Domain A trusts Domain B and Domain B trusts Domain C, then Domain A implicitly trusts Domain C. Trusts can be configured so that this type of behavior does not occur. That is, transitivity can be disabled.

One-Way vs. Two-Way   Trusts can be configured as one-way or two-way relationships. The default operation is to create *two-way trusts*. This facilitates the management of trust relationships by reducing the number of trusts that must be created. In some cases, however, you might decide that two-way trusts are not required. In one-way relationships, the trusting domain allows resources to be shared with the trusted domain.

When domains are added together to form trees and forests, an automatic transitive two-way trust is created between them. Although the default trust relationships will work well for most organizations, there are some possible reasons for managing trusts manually. First, you may want to remove trusts between domains if you are absolutely sure that you do not want resources to be shared between domains. Second, security concerns may require you to keep resources isolated. In some cases, you may actually want to create direct trusts between two domains that implicitly trust each other. Such a trust is sometimes referred to as a shortcut trust and can improve the speed at which resources are accessed across many different domains.

Perhaps the most important aspect to remember regarding trusts is that their creation only *allows* resources to be shared between domains. The trust does not grant any permissions between domains by itself. Once a trust has been established, however, systems administrators can easily assign the necessary permissions. Exercise 5.4 walks through the steps required to manage trusts.

EXERCISE 5.4

Managing Trust Relationships

In this exercise, we will see how trust relationships between domains can be assigned. In order to complete the steps in this exercise, you must have domain administrator access permissions.

1. Log on to the domain controller as a domain administrator, and open the Active Directory Domains and Trusts tool.

2. Right-click the name of a domain, and select Properties.

3. Select the Trusts tab. You will see a list of the trusts that are currently configured.

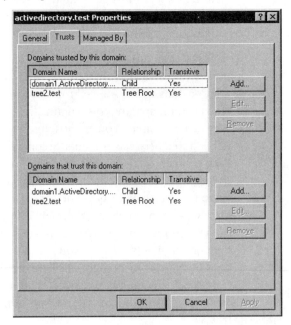

4. To modify the trust properties for an existing trust, highlight that trust and click Edit. Information about the trust's direction, transitivity, and type will be displayed, along with the names of the domains involved in the relationship. Click Cancel to exit without making any changes.

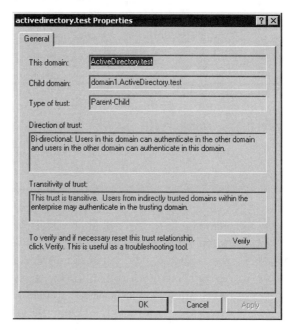

5. To create a new trust relationship, click Add. You will be prompted for the name of the domain with which the trust should be created. Enter the name of the domain along with a password that should be used to administer the trust. Note that if there is an existing trust relationship between the domains, the passwords must match. Click Cancel to continue without making any changes.

6. Exit the Trust properties for the domain by clicking Cancel.

Once the trust relationships have been established, you will be able to share resources between domains. We'll look at exactly how this is done in Chapter 8, "Active Directory Security."

Managing Global Catalog Servers

One of the best features of a distributed directory service like the Active Directory is the fact that different pieces of information can be stored throughout an organization. For example, a domain in Japan might store a list of users who operate within a company's Asian Operations business unit, while one in New York would contain a list of users who operate within its North American Operations business unit. This architecture allows systems administrators to place the most frequently accessed information on domain controllers in different domains, thereby reducing disk space requirements and replication traffic.

Microsoft ✓ *Exam* *Objective*   **Install, configure, and troubleshoot the components of Active Directory.**

- Create global catalog servers.

There is, however, a problem in dealing with information that is segmented into multiple domains. The issue involves querying information stored within the Active Directory. What would happen, for example, if a user wanted a list of all of the printers available in all domains within the Active Directory forest? In this case, the search would normally require information from at least one domain controller in each of the domains within the environment. Some of these domain controllers may be located across slow network links or may have unreliable connections. The end result would include an extremely long wait while retrieving the results of the query.

Fortunately, the Active Directory has a mechanism that speeds up such searches. Any number of domain controllers can be configured to host a copy of the Global Catalog. The Global Catalog contains all of the schema information and a subset of the attributes for all domains within the Active Directory environment. Although there is a default set of information that is normally included with the Global Catalog, systems administrators can choose to add additional information to this data store. Servers that contain a copy of the Global Catalog are known as Global Catalog servers. Now, whenever a user executes a query that requires information from multiple domains, they need only contact their nearest Global Catalog server for this information. Similarly, when users are required to authenticate across domains, they will not have to wait for a response from a domain controller that may be located across the world. The end result is increased overall performance of Active Directory queries.

Exercise 5.5 walks through the steps required to configure a domain controller as a Global Catalog server. Generally, Global Catalog servers are only useful in environments that use multiple Active Directory domains. We will cover the details involved with placing Global Catalog servers in a distributed environment in Chapter 6, "Configuring Sites and Managing Replication."

EXERCISE 5.5

Managing Global Catalog Servers

In this exercise, you will set the option that defines whether a domain controller is a Global Catalog server.

1. Open the Active Directory Sites and Services administrative tool.

2. Find the name of the local domain controller within the list of objects, and expand this object. Right-click NTDS Settings, and select Properties.

3. In the NTDS Settings Properties dialog box, type **Primary GC Server for Domain** in the Description field. Note that there is a check box that determines whether or not this computer contains a copy of the Global Catalog. If the box is checked, then this domain controller contains a subset of information from all other domains within the Active Directory environment. Select or deselect the Global Catalog check box, and then click OK to continue.

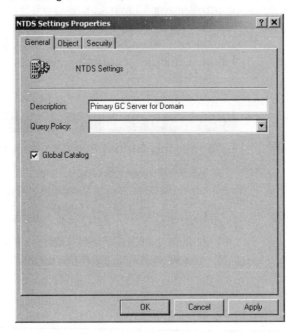

4. When finished, close the Active Directory Sites and Services administrative tool.

Summary

There are several good reasons for creating multiple domains. By using multiple domains, organizations can retain separate security databases.

However, they are also able to share resources between domains. Multiple domains provide two major benefits for the network directory services—security and availability. This is made possible through the use of the structure of the Active Directory and the administrative tools that can be used to access it. Because security information is managed by domain controllers, systems administrators can simplify operations while still ensuring that only authorized users have access to their data.

In this chapter, we looked at ways that multiple domains can interact to form Active Directory trees and forests. We saw that the simple promotion of a server to a domain controller for a new domain can create a multi-domain environment. We also saw that multiple domain trees can be combined together into Active Directory forests. Although each domain in the environment retains a separate security database, through the use of properly configured trusts, you will be able to enjoy the benefits of separate security domains while still being able to share resources.

In Chapter 6, "Configuring Sites and Managing Replication," we'll see how the components of the Active Directory can be used to manage replication operations and traffic.

Key Terms

Before you take the exam, you should be familiar with the following terms and concepts:

Active Directory Installation Wizard

domain controllers

Domain Naming Master

forests

Infrastructure Master

Primary Domain Controller (PDC) Emulator

promotion

Relative ID (RID) Master

Schema Master

single master operations

trees

transitive trusts

two-way trusts

Review Questions

1. A systems administrator creates a trust relationship between Domain A and Domain B. Which of the following statements is true?

   A. All users in Domain A can access all resources in Domain B.

   B. All users in Domain B can access all resources in Domain A.

   C. Both of the above.

   D. None of the above.

2. Which of the following tools is used to configure domainwide single master operations?

   A. Active Directory Users and Computers

   B. Active Directory Domains and Trusts

   C. Active Directory Sites and Services

   D. Computer Management

   E. None of the above

3. What is the minimum number of domain controllers required to have four domains?

   A. 0

   B. 1

   C. 2

   D. 4

   E. 8

4. Which of the following server configurations can be promoted to a domain controller?

   A. Member server

   B. Stand-alone server

   C. Domain controller

   D. Both A and B

5. Which of the following single master operations is used primarily for backwards compatibility with Windows NT servers?

A. Schema Master

B. RID Master

C. Infrastructure Master

D. PDC Emulator Master

E. None of the above

6. Implicit trusts created between domains are known as which of the following?

A. Two-way trusts

B. Transitive trusts

C. Both of the above

D. None of the above

7. Which of the following Flexible Single Master Operations (FSMOs) roles is responsible for uniquely identifying objects within the Active Directory?

A. RID Master

B. Domain Naming Master

C. Schema Master

D. Infrastructure Master

E. None of the above

8. A systems administrator wants to add a field to the information included on a User account. On which of the following servers can the change be made?

A. Any domain controller

B. Any member server

C. The Schema Master

D. None of the above

9. What is a set of domains that share a contiguous namespace called?

    A. A domain forest

    B. A domain hierarchy

    C. A domain tree

    D. A DNS zone

    E. None of the above

10. After the last domain controller in a domain has been demoted, how can the domain be re-created?

    A. By creating a new domain controller with the same name as the demoted one

    B. By creating a new domain with the same name

    C. By adding a new member server to the old domain

    D. None of the above

11. Which of the following does not depend on the DNS namespace?

    A. Organizational units

    B. Domains

    C. Domain trees

    D. Domain forests

    E. All of the above

12. Which of the following types of computers contain a copy of the Global Catalog?

    A. All Windows NT domain controllers

    B. All Active Directory domain controllers

    C. Specified Active Directory domain controllers

    D. Active Directory workstations

    E. All of the above

13. Which of the following pieces of information should you have before beginning the Active Directory Installation Wizard?

   A. Active Directory domain name

   B. Administrator password for the local computer

   C. NetBIOS name for the server

   D. DNS configuration information

   E. All of the above

14. Which type of trust is automatically created between the domains in a domain tree?

   A. Transitive

   B. Two-way

   C. Transitive two-way

   D. None of the above

15. In order to provide for fault tolerance of domain controllers, a domain must have at least how many domain controllers?

   A. 1

   B. 2

   C. 4

   D. None of the above

16. The Active Directory Installation Wizard can be accessed by typing which of the following commands?

   A. DOMAININSTALL

   B. DOMAINUPGRADE

   C. DCCONFIG

   D. DCINSTALL

   E. None of the above

17. If Domain A trusts Domain B and Domain C trusts Domain B, then Domain A trusts Domain C. This is an example of which type of trust?

    A. Bidirectional

    B. Transitive

    C. Cumulative

    D. Recursive

18. In order for resources to be shared to users in different domains, which of the following is/are required?

    A. Trust relationships

    B. Security permissions

    C. Both A and B

    D. None of the above

19. A systems administrator wants to remove a domain controller from a domain. Which of the following is the easiest way to perform the task?

    A. Use the Active Directory Installation Wizard to demote the domain controller.

    B. Use the DCPROMO/REMOVE command.

    C. Reinstall the server over the existing installation, and make the machine a member of a workgroup.

    D. Reinstall the server over the existing installation, and make the machine a member of a domain.

20. Which of the following is *true* regarding the sharing of resources between forests?

    A. All resources are automatically shared between forests.

    B. A trust relationship must exist before resources can be shared between forests.

    C. Resources cannot be shared between forests.

    D. None of the above.

Answers to Review Questions

1. D. A trust relationship only allows the possibility for the sharing of resources between domains; it does not explicitly provide any permissions.

2. A. The Active Directory Users and Computers administrative tool is used to set domain-level single master operations roles.

3. D. Every domain must have at least one domain controller; therefore, at least four domain controllers would be required.

4. D. Both member servers and stand-alone servers can be promoted to domain controllers.

5. D. The PDC Emulator Master is used primarily for compatibility with Windows NT domains.

6. C. Trusts between domains that have not been explicitly defined are known as transitive trusts.

7. A. The RID Master creates unique identifiers for every object in the domain.

8. C. The Schema Master is the only server within the Active Directory on which changes to the schema can be made.

9. C. A domain tree is made up of multiple domains that share the same contiguous namespace.

10. D. Once the last domain controller in an environment has been removed, there is no way to re-create the same domain.

11. A. OUs do not participate in the DNS namespace—they are used primarily for naming objects within a DNS domain.

12. C. Systems administrators can define which domain controllers in the environment will contain a copy of the Global Catalog (GC). Although the GC does contain information about all domains in the environment, it does not have to reside on all domain controllers.

13. E. Before beginning the promotion of a domain controller, you should have all of the information listed.

14. C. A transitive two-way trust is automatically created between the domains in a domain tree.

15. B. A minimum of two domain controllers must be present within a domain to provide for fault tolerance.

16. E. The DCPROMO command can be used to launch the Active Directory Installation Wizard. This Wizard can also be accessed by using the Configure Your Server item in the Administrative Tools folder.

17. B. The above is an example of a transitive trust.

18. C. The creation of trusts only *allows* resources to be shared. Specific permissions must be set on objects within another domain before users can access them.

19. A. The Active Directory Installation Wizard allows administrators to quickly and easily remove a domain controller from a domain without requiring the reinstallation of the operating system.

20. B. Through the creation of trust relationships, resources can be shared between domains that are in two different forests.

Chapter
6

Configuring Sites and Managing Replication

MICROSOFT EXAM OBJECTIVES COVERED IN THIS CHAPTER:

✓ **Install, configure, and troubleshoot the components of Active Directory.**

- Install Active Directory.
- Create sites.
- Create subnets.
- Create site links.
- Create site link bridges.
- Create connection objects.
- Create global catalog servers.
- Move server objects between sites.
- Transfer operations master roles.
- Verify Active Directory installation.
- Implement an organizational unit (OU) structure.

✓ **Manage and troubleshoot Active Directory replication.**

- Manage intersite replication.
- Manage intrasite replication.

Microsoft has designed the Active Directory to be an enterprisewide solution for managing network resources. In previous chapters, we focused on creating Active Directory objects based on an organization's logical design. Domain structure and OU structure, for example, should be designed based primarily on an organization's business needs.

Now, it's time to talk about how the Active Directory can map to an organization's *physical* requirements. Specifically, we must consider network connectivity between sites and the flow of information between *domain controllers* under less than ideal conditions. These constraints will determine how domain controllers can work together to ensure that the objects within the Active Directory remain synchronized, no matter how large and geographically dispersed the network is.

Fortunately, through the use of the Active Directory Sites and Services administrative tool, you can quickly and easily create the various components of an Active Directory replication topology. This includes the creation of objects called Sites, the placement of servers in sites, and the creation of connections between sites. Once you have configured *Active Directory replication* to fit your current network environment, you can sit back and allow the Active Directory to make sure that information remains consistent across domain controllers.

In this chapter, we will cover the features of the Active Directory that allow systems administrators to modify the behavior of replication based on their physical network design. Through the use of sites, systems and network administrators will be able to leverage their network infrastructure to best support Windows 2000 and the Active Directory.

This chapter covers material related to creating sites, subnets, site links, site link bridges, and connection objects, as well as on moving server objects between sites, for the "Install, configure, and troubleshoot the components of Active Directory" objective. See Chapter 3, "Installing and Configuring the Active Directory," for material on the Active Directory and its installation; Chapter 4, "Creating and Managing Organizational Units," for coverage on implementing an OU structure; and Chapter 5, "Installing and Managing Trees and Forests," for material on creating Global Catalog servers and transferring operations master roles.

Overview of Active Directory Physical Components

In an ideal situation, a high-speed network would connect computers and networking devices. In such a situation, you would be able to ensure that, regardless of the location of a network user, they would be able to quickly and easily access resources. When working in the real world, however, there are many other constraints to keep in mind. These include the following:

Network Bandwidth   Network bandwidth generally refers to the amount of data that can pass through a specific connection in a given amount of time. For example, a standard analog modem may have a bandwidth of 33.6Kbps (kilobits per second) while an average physical network connection may have a bandwidth of 100Mbps (megabits per second).

Network Cost   Cost is perhaps the single biggest factor in determining a network design. If cost were not a constraint, organizations would clearly choose to use high-bandwidth connections for all of their sites. Realistically, trade-offs in performance must be made for the sake of affordability. Some of the factors that can affect the cost of networking include the distance between networks and the types of technology available at certain sites throughout the world. Network designers must keep these factors in mind and often must settle for less than ideal connectivity.

When designing and configuring networks, certain devices can be made to automatically make data transport decisions based on an assigned network cost. In many cases, for example, there may be multiple ways to connect to a remote site. When two or more routes are available, the one with the lower cost is automatically used first.

Technological Limitations   In addition to all of the other constraints that have been presented thus far, there's one that we have little control over—the laws of physics! Although newer networking technologies are emerging very quickly, there will always be limits to how quickly and efficiently information can travel throughout the world.

All of these factors will play an important role when you make your decisions related to the implementation of the Active Directory.

When designing networks, systems and network administrators use the following terms to distinguish the types of connectivity between locations and servers:

Local Area Networks (LANs)   A *Local Area Network (LAN)* is usually characterized as a high-bandwidth network. Generally, an organization owns all of its LAN network hardware and software. Ethernet is by far the most common networking standard. Ethernet speeds are generally at least 10Mbps and can scale to multiple gigabits per second. Several LAN technologies, including routing and switching, are available to segment LANs and reduce contention for network resources.

Wide Area Networks (WANs)   The purpose of a *Wide Area Network (WAN)* is similar to that of a LAN—to connect network devices together. Unlike LANs, however, WANs are usually leased from third-party telecommunications carriers. Although extremely high-speed WAN connections are available, they are generally much too costly for organizations to implement through a distributed environment. Therefore, WAN connections are characterized by lower-speed connections and, sometimes, nonpersistent connections.

The Internet   You would have to be locked away in a server room (without network access) for a long time to not have heard about the Internet. The Internet is a worldwide public network infrastructure. It is based on the *Internet Protocol (IP)*. Access to the Internet is available through organizations known as Internet Service Providers (ISPs). As it is a public network, there is no single "owner" of the Internet. Instead, large network and telecommunications providers are constantly upgrading the infrastructure of this network to meet growing demands.

Recently, organizations have started to make use of the Internet for business purposes. For example, it's rare nowadays to see advertisements that don't direct you to one Web site or another. Through the use of technologies such as Virtual Private Networks (VPNs), organizations can use encryption and authentication technology to enable secure communications across the Internet.

Regardless of the issues related to network design and technological constraints, network users will have many different requirements and needs that must be addressed. First and foremost, network resources such as files, printers, and shared directories must be made available for use. Similarly, the resources stored within the Active Directory—and, especially, its security information—are required for many operations that occur within domains.

With these issues in mind, let's look at how you can configure the Active Directory to reach connectivity goals through the use of replication.

The focus of this chapter is on implementing sites. However, in the real world, it won't make much sense to implement sites until you have properly planned for them based on your business needs. You can find more information on planning for sites in Appendix B, "Planning the Active Directory."

Active Directory Replication

The Active Directory was designed as a scalable, distributed database that contains information about an organization's network resources. In previous chapters, we looked at how domains can be created and managed and how domain controllers are used to store Active Directory databases.

Even in the simplest of network environments, there is generally a need to have more than one domain controller. The major reasons for this include fault tolerance (if one domain controller fails, others can still provide network services) and performance (the load can be balanced between multiple domain controllers). Windows 2000 domain controllers have been designed to contain read-write copies of the Active Directory database. However, the domain controllers must also contain knowledge that is created or modified on other domain controllers since a systems administrator may make changes on only one out of many domain controllers. This raises an important point—how is information kept consistent between domain controllers?

The answer is Active Directory replication. Replication is the process by which changes to the Active Directory database are transferred between domain controllers. The end result is that all of the domain controllers within an Active Directory domain contain up-to-date information. Keep in mind that domain controllers may be located very near to each other (e.g., within the same server rack) or may be located across the world from each other. Although the goals of replication are quite simple, the real-world constraints of network connections between servers cause many limitations that must be accommodated.

In this chapter, we will look at the technical details of Active Directory replication and how the concept of sites can be used to map the logical structure of the Active Directory to a physical network topology. Let's begin by looking at the fundamental concepts on which the Active Directory is based.

Active Directory Site Concepts

One of the most important concepts regarding the design and implementation of the Active Directory focuses on the separation of the logical components from the physical components of the directory service. The logical components include the features that map to business requirements. For example, Active Directory domains, organizational units (OUs), users, groups, and computers are all designed to map to political requirements of a business.

Active Directory physical components, on the other hand, are based on technical issues. These issues will crop up, for instance, when we address the question of how the Active Directory can remain synchronized in a distributed network environment. The Active Directory uses the concept of sites to map to an organization's physical network. Stated simply, a *site* is a collection of well-connected computers. We'll define the technical implications of sites later in this chapter.

It is important to understand that there is no specified relationship between Active Directory domains and Active Directory sites. An Active Directory site can contain many domains. Alternatively, a single Active Directory domain can span multiple sites. Figure 6.1 illustrates this very important characteristic of their relationship.

FIGURE 6.1   Potential relationships between domains and sites

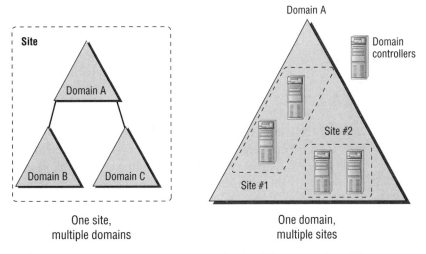

One site,
multiple domains

One domain,
multiple sites

There are two main reasons to use Active Directory sites. These are as follows:

Service Requests   Clients often require the network services of a domain controller. One of the most common reasons for this is that they need the domain controller to perform network authentication. Through the use of Active Directory sites, clients can easily connect to the domain controller that is located closest to them. By doing this, they avoid many of the inefficiencies associated with connecting to distant domain controllers or those that are located on the other side of a slow network connection. Other network services include the Licensing service (for tracking licenses associated with Microsoft and other compatible products) and such applications as messaging (such as Exchange Server 2000). All of these functions are dependent on the availability of network services. In the case of the Active Directory, clients should try to connect to the domain controllers that are located closest to them. This reduces network costs and results in increased performance. In order for this to work, however, systems administrators must define which services are available at specific sites.

Replication   As we mentioned earlier, the purpose of Active Directory replication is to ensure that the information stored on domain controllers remains synchronized. However, in environments with many domains and domain controllers, there are multiple paths of communication between them, which makes the synchronization process more complicated. One method of transferring updates and other changes to the Active Directory would be for all of the servers to communicate directly with each other as soon as a change occurs. This is not ideal, however, since it places high requirements on network bandwidth and is inefficient for many network environments that use slower and more costly WAN links. So how can we efficiently solve this problem?

Through the use of sites, the Active Directory can automatically determine the best methods for performing replication operations. Sites take into account an organization's network infrastructure and are used by the Active Directory to determine the most efficient method for synchronizing information between domain controllers. Systems administrators can make their physical network design map to Active Directory objects. Based on the creation and configuration of these objects, the Active Directory service can then manage replication traffic in an efficient way.

Whenever a change is made to the Active Directory database on a domain controller, the change is given a logical sequence number. The domain controller can then propagate these changes to other domain controllers based on replication settings. In the event that the same setting (such as a user's last name) has been changed on two different domain controllers (before replication can take place), these sequence numbers are used to resolve the conflict.

Implementing Sites and Subnets

Now that we have an idea of the goals of replication, let's do a quick overview of the various Active Directory objects that are related to physical network topology.

The basic objects that are used for managing replication include the following:

Subnets A *subnet* is a partition of a network. Subnets are usually connected through the use of routers and other network devices. All of the computers that are located on a given subnet are generally well connected.

It is extremely important to understand the concepts of TCP/IP and the routing of network information when designing the topology for Active Directory replication. See *MCSE: Windows 2000 Network Infrastructure Administration Study Guide* (Sybex, 2000) for more information on this topic.

Sites An Active Directory site is a logical object that can contain servers and other objects related to Active Directory replication. Specifically, a site is a grouping of related subnets. Sites are created to match the physical network structure of an organization.

Site Links *Site links* are created to define the types of connections that are available between the components of a site. Site links can reflect a relative cost for a network connection and can reflect the bandwidth that is available for communications.

Each of these components works together in determining how information is used to replicate data between domain controllers. Figure 6.2 provides an example of the physical components of the Active Directory.

FIGURE 6.2 Active Directory replication objects

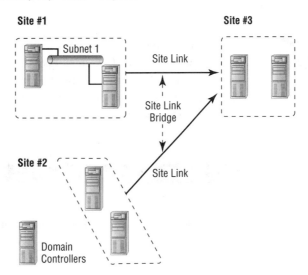

There are many issues related to configuring and managing sites. Rest assured, we'll cover each in turn throughout this chapter. Overall, the use of sites allows you to control the behavior of the Active Directory replication between domain controllers. With this background and goal in mind, let's look at how sites can be implemented to control Active Directory replication.

Creating Sites

The primary method for creating and managing Active Directory replication components is to utilize the Active Directory Sites and Services tool. Using this administrative component, you can graphically create and manage sites in much the same way as you create and manage organizational units (OUs). Exercise 6.1 walks you through the process of creating Active Directory sites.

Microsoft Exam Objective	**Install, configure, and troubleshoot the components of Active Directory.**
	• Create sites.

The exercises in this chapter have been designed to work through the use of a single domain controller and single Active Directory domain. Although you can walk through all of the steps required to create sites and related objects without using multiple domain controllers, real-world replication will generally involve the use of multiple domain controllers in multiple physical sites.

EXERCISE 6.1

Creating Sites

In this exercise, you will create new Active Directory sites. In order to complete this exercise, the local machine must be a domain controller. Also, this exercise assumes that you have not yet changed the default domain site configuration.

EXERCISE 6.1 *(continued)*

1. Open the Active Directory Sites and Services tool from the Administrative Tools program group.

2. Expand the Sites folder.

3. Right-click the Default-First-Site-Name item, and choose Rename. Rename the site to CorporateHQ.

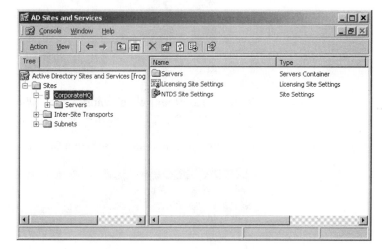

4. To create a new site, right-click the Sites object and select New Site.

5. For the name of the site, type **Austin**. Click the DEFAULTIPSITELINK item, and then click OK to create the site. Note that you cannot include spaces or other special characters in the name of a site.

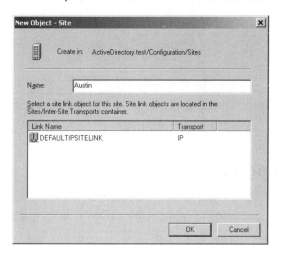

6. You will see a dialog box stating the actions that you should take to finish the configuration of this site. Click OK to continue.

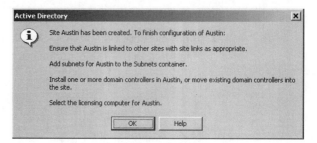

7. Create another new site and name it NewYork. Again, choose the DEFAULTIPSITELINK item.

8. When finished, close the Active Directory Sites and Services tool.

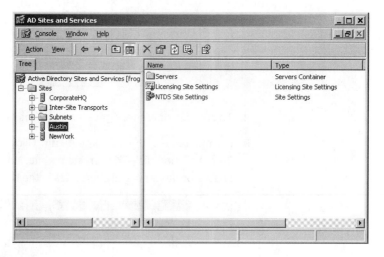

Now that you have created a couple of new sites, it's time to configure them so they can be used to manage replication operations.

Creating Subnets

Once you have created the sites that map to your network topology, it's time to define the subnets that belong with the site.

Install, configure, and troubleshoot the components of Active Directory.

- Create subnets.

Subnets are based on TCP/IP address information and take the form of a TCP/IP address and a subnet mask. For example, the TCP/IP address may be 10.120.0.0, and the subnet mask may be 255.255.0.0. This information specifies that all of the TCP/IP addresses that begin with the first two octets are part of the same TCP/IP subnet. All of the following TCP/IP addresses would be within this subnet:

- 10.120.1.5

- 10.120.100.17

- 10.120.120.120

The Active Directory Sites and Services tool expresses these subnets in a somewhat different notation. It uses the provided subnet address and appends a slash followed by the number of bits in the subnet mask. In the example above, the subnet would be defined as 10.120.0.0/16.

Generally, information regarding the definition of subnets for a specific network environment will be available from a network designer. Exercise 6.2 walks you through the steps that are required to create subnets and assign subnets to sites.

EXERCISE 6.2

Creating Subnets

In this exercise, you will create subnets and then assign them to sites. In order to complete the steps in this exercise, you must have first completed Exercise 6.1.

1. Open the Active Directory Sites and Services tool from the Administrative Tools program group.

2. Expand the Sites folder. Right-click the Subnets folder, and select New Subnet.

3. You will be prompted for information regarding the TCP/IP information for the new subnet. For the address, type **100.1.1.0**, and for the mask, type **255.255.255.0**. You will see that the Name value has been automatically calculated as 100.1.1.0/24. Click the Austin site, and then click OK to create the subnet.

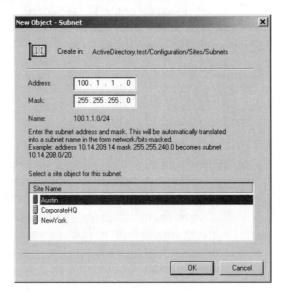

4. Right-click the newly created 100.1.1.0/24 subnet object, and select Properties. On the Subnet tab, type **Austin 100Mbit LAN** for the description. Click OK to continue.

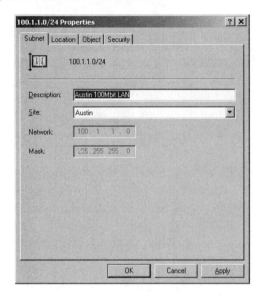

5. Create a new subnet using the following information:

- Address: 160.25.0.0

- Mask: 255.255.0.0

- Site: NewYork

- Description: NewYork 100Mbit LAN

6. Finally, create another subnet using the following information:

- Address: 176.33.0.0

- Mask: 255.255.0.0

- Site: CorporateHQ

EXERCISE 6.2 (continued)

- Description: Corporate 100Mbit switched LAN

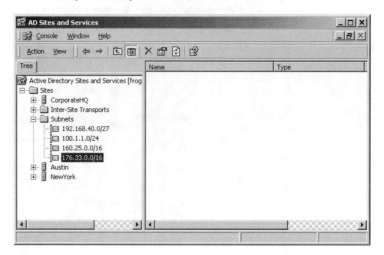

7. When finished, close the Active Directory Sites and Services tool.

So far, we have created the basic components that govern Active Directory sites: sites and subnets. We also linked these two components together by defining which subnets belong in which sites. These two steps—the creation of sites and subnets—form the basis of mapping the physical network infrastructure of an organization to the Active Directory. But wait, there's more! In addition to the basic configuration options we have covered thus far, sites can be further customized. Now, let's look at the various settings that you can make for sites.

Configuring Sites

Once you have configured Active Directory sites and defined which subnets they contain, it's time to make some additional configurations to the site structure. Specifically, you'll need to assign servers to specific sites and configure the site licensing options. Exercise 6.3 walks you through the steps necessary to accomplish this. Placing servers in sites tells the Active Directory replication services how to replicate information for various types of servers.

Later in this chapter, we'll look at the details of working with replication within sites and replication between sites.

The purpose of the *Licensing server* is to track the operating system and Microsoft BackOffice licenses within a domain. This is an important feature because it allows systems administrators to ensure that they have purchased the proper number of licenses for their network environment. Since licensing information must be recorded by servers, you can use the Active Directory Sites and Services tool to specify a License server for a site.

EXERCISE 6.3

Configuring Sites

In this exercise, you will add servers to sites and configure site licensing options. In order to complete the steps in this exercise, you must have first completed Exercises 6.1 and 6.2.

1. Open the Active Directory Sites and Services tool from the Administrative Tools program group.

2. Expand the Sites folder, and click the Austin site.

3. Right-click the Servers container, and select New ➤ Server. Type **AustinDC1** for the name of the server, and then click OK.

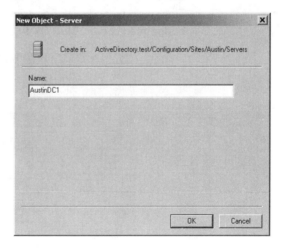

4. Create a new Server object within the CorporateHQ site, and name it CorpDC1. Note that this object will also include the name of the local domain controller.

EXERCISE 6.3 *(continued)*

5. Create two new Server objects within the NewYork site, and name them NewYorkDC1 and NewYorkDC2.

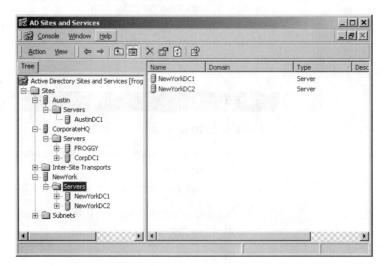

6. Right-click the NewYorkDC1 server object and select Properties. Select the IP item in the Transports Available for Intersite Data Transfer box, and click Add to make this server a preferred IP bridgehead server. Click OK to accept the settings.

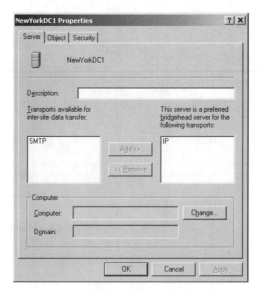

EXERCISE 6.3 *(continued)*

7. To set the Licensing server for the CorporateHQ site, click the Austin container and look in the right windowpane. Right-click the Licensing Site Settings object, and select Properties. To change the computer that will act as the Licensing server for the site, click Change. Select the name of the local domain controller from the list of available computers, and click OK. To save the settings, click OK.

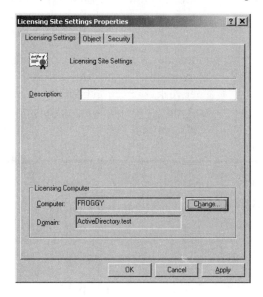

8. When finished, close the Active Directory Sites and Services tool.

With the configuration of the basic settings for sites out of the way, it's time to focus on the real details of the site topology—creating site links and site link bridges.

Configuring Replication

Sites are generally used to define groups of computers that are located within a single geographic location. In most organizations, machines that are located in close physical proximity (for example, within a single building or branch office) are well connected. A typical example is a LAN in a branch office of a company. All of the computers may be connected together using Ethernet, and routing and switching technology may be in place to reduce network congestion.

Often, however, domain controllers are located across various states, countries, and even continents. In such a situation, network connectivity is usually much slower, less reliable, and more costly than that for the equivalent LAN. Therefore, Active Directory replication must accommodate accordingly. When managing replication traffic within Active Directory sites, there are two main areas of synchronization.

Intrasite   *Intrasite replication* refers to the synchronization of Active Directory information between domain controllers that are located in the same site. In accordance with the concept of sites, these machines are usually well connected by a high-speed LAN.

Intersite   *Intersite replication* occurs between domain controllers in different sites. Usually, this means that there is a WAN or other type of costly network connection between the various machines. Intersite replication is optimized for minimizing the amount of network traffic that occurs between sites.

Microsoft ✓ *Exam* *Objective*

Manage and troubleshoot Active Directory replication.

- Manage intersite replication.
- Manage intrasite replication.

In this section, we'll look at ways to configure both intrasite and intersite replication. Additionally, we'll look at features of the Active Directory replication architecture that can be used to accommodate the needs of almost any environment.

Intrasite Replication

Intrasite replication is generally a simple process. One domain controller contacts the others in the same site when changes to its copy of the Active Directory are made. It compares the logical sequence numbers in its own copy of the Active Directory with that of the other domain controllers, then the most current information is chosen, and all domain controllers within the site use this information to make the necessary updates to their database.

Since it is assumed that the domain controllers within an Active Directory site are well connected, less attention to exactly when and how replication takes place is required. Communications between domain controllers occur using the *Remote Procedure Call (RPC) protocol*. This protocol is optimized for transmitting and synchronizing information on fast and reliable network connections. The actual directory synchronizing information is not compressed. Therefore, it provides for fast replication at the expense of network bandwidth.

Intrasite replication works well for domain controllers that are well connected. But what should be done about replication between sites? We'll cover this topic next.

Intersite Replication

Intersite replication is optimized for low-bandwidth situations and network connections that have less reliability.

Intersite replication offers several specific features that are tailored toward these types of connections. To begin with, there are two different protocols that may be used to transfer information between sites:

RPC over Internet Protocol (IP)   When connectivity is fairly reliable, the Internet Protocol is a good choice. IP-based communications require a live connection between two or more domain controllers in different sites and allow for the transfer of Active Directory information. RPC over IP was originally designed for slower WANs in which packet loss and corruption may occur often. As such, it is a good choice for low-quality connections involved in intersite replication.

Simple Mail Transfer Protocol (SMTP)   *Simple Mail Transfer Protocol (SMTP)* is perhaps best known as the protocol that is used to send e-mail messages on the Internet. SMTP was designed to use a store-and-forward mechanism through which a server receives a copy of a message, records it to disk, and then attempts to forward it to another mail server. If the destination server is unavailable, it will hold the message and attempt to resend it at periodic intervals.

This type of communication is extremely useful for situations in which network connections are unreliable or not always available. If, for instance, a branch office in Peru is connected to the corporate office by a dial-up connection that is available only during certain hours, SMTP would be a good choice.

SMTP is an inherently insecure network protocol. You must, therefore, take advantage of Windows 2000's Certificate Services functionality if you use SMTP for Active Directory replication.

Other intersite replication characteristics that are designed to address low-bandwidth situations and less reliable network connections include the compression of Active Directory information. This is helpful because changes between domain controllers in remote sites may include a large amount of information and also because network bandwidth tends to be less available and more costly. Intersite replication topology is determined through the use of site links and site link bridges and can occur based on a schedule defined by systems administrators. All of these features provide for a high degree of flexibility in controlling replication configuration.

You can configure intersite replication by using the Active Directory Sites and Services tool. Select the name of the site for which you want to configure settings. Then, right-click the NTDS Site Settings object in the right window-pane, and select Properties. By clicking the Change Schedule button, you'll be able to configure how often replication between sites will occur (see Figure 6.3).

FIGURE 6.3 Configuring intersite replication schedules

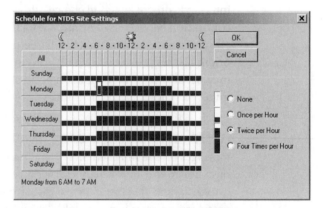

Creating Site Links and Site Link Bridges

The overall topology of intersite replication is based on the use of site links and site link bridges. Site links are logical connections that define a path between two Active Directory sites. Site links can include several descriptive elements that define their network characteristics. *Site link bridges* are used to connect site links together so that the relationship can be transitive.

Microsoft
✓ **Exam**
Objective

Install, configure, and troubleshoot the components of Active Directory.

- Create site links.
- Create site link bridges.

Figure 6.4 provides an example of site links and site link bridges.

FIGURE 6.4 An example of site links and site link bridges

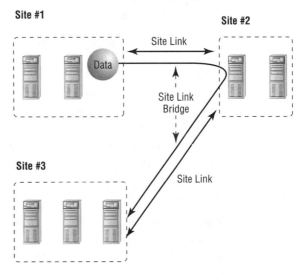

Both of these types of logical connections are used by the Active Directory services to determine how information should be synchronized between domain controllers in remote sites. So how is this information used? The Knowledge Consistency Checker (KCC) forms a replication topology based on the site topology created. This service is responsible for determining the best way to replicate information within and between sites.

When creating site links for your environment, you'll need to consider the following factors:

Transport You can choose to use either RPC over IP or SMTP for transferring information over a site link. The main determination will be based on your network infrastructure and the reliability of connections between sites.

Cost   Multiple site links can be created between sites. Site links can be assigned a cost value based on the type of connection. The systems administrator determines the cost value, and the relative costs of site links are then used to determine the optimal path for replication. The lower the cost, the more likely the link is to be used for replication.

For example, a company may primarily use a T1 link between branch offices, but it may also use a slower dial-up Integrated Services Digital Network (ISDN) connection for redundancy (in case the T1 fails). In this example, a systems administrator may assign a cost of 25 to the T1 line and a cost of 100 to the ISDN line. This will ensure that the more reliable and higher-bandwidth T1 connection is used whenever it's available but that the ISDN line is also available.

Schedule   Once you've determine how and through which connections replication will take place, it's time to determine *when* information should be replicated. Replication requires network resources and occupies bandwidth. Therefore, you will need to balance the need for consistent directory information with the need to conserve bandwidth. For example, if you determine that it's reasonable to have a lag time of six hours between when an update is made at one site and when it is replicated to all others, you might schedule replication to occur once in the morning, once during the lunch hour, and more frequently after normal work hours.

Based on these factors, you should be able to devise a strategy that will allow you to configure site links.

Exercise 6.4 walks you through the process of creating site links and site link bridges.

EXERCISE 6.4

Creating Site Links and Site Link Bridges

In this exercise, you will create links between sites. In order to complete the steps in this exercise, you must have first completed the steps in Exercises 6.1, 6.2, and 6.3.

1. Open the Active Directory Sites and Services tool from the Administrative Tools program group.

2. Expand Sites ➢ Inter-Site Transports ➢ IP object. Right-click the DEFAULTIPSITELINK item in the right pane, and select Rename. Rename the object to CorporateWAN.

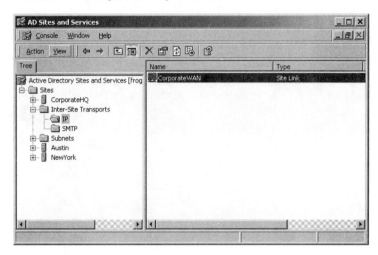

3. Right-click the CorporateWAN link, and select Properties. For the description of the link, type **T1 connecting Corporate and New York offices**. Remove the Austin site from the link. For the Cost value, type **50**, and specify that replication should occur every 60 minutes. To create the site link, click OK.

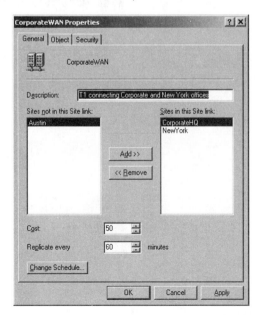

EXERCISE 6.4 *(continued)*

4. Right-click the IP folder, and select New Site Link. For the name of the link, type **CorporateDialup**. Add the Austin and CorporateHQ sites to the site link, and then click OK.

5. Right-click the CorporateDialup link, and select Properties. For the description, type **ISDN Dialup between Corporate and Austin office**. Set the Cost value to 100, and specify that replication should occur every 120 minutes.

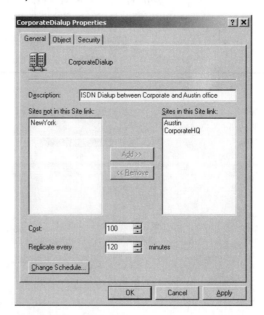

6. To specify that replication should occur only during certain times of the day, click the Change Schedule button. Highlight the area between 8:00 A.M. and 6:00 P.M. for the days Monday through Friday, and click the Replication Not Available option. This will ensure that replication traffic is minimized during normal work hours. Click OK to accept the new schedule, and then OK again to create the site link.

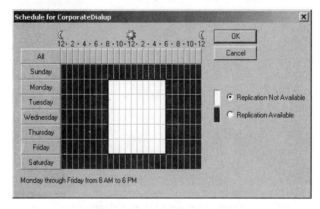

7. Right-click the IP object, and select New Site Link Bridge. For the name of the site link bridge, type **CorporateBridge**. Note that the CorporateDialup and CorporateWAN site links are already added to the site link bridge. Since there must be at least two site links in each bridge, you will not be able to remove these links. Click OK to create the site link bridge.

8. When finished, close the Active Directory Sites and Services tool.

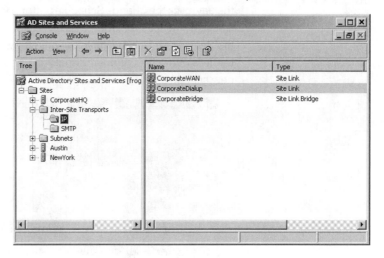

Creating Connection Objects

Generally, it is a good practice to allow the Active Directory's replication mechanisms to automatically schedule and manage replication functions. In some cases, however, you may want to have additional control over replication. Perhaps you want to replicate changes on demand (when you create new accounts). Or, you may want to specify a custom schedule for certain servers.

Microsoft ✓ *Exam* *Objective*

Install, configure, and troubleshoot the components of Active Directory.

▪ Create connection objects.

You can set up these different types of replication schedules through the use of connection objects. Connection objects can be created with the Active

Directory Sites and Services tool by expanding a server object, right-clicking the NTDS (Windows NT Directory Services) Settings object, and selecting New Active Directory Connection (see Figure 6.5). Exercise 6.5 takes you through the steps for creating connection objects in more detail.

FIGURE 6.5 Creating a new connection object

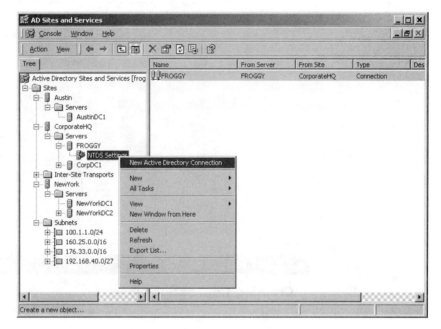

Within the properties of the connection object, which you can see in the right pane, you can specify the type of transport to use for replication (RPC over IP or SMTP), the schedule for replication, and the domain controllers that will participate in the replication (see Figure 6.6). Additionally, you will have the ability to right-click the connection object and select Replicate Now.

FIGURE 6.6 Viewing the properties of a connection object

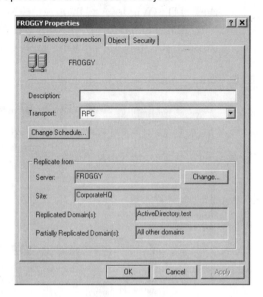

EXERCISE 6.5

Creating Connection Objects

In this exercise, you will create and configure a custom connection object to control Active Directory replication.

1. Open the Active Directory Sites and Services tool.

2. Find the site that contains the local domain controller, and expand this object.

3. Expand the name of the local domain controller. Right-click NTDS Settings, and select New Active Directory Connection. The Find Domain Controllers box will appear, showing a list of the servers that are available.

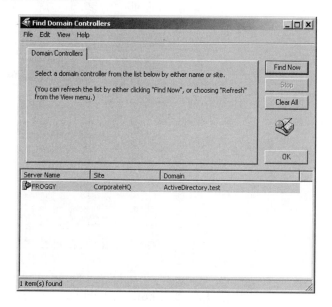

4. Highlight the name of the local server, and click OK.

5. For the name of the connection object, type **Connection**. Click OK.

6. In the right pane of the window, right-click the Connection item, and select Properties.

EXERCISE 6.5 *(continued)*

7. For the description, type **After-hours synchronization**. For the Transport, choose IP.

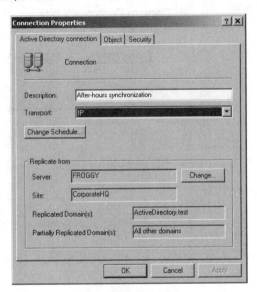

8. To modify the allowed times for replication, click the Change Schedule button. Highlight the area from 8:00 A.M. to 6:00 P.M. for all days, and then click the Once per Hour item. This will reduce the frequency of replication during normal business hours. Click OK to save the schedule.

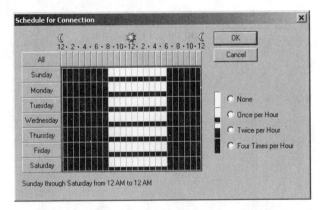

EXERCISE 6.5 *(continued)*

9. When finished, click OK to save the properties of the connection object.

10. Close the Active Directory Sites and Services tool.

Moving Server Objects between Sites

Using the Active Directory Sites and Services tool, you can easily move servers between sites. To do this, simply right-click the name of a domain controller, and select Move. You can then select the site to which you want to move the domain controller object.

Microsoft ✓ *Exam* *Objective*

Install, configure, and troubleshoot the components of Active Directory.

- Move server objects between sites.

Figure 6.7 shows the screen that you'll see when you attempt to move a server. After the server is moved, all replication topology settings will be updated automatically. If you want to choose custom replication settings, you'll need to manually create connection objects (as described earlier). See Exercise 6.6 for a detailed explanation of the steps involved in moving server objects between sites.

FIGURE 6.7   Choosing a new site for a specific server

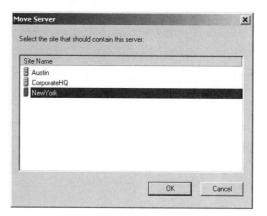

Moving Server Objects between Sites

In this exercise, you will move a server object between sites. In order to complete the steps in this exercise, you must have first completed the previous exercises in this chapter.

1. Open the Active Directory Sites and Services administrative tool.

2. Right-click the server named NewYorkDC1, and select Move.

3. Select the Austin site, and then click OK. This will move this server to the Austin site.

4. To move the server back, right-click NewYorkDC1 (now located in the Austin site) and then click Move. Select New York for the destination site.

5. When finished, close the Active Directory Sites and Services administrative tool.

Creating Bridgehead Servers

By default, all of the servers in one site will communicate with the servers in another site. You can, however, further control replication between sites by using *bridgehead servers*. This method is useful for minimizing replication traffic in larger network environments and allows you to dedicate machines that are better connected to receive replicated data. Figure 6.8 provides an example of how bridgehead servers work.

FIGURE 6.8 A replication scenario using bridgehead servers

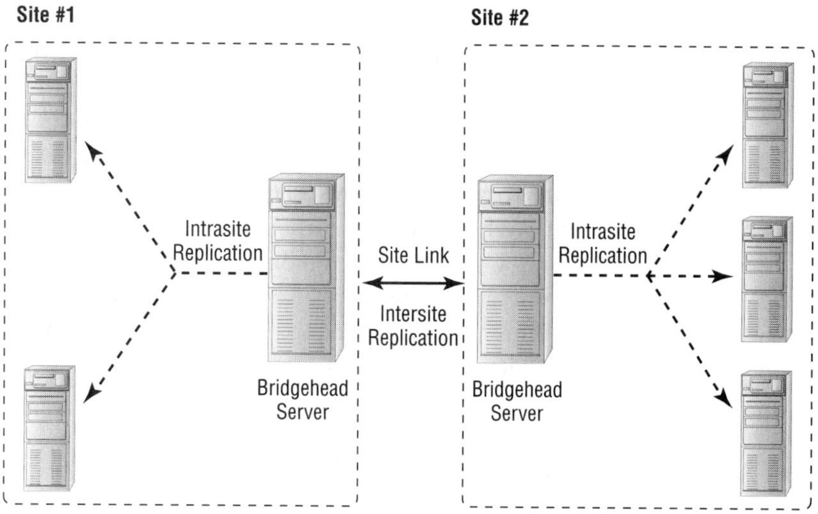

A bridgehead server is used to specify which domain controllers are preferred for transferring replication information between sites. Different bridgehead servers can be selected for RCP over IP and SMTP replication, thus allowing you to balance the load. To create a bridgehead server for a site, simply right-click a domain controller and select Properties (See Figure 6.9).

FIGURE 6.9 Specifying a bridgehead server

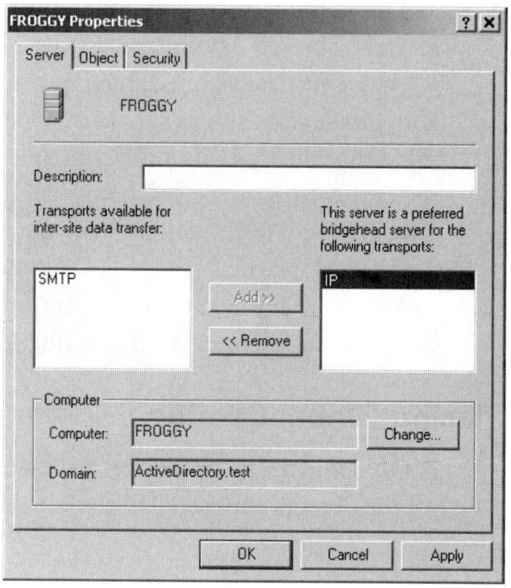

Configuring Server Topology

In environments that require the use of multiple sites, it is very important to consider the placement of servers. In so doing, you can greatly improve performance and end-user experience by reducing the time required to perform common operations such as authentication or searching the Active Directory.

There are two main issues to consider when designing a distributed Active Directory environment. The first is the placement of domain controllers within the network environment. The second is managing the use of Global Catalog (GC) servers. Finding the right balance between servers, server resources, and performance can be considered an art form for network and systems administrators. In this section, we'll look at some of the important considerations that must be taken into account when designing a replication server topology.

Placing Domain Controllers

It is highly recommended that you have at least two domain controllers in each domain of your Active Directory environment. As mentioned earlier in this chapter, the use of additional domain controllers allows for additional performance (since the servers can balance the burden of serving client requests) and provides for fault tolerance (in case one domain controller fails, the other still contains a valid and usable copy of the Active Directory database). Furthermore, the proper placement of domain controllers can increase overall network performance since clients can connect to the server closest to them instead of performing authentication and security operations across a slow WAN link.

As we just mentioned, having too few domain controllers can be a problem. However, there is such a thing as *too many* domain controllers. Keep in mind that the more domain controllers you choose to implement, the greater the replication traffic will be. As each domain controller must propagate any changes to all of the others, you can probably see how this can result in a lot of network traffic.

For more information on installing additional domain controllers for a domain, see Chapter 5, "Installing and Managing Trees and Forests."

Placing Global Catalog Servers

A *Global Catalog (GC) server* is a domain controller that contains a copy of all the objects contained in the forestwide domain controllers that compose the Active Directory database. Making a domain controller a GC server is a very simple operation, and you can change this setting quite easily. That brings us to the harder part—determining which domain controllers should also be GC servers.

The placement of domain controllers and GC servers is an important issue. Generally, you will want to make GC servers available in every site that has a slow link. However, there is a trade-off that can make having too many GC servers a bad thing. The main issue is associated with replication traffic—each GC server within your environment must be kept synchronized with the other servers. In a very dynamic environment, the additional network traffic caused by the use of GC servers can be considerable. Therefore, you will want to find a good balance between replication burdens and GC query performance in your own environment.

To create a GC server, simply expand the Server object in the Active Directory Sites and Services tool, right-click NTDS settings, and select Properties. To configure a server as a GC server, simply place a check mark in the Global Catalog box (see Figure 6.10).

FIGURE 6.10 Enabling the Global Catalog on an Active Directory domain controller

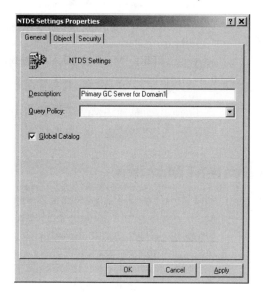

Monitoring and Troubleshooting Active Directory Replication

For the most part, domain controllers handle the processes involved with replication automatically. However, systems administrators will still need to monitor the performance of Active Directory replication. Failed network links and incorrect configurations can sometimes prevent the synchronization of information between domain controllers.

Microsoft
✓ *Exam*
Objective

Manage and troubleshoot Active Directory replication.

- Manage intersite replication.

- Manage intrasite replication.

This section covers information related to troubleshooting replication. See "Configuring Replication," a section that appears earlier in this chapter, for coverage of the "Manage intersite replication" and "Manage intrasite replication" subobjectives.

There are several ways in which you can monitor the behavior of Active Directory replication and troubleshoot the process if problems occur.

Using System Monitor

The Windows 2000 System Monitor administrative tool was designed to allow you to monitor many performance statistics associated with the use of the Active Directory. Included within the various performance statistics that may be monitored are counters related to Active Directory replication. We'll cover the details of working with the System Monitor tools of Windows 2000 in Chapter 9, "Active Directory Optimization and Reliability."

Troubleshooting Replication

A common symptom of replication problems is that information is not updated on some or all domain controllers. For example, a systems administrator creates a User account on one domain controller, but the changes are not propagated to other domain controllers. In most environments, this is a potentially serious problem as it affects network security and can prevent authorized users from accessing the resources they require.

There are several steps that you can take to troubleshoot Active Directory replication:

Verify network connectivity.   The fundamental requirement for replication to work properly in distributed environments is network connectivity. Although the ideal situation would be that all domain controllers are connected by high-speed LAN links, this is rarely the case for larger organizations. In the real world, dial-up connections and slow connections are common. If you have verified that your replication topology is setup properly, you should confirm that your servers are able to communicate. Problems such as a failed dial-up connection attempt can prevent important Active Directory information from being replicated.

Verify router and firewall configurations.   Firewalls are used to restrict the types of traffic that can be transferred between networks. Their main use is to increase security by preventing unauthorized users from transferring information. In some cases, company firewalls may block the types of network access that must be available in order for Active Directory replication to occur. For example, if a specific router or firewall prevents data from being transferred using SMTP, replication that uses this protocol will fail.

Examine the event logs.   Whenever an error in the replication configuration occurs, events are written to the Directory Service event log. By using the Event Viewer administrative tool, you can quickly and easily view the details associated with any problems in replication. For example, if one domain controller is not able to communicate with another to transfer changes, a log entry will be created. Figure 6.11 shows an example of the types of events you will see in the Directory Service log, and Figure 6.12 shows an example of a configuration error.

FIGURE 6.11 Viewing entries in the Directory Service event log

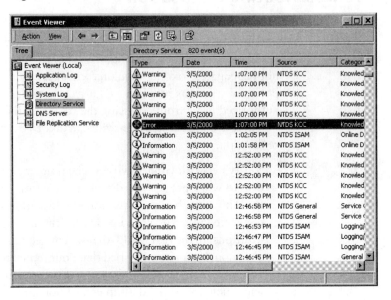

FIGURE 6.12 Examining the details of an event log entry

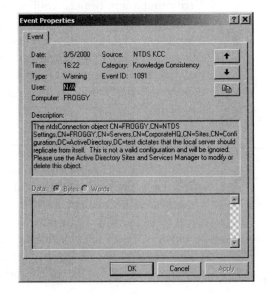

Verify site links.   Before domain controllers in different sites can communicate with each other, the sites must be connected by site links. If replication between sites is not occurring properly, verify that the proper site links are in place.

Verify that information is synchronized.   It's often easy to forget to perform manual checks regarding the replication of Active Directory information. One of the reasons for this is that Active Directory domain controllers have their own read/write copies of the Active Directory database. Therefore, you will not encounter failures in creating new objects if connectivity does not exist.

It is important to periodically verify that objects have been synchronized between domain controllers. The process might be as simple as logging on to a different domain controller and looking at the objects within a specific OU. This manual check, although it might be tedious, can prevent inconsistencies in the information stored on domain controllers, which, over time, could become an administration and security nightmare.

Verify authentication scenarios.   A common replication configuration issue occurs when clients are forced to authenticate across slow network connections. The primary symptom of the problem is that users will complain about the amount of time that it takes to log on to the Active Directory (especially during times of high volume of authentications, such as at the beginning of the workday).

Usually, this problem can be alleviated through the use of additional domain controllers or a reconfiguration of the site topology. A good way to test this is to consider the possible scenarios for the various clients that you support. Often, walking through a configuration, such as "A client in Domain1 is trying to authenticate using a domain controller in Domain2, which is located across a slow WAN connection," can be helpful in pinpointing potential problem areas.

Verify the replication topology.   The Active Directory Sites and Services tool allows you to verify that a replication topology is logically consistent. You can quickly and easily perform this task by right-clicking the NTDS Settings within a Server object and choosing All Tasks ➤ Check Replication Topology (see Figure 6.13). If any errors are present, a dialog box will alert you to the problem.

FIGURE 6.13 Verifying the Active Directory topology using the Active Directory Sites and Services tool

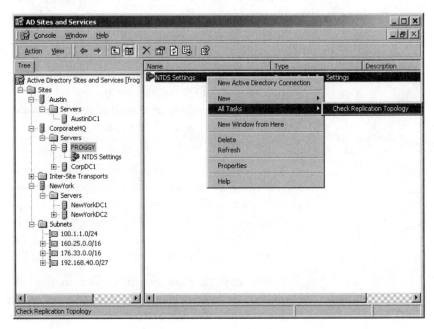

By using the above troubleshooting techniques, you will be able to diagnose and verify any problems with the configuration of your replication topology. This will ensure consistency of data between the various domain controllers in your environment.

Summary

In this chapter, we covered the very important topic of managing Active Directory replication. Although this is a behind-the-scenes type of task, the optimal configuration of replication in distributed network environments will result in better use of bandwidth and faster response of network resources. For these reasons, you should be sure that you thoroughly understand the concepts related to managing replication for the Active Directory.

Key Terms

Before you take the exam, be sure you're familiar with the following terms:

Active Directory replication

bridgehead servers

domain controllers

Global Catalog (GC) server

Internet Protocol (IP)

Intersite replication

Intrasite replication

Licensing server

Local Area Network (LAN)

Remote Procedure Call (RPC) protocol

Simple Mail Transfer Protocol (SMTP)

site

Site links

Site link bridges

subnet

Wide Area Network (WAN)

Review Questions

1. A systems administrator wants to specify that a single server within a site is to receive all replication traffic from another site. They should configure this server as a:

   A. Site

   B. Site link

   C. Site link bridge

   D. Bridgehead server

   E. None of the above

2. Which of the following is/are not required for setting up a replication scenario involving three domains and three sites?

   A. Sites

   B. Site links

   C. Connection objects

   D. Subnets

   E. None of the above

3. Which of the following services of the Active Directory is responsible for maintaining the replication topology?

   A. File Replication Service

   B. Knowledge Consistency Checker

   C. Windows Internet Name Service

   D. Domain Name System

   E. None of the above

4. Which of the following tools is used for configuring Active Directory replication topology?

   A. Active Directory Users and Computers

   B. Active Directory Domains and Trusts

   C. Active Directory Sites and Services

   D. Computer Management

   E. All of the above

5. A systems administrator wants to configure site links to be transitive. Which of the following Active Directory objects must they create?

   A. Additional sites

   B. Additional site links

   C. Bridgehead servers

   D. Site link bridges

   E. None of the above

6. Which of the following is generally *not* true regarding the domain controllers within a site?

   A. They are generally connected by a high-speed network.

   B. They must reside on the same subnets.

   C. They are generally connected by reliable connections.

   D. They may be domain controllers for different domains.

   E. None of the above.

7. Which of the following protocols is used for intrasite replication?

    A. DHCP

    B. RPC

    C. IP

    D. SMTP

    E. None of the above

8. Which of the following replication mechanisms uses a store-and-forward method for transferring replication data?

    A. IP

    B. SMTP

    C. RPC

    D. DHCP

    E. None of the above

9. An Active Directory environment consists of four sites. What is the minimum number of domains that must be present to support this configuration?

    A. 0

    B. 1

    C. 4

    D. None of the above

10. An organization's Active Directory site structure should be primarily based on its:

    A. Domain structure

    B. Political concerns

    C. Geographic distribution

    D. Physical network infrastructure

    E. None of the above

11. A systems administrator notices that one domain controller is not receiving updated Active Directory information. A possible cause for this problem is that:

   A. Network connectivity is unavailable

   B. Replication is not properly configured

   C. Sites are not properly configured

   D. Site connectors are not properly configured

   E. All of the above

12. A systems administrator suspects that there is an error in the replication configuration. How can they look for specific error messages related to replication?

   A. By using the Active Directory Sites and Services administrative tool

   B. By using the Computer Management tool

   C. By going to Event Viewer ➤ System log

   D. By going to Event Viewer ➤ Directory Service log

   E. All of the above

13. Which of the following administrative tools is most useful for measuring statistics related to replication?

   A. Active Directory Users and Computers

   B. Active Directory Domains and Trusts

   C. Active Directory Sites and Services

   D. Event Viewer

   E. Performance

14. The Active Directory distributed database is best described as which of the following types of databases?

   A. Multimaster

   B. Single-master

   C. Transitive

   D. No-master

   E. None of the above

15. Which of the following Active Directory objects is used to define the network boundaries for a site?

A. Site links

B. Site link bridges

C. Bridgehead servers

D. Subnets

E. None of the above

16. Which of the following are not characteristics of a site link?

A. Transport protocol

B. Cost

C. Route

D. Schedule

17. Regardless of the replication topology, a domain controller at a specific site is not receiving Active Directory updates. Which of the following is a possible reason for this?

A. Network connectivity has not been established for this server.

B. A firewall is preventing replication information from being transmitted.

C. There are not enough domain controllers in the environment.

D. There are too many domain controllers in the environment.

E. Both A and B.

18. Which of the following services can be configured using the Active Directory Sites and Services tool?

A. Licensing server

B. E-mail domains

C. Software installation services

D. Remote configuration services

E. All of the above

19. Which of the following network characteristics does *not* generally apply to LANs?

A. High-speed links

B. Routing

C. Switching

D. Non-persistent connections

E. All of the above

20. An Active Directory environment consists of four sites. What is the maximum number of subnets that can be created for this environment?

A. 0

B. 1

C. 4

D. 16

E. None of the above

Answers to Review Questions

1. D. Bridgehead servers receive replication information for a site and transmit this information to other domain controllers within the site.

2. C. Connection objects are only created to override the default behavior of Active Directory replication topology.

3. B. The Knowledge Consistency Checker (KCC) is responsible for establishing the replication topology and ensuring that all domain controllers are kept up-to-date.

4. C. The Active Directory Sites and Services tool is used for creating and managing the Active Directory components related to replication.

5. D. Site link bridges are designed to allow site links to be transitive. That is, they allow site links to use other site links to transfer replication information between sites.

6. B. Domain controllers may be located on various different subnets and still be part of the same site.

7. B. Remote Procedure Calls (RPCs) are used to transfer information between domain controllers within an Active Directory site.

8. B. The Simple Mail Transfer Protocol (SMTP) was designed for environments in which persistent connections may not always be available. SMTP uses the store-and-forward method to ensure that information is not lost if a connection cannot be made.

9. B. Since there is no relationship between domain structure and site structure, only one domain is required. Generally, if there is only one domain, there will be many domain controllers with at least one in each site.

10. D. Although all of the choices may play a factor in the ultimate design, the primary consideration for site structure is based on physical network topology.

11. E. All of the scenarios listed are potential causes for a failure in replication.

12. D. The Directory Service event log contains error messages and information related to replication. These details can be useful when troubleshooting replication problems.

13. E. Through the use of the Performance administrative tool, systems administrators can measure and record performance values related to Active Directory replication.

14. A. Since all domain controllers contain read-write copies of the Active Directory database, the replication is considered to be multimaster.

15. E. Subnets define the specific network segments that are well connected.

16. C. A route is not a characteristic of a site link.

17. E. A lack of network connectivity or the presence of a firewall can prevent replication from occurring properly. The number of domain controllers in an environment will not prevent the replication of information.

18. A. Systems administrators can use the Active Directory Sites and Services tool to define a Licensing server for a site.

19. D. LAN connections are generally always available. They also share all of the other characteristics mentioned in the choices.

20. E. Each site within the environment can consist of multiple subnets, based on the details of the network environment.

Chapter 7

Administering the Active Directory

MICROSOFT EXAM OBJECTIVES COVERED IN THIS CHAPTER:

✓ **Manage Active Directory objects.**

- Move Active Directory objects.
- Publish resources in Active Directory.
- Locate objects in Active Directory.
- Create and manage accounts manually or by scripting.
- Control access to Active Directory objects.
- Delegate administrative control of objects in Active Directory.

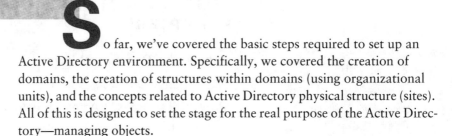

So far, we've covered the basic steps required to set up an Active Directory environment. Specifically, we covered the creation of domains, the creation of structures within domains (using organizational units), and the concepts related to Active Directory physical structure (sites). All of this is designed to set the stage for the real purpose of the Active Directory—managing objects.

In this chapter, we'll cover the actual steps required to create common Active Directory objects. Then, we'll see how these objects can be configured and managed. Finally, we'll look at ways to publish resources and methods for automating the creation of User accounts.

Although this chapter covers material related to Active Directory administration for the "Manage Active Directory objects" objective, controlling access to Active Directory objects and delegating administrative control of objects in Active Directory, topics addressed by the last two subobjectives, are covered in Chapter 8, "Active Directory Security."

Creating and Managing Active Directory Objects

The main tool used to manage the objects within the Active Directory is the *Active Directory Users and Computers tool*. Using this Microsoft Management Console (MMC) snap-in, you will be able to create, manage, and control the use of Active Directory objects.

In Chapter 4, "Creating and Managing Organizational Units," we looked at how a hierarchical structure could be created within a domain. Be sure to review that information if you're unfamiliar with OUs. The good news is that if you are familiar with the task of creating OUs, creating other Active Directory objects will be quite simple. Let's look at the details.

Overview of Active Directory Objects

By default, after you install and configure a domain controller, you will see the following sections of organization within the Active Directory Users and Computers tool:

Built-In   The Built-In container includes all of the standard groups that are installed by default when you promote a domain controller. These groups are used for administering the servers in your environment. Examples include the Administrators group, Backup Operators, and Print Operators.

Computers   By default, the Computers container contains a list of the workstations in your domain. From here, you can manage all of the computers in your domain.

Domain Controllers   This container includes a list of all of the domain controllers for the domain.

Foreign Security Principals   *Security principals* are Active Directory objects to which permissions can be applied. They are used for managing permissions within the Active Directory. We'll cover the details of working with security principals in Chapter 8, "Active Directory Security."

Foreign security principals are any objects to which security can be assigned and that are not part of the current domain.

Users   The Users container includes all of the security accounts that are part of the domain. When you first install the domain controller, there will be several groups in this container. For example, the Domain Admins group and the Administrator account are created in this container.

There are several different types of Active Directory objects that can be created and managed. The following are specific object types:

Computer   *Computer objects* are used for managing workstations in the environment.

Contact   Contacts are not security principals like Users, but they are used for specifying information about individuals within the organization. *Contact objects* are usually used in OUs to specify the main administrative contact.

Group   Groups are security principals. That is, they are created for assigning and managing permissions. Groups contain User accounts.

Organizational Unit   An Organizational Unit (OU) is created to build a hierarchy within the Active Directory domain. They are the smallest units that can be used to create administrative groupings and can be used for assigning Group Policies. Generally, the OU structure within a domain will reflect a company's business organization.

Printer   *Printer objects* map to printers.

Shared Folder   *Shared Folder objects* map to server shares. They are used for organizing the various file resources that may be available on file/print servers.

User   A *User object* is the fundamental security principal on which the Active Directory is based. User accounts contain information about individuals, as well as password and other permission information.

We'll cover the security aspects related to the use of Active Directory objects in Chapter 8, "Active Directory Security." For now, however, know that these objects are used to represent various items in your network environment. Through the use of these objects, you will be able to manage the content of your Active Directory.

Exercise 7.1 walks through the steps required to create various different objects within an Active Directory domain.

EXERCISE 7.1

Creating Active Directory Objects

In this exercise, we will create some basic Active Directory objects. In order to complete this exercise, you must have first installed and configured at least one Active Directory domain.

1. Open the Active Directory Users and Computers tool.

2. Expand the current domain to list the objects currently contained within it. You should see folders similar to those shown.

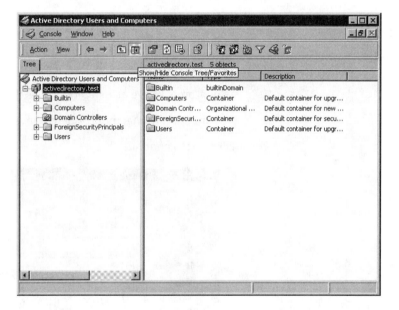

3. Create a new top-level OU by right-clicking the name of the domain and selecting New ➤ Organizational Unit. When prompted for the name of the OU, type **Corporate** and click OK.

4. Repeat step 3 to create the following top-level OUs:

   - Engineering

   - HR

   - IT

   - Marketing

   - Sales

5. Right-click the Corporate OU, and select New ➢ User. Fill in the following information:

   - First Name: Monica

   - Initials: D

   - Last Name: President

   - Full Name: (leave as default)

   - User Logon Name: mdpresident (leave default domain)

   Click Next to continue.

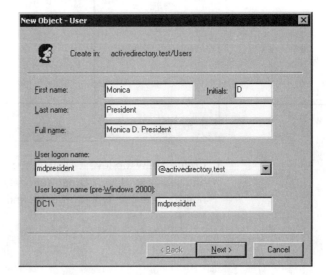

6. Enter in a password for this user, and then confirm it. Note that you can also make changes to password settings here. Click Next. You will see a summary of the user information. Click OK to create the new user.

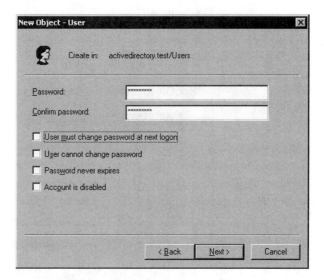

7. Create another user in the IT container with the following information:

   - First Name: John

   - Initials: Q

   - Last Name: Admin

   - Full Name: (leave as default)

   - User Logon Name: jqadmin (leave default domain)

   Click Next to continue. Assign a password. Click Next, and then click Finish to create the user.

EXERCISE 7.1 *(continued)*

8. Right-click the IT OU, and select New ➤ Contact. Use the following information to fill in the properties of the Contact object:

   - First Name: Jane

   - Initials: R

   - Last Name: Admin

   - Display Name: jradmin

   Click OK to create the new Contact object.

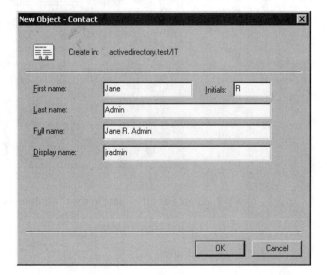

9. Right-click the IT OU, and select New ➢ Shared Folder. Enter **Soft-ware** for the name and **\\server1\applications** for the Network Path. Note that although this resource does not exist, the object can still be created. Click OK to create the Shared Folder object.

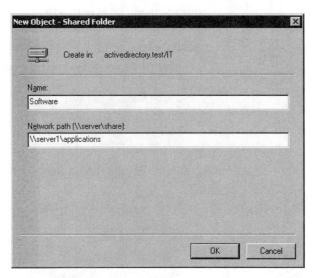

10. Right-click the HR OU, and select New ➢ Group. Type **All Users** for the Group Name (leave the Group Name (Pre-Windows 2000) field with the same value). For the Group Scope, select Global, and for the Group Type, select Security. To create the group, click OK.

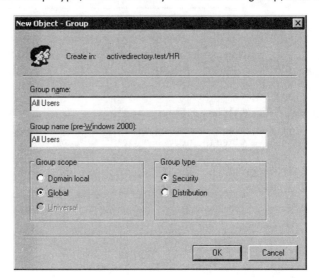

11. Right-click the Sales OU and select New ➤ Computer. Type **Workstation1** for the name of the computer. Notice that the pre-Windows 2000 name will automatically be populated and that, by default, the members of the Domain Admins group will be the only ones that will be able to add this computer to the domain. Place a check mark in the Allow Pre-Windows 2000 Computers to Use This Account box, and then click OK to create the Computer object.

12. Close the Active Directory Users and Computers tool.

Now that you are familiar with the process of creating and managing objects, let's move on to look at some additional properties that can be set for each of these items.

Managing Object Properties

Once the necessary Active Directory objects have been created, you'll probably need to make changes to their default properties. In addition to the settings you made when creating Active Directory objects, there are several more properties that can be configured. Exercise 7.2 walks you through setting various properties for Active Directory objects.

Although it may seem somewhat tedious, it's always a good idea to enter in as much information as you know about Active Directory objects when you create them. Although the name Printer1 may be meaningful to you, users will appreciate the additional information when searching for objects.

EXERCISE 7.2

Managing Object Properties

In this exercise, we will modify the properties for Active Directory objects. In order to complete the steps in this exercise, you must have first completed Exercise 7.1.

1. Open the Active Directory Users and Computers tool.

2. Expand the name of the domain, and select the IT container. Right-click the John Q. Admin User account, and select Properties.

3. Here, you will see the various Properties tabs for the User account. The basic tabs include the following:

   - General: General account information about this user

   - Address: The physical location information about this user

   - Account: User logon name and other account restrictions such as workstation restrictions and logon hours

   - Profile: Information about the user's roaming profile settings

   - Telephones: Telephone contact information for the user

   - Organization: The user's title, department, and company information

   - Member Of: Group membership information for the user

   - Dial-In: Remote Access Service (RAS) permissions for the user

   - Environment: Logon and other network settings for the user

EXERCISE 7.2 *(continued)*

- Sessions: Session limits, including maximum session time and idle session settings

- Remote Control: Sets remote control options for this user's session

- Terminal Services Profile: Sets information about the user's profile for use with Windows 2000 Terminal Services

Click OK to continue.

4. Select the HR OU. Right-click the All Users Group, and click Properties. In this dialog box, you will be able to modify the membership of the group. Click the Members tab, and then click Add. Add the Monica D. President and John Q. Admin User accounts to the Group. Click OK to save the settings and then OK to accept the group modifications.

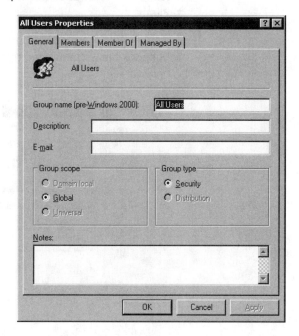

5. Select the Sales OU. Right-click the Workstation1 Computer object. Notice that you can choose to disable the account or reset it (to allow another computer to join the domain under that same name). From the right-click menu, choose Properties. You'll see the properties for the Computer object. The various tabs in this dialog box include the following:

- General: Information about the name of the computer, the role of the computer, and its description. Note that you can enable an option to allow the Local System Account of this machine to request services from other servers. This is useful if the machine is a trusted and secure computer.

- Operating System: The name, version, and service pack information for the operating system running on the computer

- Member Of: The Active Directory groups that this Computer object is a member of

- Location: A description of where the computer is physically located

- Managed By: Information about the User or Contact object that is responsible for managing this computer

After you have examined the available options, click OK to continue.

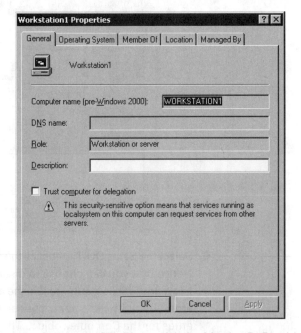

6. Select the Corporate OU. Right-click the Monica D. President User account, and choose Reset Password. You will be prompted to enter a new password and then asked to confirm it. Note that you can also force the user to change this password upon the next logon.

7. Close the Active Directory Users and Computers tool.

By now, you have probably noticed that there are a lot of common options for Active Directory objects. For example, Groups and Computers both have a Managed By tab. As was mentioned earlier, it's always a good idea to enter in as much information as possible about an object. This will help systems administrators and users alike. On the down side, however, it will tell them who is to blame when a printer no longer works!

More Active Directory Management Features

The Active Directory Users and Computers tool has a couple of other features that come in quite handy when managing many objects. The first is accessed by clicking the View menu in the MMC console and choosing Filter Options. You'll see a dialog box similar to the one shown in Figure 7.1. Here, you can choose to filter objects by their specific types within the display. For example, if you are an administrator who works primarily with User accounts and groups, you can select those specific items by placing a check mark in the list. Additionally, you can create more complex filters by choosing Create Custom Filter. That will provide you with an interface that looks similar to the Find command.

FIGURE 7.1   Filtering objects using the Active Directory Users and Computers tool

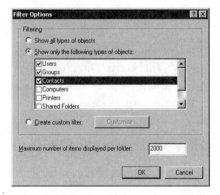

Another option in the Active Directory Users and Computers tool is to view Advanced options. You can enable the Advanced options by clicking Advanced Options in the View menu. This will add two top-level folders to the list under the name of the domain. The System folder (shown in Figure 7.2) provides a list of some additional features that can be configured to work with the Active Directory. For example, you can configure settings for the Distributed File System (DFS), IP Security policies, the File Replication Service, and more. In addition to the System folder, you'll also see the LostAndFound folder. This folder contains any files that may not have been replicated properly between domain controllers. You should check this folder periodically for any files so that you can decide whether you need to move them or copy them to other locations.

FIGURE 7.2 Advanced options in the Active Directory Users and Computers tool

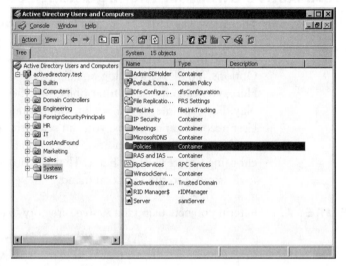

As you can see, managing Active Directory objects is generally a simple task. The Active Directory Users and Computers tool allows you to configure several objects. Let's move on to look at one more common administration function—moving objects.

Moving Active Directory Objects

One of the extremely useful features of the Active Directory Users and Computers tool is its ability to easily move users and resources.

Microsoft ✔ *Exam Objective*

Manage Active Directory objects.

- Move Active Directory objects.

Exercise 7.3 walks through the process of moving Active Directory objects.

EXERCISE 7.3

Moving Active Directory Objects

In this exercise, we will make several changes to the organization of Active Directory objects. In order to complete this exercise, you must have first completed Exercise 7.1.

1. Open the Active Directory Users and Computers tool, and expand the name of the domain.

2. Select the Sales OU, right-click Workstation 1, and select Move. A dialog box will appear. Select the IT OU, and click OK to move the Computer object to that container.

3. Click the IT OU, and verify that Workstation1 was moved.

4. Close the Active Directory Users and Computers tool.

In addition to moving objects within the Active Directory, you can also easily rename them. You can do this by right-clicking an object and selecting Rename. Note that this option does not apply to all objects. For example, in order to prevent security breaches, Computer objects cannot be renamed. Additionally, you can remove objects from the Active Directory by right-clicking them and choosing Delete.

Deleting an Active Directory object is an irreversible action. When an object is destroyed, any security permissions or other settings made for that object are removed as well. Since each object within the Active Directory contains its own security identifier (SID), simply re-creating an object with the same name will not place any permissions on it. Before you delete an Active Directory object, be sure that you will never need it again.

Publishing Active Directory Objects

One of the main goals of the Active Directory is to make resources easy to find. Two of the most commonly used resources in a networked environment are server file shares and printers. These are so common, in fact, that most organizations will have dedicated File/Print Servers. When it comes to managing these types of resources, the Active Directory makes it easy to determine which files and printers are available to users.

Microsoft ✓ *Exam* *Objective*

Manage Active Directory objects.

- Publish resources in Active Directory.
- Locate objects in Active Directory.

With that said, let's look at how Active Directory manages the publishing of shared folders and printers.

Making Active Directory Objects Available to Users

An important aspect of managing Active Directory objects is that a systems administrator can control which objects users can see. The act of making an Active Directory object available is known as *publishing*. The two main publishable objects are Printers and Shared Folders.

The general process for creating server shares and shared printers has remained unchanged from previous versions of Windows. That is, the main method is to create the various objects (a printer or a file system folder) and then to enable it for sharing. To make these resources available via the Active Directory, however, there's an additional step: Resources must be published. Once an object has been published in the Active Directory, it will be available for use by clients.

You can also publish Windows NT 4 resources through the Active Directory by creating Active Directory objects as we did in Exercise 7.3. When publishing objects in the Active Directory, you should know the server name and share name of the resource. The use of Active Directory objects offers systems administrators the ability to change the resource to which the object points without having to reconfigure or even notify clients. For example, if we move a share from one server to another, all we need to do is update the Shared Folder properties to point to the new location. Active Directory clients will still refer to the resource with the same path and name as they used before.

Without the Active Directory, Windows NT 4 shares and printers will only be accessible through the use of NetBIOS. If you're planning to disable the NetBIOS protocol in your environment, you must be sure that these resources have been published, or they will not be accessible.

Publishing Printers

Printers can be published easily within the Active Directory. Exercise 7.4 walks you through the steps required to share and publish a Printer object.

EXERCISE 7.4

Creating and Publishing a Printer

In this exercise, we will create and share a printer. Specifically, we will install and share a new, text-only printer. In order to complete the installation of the printer, you will require access to the Windows 2000 installation media (via the hard disk, a network share, or the CD-ROM drive).

1. Click Start ➤ Settings ➤ Printers. Double-click Add New Printer. This will start the Add Printer Wizard. Click Next to begin.

2. In the Network or Local Printer box, select Local Printer. Uncheck the Automatically Detect and Install My Plug and Play Printer box. Click Next.

3. In the Select the Printer Port dialog box, select Use the Following Port. From the list below that option, select LPT1: Printer Port. Click Next.

4. For the Manufacturer, select Generic, and for the printer, highlight Generic / Text Only. Click Next.

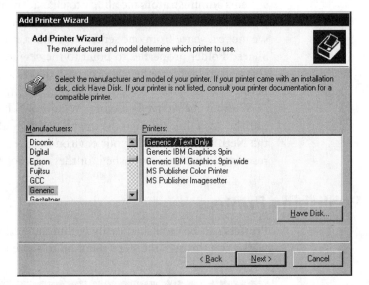

5. When asked for the name of the printer, type **Text Printer**. Click Next.

6. When prompted for the share name, select Share As and type **Text Printer**. Click Next.

7. For the Location, type **Building 203** and add the comment **This is a text-only printer**. Click Next.

8. When prompted to print a test page, select No. Click Next.

9. You will see a confirmation of the printer options you selected. Click Finish to create the printer.

Add Printer Wizard

Completing the Add Printer Wizard

You have successfully completed the Add Printer wizard.

You specified the following printer settings:

Name: Text Printer
Shared as: TextPrinter
Port: LPT1:
Model: Generic / Text Only
Default: Yes
Test page: No
Location: Building 203
Comment: This is a text-only printer.

To close this wizard, click Finish.

< Back   Finish   Cancel

EXERCISE 7.4 *(continued)*

10. Next, you will need to verify that the printer will be listed in the Active Directory. In the Printers folder, right-click the Text Printer icon and select Properties. Next, select the Sharing tab, and ensure that the List in the Directory box is checked. Note that you can also add additional printer drivers for other operating systems using this tab. Click OK to accept the settings. Close the Printers window.

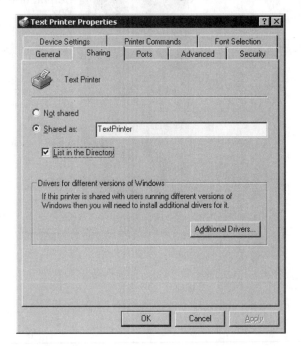

11. Now that the printer has been created and shared, we need to verify that it is available for use. To do this, click Start ≻ Search ≻ For Printers. In order to search for all printers, leave all of the options blank. Note that you can use the Features and Advanced tabs to restrict the list of printers to those that match certain requirements. Click Find Now. You should receive results that demonstrate that the printer is available through the Active Directory.

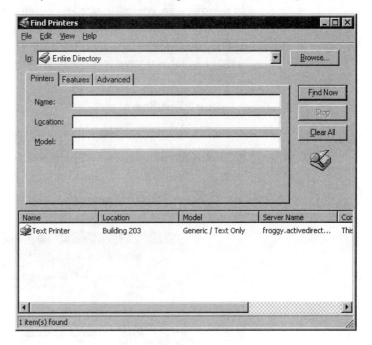

12. When finished, exit the Find dialog box.

Note that when you create and share a printer this way, an Active Directory Printer object is not displayed within the Active Directory Users and Computers tool. The printer is actually associated with the Computer object to which it is shared. Printer objects in the Active Directory are manually created for sharing printers from Windows NT 4 and earlier shared printer resources.

Publishing Shared Folders

Now that we've created and published a printer, let's look at how the same thing can be done to shared folders. Exercise 7.5 walks through the steps required to create a folder, share it, and then publish it in the Active Directory.

EXERCISE 7.5

Creating and Publishing a Shared Folder

In this exercise, we will create and publish a shared folder. This exercise assumes that you will be using the C: partition; however, you may want to change this based on your server configuration. This exercise assumes that you have completed Exercise 7.1.

1. Create a new folder in the root directory of your C: partition, and name it **Test Share**.

2. Right-click the Test Share folder, and select Sharing.

3. On the Sharing tab, select Share This Folder. For the Share Name, type **Test Share,** and for the Comment, enter **Share used for testing Active Directory**. Leave the user limit, permissions, and caching settings as their defaults. Click OK to create the share.

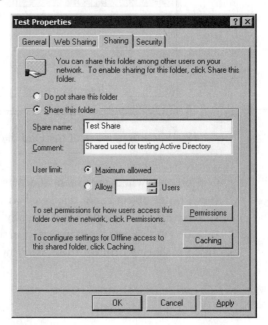

4. To verify that the share has been created, click Start ➢ Run, and type the UNC path for the local server. For instance, if the server was named DC1, you would type **\\dc1**. This will connect you to the local computer where you can view any available network resources. Verify that the Test Share folder exists, and then close the window.

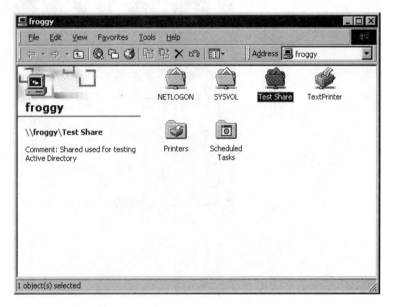

5. Open the Active Directory Users and Computers tool. Expand the current domain, and right-click the IT OU. Select New ➢ Shared Folder.

6. In the dialog box, type **Shared Folder Test** for the name of the folder. Then, type the UNC path to the share (for example, **\\DC1\Test Share**). Click OK to create the share.

7. Now that we have created the shared folder in the Active Directory, it's time to verify that it was created. To do this, right-click the name of the domain and select Find.

EXERCISE 7.5 *(continued)*

8. On the Find menu, select Shared Folders. Leave the remaining options blank to search for all Active Directory shares. (Notice that you can also use the Advanced tab to further specify information about the share you are searching for.) Click the Find Now button to obtain the results of the search.

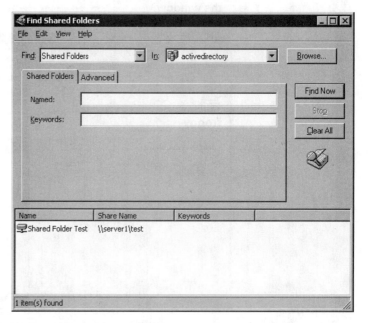

9. Close the Find dialog box, and exit the Active Directory Users and Computers tool.

Once you have created and published the shared folder, clients can use the My Network Places icon to find this object. The shared folder will be organized based on the OU in which you created the Shared Folder object. Through the use of publication, you can see how this makes it easy to manage shared folders.

Although it's beyond the scope of this book to discuss, the Windows 2000 Distributed File System (DFS) service allows for the use of hierarchical shares. The Active Directory Shared Folders object is completely compatible with this feature.

Once you have created resources, it is likely that you will want to restrict their use to only certain users and groups. We'll cover ways to do this in Chapter 8, "Active Directory Security." In addition to setting permissions for end users, you can also use the Delegation of Control Wizard to assign management permissions to objects. We covered methods for delegating control of OUs in Chapter 4, "Creating and Managing Organizational Units."

Searching the Active Directory

So far, we've created several Active Directory resources. One of the main benefits of having all of your resource information in the Active Directory is that you should be able to easily find what you're looking for. Remember, when we recommended that you should always enter in as much information as possible when creating Active Directory objects? Well, this is where that extra effort begins to pay off.

Exercise 7.6 walks through the steps required to find objects in the Active Directory.

EXERCISE 7.6

Finding Objects in the Active Directory

In this exercise, we will search for specific objects in the Active Directory. In order to complete this exercise, you must have first completed Exercise 7.1.

1. Open the Active Directory Users and Computers tool.

2. Right-click the name of the domain, and select Find.

EXERCISE 7.6 *(continued)*

3. In the Find field, select Users, Computers, and Groups. For the In setting, choose Entire Directory. This will search the entire Active Directory environment for the criteria you enter. Note that if this is a production domain and if there are many objects, this may be a time-consuming and network-intensive operation.

4. In the Name field, type **admin** and then click Find Now to obtain the results of the search.

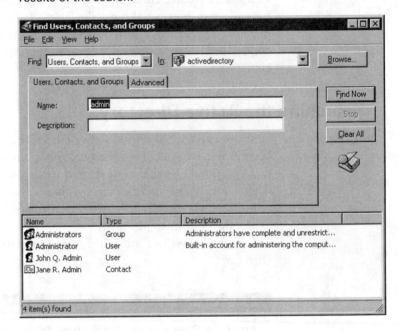

5. Now that we have found several results, let's narrow down the list. Click the Advanced tab. In the Fields drop-down list, select User ➢ Last Name. For the Condition, select Starts With, and for the Value, type **Admin**. Click Add to add this item to the search criteria. Click Find Now. Notice that this time, only the User and Contact that have the last name Admin are shown.

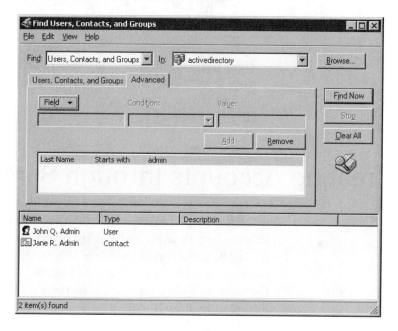

6. To filter the result set even further, click the View menu and select Filter. The filter is displayed in the row just above the Results windows. In the Name field, type **John** and press Enter. Notice that this filters the list to only the John Q. Admin User object.

7. To view more information about the User object, you can right-click it and select Properties.

EXERCISE 7.6 (continued)

8. To quickly view (and filter) more information about multiple objects, select the View menu, and choose Select Columns. By selecting fields and clicking Add, you will be able to view more information about the retrieved objects. Click OK to add the information.

9. When you are finished searching, close the Find box and exit the Active Directory Users and Computers tool.

Using the many options available in the Find dialog box, you can usually narrow down the objects you're searching for quite quickly and efficiently. Users and systems administrators alike will find this to be useful in environments of any size!

Creating Accounts through Scripting

Although the Active Directory Users and Computers tool provides an intuitive way to create and manage objects, sometimes using a GUI tool is not the best solution. Imagine the task facing a systems administrator who must create and populate several hundred User accounts. Clearly, using the point-and-click interface is inefficient. This is especially true if the information already exists in another format—such as a text file or an Excel spreadsheet.

Microsoft
✓ Exam
Objective

Manage Active Directory objects.

- Create and manage accounts manually or by scripting.

Fortunately, through the use of scripting and import/export processes, you can make this task much more manageable. In this section, we'll look at several ways to manage import users. The focus will be on an overview of methods. You'll likely need to consult other resources to carry out customizations for your own environment.

Let's start by looking at two command-line tools that can be used to import and export Active Directory objects.

CSVDE

The *Comma-Separated Value Directory Exchange (CSVDE)* tool is used to import and export Active Directory information to and from comma-separated value (CSV) text files. CSV files are commonly used to transfer information between different types of data storage systems. If we wanted to transfer information between a mainframe application and an Excel spreadsheet, we could use a CSV text file as an intermediate (since both applications can read this format).

Other than serving as a common intermediate, another useful feature of CSV files is that they can be easily edited using any standard text editor (such as the Windows Notepad) or applications that support this format (such as Microsoft Excel).

The CSVDE utility is run from the command line. It offers many options for specifying the exact information you want to import and export. Following are the results of running the CSVDE command without any commands:

```
CSV Directory Exchange


General Parameters
===================
-i               Turn on Import Mode (The default is
                    Export)
-f filename      Input or Output filename
-s servername    The server to bind to (Default to DC of
                    logged in Domain)
-v               Turn on Verbose Mode
-c FromDN ToDN   Replace occurences of FromDN to ToDN
-j               Log File Location
-t               Port Number (default = 389)
-u               Use Unicode format
-?               Help
```

```
Export Specific
===============
-d RootDN         The root of the LDAP search (Default to
                  Naming Context)
-r Filter         LDAP search filter (Default to
                  "(objectClass=*)")
-p SearchScope    Search Scope (Base/OneLevel/Subtree)
-l list           List of attributes (comma separated) to
                  look for in an LDAP search
-o list           List of attributes (comma separated) to
                  omit from input.
-g                Disable Paged Search.
-m                Enable the SAM logic on export.
-n                Do not export binary values


Import
======


-k                The import will go on ignoring 'Constraint
                  Violation' and 'Object Already Exists'
                  errors


Credentials Establishment
=========================


Note that if no credentials are specified, CSVDE will
    bind as the currently logged on user, using SSPI.

-a UserDN [Password | *]         Simple authentication
-b UserName Domain [Password | *]    SSPI bind method

Example: Simple import of current domain
    csvde -i -f INPUT.CSV

Example: Simple export of current domain
    csvde -f OUTPUT.CSV

Example: Export of specific domain with credentials
```

```
csvde -m -f OUTPUT.CSV
        -b USERNAME DOMAINNAME *
        -s SERVERNAME
        -d "cn=users,DC=DOMAINNAME,DC=Microsoft,DC=Com"
        -r "(objectClass=user)"
```

When you are planning to import new User accounts, it's always useful to first perform an export so you can view the structure of the file and the information that you'll need. You can then make changes to this file and import it later. Exercise 7.7 walks through the steps required in order to create User accounts by using the CSVDE.

EXERCISE 7.7

Modifying User Accounts Using CSVDE

In this exercise, we will use the CSVDE utility to export a list of User objects from the Active Directory. We will then make changes to this file and then import the changes back into the Active Directory.

1. Open the Active Directory Users and Computers tool, and expand the name of the Active Directory domain.

2. Create a new, top-level OU named Scripting.

3. Within the Scripting OU, create four users with the following information (for all other options, use the defaults):

   a. User #1

      First Name: Andrew

      Initials: P

      Last Name: Admin

      Logon Name: apadmin

   b. User #2

      First Name: Brian

      Initials: C

      Last Name: Manager

      Logon Name: bcmanager

c. User #3

First Name: Julie

Initials: A

Last Name: Finance

Logon Name: jafinance

d. User #4

First Name: Clara

Initials: D

Last Name: Manager

Logon Name: cdmanager

4. Click Start ➢ Run, and type **cmd**. This will open up a command prompt. Make a note of the current directory path since this is where we will be creating an export text file for later use.

5. Type the following command to export the contents of the Scripting OU (note that you will need to replace the DC= sections to reflect the name of your current domain and that the command should be typed on a single line) and obtain the results shown.

Csvde –f export.csv –v –r "(objectclass=user)"

➥–d "OU=Scripting, DC=DomainName,DC=com" –m

```
G:\WINNT\System32\cmd.exe                                    _ □ ×

G:\>csvde -f export.csv -v -r "(objectclass=user)" -d "OU=Scripting, DC=Acti
rectory, DC=Test" -m
Connecting to "(null)"
Logging in as current user using SSPI
Exporting directory to file export.csv
Searching for entries...
Writing out entries
Exporting entry: "CN=Andrew P. Admin,OU=Scripting,DC=activedirectory,DC=test
Exporting entry: "CN=Brian C. Manager,OU=Scripting,DC=activedirectory,DC=tes
Exporting entry: "CN=Julie A. Finance,OU=Scripting,DC=activedirectory,DC=tes
Exporting entry: "CN=Clara D. Manager,OU=Scripting,DC=activedirectory,DC=tes

Export Completed. Post-processing in progress...
4 entries exported

The command has completed successfully

G:\>_
```

6. Now, open the Active Directory Users and Computers tool. Expand the Scripting OU, and delete all four of the users we created previously.

7. At the command prompt, type the following command:

notepad export.csv

8. In the text file, scroll over to the column that contains the middle initial value. It may be difficult to find the value since the file is not arranged in columns. Change all of the Middle Initial values to X.

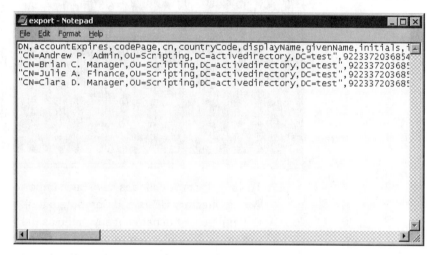

9. To save the file, click File ➢ Save. For the name of the file, type **import.csv**. Make sure that the Save as Type selection is All Files and that the Encoding value is set to ANSI.

10. Now, to import the changed file, return to the command prompt window and type the following:

csvde −i −f import.csv -v

11. Once you receive the results similar to those shown, close the command prompt.

```
G:\WINNT\System32\cmd.exe                                    _ □ ×

G:\>csvde -i -f import.csv -v
Connecting to "(null)"
Logging in as current user using SSPI
Importing directory from file "import.csv"
Loading entries
2: CN=Andrew P. Admin,OU=Scripting,DC=activedirectory,DC=test
Entry modified successfully.
3: CN=Brian C. Manager,OU=Scripting,DC=activedirectory,DC=test
Entry modified successfully.
4: CN=Julie A. Finance,OU=Scripting,DC=activedirectory,DC=test
Entry modified successfully.
5: CN=Clara D. Manager,OU=Scripting,DC=activedirectory,DC=test
Entry modified successfully.
4 entries modified successfully.

The command has completed successfully

G:\>_
```

12. To verify that the changes have been imported correctly, open the Active Directory Users and Computers tool. Within the Scripting OU, right-click the name of any of the users. Verify that the middle initials have indeed been changed to X. Notice that the display name and the name displayed in the directory do not change. These are distinct attributes in the directory. When finished, close the Active Directory Users and Computers tool.

This import process can be made much easier if you use an application that can read and properly format CSV files. Microsoft Excel is a good example. You can also cut and paste values from other Microsoft Excel spreadsheets into this same file. When used correctly, the CSVDE utility can save many hours of work (and reduce the chances for errors introduced by manual data entry).

LDIFDE

In Chapter 1, "Overview of the Active Directory," we mentioned that the main method used to query the Active Directory is through the use of the Lightweight Directory Access Protocol (LDAP). LDAP is commonly used for querying many directory sources, such as X.500-based directories and Novell Directory Services (NDS). The benefit to using this standard is that systems administrators and application developers can use a common method to access information from different types of directories.

In addition to the LDAP specification, there is a specification called the LDAP Interchange Format (LDIF). The idea behind LDIF is to provide a common data storage and transfer mechanism for working with LDAP-based data. LDIF files can contain the instructions required to create, modify, and delete objects.

The *LDIF Directory Exchange (LDIFDE)* command works similarly to the CSVDE command. The primary difference (as you have probably already guessed!) is that the intermediate file is in the LDIF format. Following are the results of running the LDIFDE command without any commands:

```
LDIF Directory Exchange

General Parameters
===================
-i                 Turn on Import Mode (The default is
                   Export)
-f filename        Input or Output filename
-s servername      The server to bind to (Default to DC
                   of logged in Domain)
-c FromDN ToDN     Replace occurences of FromDN to ToDN
-v                 Turn on Verbose Mode
-j                 Log File Location
-t                 Port Number (default = 389)
-u                 Use Unicode format
-?                 Help


Export Specific
===============
-d RootDN          The root of the LDAP search (Default to
                   Naming Context)
```

```
-r Filter        LDAP search filter (Default to
                    "(objectClass=*)")
-p SearchScope   Search Scope (Base/OneLevel/Subtree)
-l list          List of attributes (comma separated) to
                    look for in an LDAP search
-o list          List of attributes (comma separated) to
                    omit from input.
-g               Disable Paged Search.
-m               Enable the SAM logic on export.
-n               Do not export binary values


Import
======

-k               The import will go on ignoring 'Constraint
                    Violation' and 'Object Already Exists'
                    errors
-y               The import will use lazy commit for better
                    performance


Credentials Establishment
=========================
Note that if no credentials is specified, LDIFDE will bind
    as the currently logged on user, using SSPI.

-a UserDN [Password | *]             Simple authentication
-b UserName Domain [Password | *]    SSPI bind method


Example: Simple import of current domain
    ldifde -i -f INPUT.LDF


Example: Simple export of current domain
    ldifde -f OUTPUT.LDF


Example: Export of specific domain with credentials
    ldifde -m -f OUTPUT.LDF
            -b USERNAME DOMAINNAME *
```

```
-s SERVERNAME
-d "cn=users,DC=DOMAINNAME,DC=Microsoft,DC=Com"
-r "(objectClass=user)"
```

Notice that most of these options are the same as those presented for the CSVDE command. The actual operations are very similar. The major exception is that the LDIF file format is designed for use with specific applications that support this format. It is not optimized for use with Microsoft Excel or Notepad, for example.

Windows Script Host (WSH)

Although the LDIFDE and CSVDE utilities provide a good way to import and export data, sometimes you need to perform more complicated modifications to data. Suppose you wanted to programmatically change all of your usernames to conform to your company's new naming convention. These types of actions are best performed through scripting methods.

The *Windows Script Host (WSH)* was designed to allow systems administrators to quickly and easily create simple files that automate common functions. Among the various functions that can be performed by WSH are the following:

- Creating Active Directory objects, including users, groups, and printers

- Modifying or deleting Active Directory objects

- Performing network logon functions such as mapping network drives

- Starting and stopping services

- Accessing Microsoft Office or other applications and performing common tasks

WSH is actually a scripting host, as opposed to a programming language. This means that it allows for the use of many different languages. Specifically, WSH ships with support for VBScript (a simplified version of Visual Basic, optimized for scripting) and JScript (Microsoft's version of Java–Script). Additionally, third-party developers can write interpreters that allow the use of PERL and other types of scripts.

There are two main executables that are used to launch files that are compatible with WSH.

Cscript   The command-line version of the scripting host.

Wscript   The Windows GUI version of the scripting host.

WSH has a wide array of possible uses and should be a part of any systems administrator's bag of tricks. For more information on obtaining and using WSH, see `msdn.microsoft.com/scripting/`. This site includes the entire object model for WSH, sample script files, tutorials, and VBScript/JScript language references. Figure 7.3 shows an example of the site.

FIGURE 7.3   The Microsoft scripting Web site

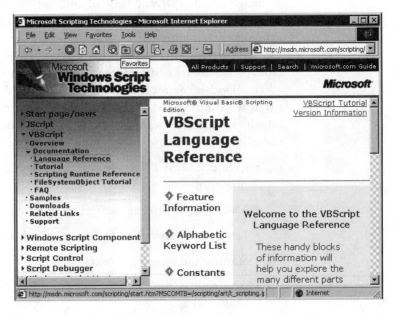

Active Directory Services Interface

The *Active Directory Services Interface (ADSI)* is designed to allow developers to programmatically view and modify objects within the Active Directory. It is based on a set of Component Object Model (COM) structures that can be used in a variety of environments. The ADSI object model can be accessed from within popular development languages, including Visual

Basic, Visual C++, Java, and Active Server Pages (ASP). This makes the use of ADSI very accessible for the vast majority of today's programmers.

In addition to supporting the Active Directory, ADSI also supports the use of the Netware 3.x Bindery, Novell Directory Services (NDS), and Windows NT 4 account databases. This broad support makes ADSI an excellent solution for migrating users from other directory services to the Active Directory. For example, a developer could quickly write an ADSI Visual Basic application that takes all of the existing groups and accounts from a Windows NT 4 domain and places them in the appropriate groups and OUs within an Active Directory domain.

It is beyond the scope of this book (and the Microsoft exam for which it prepares you) to cover programming concepts in-depth. For more information on these topics, see Microsoft's Active Directory Services Interface Web site at www.microsoft.com/ADSI and the Windows 2000 Resource Kit.

Summary

In this chapter, we took a look at several ways to create, manage, and publish objects in the Active Directory. If you're responsible for day-to-day systems administration, there's a good chance that you were already familiar with using this tool. After we created some basic objects, we used other features of the Active Directory to search for resources. Finally, we looked at ways to script the import and export of users in bulk.

The concepts and operations we covered in this chapter will be instrumental in understanding the ideas behind other Active Directory topics. A prime example is the topic of Active Directory security, which we'll cover next!

Key Terms

You should be familiar with the following key terms related to Active Directory administration:

Active Directory Services Interface (ADSI)

Active Directory Users and Computers tool

Computer objects

Contact objects

Comma-Separated Value Directory Exchange (CSVDE)

LDIF Directory Exchange (LDIFDE)

Printer objects

publishing

security principals

Shared Folder objects

User object

Windows Script Host (WSH)

Review Questions

1. Which of the following operations *cannot* be performed using the Active Directory Users and Computers tool?

   A. Renaming an organizational unit

   B. Searching for resources

   C. Renaming a group

   D. Creating a computer account

   E. None of the above

2. Which of the following operations *cannot* be performed using the Active Directory Users and Computers tool?

   A. Creating shared folders

   B. Creating printers

   C. Creating domains

   D. Creating organizational units

   E. All of the above

3. The LostAndFound and System folders do not appear in the Active Directory Users and Computers tool. What is the most likely reason for this?

   A. The user does not have permissions to view those folders.

   B. The Advanced Options item in the View menu is unselected.

   C. The local server is not a domain controller.

   D. None of the above.

4. Which of the following is not a default folder that appears in the Active Directory Users and Computers tool?

   A. Foreign Security Principals

   B. Domain Controllers

   C. Servers

   D. Computers

   E. Users

5. Restricting the display of visible object types in the Active Directory Users and Computers tool is known as:

   A. Restriction

   B. Delegation

   C. Filtering

   D. Excluding

   E. None of the above

6. Which of the following default folders includes the Print Operators and Server Operators groups?

   A. Builtin

   B. Users

   C. Foreign Security Principals

   D. Windows NT

   E. None of the above

7. Which of the following utilities creates a text file of some or all of the objects in the Active Directory that can be modified using standard text editors?

   A. LDIFDE

   B. CSVDE

   C. Active Directory Users and Computers

   D. None of the above

8. A systems administrator creates a local printer object, but it doesn't show up in the Active Directory when a user executes a search for all printers. Which of the following is a possible reason for this?

   A. The printer was not shared.

   B. The List in Directory option is unchecked.

   C. The client does not have permissions to use the printer.

   D. All of the above.

9. Shared Folder objects can refer to which of the following types of shares?

   A. Windows NT Shares

   B. Windows 2000 Shares

   C. Both A and B

   D. None of the above

10. When searching for printers using the Active Directory Users and Computers tool, which of the following tabs can be used to return a list of only those printers that can print in color?

   A. Printer Options

   B. Advanced

   C. Features

   D. General

   E. None of the above

11. The Active Directory Users and Computers tool can be used to do all of the following *except*:

   A. Create a User object

   B. Rename a User object

   C. Reset a password for a User object

   D. Rename a Computer object

   E. None of the above

12. Which of the following tools can be used to export a list of users from the Active Directory?

   A. CSVDE

   B. LDIFDE

   C. Active Directory Users and Computers

   D. All of the above

13. Which of the following allows for programmatically transferring information between a Novell Directory Services (NDS) directory and the Active Directory?

   A. WSH

   B. LDIFDE

   C. CSVDE

   D. ADSI

   E. None of the above

14. A systems administrator can determine the type of operating system a computer is using with which of the following tools?

A. Active Directory Sites and Services

B. Active Directory Domains and Trusts

C. Active Directory Users and Computers

D. DNS

E. None of the above

15. A systems administrator is using the Active Directory Users and Computers tool to view the objects within an OU. They had previously created many users, groups, and computers within this OU, but now only the users are being shown. What is a possible explanation for this?

A. Groups and Computers are not normally shown in the Active Directory Users and Computers tool.

B. Another systems administrator may have locked the group, preventing others from accessing it.

C. Filtering options have been set that specify that only User objects should be shown.

D. The Group and Computer accounts have never been used and are, therefore, not shown.

E. None of the above.

16. A systems administrator wishes to access the System folder within the Active Directory Users and Computers tool, but it does not appear in the utility. What must they do to be able to access this folder (assuming they have the appropriate permissions)?

A. Use the Delegation of Control Wizard.

B. Click View ➢ Advanced Features.

C. Click the Refresh button.

D. Modify the Properties page for the domain.

E. None of the above.

17. Which of the following default Active Directory folders can contain Computer objects?

    A. Users

    B. System

    C. Builtin

    D. Computers

    E. All of the above

18. Which of the following is not a default category of Active Directory objects in the Find dialog box?

    A. Users, Contacts, and Groups

    B. Computers

    C. Servers and Domain Controllers

    D. Organizational Units

    E. Printers

19. Which of the following default desktop icons can a Windows 2000 Professional user use to browse the Active Directory?

    A. Network Neighborhood

    B. Networks

    C. My Network Places

    D. Active Directory Browser

    E. None of the above

20. A user is having a problem with a Shared Folder located in a specific OU and wants to know who to contact. A good way to find this information is to:

A. Right-click the Shared Folder object, select Properties, and select the Managed By tab.

B. Right-click the parent OU, select Properties, and select the Managed By tab.

C. Right-click the Shared Folder object, and choose Notify Operator.

D. Both A and B.

Answers to Review Questions

1. E. All of the above operations can be carried out using the Active Directory Users and Computers tool.

2. C. Domains can only be created through the use of the Active Directory Installation Wizard.

3. B. Enabling the Advanced Options item in the View menu will allow you to see the LostAndFound and System folders.

4. C. Upon installation of the Active Directory, there is no Servers container.

5. C. Through the use of the Filtering object, systems administrators can choose which types of objects they want to see in the Active Directory Users and Computers interface.

6. A. The Builtin group contains the default server roles that are available within the domain.

7. B. The CSVDE utility creates a standard text file while the LDIFDE utility creates a file for use with LDIF-compatible applications.

8. D. All of the reasons listed are explanations why a printer may not show up within the Active Directory.

9. C. A Shared Folder refers to resources by UNC name and can point to a Windows NT or Windows 2000 share.

10. C. The Features tab can be used to specify the features of a printer object.

11. D. Computer objects can be created and deleted using the Active Directory Users and Computers tool, but they cannot be renamed.

12. D. All of the above tools can be used to export a list of users.

13. D. The Active Directory Services Interface (ADSI) presents an object model that can be used to access information from a variety of different directory services.

14. C. By right-clicking a Computer object and choosing Properties within the Active Directory Users and Computers tool, a systems administrator can view operating system information about a specific computer that is a member of the domain.

15. C. The filtering options would cause other objects to be hidden (although they still exist). Another explanation (but not one of the choices) is that a higher-level systems administrator modified the administrator's permissions using the Delegation of Control Wizard.

16. B. The System folder is shown in the Active Directory Users and Computers tool only if the Advanced Features option is enabled.

17. E. All of the default folders listed can contain Active Directory Computer objects.

18. C. There is no default option to search for servers and domain controllers.

19. C. The My Network Places icon allows users to navigate through the structure of the Active Directory (based on their permissions).

20. D. The Managed By tab is used to specify the individual who is responsible for managing the Active Directory object. In this case, the user will want to determine who manages the Shared Folder and/or the OU in which it is contained.

Chapter

8

Active Directory Security

MICROSOFT EXAM OBJECTIVES COVERED IN THIS CHAPTER:

✓ **Configure and troubleshoot security in a directory services infrastructure.**

- Apply security policies by using Group Policy.
- Create, analyze, and modify security configurations by using Security Configuration and Analysis and Security Templates.
- Implement an audit policy.

✓ **Monitor and analyze security events.**

✓ **Manage Active Directory objects.**

- Move Active Directory objects.
- Publish resources in Active Directory.
- Locate objects in Active Directory.
- Create and manage accounts manually or by scripting.
- Control access to Active Directory objects.
- Delegate administrative control of objects in Active Directory.

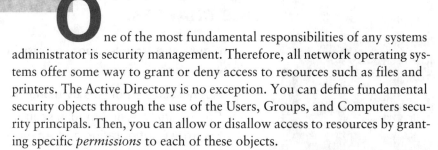

One of the most fundamental responsibilities of any systems administrator is security management. Therefore, all network operating systems offer some way to grant or deny access to resources such as files and printers. The Active Directory is no exception. You can define fundamental security objects through the use of the Users, Groups, and Computers security principals. Then, you can allow or disallow access to resources by granting specific *permissions* to each of these objects.

In this chapter, you'll learn how to implement security within the Active Directory. Through the use of Active Directory tools, you can quickly and easily configure the settings that you require in order to protect information. Note, however, that proper planning for security permissions is an important prerequisite. If your security settings are too restrictive, users may not be able to perform their job functions. Worse yet, they may try to circumvent security measures. On the other end of the spectrum, if security permissions are too lax, users may be able to access and modify sensitive company resources.

With all of this in mind, let's start looking at how you can manage security within the Active Directory.

With respect to the "Manage Active Directory objects" objective, this chapter covers material related to only the last two subobjectives. See Chapter 7, "Administering the Active Directory," for material on Active Directory administration and the remainder of the subobjectives under the "Manage Active Directory objects" objective.

In order to complete the exercises in this chapter, you should understand the basics of working with Active Directory objects. If you are not familiar with creating and managing users, groups, computers, and organizational units, you should review the information in Chapter 7, "Administering the Active Directory," before continuing.

Active Directory Security Overview

One of the fundamental design goals for the Active Directory is to define a single, centralized repository of users and information resources. The Active Directory records information about all of the users, computers, and resources on your network. Each domain acts as a security boundary, and members of the domain (including workstations, servers, and domain controllers) share information about the objects within them.

The information stored within the Active Directory determines which resources are accessible to which users. Through the use of permissions that are assigned to Active Directory objects, you can control all aspects of network security.

Many security experts state that 20 percent of real-world network security is a technical issue and that 80 percent of it is a process and policy one. Don't make the mistake of trying to solve all security problems through a point-and-click interface. You also need to establish and enforce system usage policies, physically secure your resources, and ensure that users are aware of any restrictions.

In this chapter, we'll cover the details of security as it pertains to the Active Directory. Note, however, that this is only one aspect of true network security. That is, you should always be sure that you have implemented appropriate access control settings for the file system, network devices, and other resources. Let's start by looking at the various components of network security.

Security Principals

Security principals are Active Directory objects that are assigned security identifiers (SIDs). A SID is a unique identifier that is used to manage any object to which permissions can be assigned. Security principals are assigned permissions to perform certain actions and access certain network resources.

The basic types of Active Directory objects that serve as security principals include:

User Accounts   These objects identify individual users on your network. The User account includes information such as the user's name and their password. User accounts are the fundamental unit of security administration.

Groups   There are two main types of groups: *Security groups* and *Distribution groups*. Both types of groups can contain User accounts. Security groups are used for easing the management of security permissions. Distribution groups, on the other hand, are used solely for the purpose of sending e-mail. Distribution groups are *not* considered security principals. We'll cover the details of groups in the next section.

Computer Accounts   Computer accounts identify which client computers are members of particular domains. Since these computers participate in the Active Directory database, systems administrators can manage security settings that affect the computer. Computer accounts are used to determine whether a computer can join a domain and for authentication purposes. As we'll see later in this chapter, systems administrators can also place restrictions on certain computer settings to increase security. These settings apply to the computer and, therefore, also apply to any user who is using it (regardless of the permissions granted to the User account).

Security principals can be assigned permissions so that they can access various network resources, be given user rights, and may have their actions tracked (through *auditing*, covered later in this chapter). The three types of security principals—Users, Groups, and Computers—form the basis of the Active Directory security architecture. As a systems administrator, you will likely spend a portion of your time managing permissions for these objects.

It is important to understand that, since a unique SID defines each security principal, deleting a security principal is an irreversible process. For example, if you delete a User account and then later re-create one with the same name, you will need to reassign permissions and group membership settings for the new account.

Note that other objects—such as organizational units (OUs)—do not function as security principals. What this means is that you can apply certain settings (such as Group Policy) on all of the objects within an OU. However, you cannot specifically set permissions with respect to the OU itself. The purpose of OUs is to logically organize other Active Directory objects based on business needs. This distinction is important to remember.

Understanding Users and Groups

The fundamental security principals that are used for security administration include Users and Groups. In this section, you'll learn how Users and Groups interact and about the different types of Groups that can be created.

Types of Groups

When dealing with Groups, you should make the distinction between local security principals and domain security principals. Local Users and Groups are used for assigning the permissions necessary to access the local machine. For example, we may assign the permissions necessary to restart a domain controller to a specific local Group. Domain Users and Groups, on the other hand, are used throughout the domain. These objects are available on any of the computers within the Active Directory domain and between domains that have a trust relationship.

There are two main types of Groups used in the Active Directory:

Security Groups   Security groups are considered security principals. They can contain User accounts. To make administration simpler, permissions are usually granted to groups. This allows for changing permissions easily at the level of the Active Directory (instead of at the level of the resource on which the permissions are assigned).

Security groups can be used for e-mail purposes—that is, a systems administrator can automatically e-mail all of the User accounts that exist within a group. Of course, the systems administrator must specify the e-mail addresses for these accounts.

Active Directory Contact objects can also be placed within Security groups, but security permissions will not apply to them.

Distribution Groups   Distribution groups are not considered security principals and are used only for the purpose of sending e-mail messages. You can add users to Distribution groups just as you would add them to Security groups. Distribution groups can also be placed within OUs for easier management. They are useful, for example, if you need to send e-mail messages to an entire department or business unit within the Active Directory.

Understanding the differences between Security and Distribution groups is important in an Active Directory environment. For the most part, systems administrators use Security groups for daily administration of permissions. Systems administrators who are responsible for maintaining e-mail distribution lists, on the other hand, will generally use Distribution groups to logically group members of departments and business units.

When working in native-mode domains (domains that support the use of only Windows 2000 domain controllers), Security groups can be converted to or from Distribution groups. When running in mixed-mode (which allows the use of Windows NT domain controllers), Group types cannot be changed.

Group Scope

In addition to being classified by type, each Group is also given a specific scope. The scope of a Group defines two characteristics. First, it determines the level of security that applies to a Group. Second, it determines which users can be added to the group. Group scope is an important concept in network environments because it ultimately defines which resources users will be able to access.

The three types of Group scope are as follows:

Domain Local   The scope of *Domain Local groups* extends as far as the local machine. When you're using the Active Directory Users and Computers tool, Domain Local accounts apply to the computer for which you are viewing information. Domain Local groups are used to assign permissions to local resources such as files and printers. They can contain *Global groups*, *Universal groups*, and User accounts.

Global   The scope of Global groups is limited to a single domain. Global groups may contain any of the users that are a part of the Active Directory domain in which the Global groups reside. Global groups are often used for managing domain security permissions based on job functions. For example, if we need to specify permissions for the Engineering department, we could create one or more Global groups (such as EngineeringManagers and EngineeringDevelopers). We could then assign security permissions to each group for any of the resources within the domain.

Universal   Universal groups can contain users from any domains within an Active Directory forest. Therefore, they are used for managing security across domains. Universal groups are only available when you're running the Active Directory in native mode. When managing multiple domains, it is often helpful to group Global groups within Universal groups. For instance, if I have an Engineering Global group in Domain 1 and an Engineering Global group in Domain 2, I could create a universal AllEngineers group that contains both of the Global groups. Now, whenever security permissions must be assigned to all Engineers within the organization, we only need to assign permissions to the AllEngineers Universal group.

In order to process authentication between domains, information about the membership in Universal groups is stored in the Global Catalog (GC). Keep this in mind if you ever plan to place users directly into Universal groups and bypass Global groups because all of the users will be enumerated in the GC, which will impact size and performance.

In addition to the security implications of Group scope, there are also important network replication traffic considerations. This is because domains must communicate information about Global and Universal groups in order to perform authentication. For more information on Active Directory performance, see Chapter 9, "Active Directory Optimization and Reliability."

As you can see, the main properties for each of these Group types are affected by whether Active Directory is running in mixed mode or native mode. Each of these scope levels is designed for a specific purpose and will ultimately affect the types of security permissions that can be assigned to them.

There are several limitations on Group functionality when running in mixed-mode domains. Specifically, the following limitations exist:

- Only Distribution groups can have Universal scope.

- Universal security groups are not available in mixed-mode domains.

- Changing the scope of groups is not allowed.

- There are limitations to Group nesting. Specifically, the only nesting allowed is Global groups contained in Domain Local groups.

When running in native-mode domains, you can make the following Group scope changes:

- Domain Local groups can be changed to a Universal group. This change can be made only if the Domain Local group does not contain any other Domain Local groups.

- A Global group can be changed to a Universal group. This change can be made only if the Global group is not a member of any other Global groups.

Universal groups themselves cannot be converted into any other Group scope type. Changing Group scope can be helpful when your security administration or business needs change.

Built-In Local Groups

Built-in local groups are used for performing administrative functions on the local server. Because they have pre-assigned permissions and privileges, they allow systems administrators to easily assign common management functions. The list of built-in local groups includes:

Account Operators   These users are able to create and modify Domain User and Group accounts. Members of this group are generally responsible for the daily administration of the Active Directory.

Administrators   Members of the Administrators group are given full permissions to perform any functions within the Active Directory domain and on the local computer. This includes the ability to access all files and resources that reside on any server within the domain. As you can see, this is a very powerful account.

In general, you should restrict the number of users that are included in this group since most common administration functions do not require this level of access.

Backup Operators   One of the problems associated with backing up data in a secure network environment is that there must be a way to bypass standard file system security in order to copy files. Although you could place users in the Administrators group, this usually provides more permissions than necessary. Members of the Backup Operators group are able to bypass standard file system security for the purpose of backup and recovery only. They cannot, however, directly access or open files within the file system.

Generally, the permissions assigned to the Backup Operators group are used by backup software applications and data. We'll cover the details of performing backups in Chapter 9, "Active Directory Optimization and Reliability."

Guests The Guests group is generally used for providing access to resources that generally do not require security. For example, if you have a network share that provides files that should be made available to all network users, you can assign permissions to allow members of the Guest group to access those files.

Print Operators Members of the Print Operators group are given permissions to administer all of the printers within a domain. This includes common functions such as changing the priority of print jobs and deleting items from the print queue.

Replicator The Replicator group was created to allow the replication of files between the computers in a domain. Accounts that are used for replication-related tasks are added to this group to provide them with the permissions necessary to keep files synchronized across multiple computers.

Server Operators A common administrative task is managing server configuration. Members of the Server Operators group are granted the permissions necessary to manage services, shares, and other system settings.

Users The Users group, as shown in Figure 8.1, is often used as a generic grouping for network accounts. Usually, this group is given minimal permissions and is used for the application of security settings that apply to most employees within an organization.

Additionally, there are two main User accounts that are created during the promotion of a domain controller. The first is the Administrator account. This account is assigned the password that is provided by a systems administrator during the promotion process and has full permissions to perform all actions within the domain. The second account is Guest, which is disabled by default. The purpose of the Guest account is to provide anonymous access to users who do not have an individual logon and password for use within the domain. Although this might be useful in some situations, it is generally recommended that the Guest account be disabled to increase security.

FIGURE 8.1 Contents of the default Users folder

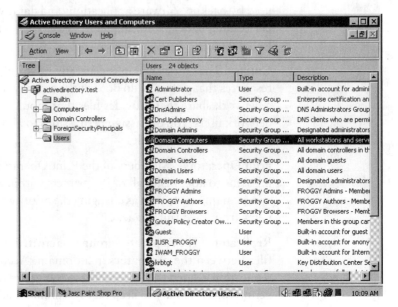

Predefined Global Groups

As we mentioned earlier in this chapter, Global groups are used for managing permissions at the domain level. The following predefined Global groups are installed in the Users folder:

Cert Publishers Certificates are used to increase security by allowing for strong authentication methods. User accounts are placed within the Cert Publishers group if they require the ability to publish security certificates. Generally, these accounts will be used by Active Directory security services.

Domain Computers All of the computers that are a member of the domain are generally members of the Domain Computers group. This includes any workstations or servers that have joined the domain but does not include the domain controllers.

Domain Admins Members of the Domain Admins group have full permissions to manage all of the Active Directory objects for this domain. This is a powerful account; therefore, membership should be restricted to only those users that require full permissions.

Domain Controllers   All of the domain controllers for a given domain are generally included within the Domain Controllers group.

Domain Guests   Generally, members of the Domain Guests group are given minimal permissions with respect to resources. Systems administrators may place User accounts in this group if they require only basic access or require temporary permissions within the domain.

Domain Users   The Domain Users group usually contains all of the User accounts for the given domain. This group is generally given basic permissions to resources that do not require higher levels of security. A common example is a public file share.

Enterprise Admins   Members of the Enterprise Admins group are given full permissions to perform actions within the entire domain forest. This includes functions such as managing trust relationships and adding new domains to trees and forests.

Group Policy Creator Owners   Members of the Group Policy Creator Owners group are able to create and modify *Group Policy* settings for objects within the domain. This allows them to enable security settings on OUs (and the objects that they contain).

Schema Admins   Members of the Schema Admins group are given permissions to modify the Active Directory schema. This, for example, allows them to create additional fields of information for User accounts. This is a very powerful function since any changes to the schema will be propagated to all of the domains and domain controllers within an Active Directory forest. Furthermore, changes to the schema cannot be undone (although additional options can be disabled).

Members of each of these groups are able to perform specific tasks related to the management of the Active Directory.

In addition to the Groups listed above, new ones might be created for specific services and applications that are installed on the server. Specifically, services that run on domain controllers and servers will be created as Security groups with Domain Local scope. For example, if a domain controller is running the DNS service (described in Chapter 2, "Integrating DNS with the Active Directory"), the DNSAdmins and DNSUpdateProxy groups will be available. Similarly, installing the DHCP service creates the DHCPUsers and DHCPAdministrators groups. The purpose of these groups will vary based on the functionality of the applications being installed.

Foreign Security Principals

In environments that consist of more than one domain, you may need to grant permissions to users that reside in multiple domains. Generally, this is managed through the use of Active Directory trees and forests. However, in some cases, you may want to provide resources to users that are contained in domains that are not part of the same forest.

The Active Directory uses the concept of *Foreign security principals* to allow permissions to be assigned to users that are not part of the same Active Directory forest. This process is automatic and does not require the intervention of systems administrators. The Foreign security principals can then be added to Domain Local groups which, in turn, can be granted permissions for resources within the domain. For more information on managing a multiple domain environment, see Chapter 5, "Installing and Managing Trees and Forests."

Managing Security and Permissions

Now that you have a good understanding of the basic issues, terms, and Active Directory objects that pertain to security, it's time to look at how you can apply this information to secure your network resources. The general practice for managing security is to assign users to groups and then grant permissions to the groups so that they can access certain resources.

For ease of management and to implement a hierarchical structure, you can place groups within OUs. You can also assign Group Policy settings to all of the objects contained within an OU. By using this method, you can combine the benefits of a hierarchical structure (through OUs) and the use of security principals. Figure 8.2 provides a diagram of this process.

FIGURE 8.2 An overview of security management

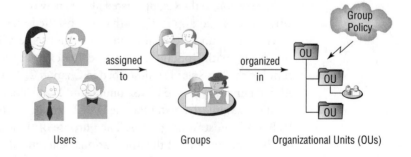

Users   Groups   Organizational Units (OUs)

The primary tool used to manage security permissions for Users, Groups, and Computers is the Active Directory Users and Computers snap-in. Using this tool, you can create and manage Active Directory objects and organize them based on your business needs. Common tasks for many systems administrators might include the following:

- Resetting a user's password (for example, in cases where they forget the password)

- Creating new user accounts (when, for instance, a new employee joins the company)

- Modifying group memberships based on changes in job requirements and functions

- Disabling user accounts (when, for example, users will be out of the office for long periods of time and will not require network resource access)

Permissions

Once you've properly grouped your users, you'll need to set the actual permissions that will affect the objects within the Active Directory. The actual permissions available will vary based on the type of object. The following provides an example of some of the permissions that can be applied to various Active Directory objects and an explanation of what each permission does:

Control Access   Changes security permissions on the object

Create Child   Creates objects within an OU (such as other OUs)

Delete Child   Deletes child objects within an OU

Delete Tree   Deletes an OU and the objects within it

List Contents   Views objects within an OU

List Object   Views a list of the objects within an OU

Read   Views properties of an object (such as a user name)

Write   Modifies properties of an object

Now that you have a good idea of the basis of the Active Directory security architecture, let's move on to covering exactly how security is implemented. We'll cover the steps required to set up permissions in the next section.

Implementing Active Directory Security

Within the Administrative Tools folder on domain controllers, you will find three useful tools for setting and managing Active Directory and domain controller security.

Microsoft
✓ *Exam*
Objective

Manage Active Directory objects.

- Control access to Active Directory objects.

- Delegate administrative control of objects in Active Directory.

The following are the three useful tools just mentioned:

Local Security Policy   The Local Security Policy settings pertain to the local computer only. These settings are useful when you have specific computers that require custom security configurations. For example, an intranet Web server may have different settings from a mission-critical database server.

Domain Security Policy   The Domain Security Policy utility is used to view security settings that apply to all of the objects within a domain. Using this utility, you can specify settings such as the audit policy, System Service settings, and other options. These settings will apply to all of the domain controllers within a domain, unless they are specifically overridden.

Domain Controller Security Policy   The options presented within the Domain Controller Security Policy are similar to those found in the Domain Security Policy utility. The major difference is that the settings you make using this tool apply only to the local domain controller rather than to all domain controllers within the domain. This tool is useful when you want to specify different settings on different domain controllers.

Figure 8.3 shows an example of the settings available within the Domain Controller Security Policy tool.

FIGURE 8.3 The Domain Controller Security Policy tool

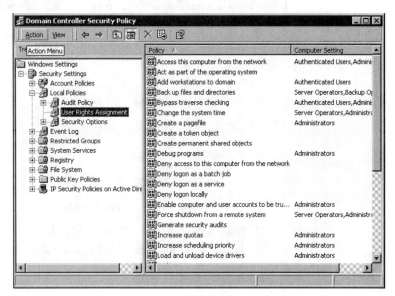

Exercise 8.1 walks you through the steps required to create and manage Users and Groups. If you are unfamiliar with basic Active Directory administration steps, you will find it useful to review Chapter 7, "Administering the Active Directory."

EXERCISE 8.1

Creating and Managing Users and Groups

In this exercise, you will create Users and Groups within the Active Directory and then place Users into Groups.

1. Open the Active Directory Users and Computers tool.

2. Create the following top-level OUs:

   - Sales

   - Marketing

   - Engineering

   - HR

3. Create the following User objects within the Sales container (use the defaults for all fields not listed):

   a. First Name: John

   Last Name: Sales

   User Logon Name: jsales

   b. First Name: Linda

   Last Name: Manager

   User Logon Name: lmanager

4. Create the following User objects within the Marketing container (use the defaults for all fields not listed):

   a. First Name: Jane

   Last Name: Marketing

   User Logon Name: jmarketing

   b. First Name: Monica

   Last Name: Manager

   User Logon Name: mmanager

5. Create the following User object within the Engineering container (use the defaults for all fields not listed):

a. First Name: Bob

   Last Name: Engineer

   User Logon Name: bengineer

6. Right-click the HR container, and select New ➢ Group. Use the name Managers for the Group, and specify Global for the Group scope and Security for the Group type). Click OK to create the Group.

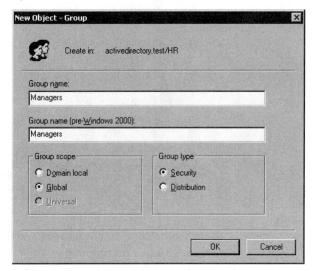

7. To assign Users to the Managers group, right-click the Group object and select Properties. Change to the Members tab, and click Add. From the list, select Linda Manager and Monica Manager, then click OK. You will see the Group membership. Click OK to finish adding the Users to the Group.

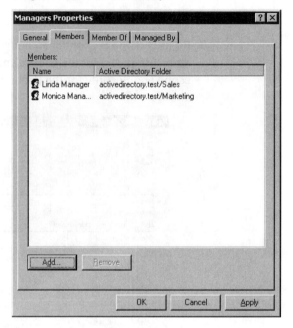

8. When finished creating Users and Groups, close the Active Directory Users and Computers tool.

Notice that you can add Users to Groups regardless of the OU in which they're contained. In Exercise 8.1, for example, we added two User accounts from different OUs into a Group that was created in a third OU. This type of flexibility allows you to easily manage User and Group accounts based on your business organization.

The Active Directory Users and Computers tool also allows you to perform common functions by simply right-clicking an object and selecting actions from the context-sensitive menu. For example, we could right-click a User account and select Add Members to Group to quickly change Group membership.

Delegating Control of Active Directory Objects

A common administrative function related to the use of the Active Directory involves managing objects. OUs can be used to logically group objects so that they can be easily managed. Once you have placed the appropriate Active Directory objects within OUs, you will be ready to delegate control of these objects.

Delegation is the process by which a higher-level security administrator assigns permissions to other users. For example, if Admin A is a member of the Domain Administrators group, they will be able to delegate control of any OU within the domain to Admin B. Exercise 8.2 walks through the steps required to delegate control of OUs.

EXERCISE 8.2

Delegating Control of Active Directory Objects

In this exercise, we will delegate control of Active Directory objects. In order to complete the steps in this exercise, you must have already completed Exercise 8.1.

1. Open the Active Directory Users and Computers tool.

2. Create a new user within the Engineering OU, using the following information (use the default settings for any fields not specified):

   a. First Name: Robert

      Last Name: Admin

      User Logon Name: radmin

3. Right-click the Sales OU, and select Delegate Control. This will start the Delegation of Control Wizard. Click Next.

4. To add users and groups to which you want to delegate control, click Add. From the list of users, select Robert Admin. Click OK and then Next to continue.

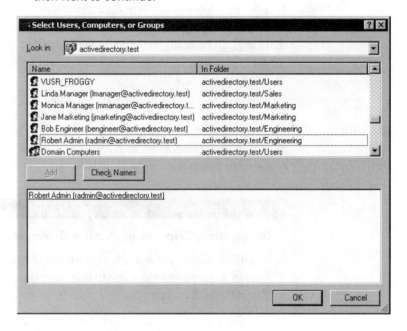

5. Select the Delegate the Following Common Tasks option, and place a check mark next to the following options:

   - Create, Delete, and Manage User Accounts

   - Reset Passwords on User Accounts

   - Read all User Information

- Create, Delete, and Manage Groups

- Modify the Membership of a Group

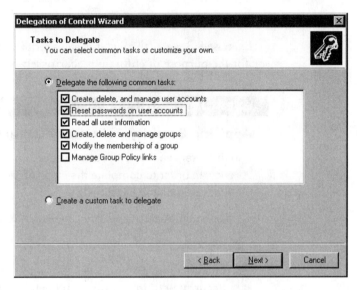

6. Click Next to continue, then click Finish to save the changes. Now, when the user Robert Admin logs on, he will be able to perform common administrative functions for all of the objects contained within the Sales OU.

7. When finished, close the Active Directory Users and Computers tool.

Using Group Policy for Security

Through the use of the Active Directory, systems administrators can define Group Policy objects and then apply them to OUs. We'll cover the details of creating, assigning, and managing Group Policy settings later in Chapter 10, "Managing Group Policy."

Microsoft ✓ *Exam* *Objective*

Configure and troubleshoot security in a directory services infrastructure.

- Apply security policies by using Group Policy.

Exercise 8.3 walks through the steps required to create a basic Group Policy for the purpose of enforcing security settings.

EXERCISE 8.3

Applying Security Policies by Using Group Policy

In this exercise, you will assign security permissions by using Group Policy. In order to complete the steps of this exercise, you must have already completed Exercise 8.1.

1. Open the Active Directory Users and Computers tool.

2. Right-click the Engineering OU, and select Properties.

3. Change to the Group Policy tab, and click New. Type **Engineering Security Settings** for the name of the new Group Policy.

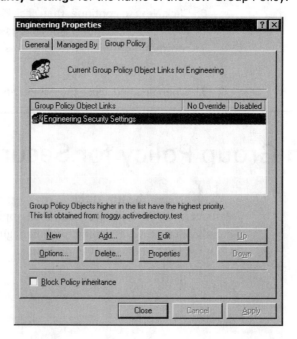

4. To specify the Group Policy settings, click Edit.

EXERCISE 8.3 *(continued)*

5. In the Group Policy window, open Computer Configuration ➤ Windows Settings ➤ Security Settings ➤ Account Policies ➤ Password Policy object.

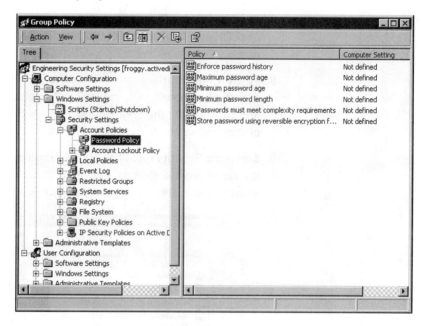

6. In the right-hand pane, double-click the Minimum Password Length setting. In the Security Policy Setting dialog box, place a check mark next to the Define This Policy Setting option. Leave the default value of 7 characters. Click OK.

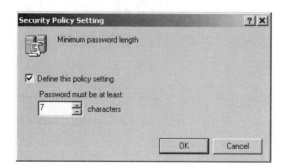

7. Open User Configuration ➢ Administrative Templates ➢ Control Panel object. Double-click Disable Control Panel, select Enabled, and then click OK.

8. Close the Group Policy window to save the settings you chose. Click OK and Close to enable the Security Group Policy for the Engineering OU.

9. To view the security permissions for a Group Policy object, right-click the Engineering OU and select Properties. On the Group Policy tab, highlight the Engineering Security Settings Group Policy object, and select Properties.

10. Select the Security tab. Click Add, and select Linda Manager from the list of users. Click Add and OK. Highlight Linda Manager, and allow this user the Read and Write permissions.

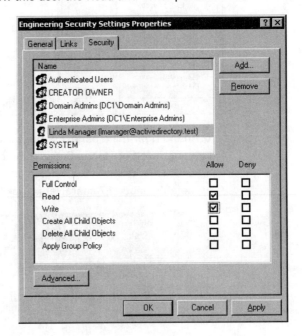

11. Click OK twice to save the changes. Linda Manager will now be able to view and change information for objects in the Sales OU.

12. When finished, close the Active Directory Users and Computers tool.

The settings that you specify will apply to all of the security principals included within the OU to which the Group Policy applies.

Using the Security Configuration and Analysis Utility

The power and flexibility of Windows-based operating systems is both a benefit and a liability. On the plus side, the many configuration options available allow users and systems administrators to modify and customize settings to their preference. On the negative side, however, the full level of functionality can cause problems. For example, novice users might attempt to delete critical system files or incorrectly uninstall programs to free up disk space. So how can these types of problems be prevented? One method is to strictly enforce the types of actions that users can perform. Since most settings for the Windows 2000 interface can be configured in the Registry, you could edit the appropriate settings using the RegEdit command.

Although you could manage security settings manually through the use of Registry changes, this process can become quite tedious. Furthermore, manually modifying the Registry is a dangerous process and one that is bound to cause problems due to human error. In order to make the creation and application of security settings easier, Microsoft has included the Security Configuration and Analysis tool with Windows 2000. This tool can be used to create, modify, and apply security settings in the Registry through the use of Security Template files. *Security Templates* allow systems administrators to define security settings once and then store this information in a file that can be applied to other computers.

Microsoft
✓ *Exam*
Objective

Configure and troubleshoot security in a directory services infrastructure.

- Create, analyze, and modify security configurations by using Security Configuration and Analysis and Security Templates.

These Template files offer a user-friendly way of configuring common settings for Windows 2000-based operating systems. For example, instead of searching through the Registry (which is largely undocumented) for specific keys, a systems administrator can choose from a list of common options. The Template file provides a description of the settings, along with information about the Registry key(s) to which the modifications must be made. Templates can be stored and applied to users and computers. For example, we could create three configurations entitled Level 1, Level 2, and Level 3. We may use the Level 3 template for high-level managers and engineers, while the Level 1 and Level 2 templates are used for all other users that require basic functionality.

The overall process for working with the Security Configuration and Analysis tool is as follows:

1. Open or create a Security Database file.

2. Import an existing Template file.

3. Analyze the local computer.

4. Make any setting changes.

5. Save any template changes.

6. Export the new template (optional).

7. Apply the changes to the local computer (optional).

There is no default icon for the *Security Configuration and Analysis utility*. In order to access it, you must manually choose this snap-in from within the Microsoft Management Console (MMC) tool. Exercise 8.4 walks you through the steps required to use the Security Configuration and Analysis utility.

EXERCISE 8.4

Using the Security Configuration and Analysis Utility

In this exercise, you will use the Security Configuration and Analysis utility to create and modify security configurations.

1. Click Start ➤ Run, type **mmc**, and press Enter. This will open a blank MMC.

2. In the Console menu, select Add/Remove Snap-In. Click Add. Select the Security Configuration and Analysis item, and then click Add. Click Close.

3. You will see that the Security Configuration and Analysis snap-in has been added to the configuration. Click OK to continue.

EXERCISE 8.4 *(continued)*

4. Within the MMC, right-click Security Configuration and Analysis, and select Open Database. Change to a local directory on your computer, and create a new Security Database file named `SecurityTest.sdb`. Note the location of this file as you'll need it in later steps. Click OK.

5. Next, you'll be prompted to open a Security Template file. By default, these files are stored within the Security\Templates directory of your Windows NT system root. From the list, select DC Security, and place a check mark in the Clear This Database before Importing box. Click Open to load the Template file.

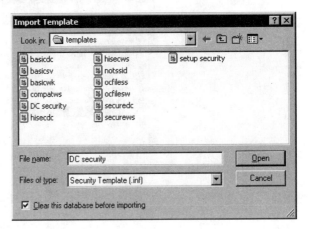

6. Now that we have created a Security Database file and opened a template, we can start performing useful security tasks. Notice that several tasks will be available. To perform an analysis on the security configuration of the local computer, right-click the Security Configuration and Analysis utility, and select Analyze Computer Now. When prompted, enter the path to a local directory with the filename SecurityTest.log. Click OK to begin the analysis process.

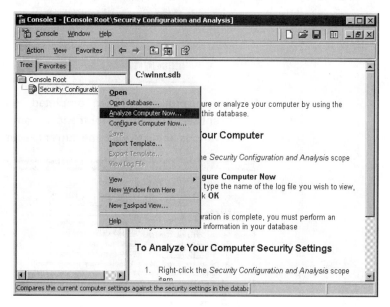

EXERCISE 8.4 *(continued)*

7. You will see the Security Configuration and Analysis utility begin to analyze your computer.

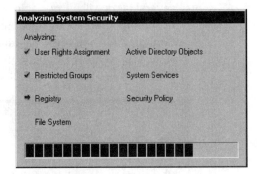

8. When the process has been completed, you will be able to view the current security settings for the local computer. Navigate through the various items to view the current security configuration.

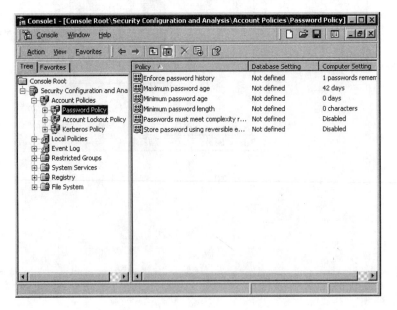

9. To make changes to this template, expand the Password Policy object under the Account Policies object. Double-click the Enforce Password History item. Place a check mark next to the Define This Policy in the Database option, and type **2** for Passwords Remembered. Click OK to make the setting change. Note that this change in setting was not enabled for the local computer—the change was implemented only within the Security Database file.

10. To save the changes to the Security Database file, right-click the Security and Configuration Analysis object, and select Save.

11. To export the current settings to a Template file, right-click the Security and Configuration Analysis object, and select Export Template. You will be prompted for the location and filename to which these settings should be saved. Be sure to choose a meaningful name so that other systems administrators will understand the purpose of this template.

EXERCISE 8.4 *(continued)*

12. So far, the configuration change we made has not yet been applied to any machines. To apply the change to the local computer, right-click the Security and Configuration Analysis object, and select Configure Computer Now. You will be prompted to enter the path for a Log file. Enter any path on the local computer, and specify `SecurityTest2.log` as the filename. Click OK. You will see the settings being applied to the local computer.

13. To quickly view the contents of the Log file for the most recent operation, right-click the Security and Configuration Analysis object, and select View Log.

14. When you are finished, exit the Security and Configuration Analysis tool by closing the MMC.

If any errors occurred during the Security Configuration and Analysis process, the results will be stored in the Log file that was created. Be sure to examine this file for any errors that might be present in your configuration.

Implementing an Audit Policy

One of the most important aspects of controlling security in networked environments is ensuring that only authorized users are able to access specific resources. Although systems administrators often spend much time in managing security permissions, it is almost always possible for a security problem to occur. Sometimes, the best way to find possible security breaches is to actually record the actions taken by specific users. Then, in the case of a security breach (the unauthorized shutdown of a server, for example), systems administrators can examine the log to find the cause of the problem. The Windows 2000 operating system and the Active Directory offer the ability to audit a wide range of actions. In this section, we'll look at how you can implement auditing for the Active Directory.

Microsoft ✓ ***Exam*** ***Objective***

Configure and troubleshoot security in a directory services infrastructure.

- Implement an audit policy.

Monitor and analyze security events.

Overview of Auditing

The act of auditing relates to the recording of specific actions. From a security standpoint, auditing is used to detect any possible misuse of network resources. Although auditing will not necessarily prevent the misuse of resources, it will help determine when security violations occurred (or were attempted). Furthermore, just the fact that others know that you have implemented auditing may prevent them from attempting to circumvent security.

There are several steps that you will need to complete in order to implement auditing using Windows 2000. These steps include the following:

- Configuring the size and storage settings for the audit logs

- Enabling categories of events to audit

- Specifying which objects and actions should be recorded in the audit log

In this section, you'll learn how to complete these steps.

Note that there are trade-offs to implementing auditing. First and foremost, recording auditing information can consume system resources. This can decrease overall system performance and use up valuable disk space. Secondly, auditing many events can make the audit log impractical to view. If too much detail is provided, systems administrators are unlikely to scrutinize all of the recorded events. For these reasons, you should always be sure to find a balance between the level of auditing details provided and the performance management implications of these settings.

Implementing Auditing

Auditing is not an all-or-none type of process. As is the case with security in general, systems administrators must choose specifically which objects and actions they want to audit.

The main categories for auditing include:

- Audit account logon events

- Audit account management

- Audit directory service access

- Audit logon events

- Audit object access

- Audit policy change

- Audit privilege use

- Audit process tracking

- Audit system events

In order to audit access to objects stored within the Active Directory, you must enable the Audit Directory Service Access option. Then, you must specify which objects and actions should be tracked. Exercise 8.5 walks through the steps required to implement auditing of Active Directory objects on domain controllers.

EXERCISE 8.5

Enabling Auditing of Active Directory Objects

In this exercise, you will enable auditing for an Active Directory domain. In order to complete the steps in this exercise, you must have already completed exercise 8.1.

1. Open the Domain Controller Security Policy tool.

EXERCISE 8.5 *(continued)*

2. Expand Security Settings ≻ Local Policies ≻ Audit Policy.

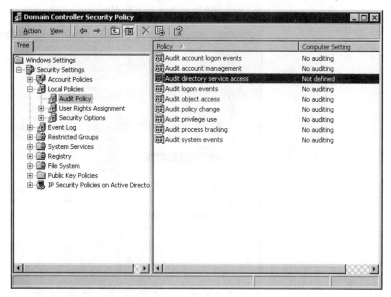

3. Double-click the setting for Audit Directory Service Access. Place a check mark next to the options for Define These Policy Settings, Success, and Failure. Click OK to save the settings.

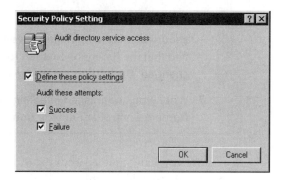

EXERCISE 8.5 *(continued)*

4. Expand Security Settings ➢ Event Log ➢ Settings for Event Logs to see the options associated with the event logs.

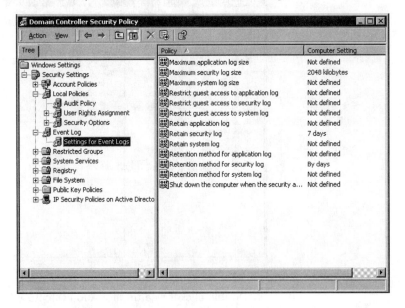

5. Double-click the Maximum Security Log Size item, and set the value to 2048KB. Click OK.

6. Double-click the Retain Security Log item, and specify that events should be overwritten after seven days. Click OK. You will be notified that the Retention Method for Security Log option will also be changed. Click OK to accept the changes.

7. When you are finished enabling auditing options, close the Domain Controller Security Configuration tool.

Once you have enabled auditing of Active Directory objects, it's time to specify exactly which actions and objects should be audited. Exercise 8.6 walks through the steps required to enable auditing for a specific OU.

EXERCISE 8.6

Enabling Auditing for a Specific OU

In this exercise, you will enable auditing for a specific OU. In order to complete the steps in this exercise, you must have already completed Exercise 8.1 and Exercise 8.5.

1. Open the Active Directory Users and Computers tool.

2. To enable auditing for a specific object, right-click the Engineering OU, and select Properties. Select the Group Policy tab.

3. Highlight the Engineering Security Settings Group Policy object, and select Properties. Select the Security tab, and then click Advanced. Select the Auditing tab. You will see the current auditing settings for this Group Policy object.

4. Click the View/Edit button. Notice that you can view and change auditing settings based on the objects and/or properties. To retain the current settings, click OK. To exit the configuration for the Engineering object, click OK three more times.

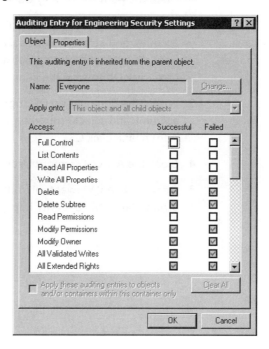

5. When you are finished with the auditing settings, close the Active Directory Users and Computers tool.

Viewing Auditing Information

One of the most important aspects of auditing is regularly monitoring the audit logs. If this step is ignored (as it often is in poorly managed environments), the act of auditing is useless. Fortunately, Windows 2000 includes the *Event Viewer* tool that allows systems administrators to quickly and easily view audited events. Using the filtering capabilities of the Event Viewer, they can find specific events of interest.

Exercise 8.7 walks through the steps required to generate some auditing events and to examine the data collected for these actions.

EXERCISE 8.7

Generating and Viewing Audit Logs

In this exercise, you will perform some actions that will be audited, and then you will view the information recorded within the audit logs. In order to complete this exercise, you must have already completed the steps in Exercise 8.1 and Exercise 8.6.

1. Open the Active Directory Users and Computers tool.

2. Within the Engineering OU, right-click the Bob Engineer User account, and select Properties. Add the middle initial A for this User account, and specify Software Developer in the Description box. Click OK to save the changes.

3. Within the Engineering OU, right-click the Robert Admin User account, and select Properties. Add a description of Engineering IT Admin, and click OK.

4. Close the Active Directory Users and Computers tool.

5. Open the Event Viewer tool from the Administrative Tools program group. Select the Security Log item.

6. You will see a list of audited events categorized under Directory Service Access. Note that you can obtain more details about a specific item by double-clicking it.

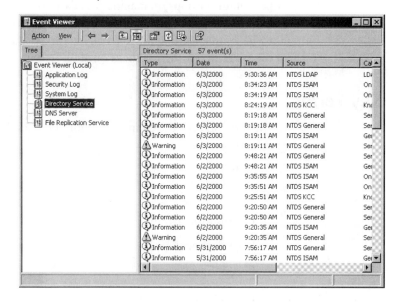

7. To modify the Log file settings, in the right-hand pane of the Computer Management window, right-click the Directory Service Access item, and choose Properties. Change the value for the Maximum Log File Size to 2048KB, and select the Overwrite Events as Needed option. This will allow you to store more audit events in the log and will ensure that events are cleared out of the log as needed. To save the new settings, click OK.

8. When you are finished viewing the security log, close the Computer Management tool.

Summary

In this chapter, we covered the important topic of security as it pertains to the Active Directory. We covered concepts such as Group types, Group scope, default Groups, managing permissions, and using Group Policy for security purposes. Thoroughly understanding each of these topics is important when implementing the Active Directory in a business environment (and when you're preparing for the exam)!

Key Terms

Before you take the exam, you should be familiar with the following terms and concepts:

auditing

Delegation

Distribution groups

Domain Local groups

Event Viewer

Foreign security principals

Global groups

Group Policy

permissions

Security Configuration and Analysis utility

Security groups

Security principals

Security Templates

Universal groups

Review Questions

1. When running in mixed mode, which of the following types of groups *cannot* be used?

    A. Universal groups

    B. Global groups

    C. Domain Local groups

    D. Computer groups

    E. None of the above

2. Which of the following is used to enable auditing for Active Directory objects?

    A. Computer Management tool

    B. Active Directory Users and Computers tool

    C. Active Directory Domains and Trusts tool

    D. Event Viewer tool

    E. All of the above

3. A systems administrator wants to allow another user the ability to change User account information for all users within a specific OU. Which of the following tools would allow them to do this most easily?

    A. Domain Security Policy

    B. Domain Controller Security Policy

    C. Computer Management

    D. Delegation of Control Wizard

    E. None of the above

4. Group Policy can be assigned to which of the following Active Directory objects?

   A. Organizational units (OUs)

   B. Users

   C. Computers

   D. Groups

   E. All of the above

5. The process by which a higher-level security authority grants permissions to other users is known as:

   A. Inheritance

   B. Transfer of control

   C. Delegation

   D. Transfer of ownership

   E. None of the above

6. A systems administrator wants to prevent users from starting or stopping a specific service on domain controllers. Which of the following tools can be used to prevent this from occurring?

   A. Active Directory Users and Computers

   B. Domain Controller Security Policy

   C. Domain Security Policy

   D. Local System Policy

   E. All of the above

7. Which of the following types of groups can contain other groups when operating in native mode?

   A. Universal groups

   B. Domain Local groups

   C. Global groups

   D. Distribution groups

   E. All of the above

8. Which of the following types of groups can contain users from multiple domains?

    A. Universal groups

    B. Domain Local groups

    C. Global groups

    D. Distribution groups

    E. All of the above

9. Which of the following features of the Security Configuration and Analysis tool helps systems administrators apply uniform security policies to users and computers?

    A. Security descriptors

    B. Domain policies

    C. Security Templates

    D. All of the above

10. Which of the following types of groups can be moved between domains?

    A. Universal groups

    B. Domain Local groups

    C. Global groups

    D. Distribution groups

    E. All of the above

11. Which of the following Active Directory objects is not considered a security principal?

    A. Users

    B. Groups

    C. Organizational units (OUs)

    D. Computers

12. Which of the following folders in the Active Directory Users and Computers tool is used when users from outside the forest are granted access to resources within a domain?

    A. Users

    B. Computers

    C. Domain Controllers

    D. Foreign Security Principals

    E. None of the above

13. Members of which of the following built-in local groups are able to bypass file system security for specific functions?

    A. Account Operators

    B. Backup Operators

    C. Guests

    D. Domain Administrators

    E. None of the above

14. Which of the following items in the Administrative Tools program group can be used to view audit logs?

    A. Event Viewer

    B. Computer Management

    C. Active Directory Users and Computers

    D. Both A and B

15. Members of which of the following groups have permissions to perform actions in multiple domains?

    A. Domain Admins

    B. Domain Users

    C. Administrators

    D. Enterprise Admins

    E. All of the above

16. Which of the following types of groups is/are not considered security principals?

   A. Global groups

   B. Domain Local groups

   C. Distribution groups

   D. Universal groups

   E. All of the above

17. To prevent the flow of security permissions from parent containers or objects to child containers or objects, a systems administrator can do which of the following?

   A. Block inheritance.

   B. Delete the parent container.

   C. Rename the parent container.

   D. None of the above.

18. A systems administrator wants to assign another user permissions to make changes to User and Group objects throughout the domain. To which of the following groups should they add the user?

   A. Backup Operators

   B. Account Operators

   C. Enterprise Admins

   D. Domain Admins

   E. All of the above

19. Which of the following objects in the Users folder is disabled by default on domain controllers?

   A. Domain Guests group

   B. Guest user

   C. Cert Publishers

   D. Administrator

   E. None of the above

20. A systems administrator wants to change the Owner of an object. How can they do this?

A. Delete the object and re-create it.

B. Rename the object.

C. Delegate control of the object.

D. Directly change the ownership of the object.

E. None of the above.

Answers to Review Questions

1. A. Universal groups are not available when running in mixed mode.

2. B. The Active Directory Users and Computers tool allows systems administrators to change auditing options and to choose which actions are audited.

3. D. The Delegation of Control Wizard is designed to assist systems administrators in granting specific permissions to other users.

4. A. Group Policy settings are assigned at the OU level and may affect other object types within that OU.

5. C. Delegation is the process of granting permissions to other users. Inheritance is the transfer of permissions and other settings from parent OUs to child OUs.

6. B. The settings made in the Domain Controller Security Policy tool apply only to domain controllers.

7. E. All of these types of groups can contain other groups when operating in native mode.

8. A and B. Universal groups and Domain Local groups can contain members from throughout the forest.

9. C. Through the use of templates, the Security Configuration and Analysis tool allows systems administrators to define various configuration settings and then apply them to various users and computers.

10. A. Universal groups can be moved between domains while all of the other group types must be re-created manually.

11. C. OUs are primarily used to organize objects within the Active Directory and do not function as security principals.

12. D. When resources are made available to users that reside in domains outside of the forest, Foreign Security Principal objects are automatically created.

13. B. Members of the Backup Operators Local group are able to bypass file system security in order to backup and restore files.

14. D. The Windows 2000 event logs can be viewed from within the Event Viewer or the Computer Management icons in the Administrative Tools program group.

15. D. Members of the Enterprise Admins group are given full permissions to manage all domains within an Active Directory forest.

16. C. Distribution groups are often used to organize users for sending e-mail, but they are not security principals.

17. A. This flow of permissions (known as inheritance) can be blocked at any level.

18. B. The user should be added to the Account Operators group. Although membership in the Enterprise Admins or Domain Admins group will provide the user with the requisite permissions, this will exceed the required functionality.

19. B. By default, the Guest user account is disabled on domain controllers.

20. D. An administrator is able to change the ownership of an object.

Chapter

9

Active Directory Optimization and Reliability

MICROSOFT EXAM OBJECTIVES COVERED IN THIS CHAPTER:

✓ **Manage Active Directory performance.**

- Monitor, maintain, and troubleshoot domain controller performance.
- Monitor, maintain, and troubleshoot Active Directory components.

✓ **Back up and restore Active Directory.**

- Perform an authoritative restore of Active Directory.
- Recover from a system failure.

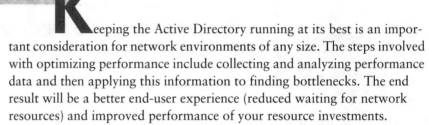

Keeping the Active Directory running at its best is an important consideration for network environments of any size. The steps involved with optimizing performance include collecting and analyzing performance data and then applying this information to finding bottlenecks. The end result will be a better end-user experience (reduced waiting for network resources) and improved performance of your resource investments.

Another important consideration when working with the Active Directory is ensuring that your system information is safely backed up. Backups are useful when data is lost due to system failures, file corruptions, or accidental modifications of information.

In this chapter, we'll look at ways in which you can use Windows 2000's performance monitoring and data protection tools to improve network operations.

Overview of Windows 2000 Performance Monitoring

When it comes to optimizing performance, a commonly used process is just plain trial and error. Although this can sometimes lead to better results, it depends on the validity of the performance measurements you have made. Does the server just *seem* to be operating faster? If that's your only guideline, it's probably time that you started collecting some hard statistics to back up that feeling! In this chapter, we'll cover tools and methods for measuring performance in Windows 2000. Specifically, we'll focus on domain controllers and the Active Directory. Before we dive into the technical details, however, we should thoroughly understand what we're trying to accomplish and how we'll meet this goal.

Microsoft Exam Objective

Manage Active Directory performance.

- Monitor, maintain, and troubleshoot domain controller performance.

- Monitor, maintain, and troubleshoot Active Directory components.

For a more detailed discussion on the topics covered by the "Manage Active Directory performance" subobjectives, see the section "Monitoring Active Directory Components" later in this chapter.

The first step in any performance optimization strategy is to be able to accurately and consistently measure performance. The insight that you'll gain from monitoring factors, such as network utilization, will be extremely useful in measuring the effects of any changes.

The overall process of performance monitoring usually involves the following steps:

1. Establish a baseline of current performance.

2. Identify bottleneck(s).

3. Plan for and implement changes.

4. Measure the effects of the changes.

5. Repeat the process, based on business needs.

Note that the performance optimization process is never really finished, since you can always try to tweak more performance out of your machines. Before you get discouraged (or change your job title to Performance Optimizer), realize that you'll reach some level of performance that you consider to be acceptable enough that it's not worth the additional effort it'll take to optimize performance further.

Now that we have an idea of the overall process, let's focus on how changes should be made. Some important ideas to keep in mind when monitoring performance include the following:

Plan changes carefully. When working in an easy-to-use GUI-based operating system like the Windows 2000 platform, it's too easy to just remove a check mark here or there and then retest the performance. You should resist the urge to do this, since some changes can cause large decreases in performance or can have an impact on functionality. Before you make haphazard changes (especially on production servers), take the time to learn about, plan for, and test your changes.

Make only one change at a time.   The golden rule of scientific experiments is that you should always keep track of as many variables as possible. When the topic is server optimization, this roughly translates into making only one change at a time.

One of the problems with making multiple system changes is that, although you may have improved performance overall, it's hard to determine exactly *which* change created the positive effects. It's also possible, for example, that changing one parameter increased performance greatly while changing another decreased it slightly. While the overall result was an increase in performance, the second, performance-reducing option should be identified so the same mistake is not made again. To reduce the chance of obtaining misleading results, always try to make only one change at a time.

Ensure consistency in measurements.   When monitoring performance, consistency in measurements is extremely important. You should strive toward having repeatable and accurate measurements. Controlling variables, such as system load at various times during the day, can help.

Let's assume, for instance, that we want to measure the number of transactions that we can simulate on the accounting database server within an hour. The results would be widely different if we ran the test during the month-end accounting close versus if we ran the test on a Sunday morning. By running the same tests when the server is under a relatively static amount of load, we will be able to get more accurate measurements.

Utilize a test environment.   Making haphazard changes in a production environment can cause serious problems. These problems will likely outweigh any benefits you could receive from making performance tweaks. To avoid negative impacts on users, attempt to make as many changes as possible within a test environment. When this isn't possible, be sure to make changes during off-peak hours. After all, the goal is to *improve* performance!

Maintain a performance history.   Earlier in this chapter, we mentioned that the performance optimization cycle is a continuous improvement process. Since many changes may be made over time, it is important to keep track of the changes that have been made and the results you experienced. Documenting this knowledge will prevent the age-old question, "What did I do to solve this last time?"

As you can see, there are a lot of factors to keep in mind when optimizing performance. Although this might seem like a lot of factors to remember, most systems administrators are probably aware of the "rules." Fortunately, the tools included with Windows 2000 can help in organizing the process and taking measurements. Now that we have a good overview of the process, let's move on to looking at the tools that can be used to set it in motion!

Using Windows 2000 Performance Tools

As performance monitoring and optimization are vital functions in network environments of any size, Windows 2000 includes several performance-related tools. The first and most useful is the Windows 2000 *System Monitor*. The Windows 2000 System Monitor was designed to allow users and systems administrators to monitor performance statistics for various operating system parameters. Specifically, information about CPU, memory, disk, and network resources can be collected, stored, and analyzed using this tool. By collecting and analyzing performance values, systems administrators will be able to identify many potential problems. As we'll see later in this chapter, the System Monitor can also be used to monitor the performance of the Active Directory and its various components.

The Windows 2000 System Monitor itself is an ActiveX control that can be placed within other applications. Examples of applications that can host the System Monitor control include Web browsers and client programs like Microsoft Word or Microsoft Excel. This can make it very easy for applications developers and systems administrators to incorporate the System Monitor into their own tools and applications.

For more common performance monitoring functions, you'll want to use the built-in Microsoft Management Console (MMC) version of the System Monitor. You can easily access the System Monitor by opening the Performance icon in the Administrative Tools program group. This will launch the MMC and will load and initialize the System Monitor.

There are many different methods of monitoring performance when using the System Monitor. One method is to look at a snapshot of current activity for a few of the most important counters. This method allows you to find areas of potential bottlenecks and monitor the load on your servers at a certain point in time. You can also save the information to a log file for historical reporting and later analysis. This type of information is useful, for example, if you want to compare the load on your servers from three months ago to the current load. We'll take a closer look at this method and many others as we examine the System Monitor in more detail.

In this section, we'll cover the basics of working with the Windows 2000 System Monitor and performance tools. Then, in the following section, we'll apply these tools and techniques when monitoring the performance of the Active Directory.

Choosing Counters

The first step in monitoring performance is to decide *what* you want to monitor. In Windows 2000, the operating system and related services include hundreds of performance statistics that can be tracked easily. All of these performance statistics fall into three main categories that you can choose to measure. These categories are as follows:

Objects   An object within the System Monitor is a collection of various performance statistics that you can monitor. Objects are based on various areas of system resources. For example, there are objects for the processor and memory, as well as for specific services such as Web service. Later in this chapter, we'll see how the Windows NT Directory Service (NTDS) object can be used to monitor performance of the Active Directory.

Counters   Counters are the actual parameters that are measured by the System Monitor. They are specific items that are grouped within objects. For example, within the Processor object, there is a counter for "% Processor Time." This counter displays one type of detailed information about the Processor object (specifically, the amount of total CPU time that is being used by all of the processes on the system).

Instances   Some counters will also have instances. An instance further identifies which performance parameter the counter is measuring. A simple example is a server with two CPUs. If you decide that you want to monitor processor usage (the Processor object) and, specifically, that you're interested in utilization (the "% Total Utilization" counter), you must still specify *which* CPU(s) you want to measure. In this example, you would have the choice of monitoring either of the two CPUs or a total value for both (using the Total instance).

You can specify which objects, counters, and instances you want to monitor by quickly and easily adding them to the System Monitor. Figure 9.1

shows the various options that are available when adding new counters to monitor using the System Monitor.

FIGURE 9.1   Adding a new System Monitor counter

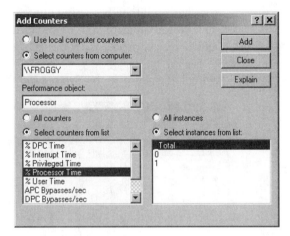

The exact items that you will be able to monitor will be based on your hardware and software configuration. For example, if you have not installed and configured the Internet Information Server (IIS) service, the options available within the Web Server objects will not be available. Or, if you have multiple network adapters or CPUs in the server, you will have the option to view each instance separately or as part of the total value.

We'll cover the details of which counters are generally most useful later in this chapter.

Viewing Performance Information

The Windows 2000 System Monitor was designed to show information in a clear and easy-to-understand format. Based on the type of performance information you're viewing, however, you might want to change the display. There are three main views that can be used to review statistics and information on performance. They are as follows:

Graph View   The Graph view is the default display that is presented when you first access the Windows 2000 System Monitor. The chart displays values using the vertical axis and time using the horizontal axis. It is useful for displaying values over a period of time and for visually seeing the changes in these values over that time period. Each of the points that are plotted on the graph is based on an average value calculated during the sample interval for the measurement being made. For example, you may notice overall CPU utilization starting at a low value at the beginning of the chart and then becoming much higher during later measurements. This would indicate that the server has become busier (specifically, with CPU-intensive processes). Figure 9.2 provides an example of the Graph view.

FIGURE 9.2 Viewing information in the System Monitor Graph view

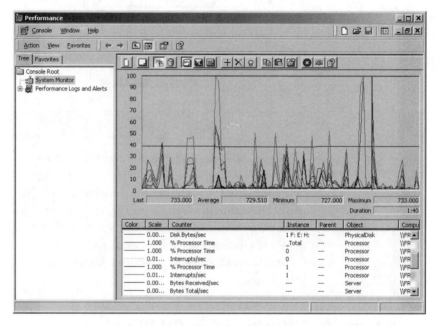

Histogram View   The Histogram view shows performance statistics and information using a set of relative bar charts. The Histogram is useful for viewing a snapshot of the latest value for a given counter. For example, if we were interested in viewing a snapshot of current system performance statistics during each refresh interval, the length of each of the bars in the display would give us a visual representation of each value. It would also allow us to visually compare each measurement relative to the others. You can also set the histogram to display an average measurement as well as minimum and maximum thresholds. Figure 9.3 shows a typical Histogram view.

FIGURE 9.3 Viewing information in the System Monitor Histogram view

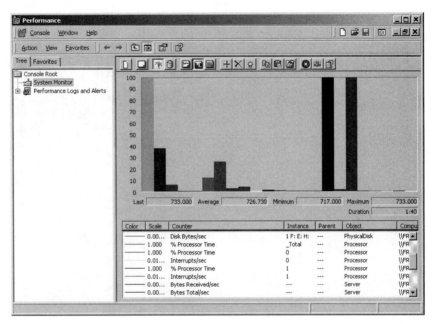

Report View Like the Histogram view, the Report view shows performance statistics based on the latest measurement or displays an average measurement as well as minimum and maximum thresholds. It is most useful for determining exact values, since it provides information in numeric terms unlike the Chart and Histogram views, which provide information graphically. Figure 9.4 provides an example of the type of information you'll see in the Report view.

FIGURE 9.4 Viewing information in the System Monitor Report view

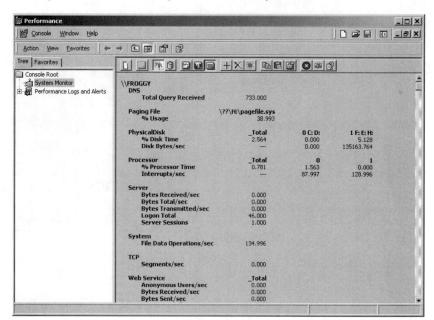

In the System Monitor, the same objects, counters, and instances may be displayed in each of the three views. This allows systems administrators to quickly and easily define the information they want to see once and then choose how it will be displayed based on specific needs.

Managing System Monitor Properties

You can specify additional settings for viewing performance information within the properties of the System Monitor. You can access these options by clicking the Properties button in the task bar or by right-clicking the System Monitor display and selecting Properties. The various tabs include the following:

General   On the General tab (shown in Figure 9.5), you can specify several options that relate to the System Monitor view. First, you can choose from among the Graph, Histogram, and Report views. Next, you can enable or disable legends (which display information about the various counters), the value bar, and the toolbar.

FIGURE 9.5   General System Monitor properties

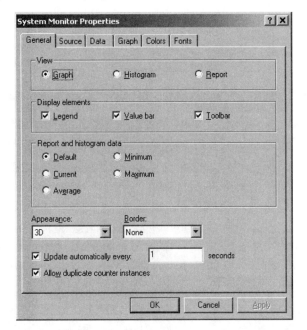

For the Report and Histogram views, you can choose which type of information is displayed. Options include default, current, average, minimum, and maximum. It's important to check these settings based on the type of information you're viewing since it will make a big difference in the type of data being collected. These options are not available for the Graph view, since the Graph view displays an average value over a period of time (the sample interval).

With the General tab, you can also choose the appearance (flat or 3-D) and border options for the display. Next, an important setting is the update interval. By default, the display will be set to update every second. If you want the update frequency to decrease, you should increase the number of seconds between updates. The final option on the General tab allows you to specify whether or not you want to allow the same counter to be displayed twice in the same view.

Source   On the Source tab, you can specify the source for the performance information you would like to view. Options include current activity (the default setting) or data from a log file. If you choose to analyze information from a log file, you can also specify the time range for which you want to view statistics. We'll cover these selections in the next section.

Data   The Data tab (shown in Figure 9.6) displays a list of the counters that have been added to the System Monitor display. These counters apply to the Chart, Histogram, and Report views. Using this interface, you can also add or remove any of the counters and change properties such as the width and style of the line and the scale used for display.

FIGURE 9.6   Viewing System Monitor Counter settings

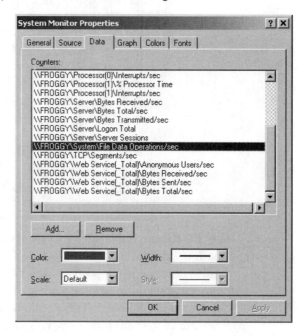

Graph   On the Graph tab, you can specify certain options that will allow you to customize the display of the System Monitor views. Specifically, you can add a title for the graph, specify a label for the vertical axis, choose to display grids, and specify the vertical scale range (see Figure 9.7).

FIGURE 9.7   Specifying System Monitor Graph settings

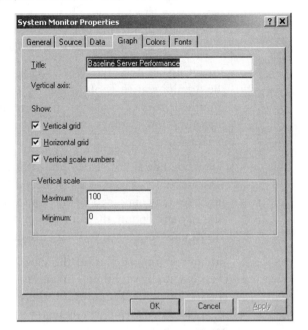

Colors   Using the Colors tab, you can specify the colors for the areas of the display such as the background and foreground.

Fonts   On the Fonts tab, you can specify the fonts that are used to display counter values in the System Monitor views. This is a useful option, and you can change settings to find a suitable balance between readability and the amount of information shown on one screen.

Now that we have an idea of the types of information System Monitor tracks and how this data is displayed, let's look at another feature—saving and analyzing performance data.

Saving and Analyzing Data with Performance Logs and Alerts

One of the most important aspects of monitoring performance is that it should be done over a given period of time. So far, we have discussed how the System Monitor can be used to view statistics in real time. We have, however, also alluded to using the System Monitor to save data for later analysis. Now let's take a look at how this is done.

When viewing information in the System Monitor, you have two main options with respect to the data on display. They are as follows:

View Current Activity When you first open the Performance icon from the Administrative Tools folder, the default option is to view data obtained from current system information. This method of viewing measures and displays various real-time statistics on the system's performance.

View Log File Data This option allows you to view information that was previously saved to a log file. Although the objects, counters, and instances may appear to be the same as those viewed using the View Current Activity option, the information itself was actually captured at a previous point in time and stored into a log file.

So how are the log files for the View Log File Data option created? The process is actually very simple. You simply access the Performance Logs and Alerts section of the Windows 2000 Performance tool. Once there, you'll see three types of items available that allow you to customize how the data is collected in the log files. Let's take a look at each type of item in turn:

Counter Logs Counter logs record performance statistics based on the various objects, counters, and instances available in the System Monitor. The values are updated based on a time interval setting and are saved to a file for later analysis.

Trace Logs Some types of information are better monitored based on the occurrence of specific events instead of the passage of specified time intervals. *Trace logs* record performance information to files based on system events. There are several trace log types that can be included in this option by default. The following types are included:

- Windows 2000 Kernel Trace Provider

- Active Directory: Netlogon

- Active Directory: SAM

- Active Directory: Kerberos

- Windows NT Active Directory Service

- Local Security Authority (LSA)

Additionally, trace logs can be examined and analyzed through the use of third-party products. These third-party programs can include custom trace log providers for use with the Windows 2000 Performance Monitoring tools. Figure 9.8 shows the types of information that can be recorded using trace logs.

FIGURE 9.8   The available settings for trace logs

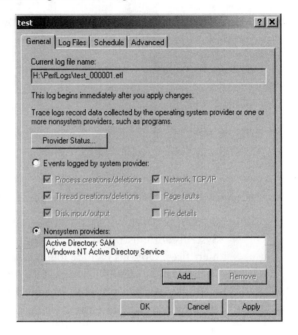

Alerts   *Alerts* monitor the standard objects, counters, and instances that are available with the Windows 2000 Performance Monitoring tools. However, they are designed to take specific actions when certain performance statistic thresholds are exceeded. For example, we could create an alert that fires every time the CPU utilization on the local server exceeds 95 percent (as shown in Figure 9.9).

FIGURE 9.9 Setting an alert on processor utilization

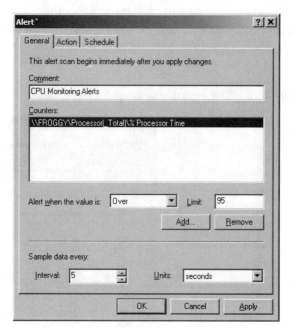

Systems administrators can configure various events to occur when an alert fires. Options include logging an entry in the application event log (which can be viewed using Event Viewer), sending a network message to a specific user or computer, starting a performance data log operation, or running a specific program (see Figure 9.10).

FIGURE 9.10   Setting alert actions

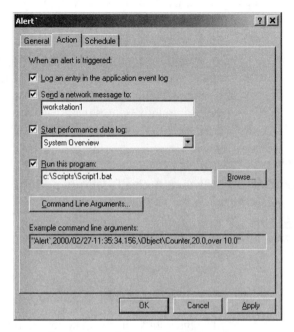

When saving performance information to files, there are two main logging methods that can be used:

Circular Logging   In circular logging, the data that is stored within a file is overwritten as new data is entered into the log. This is a useful method of logging if you only want to record information for a certain time frame (for example, the last four hours). Circular logging also conserves disk space by ensuring that the performance log file will not continue to grow over certain limits.

Linear Logging   In linear logging, data is never deleted from the log files, and new information is added to the end of the log file. The result is a log file that continually grows, but the benefit is that historical information is retained.

Now that we have an idea of the types of functions that are supported by the Windows 2000 Performance tool, let's move on to look at how this information can be applied to the task at hand—monitoring and optimizing the Active Directory.

Monitoring Active Directory Components

The Active Directory utilizes many different types of server resources in order to function properly. For example, it uses memory to increase the speed of accessing data, CPU time to process information, and network resources to communicate with clients and Active Directory domain controllers. Additionally, it uses disk space for storing the Active Directory data store itself and the Global Catalog (GC).

Microsoft ✓ *Exam* *Objective*	**Manage Active Directory performance.** • Monitor, maintain, and troubleshoot domain controller performance. • Monitor, maintain, and troubleshoot Active Directory components.

The types and amount of system resources consumed by the Active Directory is based on many factors. Some of the more obvious factors include the size of the Active Directory data store and how many users are supported in the environment. Other factors include the replication topology and the domain architecture. As you can see, all of the design issues we discussed in earlier chapters of this book will play a role in the overall performance of domain controllers and the Active Directory.

So how do all of these Active Directory requirements impact the server overall? That's a great question that all systems administrators should ask. Although the answer isn't always simple to determine, the System Monitor is usually the right tool for the job. In this section, we'll look at how you can use Windows 2000's performance tools to monitor and optimize the performance of the Active Directory.

Monitoring Domain Controller Performance

When it comes to performance, domain controllers have the same basic resource requirements as the other machines in your environment. The major areas to monitor for computers include the following:

- Processor (CPU) time

- Memory

- Disk I/O
- Disk space
- Network utilization

When you're deciding to monitor performance, you should carefully determine which statistics will be of most use. For example, if you're measuring the performance of a database server, CPU time and memory may be the most important. However, some applications may have high disk I/O and network requirements. Choosing what to monitor can be difficult since there are so many different options available. Table 9.1 provides an example of some common System Monitor counters and objects you might want to choose.

TABLE 9.1 Useful Counters for Monitoring Domain Controller Performance

Object	Counter	Notes
Memory	Available MB	Displays the number of megabytes of physical memory (RAM) that is available for use by processes.
Memory	Pages/sec	Indicates the number of pages of memory that must be read from or written to disk per second. A high number may indicate that more memory is needed.
Network Interface	Bytes Total/Second	Measures the total number of bytes sent to or received by the specified network interface card.
Network Interface	Packets Received Errors	Specifies the number of received network packets that contained errors. A high number may indicate that there are problems with the network connection.

TABLE 9.1 Useful Counters for Monitoring Domain Controller Performance *(continued)*

Object	Counter	Notes
Network Segment	% Net Utilization	Specifies the percentage of total network resources being consumed. A high value may indicate network congestion. NOTE: You must have the Network Monitor agent installed on the local computer in order to view this counter.
Paging File	% Usage	Indicates the amount of the Windows virtual memory file (paging file) that is in use. If this is a large number, the machine may benefit from a RAM upgrade.
Physical Disk	Disk Reads/sec Disk Writes/sec	Indicates the amount of disk activity on the server.
Physical Disk	Avg. Disk Queue Length	Indicates the number of disk read or write requests that are waiting in order to access the disk. If this value is high, disk I/O could potentially be a bottleneck.
Processor	% Processor Time	Indicates the overall CPU load on the server. High values generally indicate processor-intensive tasks. In machines with multiple processors, each processor can be monitored individually, or a total value can be viewed.

TABLE 9.1 Useful Counters for Monitoring Domain Controller Performance *(continued)*

Object	Counter	Notes
Server	Bytes Total/sec	Specifies the number of bytes sent by the Server service on the local machine. A high value usually indicates that the server is responsible for fulfilling many outbound data requests (such as a file/print server).
Server	Server Sessions	Indicates the number of users that may be accessing the server.
System	Processor Queue Length	Specifies the number of threads that are awaiting CPU time. A high number might indicate that a reduction in available CPU resources is creating a potential bottleneck.
System	Processes	Indicates the number of processes currently running on the system.
Web Service	Bytes Total/sec	Indicates the number of bytes of data that has been transmitted to or from the local Web service. This option is only available if Internet Information Server (IIS) is installed and the Web server is running.

Keep in mind that this list is not by any means a complete list of the items of interest—it's just a good guideline for some of the more common items that you may want to include. The key to determining what to monitor is to first understand the demands imposed by applications or services and then make appropriate choices. When monitored and interpreted properly, these performance values can be extremely useful in providing insight into overall system performance.

Now that we've covered the topic of domain controller performance, let's look at the performance of the Active Directory itself.

Monitoring Active Directory Performance with System Monitor

As you may have already guessed, the Windows 2000 operating system automatically tracks many performance statistics that are related to the Active Directory. You can easily access these same statistics by using the System Monitor. The specific counters you'll want to monitor are part of the NTDS object and are based on several different functions of the Active Directory, including those that follow:

- The Address Book (AB)

- The Directory Replication Agent (DRA)

- The Directory Service (DS)

- The Key Distribution Center (KDC)

- The Lightweight Directory Access Protocol (LDAP)

- The NTLM Authentications

- The Security Accounts Manager (SAM)

- The Extended Directory Services (XDS)

Each of these objects can be useful when monitoring specific aspects of the Active Directory. The specific counters you choose to monitor will depend on the aspects of Active Directory performance you're planning to examine. For example, if you want to measure performance statistics related to Active Directory replication (covered in Chapter 6, "Configuring Sites and Managing Replication"), you will probably want to monitor the Directory Replication Agent counters. Similarly, if you're interested in performance loads generated by Windows NT computers, you will want to monitor NTLM authentications and the Secure Accounts Manager.

Perhaps the best way to learn about the various types of objects, counters, and instances that are related to the Active Directory is by actually measuring these values and saving them for analysis. Exercise 9.1 walks you through the steps of working with various features of the Windows 2000 System Monitor.

EXERCISE 9.1

Monitoring Domain Controller and Active Directory Performance with Windows 2000 System Monitor

In this exercise, you will use various features of the Windows 2000 System Monitor to analyze performance information on a Windows 2000 domain controller.

1. Open the Performance tool from the Administrative Tools program group.

2. In the left pane, right-click the System Monitor item and select Rename. Type **Domain Controller Performance**, and press Enter.

3. Click the Add Counter button (the button with the "+" sign). Select Use Local Computer Counters. Choose the Processor object, and then click Select Counters from List. Select the % Processor Time counter and the _Total instance. Note that you can click the Explain button to find more information about the various parameters that are available. Click the Add button to add the counter to the chart.

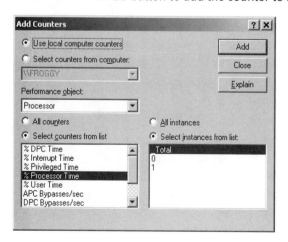

4. Add the following counters to the display by using the same process as in step 3.

Counter	Object	Instance
Total Query Received	DNS	N/A
Packets Sent in Bytes	FileReplicaConn	N/A
Pages/sec	Memory	N/A
Page Faults/sec	Memory	N/A
DRA Inbound Properties Total/sec	NTDS	N/A
DRA Outbound Bytes Total/sec	NTDS	N/A
DS % Searches from LDAP	NTDS	N/A
DS Directory Reads/sec	NTDS	N/A
DS Directory Searches/sec	NTDS	N/A
LDAP Client Sessions	NTDS	N/A
NTLM Authentications	NTDS	N/A
% Usage	Paging File	_Total
% Disk Time	Physical Disk	_Total
Bytes Total/sec	Server	N/A
File Data Operations/sec	System	N/A
Bytes Total/sec	SMTP Server	_Total

5. When you are finished adding these counters, click the Close button.

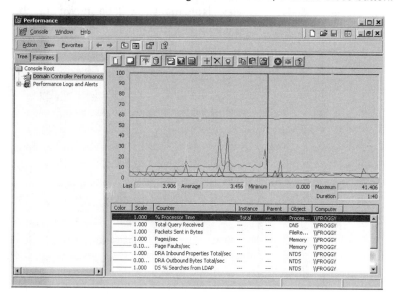

6. Click the View Histogram button to view information in the Histogram view. Click the various counters in the bottom pane of the display to view the actual statistical values for last, average, minimum, and maximum.

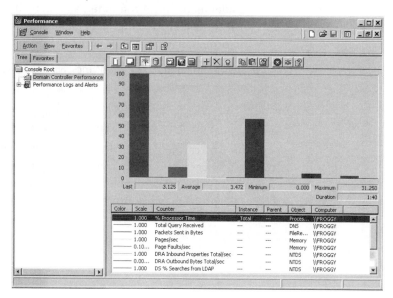

7. Click the View Report button to view information in the Report view. Note that you will be shown only the latest values for each of the counters that have been selected.

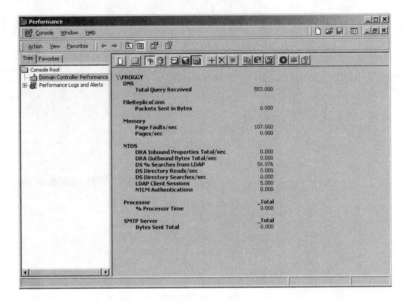

8. Click the View Chart button to return to the Graph view. Right-click the chart, and select Save As. Save the chart as a Web page to a folder on the local computer, and name it Domain Controller Performance.htm. You can open this file later if you want to record information for the same counters.

9. When finished, close the Windows 2000 System Monitor.

It is useful to have a set of performance monitor counters saved to files so you can quickly and easily monitor the items of interest. For example, you may want to create a System Monitor file that includes statistics related to database services while another focuses on network utilization. In that way, whenever a performance problem occurs, you can quickly determine the cause of the problem (without having to create a System Monitor chart from scratch).

Monitoring Active Directory Performance Using Performance Logs and Alerts

In addition to using the System Monitor functionality of the Windows 2000 Performance tool, you can also monitor Active Directory performance statistics by using the *Performance Logs* and Alerts functionality. Exercise 9.2 walks you through the steps for using these features to monitor the Active Directory.

EXERCISE 9.2

Using Performance Logs and Alerts to Monitor Active Directory Performance

In this exercise, you will use the Performance Logs and Alerts features of the Windows 2000 Performance tool. Specifically, you will create a counter log file, record performance statistics, and then later analyze this information using the System Monitor. In order to complete the steps in this exercise, you must have first completed the steps in Exercise 9.1.

1. Open the Performance tool from the Administrative Tools program group.

2. Under Performance Logs and Alerts, right-click Counter Logs and select New Log Settings From. Select the `Domain Controller Performance.htm` file that you created in Exercise 9.1.

3. You will see a warning that notifies you that some settings will be set at their defaults. Click OK to continue.

4. For the name of the new counter log, type **Domain Controller Log** and click OK. You will see that the default counters from the System Monitor settings are automatically added to this counter log. On the General tab, set the refresh interval to one second.

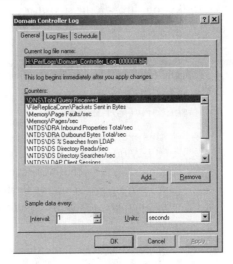

5. Click the Log Files tab. Verify that the log filename and location are appropriate. Also, note that you have an option to automatically generate log filenames. Leave the default setting at nnnnnn and the start number at one. Change the log file type to Binary Circular File and verify that the log file size is limited to 1000KB.

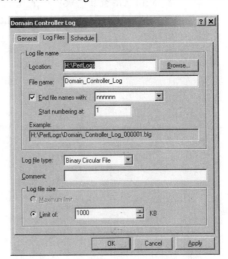

6. Click the Schedule tab and select Manually (Using the Shortcut Menu) for both the Start Log and Stop Log options. Leave all other settings at their defaults.

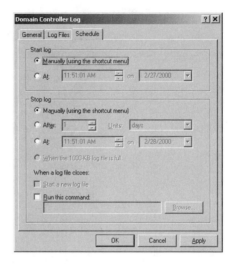

7. Click OK to create the counter log.

8. To start recording data for the counter log, right-click the Domain Controller Log item in the right windowpane and select Start. You will notice that the icon turns green. If your computer is not actively working (such as one in a test environment), you can simulate activity by running applications and searching the Active Directory.

9. Wait at least two minutes for the data collection to occur, and then right-click the Domain Controller Log item and select Stop. The icon will turn red.

10. Click the System Monitor in the left pane, and click the View Log File Data button. Select the file named Domain_Controller_Log_ 000001.log from the directory in which you stored the counter data, and click Open. The Graph view will automatically be populated.

11. To filter the values displayed, right-click the chart and select Properties. On the Source tab, change the Time Range values to view only a specific amount of data. Note that you can only choose times that are within the sampling interval. Click OK to restrict the data.

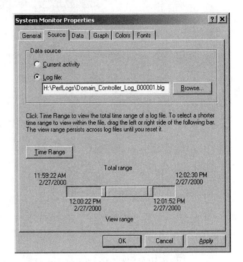

12. Examine the Chart, Histogram, and Report views. When finished, close the System Monitor.

By saving historical performance information, you can get a good idea of how your systems have performed over time. The next time your users complain about slow performance, you'll have some hard statistics to help you to determine the problem!

Other Performance Monitoring Tools

The System Monitor allows you to monitor various different parameters of the Windows 2000 operating system and associated services and applications. However, there are three other tools that can be used for monitoring performance in Windows 2000. They are the *Network Monitor*, the Event Viewer, and the *Task Manager*. All three of these tools are useful for monitoring different areas of overall system performance and for examining details related to specific system events. In this section, we'll take a quick look at these tools and how they can best be used.

The Network Monitor

Although the System Monitor is a great tool for viewing overall network performance statistics, it doesn't give you much insight into what types of network traffic are traveling on the wire. That's where the Network Monitor comes in. There are two main components to the Network Monitor: the Network Monitor Agent and the Network Monitor tool itself.

The Network Monitor Agent is available for use with Windows 2000 Professional and Server computers. You can install it by using the Add/Remove Programs Control Panel applet. It allows for the tracking of network packets. When you install the Network Monitor Agent, you will also be able to access the Network Segment System Monitor counter.

On Windows 2000 Server computers, you'll see the Network Monitor icon appear in the Administrative Tools program group. You can use the Network Monitor tool to capture data as it travels on your network (see Figure 9.11).

The version of Network Monitor that is available for free with Windows 2000 Server only allows the capture of information destined to or from the local computer. The full version of Network Monitor is available with Systems Management Server (SMS). This version places the network adapter in promiscuous mode and allows it to capture all data transferred on the network. For more information, see www.microsoft.com/management.

FIGURE 9.11   Viewing performance statistics using the Network Monitor

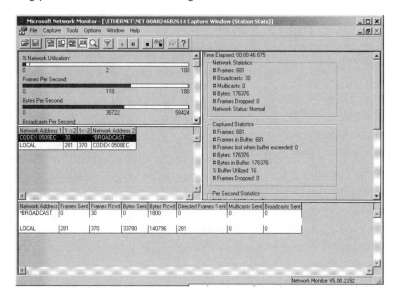

Once you have captured the data of interest, you can save it to a capture file or further analyze it using the Network Monitor. Figure 9.12 shows the level of detail that can be obtained by examining the packets that have been captured. Experienced network and systems administrators can use this information to determine how applications are communicating and the types of data that are being passed via the network.

FIGURE 9.12 Displaying the details of network packets using the Network Monitor

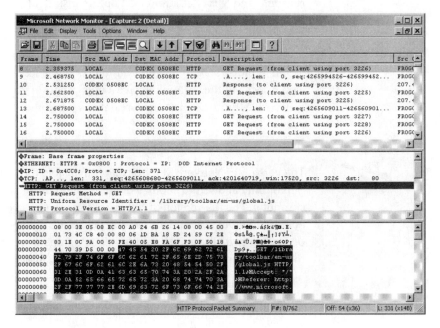

The Task Manager

The System Monitor is designed to allow you to monitor specific aspects of system performance over time. But what do you do if you want to get a quick snapshot of what the local system is doing? Clearly, creating a System Monitor chart, adding counters, and choosing a view is overkill. Fortunately, the Windows 2000 Task Manager has been designed to provide a quick overview of important system performance statistics without requiring any configuration. Better yet, it's always readily available.

The Task Manager can be easily accessed in several ways, including the following methods:

- Click Start ➢ Run, and type **taskmgr**

- Right-click the Windows taskbar, and then click Task Manager

- Press Ctrl+Alt+Del, and then select Task Manager

- Press Ctrl+Shift+Esc

Each of these methods makes accessing a snapshot of the current system performance just a few short steps away.

Once you access the Task Manager, you will see the following three tabs:

Applications   The Applications tab shows you a list of the applications currently running on the local computer. This is a good place to check to determine which programs are running on the system. It is also useful for shutting down any applications that are marked as [Not Responding] (meaning that either the application has crashed or that it is performing operations and not responding to Windows 2000).

Processes   The Processes tab shows you all of the processes that are currently running on the local computer. By default, you'll be able to view how much CPU time and memory are being used by a particular process. By clicking any of the columns, you can quickly sort by the data values in that particular column. This is useful, for example, if you want to find out which processes are using the most memory on your server.

By accessing the objects in the View menu, you can add additional columns to the Processes tab. Figure 9.13 shows a list of the current processes running on a Windows 2000 Server computer.

FIGURE 9.13 Viewing process statistics and information using the Task Manager

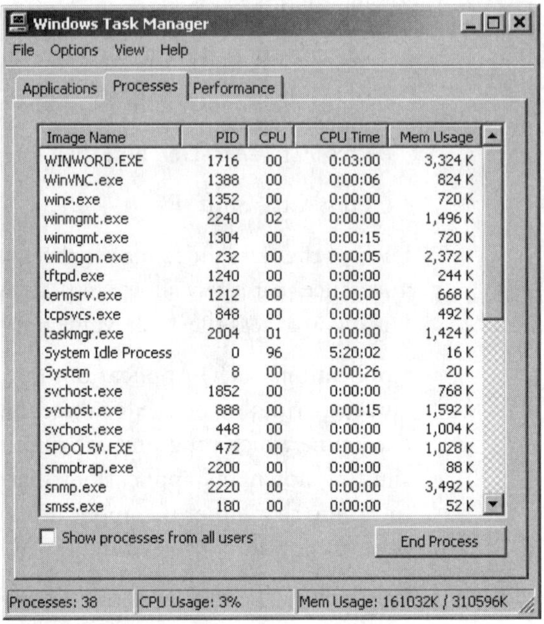

Performance One of the problems with using the System Monitor to get a quick snapshot of system performance is that you have to add counters to a chart. Most systems administrators (myself included!) are too busy to take the time to do this when all that is needed is basic CPU and memory information. That's where the Performance tab of the Task Manager comes in. Using the Performance tab, you can view details about how memory is allocated on the computer and how much of the CPU is utilized (see Figure 9.14).

FIGURE 9.14   Viewing CPU and memory performance information using the Task Manager

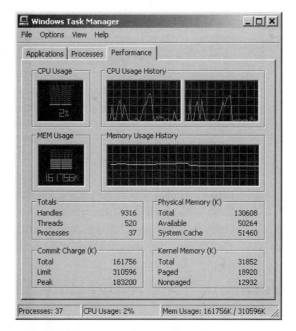

As you can see, the Task Manager is very useful for quickly providing important information about the system. Once you get used to using the Task Manager, you won't be able to get by without it!

The Event Viewer

The Event Viewer is also useful for monitoring information regarding the Active Directory. Specifically, the Directory Service log can be used to view any information, warnings, or alerts related to the proper functioning of the directory services. For example, if there is an error in the Active Directory configuration that is preventing replication between domain controllers, you will see specific events and information that can help narrow down the problem. Therefore, the Event Viewer is an excellent tool when troubleshooting problems in the behavior of the Active Directory.

In addition to the use of the Directory Service log, you can use the application and system logs to monitor other aspects of the system. In general, you should make it a habit to routinely monitor these logs for any warnings or errors.

Optimizing the Active Directory

Using the Active Directory performance statistics that you gather, you can identify areas of potential bottlenecks. The specific counters and acceptable values that you use will, however, be based on your specific hardware, software, network, and business requirements. In general, the statistics available via the System Monitor are useful for determining if a hardware upgrade will be useful or if some configuration options should be changed. The specific types of changes that can be made must be evaluated based on an Active Directory subsystem.

Throughout this book, we have included information on optimizing specific Active Directory performance parameters as they pertain to the various topics covered. For example, we covered the details related to monitoring DNS in Chapter 2, "Integrating DNS with the Active Directory," and we'll cover the specifics related to monitoring software deployment in Chapter 11, "Software Deployment through Group Policy."

Troubleshooting Active Directory Performance Monitoring

Monitoring performance is not always an easy process. As I mentioned earlier, the act of performance monitoring can use up system resources. One of the problems that may then occur is that the System Monitor is not able to obtain performance statistics and information quickly enough. If this occurs, you'll receive an error message similar to that shown in Figure 9.15. In this case, the suggestion is to increase the sample interval. This will reduce the number of statistics System Monitor has to record and display and may prevent the loss of any performance information.

FIGURE 9.15 A System Monitor error message

Sometimes, when you're viewing performance information in the Chart or Histogram view, the data is either too small (the bar or line is too close to the baseline) or too large (the bar or line is above the maximum value). In either case, you'll want to adjust the scale for the counter so that you can accurately see information in the display. For example, if the scale for the number of logons is 1 when it displays values from 0–100 and you frequently have more than 100 users per server, you might want to change the scale to a value less than1. If you choose one-tenth, you will be able to accurately see up to 1,000 user logons in the Chart and Histogram views. You can adjust the scale by right-clicking the properties of the System Monitor display, selecting Properties, and then accessing the Data tab.

Troubleshooting Reliability

The Windows 2000 operating system platform has been designed to provide high availability and uptime for mission-critical tasks. Occasionally, however, you might experience intermittent server crashes on one or more of the domain controllers or other computers in your environment.

The most common cause of such problems is a hardware configuration issue. Poorly written device drivers and unsupported hardware can cause problems with system stability. Similarly, a failed hardware component (such as system memory) can cause problems, as well. Usually, third-party hardware vendors provide utility disks with their computers that can be used for performing hardware diagnostics on machines. This is a good first step to resolving intermittent server crashes.

When these utility disks are used in combination with the troubleshooting tips provided in this and other chapters of this book, you should be able to pinpoint most Active Directory-related problems that might occur on your network.

Backup and Recovery of the Active Directory

If you have deployed the Active Directory in your network environment, there's a good chance that your users depend on it to function properly in order to do their jobs. From network authentications to file access to print and Web services, the Active Directory can be a mission-critical component of your business. Therefore, the importance of backing up the Active Directory data store should be evident.

Microsoft Exam Objective

Back up and restore Active Directory.

- Perform an authoritative restore of Active Directory.
- Recover from a system failure.

NOTE

See the subsection "Restoring the Active Directory" later in this chapter for coverage of the material related to the "Recover from a system failure" subobjective.

There are several reasons to back up data, including the reasons that follow:

Protect against hardware failures.   Computer hardware devices have finite lifetimes, and all hardware will eventually fail. Some types of failures, such as corrupted hard disk drives, can result in significant data loss.

Protect against accidental deletion or modification of data.   Although the threat of hardware failures is very real, in most environments, mistakes in modifying or deleting data are much more common. For example, suppose a systems administrator accidentally deletes all of the objects within a specific OU. Clearly, it's very important to be able to retrieve this information from a backup.

Keep historical information.   Users and systems administrators sometimes modify files but then later find that they require access to an older version of the file. Or, a file is accidentally deleted, but a user does not discover that fact until much later. By keeping backups over time, you can recover information from these prior backups when necessary.

Protect against malicious deletion or modification of data.   Even in the most secure environments, it is conceivable that unauthorized users (or authorized ones with malicious intent!) could delete or modify information. In such cases, the loss of data might require valid backups from which to restore critical information.

Windows 2000 includes a Backup utility that is designed to back up operating system files and the Active Directory data store. It allows for basic backup functionality such as scheduling backup jobs and selecting which files to back up.

Figure 9.16 shows the main screen for the Windows 2000 Backup utility.

FIGURE 9.16   The main screen of the Windows 2000 Backup utility

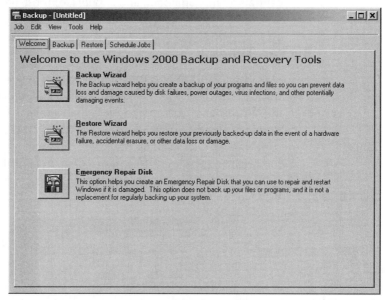

In this section, we'll look at the details of using the Windows 2000 Backup utility and how the Active Directory can be restored when problems do occur.

Overview of the Windows 2000 Backup Utility

Although the general purpose behind performing backup operations—protecting information—is straightforward, there are many different options that systems administrators must consider when determining the optimal backup and recovery scenario for their environment. Factors include what to back up, how often to back up, and when the backups should be performed.

In this section, we'll look at how the Windows 2000 Backup utility makes it easy to implement a backup plan for many network environments.

Although the Windows 2000 Backup utility provides the basic functionality required to back up your files, you may want to investigate third-party products that provide additional functionality. These applications can provide options for specific types of backups (such as those for Exchange Server and SQL Server), as well as Disaster Recovery options, networking functionality, centralized management, and support for more advanced hardware.

Backup Types

One of the most important issues when dealing with backups is keeping track of which files have been backed up and which files need to be backed up. Whenever a backup of a file is made, the Archive bit for the file is set. You can view the attributes of system files by right-clicking them, and selecting Properties. By clicking Advanced, you will see the option File Is Ready for Archiving. Figure 9.17 shows an example of the attributes for a file.

FIGURE 9.17 Viewing the Archive attributes for a file

Although it is possible to back up all of the files in the file system during each backup operation, it's sometimes more convenient to back up only selected files (such as those that have changed since the last back up operation). There are several types of back ups that can be performed:

Normal *Normal backups* back up all of the selected files and then mark them as backed up. This option is usually used when a full system backup is made.

Copy *Copy backups* back up all of the selected files, but do not mark them as backed up. This is useful when you want to make additional backups of files for moving files off-site or making multiple copies of the same data or for archival purposes.

Incremental   *Incremental backups* copy any selected files that are marked as ready for backup and then mark the files as backed up. When the next incremental backup is run, only the files that are not marked as having been backed up are stored. Incremental backups are used in conjunction with full (normal) backups. The general process is to make a full backup and then to make subsequent incremental backups. The benefit to this method is that only files that have changed since the last full or incremental backup will be stored. This can reduce backup times and disk or tape storage space requirements.

When recovering information from this type of backup method, a systems administrator will be required to first restore the full backup and then to restore each of the incremental backups.

Differential   *Differential backups* are similar in purpose to incremental backups with one important exception: Differential backups copy all files that are marked for backup but do not mark the files as backed up. When restoring files in a situation that uses normal and differential backups, you only need to restore the normal backup and the latest differential backup.

Figure 9.18 provides an example of the differences between the normal, incremental, and differential backup types.

FIGURE 9.18   Differences between the normal, incremental, and differential backup types

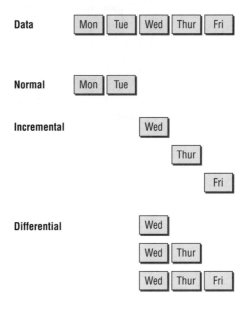

Daily *Daily backups* back up all files that have changed during the current day. This operation uses the file time/date stamps to determine which files should be backed up and does not mark the files as having been backed up.

Note that systems administrators might choose to combine normal, daily, incremental, and differential backup types as part of the same backup plan. In general, however, it is sufficient to use only one or two of these methods (for example, normal backups with incremental backups). If you require a combination of multiple backup types, be sure that you fully understand which types of files are being backed up. Figure 9.19 shows the options available when selecting a backup type.

FIGURE 9.19 Selecting the type of backup to perform

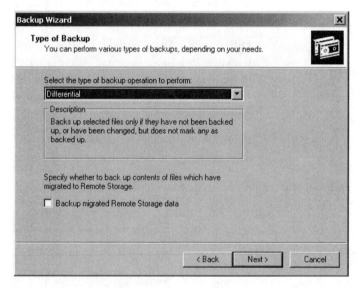

Another option is to create an Emergency Repair Disk (ERD). In the event that boot or configuration information is lost, the ERD and Windows 2000 Repair process can be used to restore a system.

Backing Up System State Information

When planning to back up and restore the Active Directory, the most important component is known as the *System State*. System State information includes the components that the Windows 2000 operating system relies on for normal operations. The Windows 2000 Backup utility offers the ability to back up the System State to another type of media (such as a hard disk, network share, or tape device). Specifically, it will back up the following components for a Windows 2000 domain controller (see Figure 9.20):

Active Directory   The Active Directory data store is at the heart of the Active Directory. It contains all of the information necessary to create and manage network resources such as users and computers. In most environments that use the Active Directory, users and systems administrators rely on the proper functioning of these services in order to do their jobs.

Boot Files   These are the files required for booting the Windows 2000 operating system and can be used in the case of boot file corruption.

COM+ Class Registration Database   Applications that run on a Windows 2000 computer might require the registration of various share code components. As part of the System State backup process, Windows 2000 will store all of the information related to Component Object Model+ (COM+) components so that this information can be quickly and easily restored.

Registry   The Windows 2000 Registry is a central repository of information related to the operating system configuration (such as desktop and network settings), user settings, and application settings. Therefore, the Registry is absolutely vital to the proper functioning of Windows 2000.

SysVol   The SysVol directory includes data and files that are shared between the domain controllers within an Active Directory domain. This information is relied upon by many operating system services for proper functioning.

FIGURE 9.20 Backing up the Windows 2000 System State information

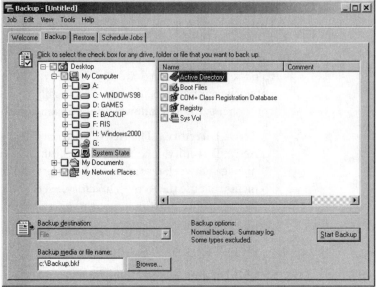

When you back up the System State information, the Windows 2000 Backup utility automatically backs up all of these types of files.

Scheduling Backups

In addition to the ability to specify which files to back up, you can schedule back up jobs to occur at specific times. Planning *when* to perform backups is just as important as deciding what to back up. Performing backup operations can reduce overall system performance; therefore, you should plan to back up information during times of minimal activity on your servers. Figure 9.21 shows the Schedule functionality of the Window 2000 Backup utility.

FIGURE 9.21 Scheduling jobs using the Windows 2000 Backup utility

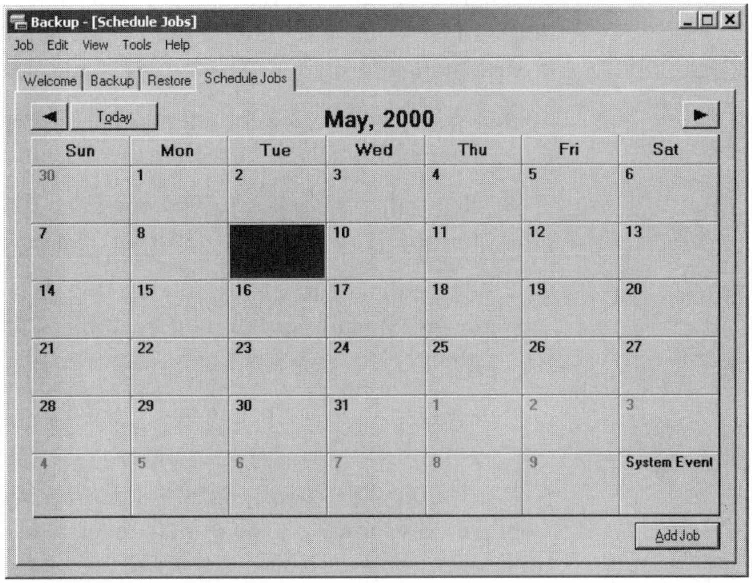

To add a backup operation to the schedule, you can simply click the Add Job button. This will start the Windows 2000 Backup Wizard (which we'll cover later in this chapter).

Restoring System State Information

In some cases, the Active Directory data store or other System State information may become corrupt or unavailable. This could be due to many different reasons. A hard disk failure might, for example, result in the loss of data. Or, the accidental deletion of an OU and all of its objects might require a restore operation to be performed.

The actual steps involved when restoring System State information are based on the details of what has caused the data loss and what effects this data loss has had on the system. In the best case (relatively speaking, of course), the System State information is corrupt or inaccurate, but the operating system can still boot. If this is the case, all that must be done is to boot into a special *Directory Services Restore Mode* and then restore the System State information from a backup. This process will replace the current System State information with that from the backup. Therefore, any changes that have been made since the last backup will be completely lost and must be redone.

In a worst-case scenario, all of the information on a server has been lost or a hardware failure is preventing the machine from properly booting. If this is the case, there are several steps that you must take in order to recover System State information. These steps include the following:

1. Fix any hardware problem that might prevent the computer from booting (for example, replace any failed hard disks).

2. Reinstall the Windows 2000 operating system. This should be performed like a regular installation on a new system.

3. Reinstall any device drivers that may be required by your backup device. If you backed up information to the file system, this will not apply.

4. Restore the System State information using the Windows 2000 Backup utility.

We'll cover the technical details of performing restores later in this section. For now, however, you should understand the importance of backing up information and, whenever possible, testing the validity of backups.

Backing Up the Active Directory

The Windows 2000 Backup utility makes it easy to back up the System State as part of a normal backup operation. Exercise 9.3 walks through the process of backing up the Active Directory.

EXERCISE 9.3

Backing Up the Active Directory

In this exercise, you will back up the Active Directory. In order to complete this exercise, the local machine must be a domain controller, and you must have sufficient free space to back up the System State (usually at least 300MB).

1. Open the Backup utility by clicking Start ➤ Programs ➤ Accessories ➤ System Tools ➤ Backup.

2. To start the backup process using the Backup Wizard, click the Backup Wizard button.

3. Click Next to start the backup process.

4. In the What to Backup dialog box, select Only Back Up the System State Data. Note that there are also options to back up all files on the computer and to back up only specific information. Click Next to continue.

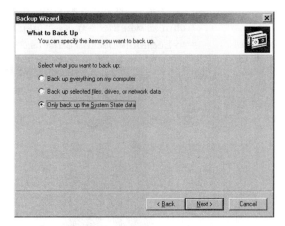

5. Next, you'll need to select where you want to back up this information. If you have a tape drive installed on the local computer, you'll have the option to back up to tape. Otherwise, the option will be disabled, and you can only select File. Select File for the backup media type, and then enter the full path and filename for the backup file. The default file extension for a Windows 2000 Backup file is .BKF. You should ensure that the selected folder has sufficient space to store the System State information (which is usually more than 300MB). Click Next to continue.

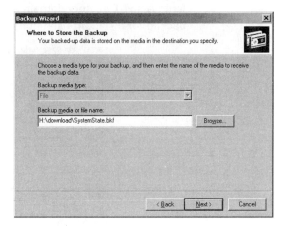

6. The Windows 2000 Backup Wizard will now display a summary of the options you selected for backup. Verify that the files to be backed up and the location information are correct. Note that by clicking the Advanced button, you can select from among different backup types (such as copy, differential, and incremental) and can choose whether remote storage files will be backed up. Click Finish to begin the backup process.

7. The backup process will begin, and the approximate size of the backup will be calculated. On most systems, the backup operation will take at least several minutes. The exact amount of time required will be based on server load, server hardware configuration, and the size of the System State information. For example, backing up the System State on a busy domain controller for a large Active Directory domain will take much longer than a similar backup for a seldom-used domain controller in a small domain.

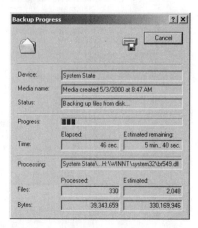

8. When the backup operation has completed, you will see information about the overall backup process. You can click the Report button to see information about the backup process (including any errors that might have occurred). Optionally, you can save this report as a text file to examine the information later.

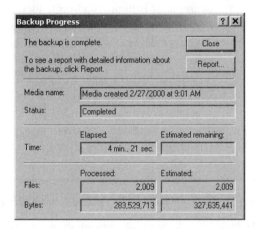

9. When finished, click Close and then close the Backup application.

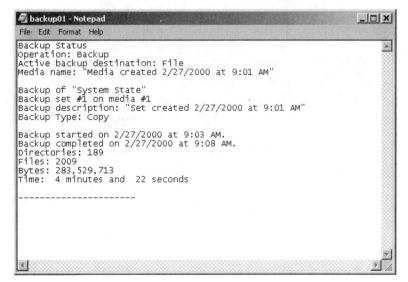

Now that we've walked through the steps required to back up the Active Directory, it's time to look at methods for restoring System State information, should the need arise.

Restoring the Active Directory

The Active Directory has been designed with fault tolerance in mind. For example, it is highly recommended that each domain have at least two domain controllers. Each of these domain controllers contains a copy of the Active Directory data store. Should one of the domain controllers fail, the other one can take over the functionality. When the failed server is repaired, it can then be promoted to a domain controller in the existing environment. This process effectively restores the failed domain controller without incurring any downtime for end users. For more information on promoting domain controllers, see Chapter 3, "Installing and Configuring the Active Directory."

Microsoft ✓ ***Exam Objective***

Back up and restore Active Directory.

- Perform an authoritative restore of Active Directory.
- Recover from a system failure.

See the material in the preceding subsections of the "Backup and Recovery of the Active Directory" section for coverage of the material related to the "Perform an authoritative restore of Active Directory" subobjective.

In some cases, you might need to restore the Active Directory from backup media. For example, suppose a systems administrator accidentally deletes several hundred users from the domain. He does not realize this until the change has been propagated to all of the other domain controllers. Manually re-creating the accounts is not an option since the objects' security identifiers will be different (and all permissions must be reset). Clearly, a method for restoring from backup is the best solution.

There are several features in Windows 2000 for solving boot-related problems and for reinstalling the operating system to fix corrupted files. These techniques are beyond the scope of this book (which focuses on restoring the Active Directory). For more information on using the Recovery Console and the Installation Repair options, see *MCSE: Windows 2000 Server Study Guide* (Sybex, 2000).

Overview of Authoritative Restore

Restoring the Active Directory and other System State information is an important process should system files or the Active Directory data store become corrupt or otherwise unavailable. Fortunately, the Windows 2000 Backup utility allows for easily restoring the System State information from a backup, should the need arise.

We mentioned earlier that in the case of the accidental deletion of information from the Active Directory, you may need to restore the Active Directory data store from a recent backup. But what happens if there is more than one domain controller in the environment? Even if you did perform a restore, the information on this domain controller would be seen as outdated and it would be overwritten by the data from another domain controller (for more information on the replication process, see Chapter 6, "Configuring Sites and Managing Replication"). And, this data from the older domain controller is exactly the information you want to replace.

Fortunately, Windows 2000 and the Active Directory allow you to perform what is called an *authoritative restore*. The authoritative restore process specifies a domain controller as having the authoritative (or master) copy of the Active Directory data store. When other domain controllers communicate with this domain controller, their information will be overwritten with the Active Directory data stored on the local machine.

Now that we have an idea of how an authoritative restore is supposed to work, let's move on to looking at the details of performing the process.

Performing an Authoritative Restore

When restoring Active Directory information on a Windows 2000 domain controller, the Active Directory services must not be running. This is because the restore of System State information requires full access to system files and the Active Directory data store. If you attempt to restore System State information while the domain controller is active, you will see the error message shown in Figure 9.22.

When recovering System State information using Windows 2000 Backup, you have the option of restoring data to an alternate location. However, this operation will only copy some components from the System State backup, and it will not restore the Active Directory.

FIGURE 9.22 Attempting to restore System State while a domain controller is active

In general, restoring data and operating system files is a straightforward process. It is important to note that restoring a System State backup will replace the existing Registry, SysVol, and Active Directory files. Exercise 9.4 walks you through the process of restoring System State and Active Directory information. This process uses the ntdsutil utility to set the authoritative restore mode for a domain controller after the System State is restored, but before the domain controller is rebooted.

Any changes made to the Active Directory since the backup performed in Exercise 9.3 will be lost after the completion of Exercise 9.4.

EXERCISE 9.4

Restoring the System State and the Active Directory

In this exercise, you will restore the Active Directory. In order to complete this process, you must have first completed the steps in Exercise 9.3.

1. Reboot the local machine. During system startup, press the F8 key to enter the Windows 2000 Server boot options.

2. From the boot menu, choose Directory Services Restore Mode "Windows 2000 Domain Controllers Only" and press Enter. The operating system will begin to boot in safe mode.

3. Log on to the computer as a member of the *local* Administrators group. Note that you cannot log on using any Active Directory accounts since network services and the Active Directory have not been started.

4. You will see a message warning you that the machine is running in safe mode and that certain services will not be available. For example, a minimal set of drivers has been loaded, and you will not have access to the network. Click OK to continue.

5. When the operating system has finished booting, open the Backup utility by clicking Start ➢ Programs ➢ Accessories ➢ System Tools ➢ Backup.

6. On the main screen of the Backup utility, click the Restore Wizard icon.

7. Click Next to begin the Restore Wizard.

8. Expand the File item by clicking the plus sign. Expand the Media item, and then click the plus sign next to the System State icon.

9. Enter the path and filename of the backup file that you created in Exercise 9.3. The Backup utility will scan the file for the appropriate backup information.

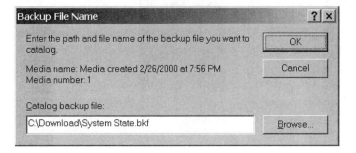

Backup File Name

Enter the path and file name of the backup file you want to catalog.

Media name: Media created 2/26/2000 at 7:56 PM
Media number: 1

Catalog backup file:

C:\Download\System State.bkf

OK

Cancel

Browse...

10. Place a check mark next to the System State item, and then click Next.

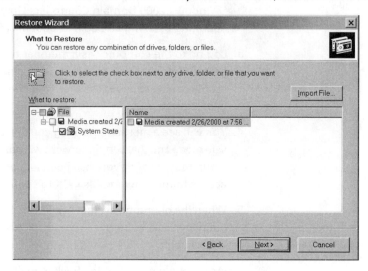

11. The Restore Wizard will display a summary of the recovery options that you selected.

12. Click the Advanced button to specify the location for the restored files. The options include the original location, an alternate location, or a single folder. Verify that the original location option is selected, and then click Next.

13. You will then be prompted to specify how you want files to be restored. Select the Always Replace the File on the Disk option, and click Next.

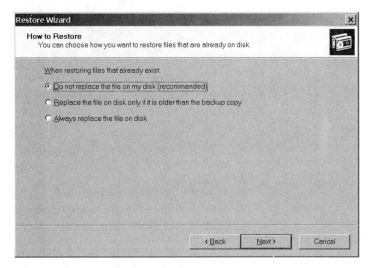

14. For the Advanced Restore Options dialog box, use the default settings (none of the boxes checked). Click Next.

15. To begin the restore operation, click Finish. Windows 2000 Backup will begin to restore the System State files to the local computer.

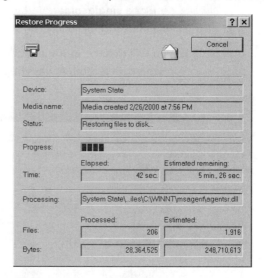

16. Once the System State information has been restored, you will see statistics related to the recovery operation. To view detailed information, click the Report button. When you are finished, click Close.

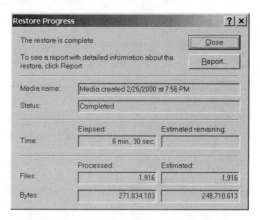

17. You will be prompted about whether or not you want to restart the computer. Select No. Close the Windows 2000 Backup application.

18. Now, you will need to place the domain controller in authoritative restore mode. To do this, click Start ➢ Run and type **cmd**. At the command prompt, type **ntdsutil** and press Enter. Note that you can type the question mark symbol, "?," and press Enter to view help information for the various commands available with the ntdsutil application.

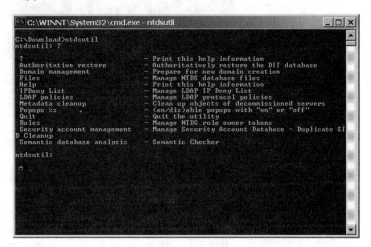

19. At the ntdsutil prompt, type **authoritative restore** and press Enter.

20. At the authoritative restore prompt, type **restore database** and press Enter. You will be asked whether or not you want to perform an authoritative restore. Click Yes.

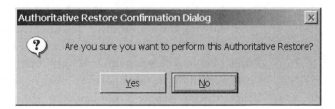

21. The ntdsutil application will begin the authoritative restore process. When the process has completed, type **quit** twice to exit ntdsutil. Then, close the command prompt by typing **exit**.

```
C:\WINNT\System32\cmd.exe - ntdsutil                              _ □ X
Help                           - Print this help information
Quit                           - Return to the prior menu
Restore database               - Authoritatively restore entire database
Restore database verinc %d     - ... and override version increase
Restore subtree %s             - Authoritatively restore a subtree
Restore subtree %s verinc %d   - ... and override version increase

authoritative restore: restore database

Opening DIT database... Done.

The current time is 02-28-00 22:25.03.
Most recent database update occured at 02-26-00 20:01.14.
Increasing attribute version numbers by 300000.

Counting records that need updating...
Records found: 0000001422
Done.

Found 1422 records to update.

Updating records...
Records remaining: 0000000000
Done.

Successfully updated 1422 records.

Authoritative Restore completed successfully.

authoritative restore: _
```

22. Finally, click Start ➢ Shut Down, and restart the computer. Following a reboot of the operating system, the Active Directory and System State information will be current to the point of the last backup.

In addition to restoring the entire Active Directory database, you can also restore just specific subtrees within the Active Directory using the RESTORE SUBTREE command. This allows you to restore specific information and is useful in the case of an accidental deletion of isolated material.

Following the authoritative restore process, the Active Directory should be updated to the time of the last backup. Furthermore, all other domain controllers for this domain will have their Active Directory information overwritten by the results of the restore operation. The end result is an Active Directory environment that has been recovered from media.

Summary

Although it's only one among the seemingly endless tasks performed by systems administrators, optimization and reliability of Active Directory domain controllers is an important factor in the overall health of a network environment. In this chapter, we covered methods for monitoring the performance of domain controllers. Based on this information, we looked at how systems administrators can optimize the performance of domain controllers to ensure that end users receive adequate performance.

Then, we covered another important topic—backing up and restoring System State information using the Windows 2000 Backup utility. Through the use of Wizards and prompts, this Backup tool can simplify an otherwise tedious process. Should the need arise to restore System State information, you should be able to quickly and easily restore it from a valid backup set.

Understanding the issues related to the reliability and performance of the Active Directory and domain controllers is vital to a smoothly running network environment.

Key Terms

Before you take the exam, you should be familiar with the following terms and concepts:

Alerts

authoritative restore

Copy backups

Daily backups

Differential backups

Directory Services Restore Mode

Incremental backups

Network Monitor

Normal backups

Performance Logs

System Monitor

Performance Logs

System Monitor

System State

Task Manager

Trace logs

Review Questions

1. Which of the following backup types backs up all of the selected files, without regard to the Archive bit setting?

   A. Normal

   B. Daily

   C. Copy

   D. All of the above

2. A systems administrator wants to configure the operating system to generate an item in the Windows 2000 event log whenever the CPU utilization for the server exceeds 95 percent. Which of the following items within the Performance tool can they use to do this?

   A. System Monitor

   B. Trace logs

   C. Counter logs

   D. Alerts

   E. All of the above

3. Which of the following System Monitor views displays performance information over a period of time?

   A. Chart

   B. Histogram

   C. Report

   D. Current Activity

   E. None of the above

4. Which of the following types of backup operations should be used when creating a backup of all of the files that have changed since the last full backup?

   A. Differential

   B. Copy

   C. Incremental

   D. Normal

   E. None of the above

5. Which of the following features of the Performance tool is the best choice for saving performance counter information to disk for later analysis?

   A. Trace logs

   B. Alerts

   C. Histogram view

   D. Counter logs

   E. None of the above

6. Which of the following operations on a domain controller requires the operating system to be booted in Directory Services Repair Mode.

   A. Backing up the Active Directory

   B. Backing up system files

   C. Restoring the Active Directory

   D. All of the above

7. A systems administrator boots the operating system using the Directory Services Repair Mode. They attempt to log in using a Domain Administrator account, but are unable to do so. What is the most likely reason for this?

   A. The account has been disabled by another domain administrator.

   B. The permissions on the domain controller do not allow users to log on locally.

   C. The Active Directory service is unavailable, and they must use the local Administrator password.

   D. Another domain controller for the domain is not available to authenticate the login.

   E. All of the above.

8. Which of the following types of backup operations should be used to back up all of the files that have changed since the last full backup or incremental backup?

   A. Differential

   B. Copy

   C. Incremental

   D. Normal

   E. None of the above

9. Following an authoritative restore of the entire Active Directory database, what will happen to the copy of the Active Directory on other domain controllers for the same domain?

   A. The copies of the Active Directory on other domain controllers will be overwritten.

   B. The information on all domain controllers will be merged.

   C. The other domain controllers will be automatically demoted.

   D. None of the above.

10. Which of the following tabs of the System Monitor Properties dialog box can be used to specify that performance data is to be viewed from a log file?

A. Log File

B. General

C. Settings

D. Source

E. Data

11. Which of the following ntdsutil commands is used to perform an authoritative restore of the entire Active Directory database?

A. RESTORE ACTIVE DIRECTORY

B. RESTORE DATABASE

C. RESTORE SUBTREE

D. RESTORE ALL

E. None of the above

12. If the Windows 2000 Server computer fails to boot properly, a systems administrator can use which of the following to restore Windows 2000 configuration information?

A. The Emergency Repair Disk

B. The System Partition Disk

C. Any other partition on the computer

D. None of the above

13. A systems administrator suspects that one or more computers are generating excessive PING traffic on the network. Which of the following tools can they use to determine which computer(s) are causing the problem?

   A. Task Manager

   B. System Monitor

   C. Event Viewer

   D. Network Monitor

   E. None of the above

14. Which of the following tools provides a quick overview of system performance, including details on overall memory usage and CPU utilization?

   A. Task Manager

   B. System Monitor

   C. Event Viewer

   D. Network Monitor

   E. None of the above

15. Which of the following is not backed up as part of the Windows 2000 System State on a domain controller?

   A. Registry

   B. COM+ Registration information

   C. Boot files

   D. Active Directory database information

   E. None of the above

16. Which of the following System Monitor objects can be used to measure performance statistics related to the Active Directory?

   A. Directory Services

   B. LDAP

   C. Network

   D. Replication

   E. NTDS

17. A systems administrator wants to measure performance related to Windows NT 4 logons. Which of the following counters of the NTDS object could provide this information?

   A. Directory Replication Agent (DRA)

   B. Directory Service (DS)

   C. NTLM Authentications

   D. Lightweight Directory Access Protocols (LDAP)

   E. None of the above

18. Which of the following functions of the Windows 2000 Backup utility can be used to schedule backups to occur during off-peak hours?

   A. Incremental backups

   B. Authoritative restore

   C. Non-authoritative restore

   D. None of the above

19. Which of the following tabs of the System Monitor Properties dialog box can be used to enable the display of vertical and horizontal grid lines in the Graph view?

A. Log File

B. General

C. Settings

D. Source

E. Graph

20. A systems administrator suspects that a domain controller is not operating properly. Where can they look for more information regarding any problems that may be occurring?

A. Task Manager

B. Network Monitor

C. System Monitor

D. Event Viewer

E. None of the above

Answers to Review Questions

1. D. Normal, daily, and copy backup operations do not use the Archive bit to determine which files to back up.

2. D. Alerts fire in response to certain performance-related parameters, as defined by systems administrators. You can configure an alert to perform several different types of actions, including writing to the Windows 2000 event log.

3. A. Using the Graph view, you can view performance information over a period of time (as defined by the sample interval). The Histogram and Report views are designed to show the latest performance statistics and average values.

4. A. Differential backup operations copy files without marking them as backed up. Therefore, they are used when a systems administrator wants to back up all of the files that have changed since the last full backup.

5. D. Counter logs are designed to track and record performance information to a file for later analysis.

6. C. Directory Services Repair Mode is only required for restoring System State information, and backups of this information can occur while the operating system is running.

7. C. When booting in Directory Services Repair Mode, the Active Directory is not started, and network services are disabled. Therefore, the systems administrator must use a local account in order to log in.

8. C. Incremental backup operations copy files and mark them as having been backed up. Therefore, they are used when a systems administrator wants to back up only the files that have changed since the last full or incremental backup.

9. A. In an authoritative restore of the entire Active Directory database, the restored copy will override information stored on other domain controllers.

10. D. By using the Source tab, you can specify that performance information is based on either current activity or data from a log file.

11. B. The RESTORE DATABASE command instructs the ntdsutil application to perform an authoritative restore of the entire Active Directory database.

12. A. The Emergency Repair Disk contains information that can be used to fix a corrupted Windows 2000 installation, but it is not a bootable floppy. If the system does not boot normally, you must use the Windows 2000 installation floppy disks or CD-ROM in order to repair the installation.

13. D. Through the use of the Network Monitor application, you can view all of the network packets that are being sent to or from the local server. Based on this information, you can determine the source of certain types of traffic, such as PINGs.

14. A. The Task Manager is an excellent tool for gaining a quick overview of system performance. It includes information on the running applications and processes, as well as performance-related information. For more details, you should use the System Monitor.

15. E. All of the information listed is backed up as part of a System State backup operation.

16. E. The various counters that are part of the NTDS object provide information about the performance of various aspects of the Active Directory.

17. C. Windows NT 4 clients use the NTLM authentication method. By measuring this counter, you can determine how many authentication requests are being generated from non-Windows 2000 computers.

18. D. By using the Schedule tab in the Windows 2000 Backup utility, you can create backup jobs and designate when they are to be run.

19. E. The Graph tab can be used to specify several different display options, including the display of vertical and/or horizontal grid lines.

20. D. The Event Viewer is the best tool for viewing information, warnings, and alerts related to Windows 2000 functions.

Chapter

10

Managing Group Policy

MICROSOFT EXAM OBJECTIVES COVERED IN THIS CHAPTER:

✓ **Implement and troubleshoot Group Policy.**

- Create a Group Policy object (GPO).
- Link an existing GPO.
- Delegate administrative control of Group Policy.
- Modify Group Policy inheritance.
- Filter Group Policy settings by associating security groups to GPOs.
- Modify Group Policy.

✓ **Manage and troubleshoot user environments by using Group Policy.**

- Control user environments by using administrative templates.
- Assign script policies to users and computers.

✓ **Manage network configuration by using Group Policy.**

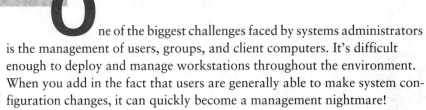

One of the biggest challenges faced by systems administrators is the management of users, groups, and client computers. It's difficult enough to deploy and manage workstations throughout the environment. When you add in the fact that users are generally able to make system configuration changes, it can quickly become a management nightmare!

For example, imagine that a user notices that they do not have enough disk space to copy a large file. Instead of seeking help from the IT help desk, they decide to do a little cleanup of their own. Unfortunately, this cleanup operation involves the deletion of many critical system files! Or, consider the case of users changing system settings "just to see what they do." Relatively minor changes, such as modifications of TCP/IP bindings or desktop settings, can cause hours of support headaches. Now, multiply these problems by hundreds (or even thousands) of end users. Clearly, there should be a way for systems administrators to limit the options available to users of client operating systems.

So how do you prevent small problems like these from occurring in a Windows 2000 environment? Fortunately, there's a solution that's readily available and easy to implement. One of the most important system administration features in Windows 2000 and the Active Directory is the use of *Group Policy*. Through the use of *Group Policy objects (GPOs)*, administrators can quickly and easily define restrictions on common actions and then apply these at the site, domain, or organizational unit (OU) level. In this chapter, we will examine how Group Policies work and then look at how they can be implemented within an Active Directory environment.

An Introduction to Group Policy

One of the strengths of Windows-based operating systems is their flexibility. End users and systems administrators can configure many different options to suit the network environment and their personal tastes. However, this flexibility comes at a price—there are many options that generally should not be changed by end users. For example, TCP/IP configuration and security policies should remain consistent for all client computers.

In previous versions of Windows, system policies were available for restricting some functionality at the desktop level. Settings could be made for users or computers. However, these settings focused primarily on preventing the user from performing such actions as changing their desktop settings. These changes were managed through the modification of Registry keys. This method made it fairly difficult for systems administrators to create and distribute policy settings. Furthermore, the types of configuration options available in the default templates were not always sufficient, and system administrators often had to dive through cryptic and poorly documented Registry settings to make the changes they required.

Windows 2000's Group Policies are designed to allow systems administrators to customize end user settings and to place restrictions on the types of actions that users can perform. Group Policies can be easily created by systems administrators and then later applied to one or more users or computers within the environment. Although they ultimately do affect Registry settings, it is much easier to configure and apply settings through the use of Group Policy than it is to manually make changes to the Registry. For ease of management, Group Policy settings can be managed from within the Active Directory environment, utilizing the structure of users, groups, and OUs.

There are several different potential uses for Group Policies. We covered one of them, managing security settings, in Chapter 8, "Active Directory Security." And, we'll cover the use of Group Policies for software deployment in Chapter 11, "Software Deployment through Group Policy." The focus of this chapter will be on the technical background of Group Policies and how they apply to general configuration management.

Let's begin by looking at how Group Policies function.

Group Policy Settings

Group Policy settings are based on Group Policy *administrative templates*. These templates provide a list of user-friendly configuration options and specify the system settings to which they apply. For example, the option to enforce a desktop setting for a user or computer would map to a specific Registry key that maintains this value. When the option is set, the appropriate change is made in the Registry of the affected user(s) and computer(s).

By default, Windows 2000 comes with several Administrative Template files that can be used for managing common settings. Additionally, systems administrators and application developers can create their own Administrative Template files to set options for specific functionality.

Most Group Policy items have three different settings options:

Enabled Specifies that a setting for this Group Policy object has been configured. Some settings will require values or options to be set.

Disabled Specifies that this option is disabled for client computers. Note that disabling an option *is* a setting. That is, it specifies that the systems administrator wants to disallow certain functionality.

Not Configured Specifies that these settings have been neither enabled nor disabled. Not Configured is the default option for most settings. It simply states that this Group Policy will not specify an option and that settings from other policy settings may take precedence.

The specific options available (and their effects) will depend on the setting. Often, additional information is required. For example, when setting the Account Lockout policy, you must specify how many bad login attempts may be made before the account is locked out. With this in mind, let's look at the types of user and computer settings that can be managed.

User and Computer Settings

Group Policy settings can apply to two types of Active Directory objects: Users and Computers. Since both Users and Computers can be placed into groups and organized within OUs, this type of configuration simplifies the management of hundreds, or even thousands, of computers.

The main types of settings that can be made within User and Computer Group Policies are as follows:

Software Settings Software settings apply to specific applications and software that might be installed on the computer. Systems administrators can use these settings to make new applications available to end users and control the default configuration for these applications. For more information on configuring software settings using Group Policy, see Chapter 11, "Software Deployment through Group Policy."

Windows Settings   Windows settings options allow systems administrators to customize the behavior of the Windows operating system. The specific options that are available here differ for users and computers. For example, the User-specific settings allow the configuration of Internet Explorer (including the default home page and other settings), while the computer settings include security options such as account policy and event log options.

Administrative Templates   The options available in administrative templates are used to further configure user and computer settings. In addition to the default options available, systems administrators can create their own administrative templates with custom options.

Figure 10.1 provides an example of the types of options that can be configured with Group Policy.

FIGURE   10.1   Group Policy configuration options

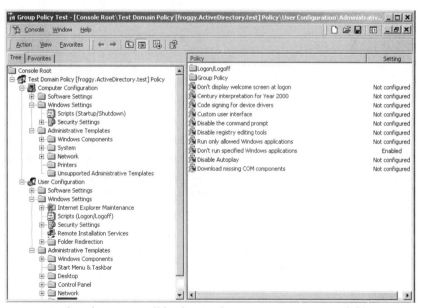

Later in this chapter, we'll look into the various options available in more detail.

Group Policy Objects

So far, we have been talking about what Group Policies are designed to do. Now, it's time to drill down into determining exactly how they can be set up and configured.

For ease of management, Group Policies may be contained in items called Group Policy objects (GPOs). GPOs act as containers for the settings made within Group Policy files, which simplifies the management of settings. For example, as a systems administrator, you might have different policies for users and computers in different departments. Based on these requirements, you could create a GPO for members of the Sales department and another for members of the Engineering department. Then you could apply the GPOs to the OU for each department.

Another important concept is that Group Policy settings are hierarchical. That is, Group Policy settings can be applied at three different levels:

Sites   At the highest level, GPOs can be configured to apply to entire sites within an Active Directory environment. These settings apply to all of the domains and servers that are part of a site. Group Policy settings that are managed at the site level may apply to more than one domain. Therefore, they are useful when you want to make settings that apply to all of the domains within an Active Directory tree or forest. For more information on sites, see Chapter 6, "Configuring Sites and Managing Replication."

Domains   Domains are the second level to which GPOs can be assigned. GPO settings that are placed at the domain level will apply to all of the User and Computer objects within the domain. Usually, systems administrators will make master settings at the domain level.

Organizational Units   The most granular level of settings for GPOs is at the OU level. By configuring Group Policy options for OUs, systems administrators can take advantage of the hierarchical structure of the Active Directory. If the OU structure is planned well, it will be easy to make logical GPO assignments for various business units at the OU level.

Based on the business need and the organization of the Active Directory environment, systems administrators might decide to set up Group Policy settings at any of these three levels. Since the settings are cumulative by default, a User object might receive policy settings from the site level, from the domain level, and from the organizational units in which it is contained. Group Policy settings can also be applied to the local computer (in which case the Active Directory is not used at all), but this limits the manageability of the Group Policy settings.

Group Policy Inheritance

In most cases, Group Policy settings will be cumulative. For example, a GPO at the domain level might specify that all users within the domain must change their passwords every 60 days, and a GPO at the OU level might specify the default desktop background for all users and computers within that OU. In this case, both settings will apply, and users within the OU will be forced to change their password every 60 days and have the default desktop setting.

So what happens if there's a conflict in the settings? For example, suppose a GPO at the site level specifies that users are to change passwords every 60 days while one at the OU level specifies that they must change passwords every 90 days. This raises an important point about *inheritance*. By default, the settings at the most specific level (in this case, the OU, which contains the User object) will override those at more general levels.

Although the default behavior is for settings to be cumulative and inherited, systems administrators can modify this behavior. There are two main options that can be set at the various levels to which GPOs might apply:

Block Policy Inheritance   The Block Policy Inheritance option specifies that Group Policy settings for an object are not inherited from its parents. This might be used, for example, when a child OU requires completely different settings from a parent OU. Note, however, that blocking policy inheritance should be managed carefully, since this option allows other systems administrators to override the settings made at higher levels.

Force Policy Inheritance   The Force Policy Inheritance option can be placed on a parent object and ensures that all lower-level objects inherit these settings. In some cases, systems administrators want to ensure that Group Policy inheritance is not blocked at other levels. For example, suppose it is corporate policy that all Network accounts are locked out after five incorrect password attempts. In this case, you would not want lower-level systems administrators to override the option with other settings.

This option is generally used when systems administrators want to globally enforce a specific setting. For example, if a password expiration policy should apply to all users and computers within a domain, a GPO with the Force Policy Inheritance option enabled could be created at the domain level.

One final case must be considered: If there is a conflict between the computer and user settings, the user settings will take effect. If, for instance, there is a default desktop setting applied for the Computer policy, and there is a different default desktop setting for the User policy, the one specified in the User object will take effect. This is because the user settings are more specific, and it allows systems administrators to make changes for individual users, regardless of the computer they're using.

Implementing Group Policy

Now that we've covered the basic layout and structure of Group Policies and how they work, let's look at how they can be implemented in an Active Directory environment. In this section, we'll start by creating GPOs. Then, we'll apply these GPOs to specific Active Directory objects.

Microsoft
✓ *Exam*
Objective

Implement and troubleshoot Group Policy.

- Create a Group Policy object (GPO).
- Link an existing GPO.
- Modify Group Policy.

Manage and troubleshoot user environments by using Group Policy.

- Control user environments by using administrative templates.
- Assign script policies to users and computers.

See the section "Managing Group Policy" later in this chapter for coverage of the material related to the "Assign script policies to users and computers" subobjective.

Creating GPOs

Although there is only one Group Policy editing application included with Windows 2000, there are several ways to access it. This is because systems administrators may choose to apply the Group Policy settings at different levels within the Active Directory. In order to create GPOs at different levels, you can use the following tools:

Active Directory Sites and Services   Used for linking GPOs at the site level.

Active Directory Users and Computers   Used for linking GPOs at the domain or OU level.

MMC Group Policy Snap-In   By directly configuring the Microsoft Management Console (MMC) Group Policy snap-in, you can access and edit GPOs at any level of the hierarchy. This is also a useful option since it allows you to modify the local Group Policy settings and create a custom console that is saved to the Administrative Tools program group.

Exercise 10.1 walks you through the process of creating a custom MMC snap-in for editing Group Policy settings.

You should be careful when making Group Policy settings since certain options might prevent the proper use of systems on your network. Always test Group Policy settings on a small group of users before deploying GPOs throughout your organization. You'll probably find that some settings need to be changed in order to be effective.

EXERCISE 10.1

Creating a Group Policy Object Using MMC

In this exercise, we will create a custom Group Policy snap-in for managing user and computer settings.

1. Click Start ➤ Run, type **mmc**, and press Enter.

2. On the Console menu, click Add/Remove Snap-In.

3. Click the Add button. Select Group Policy from the list, and click Add.

4. For the Group Policy Object setting, click Browse. Note that you can set the scope to Domains/OUs, Sites, or Computers. On the Domains/OUs tab, click the New Policy button (located to the right of the Look In drop-down list).

5. To name the new object, type **Test Domain Policy**. Click OK to open the Policy object.

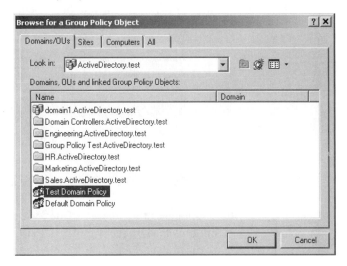

6. Place a check mark next to the Allow the Focus of the Group Policy Snap-In to Be Changed When Launching from the Command Line option. This will allow the context of the snap-in to be changed when you launch the MMC item.

7. Click Finish to create the Group Policy object. Click Close in the Add Standalone Snap-In dialog box. Finally, click OK to add the new snap-in.

8. Next, we'll make some changes to the default settings for this new GPO. Open the following items: Test Domain Policy ➤ Computer Configuration ➤ Windows Settings ➤ Security Settings ➤ Local Policies ➤ Security Options.

EXERCISE 10.1 *(continued)*

9. Double-click the Do Not Display Last User Name in Logon Screen option. Place a check mark next to the Define This Policy Setting in the Template option, and then select Enabled. Click OK to save the setting.

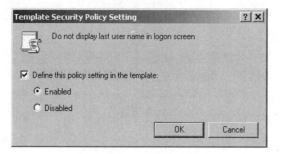

10. Double-click the Message Title for Users Attempting to Log On option. Place a check mark next to the Define This Policy Setting in the Template option, and then type the following: **By logging onto this domain, you specify that you agree to the usage policies as defined by the IT department**. Click OK to save the setting.

11. Double-click the Message Title for Users Attempting to Log On option. Place a check mark next to the Define This Policy Setting in the Template option, and then type **Test Policy Logon Message**. Click OK to save the setting.

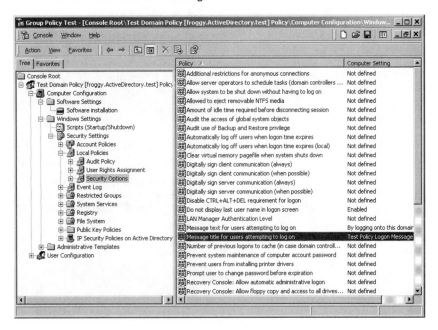

12. Now, to make changes to the User settings, expand the following objects: Test Domain Policy ➢ User Configuration ➢ Administrative Templates ➢ Start Menu & Task Bar.

13. Double-click the Add Logoff to the Start Menu option. Note that you can get a description of the purpose of this setting by clicking the Explain tab. Select Enabled, and then click OK.

14. Expand the following objects: Test Domain Policy ➢ User Configuration ➢ Administrative Templates ➢ System.

EXERCISE 10.1 *(continued)*

15. Double-click the Don't Run Specified Windows Applications option. Select Enabled, and then click the Show button. To add to the list of disallowed applications, click the Add button. When prompted to enter the item, type **wordpad.exe**. To save the setting, click OK three times.

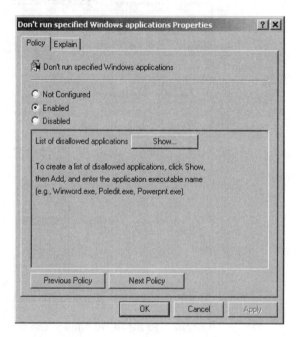

16. To change network configuration settings, click Test Domain Policy ➢ User Configuration ➢ Administrative Templates ➢ Network ➢ Offline Files. Note that you can change the default file locations for several different network folders.

17. To change script settings (which we will cover later in this chapter), click Test Domain Policy ➢ Computer Configuration ➢ Windows Settings ➢ Scripts (Startup/Shutdown). Note that you can add script settings by double-clicking either the Startup and/or the Shutdown item.

18. The changes you have made for this GPO are automatically saved. You can optionally save this customized MMC console by selecting Save As from the Console menu. Then provide a name for the new MMC snap-in (such as "Group Policy Test"). You will now see this item in the Administrative Tools program group.

19. When you are finished modifying the Group Policy settings, close the MMC tool.

Note that Group Policy changes do not take effect until the next user logs in. That is, users that are currently working on the system will not see the effects of the changes until they log off and log in again.

Now that we've seen how to create a custom MMC snap-in for modifying Group Policy, let's look at how GPOs can be linked to Active Directory objects.

Linking GPOs to the Active Directory

The creation of a GPO is the first step in assigning Group Policies. The second step is to link the GPO to a specific Active Directory object. As mentioned earlier in this chapter, GPOs can be linked to sites, domains, and OUs.

Exercise 10.2 walks through the steps required to assign a GPO to an OU within the local domain.

Linking GPOs to the Active Directory

In this exercise, we will link the Test Domain Policy GPO to an OU. In order to complete the steps in this exercise, you must have first completed Exercise 10.1.

1. Open the Active Directory Users and Computers tool.

2. Create a new top-level OU called Group Policy Test.

3. Right-click the Group Policy Test OU, and click Properties.

4. Select the Group Policy tab. To add a new policy at the OU level, click Add. In the Look In drop-down list, select the name of the local domain. Select the Test Domain Policy GPO, and then click OK.

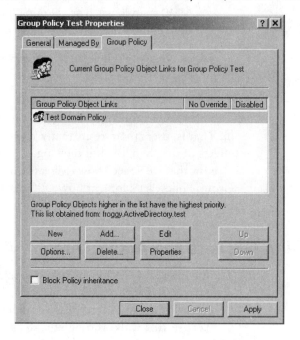

5. Note that you can also add additional GPOs to this OU. When multiple GPOs are assigned, you can also control the order in which they apply by using the Up and Down buttons. Finally, you can edit the GPO by clicking the Edit button, and you can remove the link (or, optionally, delete the GPO entirely) by clicking the Delete button.

6. To save the GPO link, click OK. When finished, close the Active Directory Users and Computers tool.

Note that the Active Directory Users and Computers tool offers a lot of flexibility in assigning GPOs. We could create new GPOs, add multiple GPOs, edit them directly, change priority settings, remove links, and delete GPOs all from within this interface. In general, creating new GPOs using the Active Directory Sites and Services or the Active Directory Users and Computers tool is the quickest and easiest way to create the settings you need.

To test the Group Policy settings, you can simply create a User or Computer account within the Group Policy Test OU that we created in Exercise 10.2. Then, using another computer that is a member of the same domain, log on as the newly created user. First, you should see the pre-logon message that we set in Exercise 10.1. After logging on, you'll also notice that the other changes have taken effect. For example, you will not be able to run the WordPad.exe program.

When testing Group Policy settings, it is very convenient to use the Terminal Services functionality of Windows 2000. Although it is beyond the scope of this book to describe the use and configuration of Terminal Services in detail, this feature allows you to have multiple simultaneous logon sessions to the same computer. With respect to Group Policy, it is useful when you want to modify Group Policy settings and then quickly log on under another User account to test them. For more information on using Terminal Services, see *MCSE: Windows 2000 Server Study Guide* (Sybex, 2000).

Using Administrative Templates

There are many different options that can be modified by Group Policy settings. Microsoft has included some of the most common and useful items by default, and they're made available when you create new GPOs or when you edit existing ones. You can, however, create your own templates and include them in the list of settings.

By default, there are several templates that are included with Windows 2000. These are as follows:

Common.adm   Contains the policy options that are common to both Windows 95/98 and Windows NT 4 computers.

Inetres.adm   Contains the policy options for configuring Internet Explorer options on Windows 2000 client computers.

System.adm   Includes common configuration options and settings for Windows 2000 client computers.

Windows.adm   Contains policy options for Windows 95/98 computers.

Winnt.adm   Contains policy options that are specific to the use of Windows NT 4.

These Administrative Template files are stored within the `inf` subdirectory of the system root directory. It is important to note that the use of the `Windows.adm`, `Winnt.adm`, and `Common.adm` files is not supported in Windows 2000. These files are primarily provided for backward compatibility with previous versions of Windows.

The `*.adm` files are simple text files that follow a specific format that is recognized by the Group Policy editor. Following is an excerpt from the `system.adm` file:

```
CATEGORY !!WindowsComponents
    CATEGORY !!WindowsExplorer
    KEYNAME "Software\Microsoft\Windows\CurrentVersion
            \Policies\Explorer"


    POLICY !!ClassicShell
        EXPLAIN !!ClassicShell_Help
        VALUENAME "ClassicShell"
    END POLICY



    POLICY !!NoFolderOptions
        EXPLAIN !!NoFolderOptions_Help
        VALUENAME "NoFolderOptions"
    END POLICY

    POLICY !!NoFileMenu
            EXPLAIN !!NoFileMenu_Help
        VALUENAME "NoFileMenu"
        END POLICY

    POLICY !!NoNetConnectDisconnect
            EXPLAIN !!NoNetConnectDisconnect_Help
        VALUENAME "NoNetConnectDisconnect"
    END POLICY
```

```
POLICY !!NoShellSearchButton
    EXPLAIN !!NoShellSearchButton_Help
    VALUENAME "NoShellSearchButton"
      END POLICY


POLICY !!NoViewContextMenu
        EXPLAIN !!NoViewContextMenu_Help
    VALUENAME "NoViewContextMenu"
    END POLICY
```

Notice that the various options that are available for modification are specified within the Administrative Template file. If necessary, systems administrators can create custom Administrative Template files that include more options for configuration.

To add new administrative templates when modifying GPOs, simply right-click the Administrative Templates object and select Add/Remove Templates (see Figure 10.2).

FIGURE 10.2   Adding administrative templates when creating GPOs

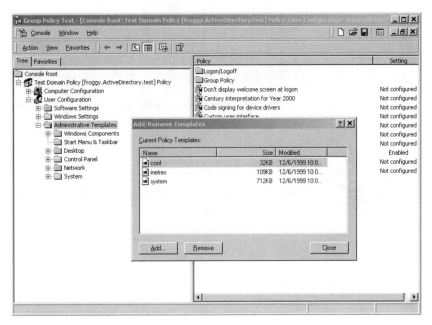

Managing Group Policy

Once you have implemented GPOs and applied them to sites, domains, and OUs within the Active Directory, it's time to look at some ways to manage them. In this section, we'll look at how multiple GPOs can interact with one another and ways you can provide security for GPO management. These are very important features of working with the Active Directory, and the proper planning of Group Policy can greatly reduce the time the help desk spends troubleshooting common problems.

Microsoft ✓ *Exam Objective*

Implement and troubleshoot Group Policy.

- Delegate administrative control of Group Policy.
- Modify Group Policy inheritance.
- Filter Group Policy settings by associating security groups to GPOs.

Manage and troubleshoot user environments by using Group Policy.

- Control user environments by using administrative templates.
- Assign script policies to users and computers.

Manage network configuration by using Group Policy.

See the section "Implementing Group Policy" earlier in this chapter for coverage of the material related to the "Control user environments by using administrative templates" subobjective.

Managing GPOs

One of the benefits of GPOs is that they're modular and can apply to many different objects and levels within the Active Directory. This can also be one of the drawbacks of GPOs, if they're not managed properly. A common administrative function related to the use of GPOs is finding all of the Active Directory links for each of these objects. This can be done when viewing the properties of a GPO by clicking the Links tab. As shown in Figure 10.3, clicking the Find Now button will show which objects are using a particular GPO.

FIGURE   10.3   Viewing GPO links to the Active Directory

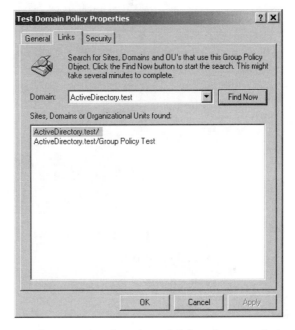

In addition to the common function of delegating permissions on OUs, you can also set permissions regarding the modification of GPOs. One method is to add users to the Group Policy Creator/Owners built-in security group. The members of this group are able to modify security policy.

Filtering Group Policy

Another method of securing access to GPOs is to set permissions on the GPOs themselves. This is done by selecting the Group Policy tab for an object with the GPO assigned, and then clicking Properties. By clicking the Security tab, you can view the specific permissions that are set on the GPO itself (see Figure 10.4).

FIGURE 10.4 GPO security settings

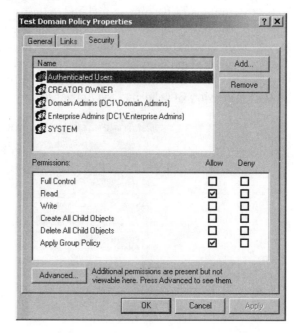

The permissions options include:

- Full Control

- Read

- Write

- Create All Child Objects

- Delete All Child Objects

- Apply Group Policy

Of these, the Apply Group Policy setting is particularly important since it is used for filtering the scope of the GPO. *Filtering* is the process by which selected security groups are included or excluded from the effects of the GPOs. To specify that the settings should apply to a GPO, you should grant at least the Apply Group Policy and Read settings. These settings will only be applied if the security group is also contained within a site, domain, or OU to which the GPO is linked. In order to disable GPO access for a group, choose Deny for both of these settings. Finally, if you do not want to specify either Allow or Deny effects, leave both boxes blank. This is effectively the same as having no setting. See Exercise 10.3 for more detailed instructions.

Filtering Group Policy Using Security Groups

In this exercise, you will filter Group Policy using security groups. In order to complete the steps in this exercise, you must have first completed Exercises 10.1 and 10.2.

1. Open the Active Directory Users and Computers administrative tool.

2. Create two new Global Security groups within the Group Policy Test OU, and name them PolicyEnabled and PolicyDisabled.

3. Right-click the Group Policy Test OU, and select Properties. Select the Group Policy tab.

4. Highlight Test Domain Policy, and select Properties.

5. On the Security tab, click Add, and select the PolicyEnabled and the PolicyDisabled groups. Click OK.

6. Highlight the PolicyDisabled group, and select Deny for the Read and Apply Group Policy permissions. This will prevent users in the PolicyDisabled group from being affected by this policy.

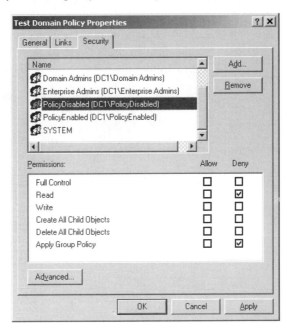

EXERCISE 10.3 *(continued)*

7. Highlight the PolicyEnabled group, and select Allow for the Read and Apply Group Policy permissions. This will ensure that users in the PolicyEnabled group will be affected by this policy.

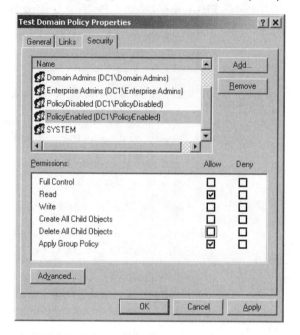

8. Click OK to save the Group Policy settings. You will be warned that Deny takes precedence over any other security settings. Select Yes to continue.

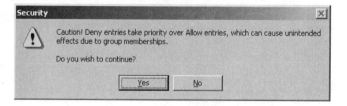

9. Click OK to save the change to the properties of the OU.

10. When finished, close the Active Directory Users and Computers administrative tool.

Through the use of these settings, you can ensure that only the appropriate individuals will be able to modify GPO settings.

Delegating Administrative Control of GPOs

So far, we have talked about how Group Policy can be used to manage user and computer settings. What we haven't done is determine who can modify GPOs themselves. It's very important to establish the appropriate security on GPOs themselves for two main reasons. First, if the security settings aren't set properly, users and systems administrators can easily override them. This defeats the purpose of having the GPOs in the first place! Second, having many different systems administrators creating and modifying GPOs can become extremely difficult to manage. When problems arise, the hierarchical nature of GPO inheritance can make it difficult to pinpoint the problem.

Fortunately, through the use of the Delegation of Control Wizard, determining security permissions for GPOs is a simple task. We looked at the usefulness of the Delegation of Control Wizard in Chapter 7, "Administering the Active Directory" and in Chapter 8, "Active Directory Security." Exercise 10.4 walks you through the steps required to grant the appropriate permissions to a User account. Specifically, the process involves delegating the ability to manage Group Policy links on an Active Directory object (such as an OU).

EXERCISE 10.4

Delegating Administrative Control of Group Policy

In this exercise, you will delegate permissions to manage Group Policies of an OU. In order to complete this exercise, you must have first completed Exercises 10.1 and 10.2.

1. Open the Active Directory Users and Computers tool.

EXERCISE 10.4 *(continued)*

2. Expand the local domain, and create a user named Policy Admin within the Group Policy Test OU.

3. Right-click the Group Policy Test OU, and select Delegate Control.

4. Click Next to start the Delegation of Control Wizard.

5. On the Users or Groups page, click Add. Select the Policy Admin account, and click OK. Click Next to continue.

6. On the Tasks to Delegate step, select Delegate the Following Common Tasks, and place a check mark next to the Manage Group Policy Links item. Click Next to continue.

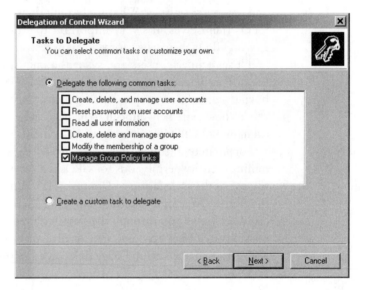

7. Finally, click Finish to complete the Delegation of Control Wizard and assign the appropriate permissions. Specifically, this will allow the Policy Admin user to create GPO links to this OU (and, by default, any child OUs).

8. When finished, close the Active Directory Users and Computers tool.

Controlling Inheritance and Filtering Group Policy

Controlling inheritance is an important function when managing GPOs. Earlier in this chapter, we discussed the fact that, by default, GPO settings flow from higher-level Active Directory objects to lower-level ones. For example, the effective set of Group Policy settings for a user might be based on GPOs assigned at the site level, the domain level, and in the OU hierarchy. In general, this is probably the behavior you would want.

In some cases, however, you might want to block Group Policy inheritance. This can be easily accomplished by selecting the properties for the object to which a GPO has been linked. On the Group Policy tab, you will be able to set several useful options regarding inheritance. The first (and most obvious) option is the Block Policy Inheritance check box located at the bottom of the Group Policy tab (see Figure 10.5). By enabling this option, you are effectively specifying that this object starts with a clean slate. That is, no other Group Policy settings will apply to the contents of this Active Directory site, domain, or OU.

FIGURE 10.5 Blocking GPO inheritance

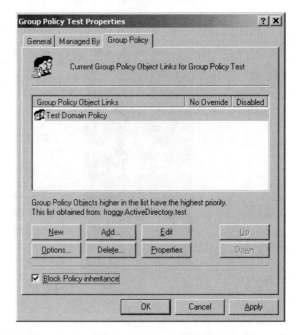

There is, however, a way that systems administrators can force inheritance. This is done using the No Override option and is generally set to prevent other systems administrators from making changes to default policies. You can set the No Override option (shown in Figure 10.6) by clicking the Options button on the Group Policy tab for the object to which the GPO applies. Notice that you can also choose to temporarily disable a GPO. This is useful during troubleshooting and when attempting to determine which GPOs are causing certain behavior.

FIGURE 10.6 Setting the No Override GPO option

Exercise 10.5 walks through the steps required to manage inheritance and filtering of GPOs.

Managing Inheritance and Filtering of GPOs

In this exercise, you will modify the behavior of Group Policy inheritance and filtering.

1. Open the Active Directory Users and Computers administrative tool.

2. Create a top-level OU called Parent.

3. Right-click the Parent OU, and select Properties. Select the Group Policy tab, and click the New button to create a new GPO. Name the new object Master GPO.

4. Click the Options button. Place a check mark next to the No Override option. This will ensure that administrators of OUs contained within the Parent OU will not be able to override the settings defined in this GPO. To save the settings, click OK. Notice that a check mark appears next to the Master GPO in the No Override column in the list of Group Policy object links.

5. Create another GPO for the parent OU, and name it Optional GPO. Click the Apply button to save the changes.

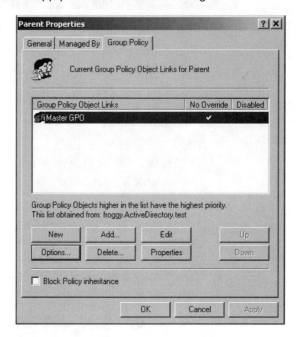

6. Within the parent OU, create another OU called Child.

EXERCISE 10.5 *(continued)*

7. Right-click the Child OU, and select Properties. Select the Group Policy tab, and place a check mark in the Block Policy Inheritance check box. This option will prevent the inheritance of GPO settings from the Parent OU for the Optional GPO settings. Note that since the No Override setting for the Master GPO was enabled on the Parent OU, the settings in the Master GPO will take effect on the Child OU regardless of the setting of the Block Policy Inheritance box.

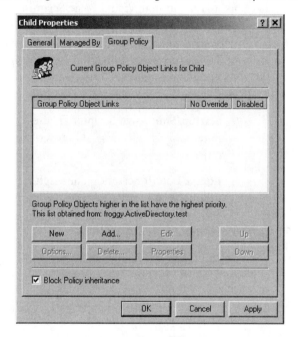

8. When finished, close the Active Directory Users and Computers tool.

Assigning Script Policies

There are several changes and settings that systems administrators might want to make during the startup of a computer or during the logon for a user. Perhaps the most common operation for logon scripts is mapping network drives. Although users can manually map network drives, providing this functionality within login scripts ensures that mappings stay consistent and that users need only remember the drive letters for their resources.

Script policies are specific options that are part of Group Policy settings for users and computers. These settings direct the operating system to the specific files that should be processed during the startup/shutdown or logon/logoff processes. The scripts themselves may be created through the use of the *Windows Script Host (WSH)* or may be standard batch file commands. WSH is a utility included with the Windows 2000 operating system. It allows developers and systems administrators to quickly and easily create scripts using the familiar Visual Basic Scripting Edition (VBScript) or JScript (Microsoft's implementation of JavaScript). Additionally, WSH can be expanded to accommodate other common scripting languages.

To set script policy options, you simply edit the Group Policy settings. As shown in Figure 10.7, there are two main areas for setting script policy settings:

Startup/Shutdown Scripts These settings are located within the Computer Configuration ➢ Windows Settings ➢ Scripts (Startup/Shutdown) object.

Logon/Logoff Scripts These settings are located within the User Configuration ➢ Windows Settings ➢ Scripts (Logon/Logoff) object.

FIGURE 10.7 Viewing script policy settings

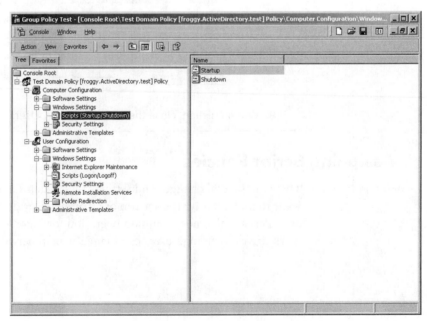

To assign scripts, simply double-click the setting. The Startup Properties dialog box appears, as shown in Figure 10.8. To add a script filename, click the Add button. You will be asked to provide the name of the script file (such as `MapNetworkDrives.vbs` or `ResetEnvironment.bat`). Note that you can change the order in which the scripts are run by using the Up and Down buttons. The Show Files button will open the directory folder in which you should store the Logon files. In order to ensure that the files are replicated to all domain controllers, you should be sure that you place the files within the *SysVol* share.

FIGURE 10.8 Setting scripting options

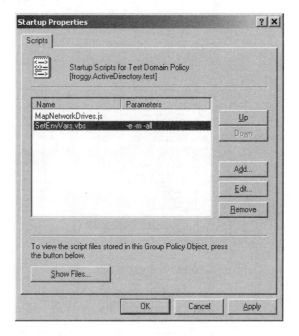

Managing Network Configuration

Group Policies are also useful in network configuration. Although there are many different methods for handling network settings at the protocol level (such as Dynamic Host Configuration Protocol, or DHCP), Group Policy allows administrators to set which functions and operations are available to users and computers.

Figure 10.9 shows some of the features that are available for managing Group Policy settings. The paths to these settings are as follows:

Computer Network Options   These settings are located within the Computer Configuration ➤ Administrative Templates ➤ Network folder.

User Network Options   These settings are located within the User Configuration ➤ Administrative Templates ➤ Network folder.

FIGURE 10.9 Viewing Group Policy network configuration options

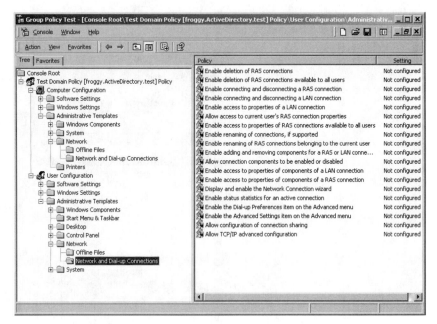

Some examples of the types of settings available include the following:

- The ability to allow or disallow the modification of network settings. In many environments, the improper changing of network configurations and protocol settings is a common cause of help desk calls.

- The ability to allow or disallow the creation of Remote Access Service (RAS) connections. This option is very useful, especially in larger networked environments, since the use of modems and other WAN devices can pose a security threat to the network.

- Setting of Offline files and folders options. This is especially useful for keeping files synchronized for traveling users and is commonly configured for laptops.

Through the use of these configuration options, systems administrators can maintain consistency for users and computers and can avoid many of the most common troubleshooting calls.

Troubleshooting Group Policy

Due to the wide variety of configurations that are possible when establishing Group Policy, you should be aware of some common troubleshooting methods. These methods will help isolate problems in policy settings or *GPO links*.

A possible problem with GPO configuration is that logons and system startups may take a long time. This occurs especially in large environments when the Group Policy settings must be transmitted over the network and, in many cases, slow WAN links. In general, the number of GPOs should be limited because of the processing overhead and network requirements during logon. By default, GPOs are processed in a synchronous manner. This means that the processing of one GPO must be completed before another one is applied (as opposed to asynchronous processing, where they can all execute at the same time).

Other common issues might include unexpected settings of Group Policy options. When this occurs, there are several options that systems administrators should verify.

Locate Active Directory GPO Links   To find out where GPOs are being used, you can quickly and easily use the Links tab in the Properties dialog box of the GPOs.

Verify GPO Configuration   Since GPOs can be assigned to sites, domains, and OUs, systems administrators should be sure to carefully plan for the inheritance of Group Policy settings. And while careful planning and maintenance of GPOs is important, it's just as important to determine the ramifications of moving and reconfiguring objects of the Active Directory. For example, moving an OU or redefining a site can cause large changes in the effective Group Policy settings.

Attempt to "Disable" Certain GPOs   When certain settings are causing problems, it can be difficult to isolate the GPOs from which the settings are being made. One method for troubleshooting GPO problems is to systematically disable and enable various combinations of GPOs. By doing this, you can determine which GPO(s) is causing the problems.

Through the use of these various techniques, you should be able to track down even the most elusive Group Policy problems. Remember, however, that good troubleshooting skills do not replace the need for adequate planning and maintenance of GPO settings!

Summary

In this chapter, we examined the Active Directory's solution to a common headache for many systems administrators: policy settings. Specifically, we discussed the functionality issues related to the use of Group Policy. Through the use of GPOs, administrative templates, and Active Directory links, the task of locking down certain operations and preconfiguring user settings is very easy.

With these ideas in mind, it's time to move on to another exciting application of Group Policy: software deployment.

Key Terms

Before you take the exam, you should be familiar with the following terms and concepts:

administrative templates

Filtering

GPO links

Group Policy

Group Policy Objects (GPOs)

inheritance

Script policies

Windows Script Host (WSH)

Review Questions

1. GPOs can be assigned at all of the following levels *except*:

    A. Sites

    B. Domains

    C. Organizational units (OUs)

    D. Local system

    E. None of the above

2. Which of the following can a systems administrator modify to create custom Group Policy options?

    A. Inheritance

    B. Delegation

    C. No Override

    D. Administrative templates

    E. None of the above

3. Script policies can be set for which of the following events?

    A. Logon

    B. Logoff

    C. Startup

    D. Shutdown

    E. All of the above

4. Script policies can be written in which of the following languages?

    A. Visual Basic Scripting Edition (VBScript)

    B. JScript

    C. Other Windows Script Host (WSH) languages

    D. Batch files

    E. All of the above

5. The process of assigning permissions to set Group Policy for objects within an OU is known as:

    A. Promotion

    B. Inheritance

    C. Delegation

    D. None of the above

6. Which of the following Properties tabs for a GPO can be used to find out which Active Directory objects that GPO applies to?

    A. General

    B. Security

    C. Links

    D. Auditing

    E. None of the above

7. The process by which lower-level Active Directory objects inherit Group Policy settings from higher-level ones is known as:

    A. Delegation

    B. Inheritance

    C. Cascading permissions

    D. Overriding

    E. None of the above

8. To disable GPO settings for a specific security group, which of the following permissions should be applied?

    A. Deny Read

    B. Allow Read

    C. Enable Apply Group Policy

    D. Disable Apply Group Policy

    E. Both A and D

9. Group Policy settings can be used to manage which of the following settings?

   A. Network Configuration settings

   B. Desktop settings

   C. Password settings

   D. All of the above

10. A systems administrator wants to prevent the application of a Group Policy on an OU without deleting its link. Which option can they use to do this?

    A. The No Override option

    B. The Block Policy Inheritance option

    C. The Disable option

    D. None of the above

11. A systems administrator wants to ensure that certain GPOs applied at the domain level are not overridden at lower levels. Which option can they use to do this?

    A. The No Override option

    B. The Block Policy Inheritance option

    C. The Disable option

    D. None of the above

12. GPOs assigned at which of the following level(s) will override GPO settings at the domain level?

    A. OU

    B. Site

    C. Domain

    D. Both OU and site

    E. None of the above

13. A systems administrator wants to ensure that only the GPOs set at the OU level affect the Group Policy settings for objects within the OU. Which option can they use to do this (assuming that all other GPO settings are the defaults)?

    A. The No Override option

    B. The Block Policy Inheritance option

    C. The Disable option

    D. None of the above

14. Which of the following Properties tabs for GPOs can be used to find the specific objects to which Group Policy settings apply?

    A. General

    B. Security

    C. Links

    D. Auditing

    E. None of the above

15. Which of the following default security groups is used primarily for creating and managing Group Policy settings?

    A. Domain Admins

    B. Enterprise Admins

    C. Account Operators

    D. Backup Operators

    E. None of the above

16. Which of the following GPO assignments does not use the Active Directory?

    A. Domains

    B. OUs

    C. Sites

    D. Local computer

    E. None of the above

17. In order to be accessible to other domain controllers, logon/logoff and startup/shutdown scripts should be placed in which of the following shares?

   A. Winnt

   B. System

   C. C$

   D. SysVol

   E. None of the above

18. Which of the following types of scripts apply to User Configuration?

   A. Logon and shutdown

   B. Logon and startup

   C. Logon and logoff

   D. Startup and shutdown

   E. None of the above

19. What is the name of the GPO that is created when a new domain is created?

   A. Test Group Policy

   B. Domain Policy

   C. Temporary Domain Policy

   D. Default Domain Policy

   E. None of the above

20. A GPO link at which of the following levels can affect more than one domain?

   A. Sites

   B. OUs

   C. Domains

   D. Local computer

   E. None of the above

Answers to Review Questions

1. E. GPOs can be set at all of the levels listed.

2. D. Administrative templates are used to specify the options available for setting Group Policy.

3. E. Script policies can be set for any of the events listed.

4. E. The Windows Script Host (WSH) can be used with any of the above languages. Additionally, standard batch files can also be used.

5. C. The Delegation of Control Wizard can be used to allow other systems administrators permission to add GPO links to an Active Directory object.

6. C. The Links tab shows the objects to which the GPO applies.

7. B. Inheritance is the process by which lower-level Active Directory objects inherit GPO settings from higher-level ones.

8. E. To disable the application of Group Policy on a security group, both the Read and Enable Group Policy options should be disabled.

9. D. LAN/WAN, RAS, desktop, and password settings are a few of the options that can be set using Group Policy.

10. C. Systems administrators can disable a GPO without removing its link to Active Directory objects. This prevents the GPO from having any effects on Group Policy.

11. A. The No Override option ensures that the Group Policy settings cannot be changed by the settings of lower-level Active Directory objects.

12. A. GPOs at the OU level take precedence over GPOs at the domain level. GPOs at the domain level, in turn, take precedence over GPOs at the site level.

13. B. The Block Policy Inheritance option prevents Group Policies of higher-level Active Directory objects from applying to lower-level objects as long as the No Override option is not set.

14. B. The settings on the Security tab allow systems administrators to determine to which security groups GPOs apply.

15. E. Members of the Group Policy Creator/Owners group are able to modify Group Policy settings.

16. D. Group Policy settings applied to the local computer do not require the use of the Active Directory.

17. D. By default, the contents of the SysVol share are made available to all domain controllers. Therefore, scripts should be placed in these directories.

18. C. Logon and logoff scripts are specified as part of the User Configuration section within the Group Policy Editor.

19. D. The Default Domain Policy GPO is created during the creation of a new domain.

20. A. GPO links at the site level affect all of the domains that are part of a site.

Chapter 11

Software Deployment through Group Policy

MICROSOFT EXAM OBJECTIVES COVERED IN THIS CHAPTER:

✓ **Manage and troubleshoot software by using Group Policy.**

- Deploy software by using Group Policy.
- Maintain software by using Group Policy.
- Configure deployment options.
- Troubleshoot common problems that occur during software deployment.

Throughout this book, we have been discussing the importance of implementing and administering a network environment based on the Windows 2000 operating system. Although the proper configuration of the Active Directory and client and server operating systems is very important, the real power of the computer for end users is in the applications they use. From simple word processors to spreadsheets and client-server applications, applications are what all types of users within a typical business require to help them complete their jobs.

From an end user's viewpoint, it's very easy to take software for granted. For example, many of us have come to expect our computers to run messaging applications, productivity applications, and (for people like us) games. However, from the view of systems administrators and help desk staff, deploying and maintaining software can be a troublesome and time-consuming process. Regardless of how much time is spent installing, updating, reinstalling, and removing applications based on users' needs, there seems to be no end to the process!

Fortunately, Windows 2000 and the Active Directory provide many improvements to the process of deploying and managing software. Through the use of Group Policy objects and the Microsoft Installer (MSI), software deployment options can be easily configured. The applications themselves can be made available to any users that are part of the Active Directory environment. Furthermore, systems administrators can automatically assign applications to users and computers and allow programs to be installed automatically when they are needed.

In this chapter, we'll look at how Windows 2000 and the Active Directory can be used to deploy and manage software throughout the network.

Overview of Software Deployment

It's difficult enough to manage applications on a stand-alone computer. It seems that the process of installing, configuring, and uninstalling applications is never finished! Add in the hassle of computer reboots and reinstalling corrupted applications, and the reduction in productivity can be very real.

When managing software in network environments, there are even more concerns. First and foremost, systems administrators must determine which applications specific users require. Then, IT departments must purchase the appropriate licenses for the software and acquire any necessary media. Next comes the fun part—actually installing the applications on users' machines. This process generally involves help desk staff visiting computers or requiring end users to install the software themselves. Both processes entail several potential problems, including inconsistency in installation and lost productivity from downtime experienced when installing applications. As if this wasn't enough, we haven't even discussed managing software updates and removing unused software!

One of the key design goals for the Active Directory was to reduce some of the headaches involved in managing software and configurations in a networked environment. To that end, Windows 2000 offers several features that can make the task of deploying software easier and less prone to errors. Before we dive into the technical details, though, let's examine the issues related to software deployment.

The Software Management Life Cycle

Although it may seem that the use of a new application requires only the installation of the necessary software, the overall process of managing applications involves many more steps. When managing software applications, there are three main phases to the life cycle of applications:

Deploying Software   The first step in using applications is to install them on the appropriate client computers. Generally, some applications are deployed during the initial configuration of a PC, and others are deployed when they are requested. In the latter case, this often used to mean that systems administrators and help desk staff would have to visit client computers and manually walk through the installation process.

It is very important to understand that the ability to easily deploy software does not necessarily mean that you have the right to do so! Before you install software on client computers, you must make sure that you have the appropriate licenses for the software. Furthermore, it's very important to take the time to track application installations. As many systems administrators have discovered, it's much more difficult to inventory software installations after they've been performed.

Maintaining Software   Once an application is installed and in use on client computers, there's a need to ensure that the software is maintained. Changes due to bug fixes, enhancements, and other types of updates must be applied in order to ensure that programs are kept up-to-date. As with the initial software deployment, software maintenance can be a tedious process. Some programs require that older versions be uninstalled before updates are added. Others allow for automatically upgrading over existing installations. Managing and deploying software updates can consume a significant amount of time for IT staff.

Removing Software   At the end of the life cycle for many software products is the actual removal of unused programs. Removing software is necessary when applications become outdated or when users no longer require their functionality. One of the traditional problems with uninstalling applications is that many of the installed files may not be removed. Furthermore, the removal of shared components can sometimes cause other programs to stop functioning properly. Also, users often forget to uninstall applications that are no longer needed, and these programs continue to occupy disk space and consume valuable system resources.

Each of these three phases of the software maintenance life cycle is managed by the Microsoft Installer application. Now that we have an overview of the process, let's move on to looking at the actual steps involved in deploying software using Group Policy.

The Windows Installer

If you've installed newer application programs (such as Microsoft Office 2000), you probably noticed the updated setup and installation routines. Applications that comply with the updated standard use the *Windows Installer* specification and software packages for deployment. Each package contains information about various setup options and the files required for installation. Although the benefits may not seem dramatic on the surface, there's a lot of new functionality under the hood!

The Windows Installer was created to solve many of the problems associated with traditional application development. It has several components, including the Installer service (that runs on Windows 2000 Server and Professional computers), the Installer program (`msiexec.exe`) that is responsible for executing the instructions in a *Windows Installer package*, and the specifications for third-party developers to use to create their own packages. Within each installation package file is a relational structure (similar to the structure of tables in databases) that records information about the programs contained within the package.

In order to appreciate the true value of the Windows Installer, let's start by looking at some of the problems with "traditional" software deployment mechanisms. Then we'll move on and look at how the Windows Installer addresses many of these problems.

Application Installation Issues

Before Windows 2000 and the Windows Installer, applications were installed using a setup program that managed the various operations required for a program to operate. These operations included copying files, changing Registry settings, and managing any other operating system changes that might be required (such as starting or stopping services). However, this method included several problems:

- The setup process was not robust, and aborting the operation often left many unnecessary files in the file system.

- The process of uninstalling an application often left many unnecessary files in the file system and remnants in the Windows Registry and operating system folders. Over time, this would result in reduced overall system performance and wasted disk space.

- There was no standard method for applying upgrades to applications, and installing a new version often required users to uninstall the old application, reboot, and then install the new program.

- Conflicts between different versions of dynamic link libraries (DLLs)—shared program code used across different applications— could cause the installation or removal of one application to break the functionality of another.

Benefits of the Windows Installer

Because of the many problems associated with traditional software installation, Microsoft has created a new standard known as the Windows Installer. This new system provides for better manageability of the software installation process and, as we'll see later in this chapter, allows systems administrators more control over the deployment process. Specifically, benefits of the Windows Installer include the following:

Improved Software Removal   The process of removing software is an important one since remnants left behind during the uninstall process can eventually clutter up the Registry and file system. During the installation process, the Windows Installer keeps track of all of the changes made by a setup package. When it comes time to remove an application, all of these changes can then be rolled back.

More Robust Installation Routines   If a typical setup program is aborted during the software installation process, the results are unpredictable. If the actual installation hasn't yet begun, then the Installer generally removes any temporary files that may have been created. If, however, the file copy routine starts before the system encounters an error, it is likely that the files will not be automatically removed from the operating system. In contrast, the Windows Installer allows you to roll back any changes when the application setup process is aborted.

Ability to Use Elevated Privileges   Installing applications usually requires the user to have Administrator permissions on the local computer since file system and Registry changes are required. When installing software for network users, systems administrators thus have two options. The first is to log off of the computer before installing the software, then log back on as a user who has Administrator permissions on the local computer. This method is tedious and time-consuming. The second is to temporarily give users Administrator permissions on their own machines. This method could cause security problems and requires the attention of a systems administrator.

Through the use of the Installer service, the Windows Installer is able to use temporarily elevated privileges to install applications. This allows users, regardless of their security settings, to execute the installation of authorized applications. The end result is the saving of time *and* the preservation of security.

Support for Repairing Corrupted Applications   Regardless of how well a network environment is managed, critical files are sometimes lost or corrupted. Such problems can prevent applications from running properly and cause crashes. Windows Installer packages support the ability to verify the installation of an application and, if necessary, replace any missing or corrupted files. This saves time and the end-user headaches associated with removing and reinstalling an entire application to replace just a few files.

Prevention of File Conflicts   Generally, different versions of the same files should be compatible with each other. In the real world, however, this isn't always the case. A classic problem in the Windows world is the case of one program replacing DLLs that are used by several other programs. Windows Installer accurately tracks which files are used by certain programs and ensures that any shared files are not improperly deleted or overwritten.

Automated Installations   A typical application setup process requires end users or systems administrators to respond to several prompts. For example, a user may be able to choose the program group in which icons will be created and the file system location to which the program will be installed. Additionally, they may be required to choose which options are installed. Although this type of flexibility is useful, it can be tedious when rolling out multiple applications. By using features of the Windows Installer, however, users are able to specify setup options before the process begins. This allows systems administrators to ensure consistency in installations and saves time for users.

Advertising and On-Demand Installations   One of the most powerful features of the Windows Installer is its ability to perform on-demand installations of software. Prior to Windows Installer, application installation options were quite basic—either a program was installed or it was not. When setting up a computer, systems administrators would be required to guess which applications the user *might* need and install them all.

The Windows Installer supports a function known as advertising. Advertising makes applications appear to be available via the Start menu. However, the programs themselves may not actually be installed on the system. When a user attempts to access an advertised application, the Windows Installer automatically downloads the necessary files from a server and installs the program. The end result is that applications are installed only when needed, and the process requires no intervention from the end user. We'll cover the details of this process later in this chapter.

To anyone that's had the pleasure of managing many software applications in a network environment, all of these features of the Windows Installer are likely to be welcome ones. They also make life easier for end users and application developers who can focus on the "real work" their jobs demand.

Windows Installer File Types

When performing software deployment with the Windows Installer in Windows 2000, there are several different file types you may encounter. These are as follows:

Windows Installer Packages (.MSI)   In order to take full advantage of Windows Installer functionality, applications must include Windows Installer packages. These packages are normally created by third-party application vendors and software developers and include the information required to install and configure the application and any supporting files.

Transformation Files (.MST)   *Transformation files* are useful when customizing the details of how applications are installed. When a systems administrator chooses to assign or publish an application, they may want to specify additional options for the package. If, for instance, a systems administrator wants to allow users to install only the Microsoft Word and Microsoft PowerPoint components of Office 2000, they could specify these options within a transformation file. Then, when users install the application, they will be provided with only the options related to these components.

Patches (.MSP)   In order to maintain software, *patches* are often required. Patches may make Registry and/or file system changes. Patch files are used for minor system changes and are subject to certain limitations. Specifically, a patch file cannot remove any installed program components and cannot delete or modify any shortcuts created by the user.

Initialization Files (.ZAP) In order to provide support for publishing non–Windows Installer applications, *initialization files* can be used. These files provide links to a standard executable file that is used to install an application. An example might be \\server1\software\program1\ setup.exe. These files can then be published and advertised, and users can access the *Add/Remove Programs* icon to install them over the network.

Application Assignment Scripts (.AAS) *Application assignment scripts* store information regarding the assignment of programs and any settings that are made by the systems administrator. These files are created when Group Policy is used to create software package assignments for users and computers.

Each of these types of files provides functionality that allows for the customization of software deployment. Windows Installer packages have special properties that can be viewed by right-clicking the file and choosing Properties (see Figure 11.1).

FIGURE 11.1 Viewing the properties of a Windows Installer (.MSI) package file

Deploying Applications

The functionality provided by Windows Installer offers many advantages to end users who install their own software. That, however, is just the tip of the iceberg in a networked environment. As we'll see later in this chapter, the various features of Windows Installer and compatible packages allow systems administrators to centrally determine applications that users will be able to install.

There are two main methods of making programs available to end users using the Active Directory. They are *assigning* and *publishing*. In this section, we'll look at how the processes of assigning and publishing applications can make life easier for IT staff and users alike. The various settings for assigned and published applications are managed through the use of Group Policy objects (GPOs).

Assigning Applications

Software applications can be assigned to users and computers. Assigning a software package makes the program available for automatic installation. The applications themselves advertise their availability to the affected users or computers by placing icons within the Programs folder of the Start menu.

When applications are assigned to a user, programs will be advertised to the user, regardless of which computer they are using. That is, icons for the advertised program will appear within the Start menu, regardless of whether the program is installed on the computer or not. If the user clicks on an icon for a program that has not yet been installed on the local computer, the application will automatically be accessed from a server and will be installed on the computer.

When an application is assigned to a computer, the program is made available to any users of the computer. For example, all users that log on to a computer that has been assigned Microsoft Office 2000 will have access to the components of the application. If the user did not previously install Microsoft Office, they will be prompted for any required setup information when the program is first run.

Generally, applications that are required by the vast majority of users should be assigned to computers. This reduces the amount of network bandwidth required to install applications on demand and improves the end user experience by preventing the delay involved when installing an application the first time it is accessed. Any applications that may be used by only a few users (or those with specific job tasks) should be assigned to users.

Publishing Applications

When applications are published, the programs are advertised, but no icons are automatically created. Instead, the applications are made available for installation using the Add/Remove Programs icon in the Control Panel. Software can be published only to users (not computers). The list of available applications is stored within the Active Directory, and client computers can query this list when they need to install programs. For ease of organization, applications can be grouped into *categories*.

Both publishing and assigning applications greatly ease the process of deploying and managing applications in a network environment.

Implementing Software Deployment

So far, we have discussed the issues related to software deployment and management from a high level. Now it's time to drill down into the actual steps required to deploy software using the features of the Active Directory. In this section, we will walk through the steps required to create an application distribution share point, to publish and assign applications, and to verify the installation of applications.

Microsoft
✓ *Exam*
Objective

Manage and troubleshoot software by using Group Policy.

- Deploy software by using Group Policy.

- Maintain software by using Group Policy.

Preparing for Software Deployment

Before you can install applications on client computers, you must make sure that the necessary files are available to end users. In many network environments, systems administrators create shares on file servers that include the installation files for many applications. Based on security permissions, either end users or systems administrators can then connect to these shares from a client computer and install the needed software. The efficient organization of these shares can save the help desk from having to carry around a library of CD-ROMs and can allow for installing applications easily on many computers at once.

Microsoft Exam Objective

Manage and troubleshoot software by using Group Policy.

- Troubleshoot common problems that occur during software deployment.

Exercises 11.1 and 11.2 provide hands-on experience related to the "Manage and troubleshoot software by using Group Policy" objective and its "Troubleshoot common problems that occur during software deployment" subobjective, but see the section "Optimizing and Troubleshooting Software Deployment" later in this chapter for more detailed text coverage of this objective and subobjective.

One of the problems in network environments is that users frequently install applications whether or not they really require them. They may stumble upon applications that are stored on common file servers and install them out of curiosity. These actions can often decrease productivity and may violate software licensing agreements. You can help avoid this by placing all of your application installation files in hidden shares (for example, "software$").

Exercise 11.1 walks you through the process of creating a software distribution share point.

EXERCISE 11.1

Creating a Software Deployment Share

In this exercise, you will prepare for software deployment by creating a directory share and placing certain types of files in this directory. In order to complete the steps in this exercise, you must have access to the Microsoft Office 2000 installation files (via CD-ROM or through a network share) and 600MB of free disk space.

1. Using Windows Explorer, create a folder called Software for use with application sharing. Be sure that the volume on which you create this folder has at least 600MB of available disk space.

EXERCISE 11.1 *(continued)*

2. Within the Software folder, create a folder called Admin Tools.

3. Copy the `adminpak.msi` file from the `%systemroot%\system32` folder to the Admin Tools folder that you created in step 2.

4. Within the Software folder, create a folder called Office 2000.

5. Copy all of the installation files for Microsoft Office 2000 from the CD-ROM or network share containing the files to the Office 2000 folder that you created in step 4.

6. Right-click the Software folder (created in step 1), and select the Sharing tab. Choose Share This Folder, and provide a share name of Software and a comment of Software Distribution Share Point. Leave all other options as the default, and click OK to create the share.

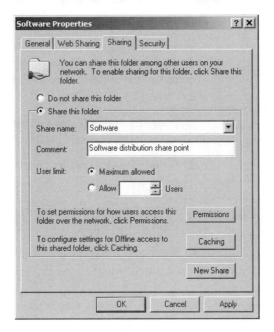

Once you have created an application distribution share, it's time to actually publish and assign the applications. We'll look at that topic next.

Publishing and Assigning Applications

As we mentioned earlier in this chapter, software packages can be made available to users through the use of publishing and assigning. Both of these operations allow systems administrators to leverage the power of the Active Directory and, specifically, Group Policy objects (GPOs) to determine which applications are available to users. Additionally, the organization provided by OUs can help group users based on their job functions and software requirements.

The general process involves creating a GPO that includes software deployment settings for users and computers and then linking this GPO to Active Directory objects. If you're unfamiliar with creating and linking GPOs, see Chapter 10, "Managing Group Policy." Exercise 11.2 walks you through the steps required to publish and assign applications.

EXERCISE 11.2

Publishing and Assigning Applications Using Group Policy

In this exercise, you will create and assign applications to specific Active Directory objects using Group Policy objects. In order to complete the steps in this exercise, you must have first completed Exercise 11.1.

1. Open the Active Directory Users and Computers tool from the Administrative Tools program group.

2. Expand the domain, and create a new top-level OU called Software.

3. Within the Software OU, create a user named Jane User with a login name of juser (choose the defaults for all other options).

4. Right-click the Software OU, and select Properties.

EXERCISE 11.2 *(continued)*

5. Select the Group Policy tab, and click New. For the name of the new GPO, type **Software Deployment**.

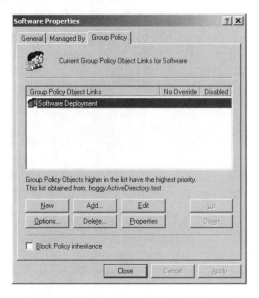

6. To edit the Software Deployment GPO, click Edit. Expand the Computer Configuration ➤ Software Settings object.

7. Right-click the Software Installation item, and select New ➤ Package. Navigate to the Software share that you created in Exercise 11.1. Within the Software share, double-click the Office 2000 folder, and select the Data1 file. Click Open.

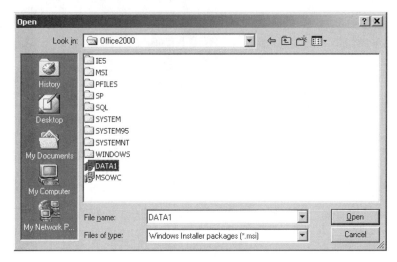

EXERCISE 11.2 *(continued)*

8. In the Deploy Software dialog box, choose Advanced Published or Assigned, and click OK. Note that the Published option is unavailable since applications cannot be published to computers.

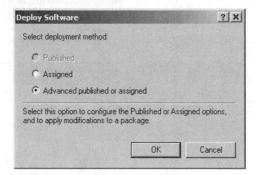

9. To examine the Deployment options of this package, click the Deployment tab. Accept the default settings by clicking OK.

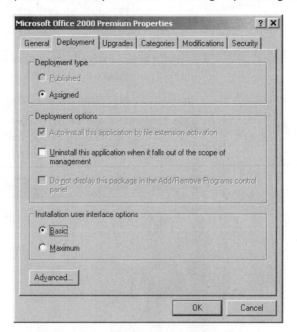

EXERCISE 11.2 *(continued)*

10. Within the Group Policy Editor, expand the User Configuration ➢ Software Settings object.

11. Right-click the Software Installation item, and select New ➢ Package. Navigate to the Software share that you created in Exercise 11.1. Within the Software share, double-click the Admin Tools folder, and select the `adminpak.msi` file. Click Open.

12. For the Software Deployment option, select Published and click OK.

13. Close the Group Policy Editor, and then click Close to close the Properties of the Software OU.

The overall process involved with deploying software using the Active Directory is quite simple. However, you shouldn't let the intuitive graphical interface fool you—there's a lot of power under the hood of these software deployment features! Once you've properly assigned and published applications, it's time to see the effects of your work.

Verifying Software Installation

In order to ensure that the settings you made in the GPO for the Software OU have taken place, you can log in to the domain from a Windows 2000 Professional computer that is within the OU to which the software settings apply. When you log in, you will notice two changes. First, Microsoft Office 2000 will be installed on the computer (if it was not installed already). In order to access the Office 2000 applications, all a user would need to do is click one of the icons within the Program group of the Start menu (for example, the Microsoft Word icon). Note also that these applications will be available to any of the users who log on to this machine. Also, the settings apply to any computers that are contained within the Software OU and to any users who log on to these computers.

The second change may not be as evident, but it is equally useful. We assigned the Windows 2000 Administrative Tools program to the Software OU. We also created an account named juser within that OU. When you log on to a Windows 2000 Professional computer that is a member of the domain and use the juser account, you will be able to automatically install

any of the published applications. You can do this by accessing the Add/
Remove Programs icon in the Control Panel. By clicking Add New Programs, you will see a display similar to that shown in Figure 11.2.

FIGURE 11.2   Installing published applications in Add/Remove Programs

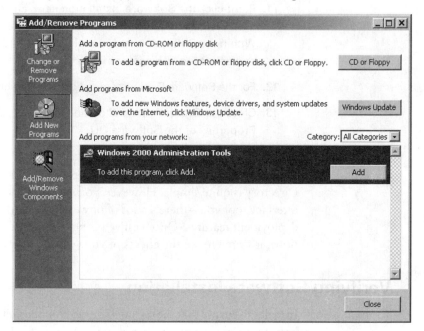

By clicking the Add button, you will automatically begin the installation
of the Windows 2000 Administration Tools (see Figure 11.3). This is a useful
way of allowing systems administrators to use the Windows 2000 Administration Tools to remotely manage Windows 2000 Server computers.

FIGURE 11.3 The automatic installation of Windows 2000 Administration Tools

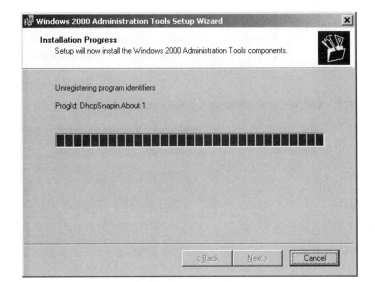

Configuring Software Deployment Settings

In addition to the basic operations of assigning and publishing applications, there are several other options for specifying the details of how software is deployed. You can access these options from within a GPO by right-clicking the Software Installation item (located within Software Settings in User Configuration or Computer Configuration). In this section, we will examine the various options that are available and their effects on the software installation process.

Microsoft ✓ *Exam* *Objective*

Manage and troubleshoot software by using Group Policy.

- Configure deployment options.

Managing Package Defaults

On the General tab of the Software Installation Properties dialog box, you'll be able to specify some defaults for any packages that you create within this GPO. Figure 11.4 shows the General options for managing software installation settings.

FIGURE 11.4 General settings for software settings

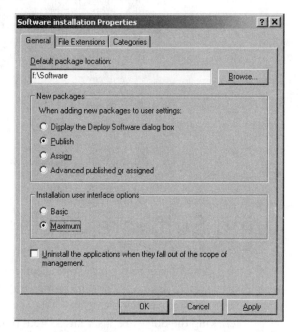

The various options available include the following:

Default Package Location This setting specifies the default file system or network location for software installation packages. This is useful if you are already using a specific share on a file server for hosting the necessary installation files.

New Packages Options This setting specifies the default type of package assignment that will be used when adding a new package to either the user or computer settings. If you'll be assigning or publishing multiple packages, it may be useful to set a default here.

Installation User Interface Options   When an application is being installed, systems administrators may or may not want end users to see all of the advanced installation options. If Basic is chosen, the user will only be able to configure the minimal settings (such as the installation location). If Maximum is chosen, all of the available installation options will be displayed. The specific installation options available will depend on the package itself.

Uninstall the Applications When They Fall Out of the Scope of Management   So far, we have discussed how applications can be assigned and published to users or computers. But what happens when effective GPOs change? For example, suppose that User A is currently located within the Sales OU. A GPO that assigns the Microsoft Office 2000 suite of applications is linked to the Sales OU. Now, I decide to move User A to the Engineering OU, which has no software deployment settings. Should the application be uninstalled, or should it remain?

If the Uninstall the Applications When They Fall Out of the Scope of Management option is checked, applications will be removed if they are not specifically assigned or published within GPOs. In our earlier example, this means that Office 2000 would be uninstalled for User A. If, however, the box is left unchecked, the application would remain installed.

Now, let's look at some more options that are available for managing software settings.

Managing File Extension Mappings

One of the potential problems associated with the use of many different file types is that it's difficult to keep track of which applications work with which files. For example, if I received a file with the extension .ABC, I would have no idea which application I would need to view it. And, Windows would not be of much help, either!

Fortunately, through software deployment settings, systems administrators can specify mappings for specific *file extensions*. For example, I could specify that whenever users attempt to access a file with the extension .VSD, the operating system should attempt to open the file using the Visio diagramming software. If Visio is not installed on the user's machine, the computer could automatically download and install it (assuming that the application has been properly advertised).

This method allows users to have applications automatically installed when they are needed. The following is an example of the sequence of events that might occur:

- A user receives an e-mail message that contains an Adobe Acrobat file attachment.

- The Windows 2000 computer realizes that Adobe Acrobat, the appropriate viewing application for this type of file, is not installed. However, it also realizes that a file extension mapping is available within the Active Directory software deployment settings.

- The client computer automatically requests the Adobe Acrobat software package from the server and uses the Windows Installer to automatically install the application.

- The Windows 2000 computer opens the attachment for the user.

Notice that all of these steps were carried out without any further interaction with the user! You can manage file extension mappings by viewing the properties for any package that you have defined within the Group Policy settings. Figure 11.5 shows how file extension settings can be managed. By default, the list of file extensions that you'll see is based on the specific software packages you have added to the current GPO.

FIGURE 11.5 Managing file extensions

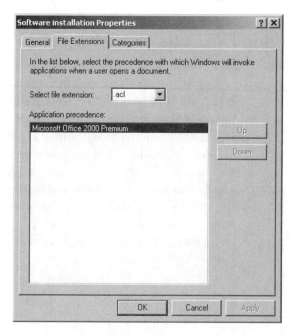

Creating Application Categories

In many network environments, the list of supported applications can include hundreds of items. For users that are searching for only one specific program, searching through a list of all of these programs can be difficult and time-consuming.

Fortunately, there are methods for categorizing the applications that are available on your network. You can easily manage the application categories for users and computers by right-clicking the Software Installation item, selecting Properties, and then clicking the Categories tab. Figure 11.6 shows you how application categories can be created. It is useful to use category names that are meaningful to users as it will make it easier for them to find the programs they're looking for.

FIGURE 11.6 Creating application categories

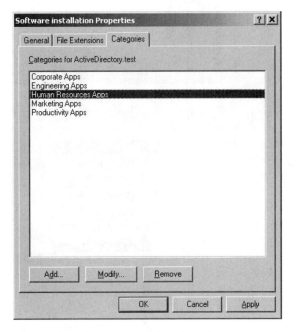

Once the software installation categories have been created, you can view them by opening the Add/Remove Programs item in the Control Panel. When you click Add New Programs, you'll see that there are several options in the Category drop-down list (see Figure 11.7). Now, when you select the properties for a package, you will be able to assign the application to one or more of the categories (as shown in Figure 11.8).

FIGURE 11.7 Viewing application categories in Add/Remove Programs

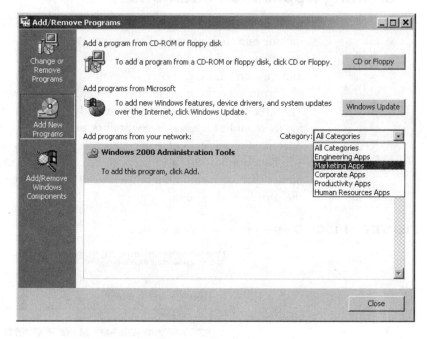

FIGURE 11.8 Specifying categories for application packages

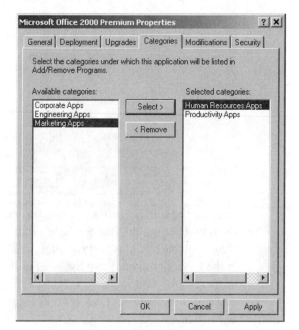

Removing Programs

As we discussed in the beginning of the chapter, an important phase in the software management life cycle is the removal of applications. Fortunately, using the Active Directory and Windows Installer packages, the process is simple. To remove an application, you can right-click the package within the Group Policy settings and select All Tasks ➢ Remove (see Figure 11.9).

FIGURE 11.9   Removing a software package

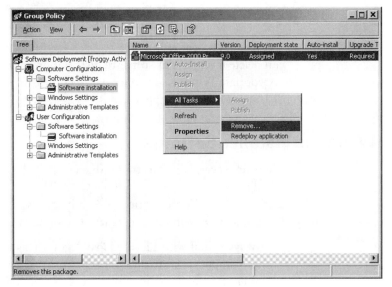

When choosing to remove a software package from a GPO, you have two options:

Immediately Uninstall the Software from Users and Computers
Systems administrators can choose this option to ensure that an application is no longer available to users that are affected by the GPO. When this option is selected, the program will be automatically uninstalled from users and/or computers that have the package. This option might be useful, for example, if the licensing for a certain application has expired or if a program is no longer on the approved applications list.

Allow Users to Continue to Use the Software, but Prevent New Installations   This option prevents users from making new installations of a package, but it does not remove the software if it has already been installed for users. This is a good option if the company has run out of additional licenses for the software, but the existing licenses are still valid.

Figure 11.10 shows the two removal options that are available.

FIGURE 11.10 Software removal options

If you no longer require the ability to install or repair an application, you can delete it from your software distribution share point by deleting the appropriate Windows Installer package files. This will free up additional disk space for newer applications.

Windows Installer Settings

There are several options that influence the behavior of the Windows Installer, which can be set within a GPO. These options are accessed by navigating to User Configuration ➤ Administrative Templates ➤ Windows Components ➤ Windows Installer. The options include the following:

Always Install with Elevated Privileges   This policy allows users to install applications that require elevated privileges. For example, if a user does not have the permissions necessary to modify the Registry, but the installation program must make Registry changes, this policy will allow the process to succeed.

Search Order   This setting specifies the order in which the Windows Installer will search for installation files. The options include n (for network shares), m (for searching removal media), and u (for searching the Internet for installation files).

Disable Rollback   When this option is enabled, the Windows Installer does not store the system state information that's required to roll back the installation of an application. Systems administrators may choose this option to reduce the amount of temporary disk space required during installation and to increase the performance of the installation operation.

However, the drawback is that the system cannot roll back to its original state if the installation fails and the application needs to be removed.

Disable Media Source for Any Install   This option disallows the installation of software using removable media (such as CD-ROM, DVD, or floppy diskettes). It is useful for ensuring that users install only approved applications.

With these options, systems administrators can control how the Windows Installer operates for specific users who are affected by the GPO.

Optimizing and Troubleshooting Software Deployment

Although the features in Windows 2000 and the Active Directory make software deployment a relatively simple task, there are still many factors that systems administrators should consider when making applications available on the network. In this section, we will discuss some common methods for troubleshooting problems with software deployment in Windows 2000 and optimizing the performance of software deployment.

Microsoft
✓ *Exam*
Objective

Manage and troubleshoot software by using Group Policy.

- Troubleshoot common problems that occur during software deployment.

Specific optimization and troubleshooting methods include those that follow:

Test packages before deployment.   The use of the Active Directory and GPOs makes publishing and assigning applications so easy that systems administrators may be tempted to make many applications available to users immediately. However, the success of using the Windows Installer is at least partially based on the quality of the programming of developers and third-party software vendors.

Before unleashing an application on the unsuspecting user population, you should always test the programs within a test environment using a few volunteer users and computers. The information gathered during these tests can be invaluable in helping the help desk, systems administrators, and end users during a large-scale deployment.

Manage Group Policy scope and links.   One of the most flexible aspects of deploying software with the Active Directory is the ability to assign Group Policy settings to users and computers. Since it is so easy to set up GPOs and link them to Active Directory objects, it might be tempting to modify all of your existing GPOs to meet the current software needs of your users. Note, however, that this can become difficult to manage.

An easier way to manage multiple sets of applications may be to create separate GPOs for specific groups of applications. For example, one GPO could provide all end user productivity applications (such as Microsoft Office 2000 and Adobe Acrobat Reader) while another GPO could provide tools for users in the Engineering department. Now, whenever the software requirements for a group changes, systems administrators can just enable or disable specific GPOs for the OU that contains these users.

Rollout software in stages.   Installing software packages over the network can involve high bandwidth requirements and reduce the performance of production servers. If you're planning to roll out a new application to several users or computers, it's a good idea to deploy the software in stages. This process involves publishing or assigning applications to a few users at a time, through the use of GPOs and OUs.

Verify connectivity with the software distribution share.   If clients are unable to communicate with the server that contains the software installation files, the Windows Installer will be unable to automatically copy the required information to the client computer, and installation will fail. You should always ensure that clients are able to communicate with the server and verify the permissions on the software installation share.

Organize categories.   The list of applications that are available in a typical network environment can quickly grow very large. From standard commercial desktop applications and utilities to custom client-server applications, it's important to organize programs based on functionality. Be sure to group software packages into categories that end users will clearly recognize and understand when searching for applications.

Create an installation log file. By using the `msiexec.exe` command, you can create an installation log file that records the actions attempted during the installation process and any errors that may have been generated.

Reduce redundancy. In general, it is better to ensure that applications are not assigned or published to users through multiple GPOs. For example, if a user almost always logs on to the same workstation and requires specific applications to be available, you may consider assigning the applications to both the user and the computer. Although this scenario will work properly, it can increase the amount of time spent during logon and the processing of the GPOs. A better solution would be to assign the applications to only the computer (or, alternatively, to only the user).

Manage software distribution points. When users require applications, they will depend on the availability of installation shares. One method by which to ensure greater performance and availability of these shares is to use the Windows 2000 Distributed File System (DFS). The features of DFS allow for fault tolerance and the ability to use multiple servers to share commonly used files from a single logical share point. The end result is increased uptime, better performance, and easier access for end users. Additionally, the underlying complexity of where certain applications are stored is isolated from the end user.

Encourage developers and vendors to create Microsoft Installer packages. Many of the benefits of the software deployment features in Windows 2000 rely on the use of Microsoft Installer (MSI) packages. To ease the deployment and management of applications, ensure that in-house application developers and third-party independent software vendors use Microsoft Installer packages that were created properly. The use of MSI packages will greatly assist systems administrators and end users in assigning and managing applications throughout the life cycle of the product.

Enforce consistency using MSI options. One of the problems with applications and application suites (such as Microsoft Office 2000) is that end users can choose to specify which options are available during installation. While this might be useful for some users, it can cause compatibility and management problems. For example, suppose a manager sends a spreadsheet containing Excel pivot tables to several employees. Some employees are able to access the pivot tables (since they chose the default installation options), but others cannot (since they chose not install this feature). The users that cannot properly read the spreadsheet will likely generate help desk calls and require assistance to add in the appropriate components.

One way to avoid problems such as these is to enforce standard configurations for applications. For example, we may choose to create a basic and an advanced package for Microsoft Office 2000. The Basic package would include the most-used applications such as Microsoft Word, Microsoft Outlook, and Microsoft Excel. The advanced package would include these applications, plus Microsoft PowerPoint and Microsoft Access.

Create Windows Installer files for older applications.   Although there is no tool included with Windows 2000 to automatically perform this task, it will generally be worth the time to create Windows Installer files for older applications. This is done through the use of third-party applications that are designed to monitor the Registry, file system, and other changes that an application makes during the setup process. These changes can then be combined into a single MSI package for use in software deployment.

By carefully planning for software deployment and using some of the advanced features of Windows 2000, you can make software deployment a smooth and simple process for systems administrators and end users alike.

Summary

The real reason for deploying and managing networks in the first place is to make the applications that they support available. End users are often much more interested in being able to do their jobs using the tools they require than in worrying about network infrastructure and directory services. In the past, software deployment and management have been troublesome and time-consuming tasks.

In this chapter, we covered ways in which new Windows 2000 features can be used to manage the tasks related to software deployment. Through the use of several features, including the Active Directory, Group Policy objects, and the Windows Installer, the tasks associated with deploying, managing, and removing applications is much more reliable. Furthermore, systems administrators can control software deployment options from within the warmth and comfort of an Active Directory console—a great improvement over the days of carrying around stacks of CD-ROMs to client computers.

When implemented correctly, the use of the Active Directory software deployment features can save much time, reduce headaches, and improve the end-user experience.

Key Terms

When working with the software deployment features made available by Windows 2000 and the Active Directory, you should be familiar with the following terms:

Add/Remove Programs

Application assignment scripts

assigning

categories

file extensions

initialization files

patches

publishing

Transformation files

Windows Installer

Windows Installer packages

Review Questions

1. A systems administrator wants to group applications based on various types of programs. Which of the following software deployment features should they use?

   A. Categories

   B. File extensions

   C. Assigning

   D. Publishing

   E. None of the above

2. Which of the following tools is used to install published applications?

   A. Active Directory Users and Computers

   B. Active Directory Domains and Trusts

   C. Add/Remove Programs Control Panel applet

   D. Computer Management

   E. All of the above

3. A systems administrator has created a Software Deployment GPO. Which tool can they use to link this GPO to an existing OU?

   A. Active Directory Users and Computers

   B. Active Directory Domains and Trusts

   C. Add/Remove Programs Control Panel applet

   D. Computer Management

   E. All of the above

4. A systems administrator wants to ensure that all users of a particular workstation will be able to run Microsoft Office 2000. Which of the following should they do?

   A. Assign the application to the computer.

   B. Assign the application to users.

   C. Publish the application to the computer.

   D. Publish the application to users.

   E. All of the above.

5. A systems administrator wants to ensure that a particular user will have access to Microsoft Office 2000 regardless of the computer to which they log on. Which of the following should they do?

   A. Assign the application to all computers within the environment and specify that only this user should have access to it.

   B. Assign the application to the user.

   C. Publish the application to all computers within the environment and specify that only this user should have access to it.

   D. Publish the application to the user.

   E. All of the above.

6. A systems administrator wants to ensure that a particular group of users will be able to install Microsoft Office 2000 by using the Add/Remove Programs icon in the Control Panel. Which of the following should they do?

   A. Assign the application to their computers.

   B. Assign the application to the users.

   C. Publish the application to their computers.

   D. Publish the application to the users.

   E. All of the above.

7. Which of the following statements regarding application categories is incorrect?

    A. Application categories are hierarchical.

    B. Application categories apply only to Microsoft applications.

    C. Application categories cannot be changed.

    D. All of the above.

8. Which of the following operations is supported by the Windows Installer?

    A. Software deployment

    B. Software removal

    C. Software patches

    D. All of the above

9. The files required to install published and assigned applications are stored within:

    A. The Active Directory data store

    B. File shares

    C. The Global Catalog

    D. None of the above

10. In order to install applications, a user must have which of the following permissions?

    A. Ability to modify the Registry

    B. Local Administrator permissions

    C. Ability to create directories

    D. None of the above

11. Which of the following types of files store information about Group Policy software assignments?

   A. .MSI

   B. .MST

   C. .ZAP

   D. .AAS

   E. None of the above

12. Which of the following Windows Installer settings prevents recovering from a failed installation?

   A. Always Install with Elevated Privileges

   B. Disable Rollback

   C. Disable Search Order

   D. Disallow Uninstall

   E. None of the above

13. Windows 2000 Remote Installation Services (RIS) can be used to install which of the following operating systems:

   A. Windows NT 4 Workstation

   B. Windows 2000 Professional

   C. Windows 2000 Server

   D. Windows 2000 Advanced Server

   E. All of the above

14. Which of the following statements is true regarding the actions that occur when a software package is removed from a GPO that is linked to an OU?

   A. The application will be automatically uninstalled for all users with the OU.

   B. Current application installations will be unaffected by the change.

   C. The systems administrator may determine the effect.

   D. None of the above.

15. When a software deployment package is created, which of the following steps must be performed manually in order to make the installation files available to end users?

    A. Refreshing the Active Directory

    B. Synchronizing all domain controllers

    C. Rebuilding the Global Catalog

    D. Copying the required files to an appropriate file share.

    E. None of the above

16. A systems administrator wants to define the application that will be installed when a user opens a file named `MarketingInfo.ppt`. Which of the following configuration options should they use?

    A. Categories

    B. Publishing options

    C. Assignment options

    D. File extensions

    E. None of the above

17. Which of the following types of files is used to modify the options for an existing Windows Installer package?

    A. .MSI

    B. .MST

    C. .ZAP

    D. .AAS

    E. None of the above

18. An applications developer wants to create a patch for an existing application. Which of the following types of files should they create?

A. .MSI

B. .MSP

C. .ZAP

D. .AAS

E. None of the above

19. How can a systems administrator get more information about a specific Windows Installer setup file?

A. By right-clicking the file and selecting Properties in Windows Explorer

B. By issuing a search within the Active Directory

C. By querying the Global Catalog

D. None of the above

20. How can a systems administrator create a Windows Installer package from a legacy setup program?

A. By right-clicking the Setup.exe file for the application and choosing Migrate

B. By right-clicking the Setup.exe file for the application and choosing Upgrade to Windows Installer

C. By adding the application to the Active Directory

D. None of the above

Answers to Review Questions

1. A. The purpose of application categories is to logically group applications in the Add/Remove Programs Control Panel applet.

2. C. End users can install applications using the Add/Remove Programs icon in the Control Panel.

3. A. Group Policy links can be created within the Active Directory Users and Computers tool.

4. A. Assigning the application to the computer will ensure that all users who access the workstation will have access to Microsoft Office 2000.

5. B. Assigning the application to the user ensures that the user will have access to Microsoft Office 2000, regardless of the computer they use.

6. D. When applications are published to users, they can easily install the programs using the Add/Remove Programs icon in the Control Panel.

7. D. All of the statements listed regarding application categories are untrue.

8. D. The Windows Installer supports all of the operations listed.

9. B. Published and assigned applications must be stored within a share on a file server and must be accessible to client computers.

10. D. The Windows Installer is able to use the Installer service to bypass user permissions for installing software. Therefore, the user performing the installation is not required to have any of the permissions listed.

11. D. Application assignment script (.AAS) files store information regarding application assignments.

12. B. Disabling rollback can improve performance and reduce disk space requirements, but this option prevents rolling back from a failed installation.

13. B. RIS only supports the automated installation of Windows 2000 Professional.

14. C. The systems administrator can specify whether the application will be uninstalled or if future installations will be prevented.

15. D. It is the responsibility of the systems administrator to copy installation files to a software deployment share point and ensure that users can access these files.

16. D. File extension settings can be used to specify the applications that are installed when specific file types are accessed.

17. B. Transformation (.MST) files are used to modify the options of a setup package.

18. B. Patch (.MSP) files are used to update existing applications.

19. A. Details about .MSI files can be viewed by right-clicking the file and selecting Properties. The other options may be available, but only if software deployment is configured within the Active Directory.

20. D. These applications and utilities must be obtained from third-party software vendors and are not included with the Windows 2000 operating system.

Chapter

12

Installing and Configuring RIS

MICROSOFT EXAM OBJECTIVES COVERED IN THIS CHAPTER:

✓ **Deploy Windows 2000 by using Remote Installation Services (RIS).**

- Install an image on a RIS client computer.
- Create a RIS boot disk.
- Configure remote installation options.
- Troubleshoot RIS problems.
- Manage images for performing remote installations.

✓ **Configure RIS security.**

- Authorize a RIS server.
- Grant computer account creation rights.
- Prestage RIS client computers for added security and load balancing.

If you ask a systems administrator about the most painful parts of their job, you're likely to hear about the pain associated with hardware and software rollouts. Deploying new computers begins with the installation of the operating system. In most environments, this involves having a member of the IT staff sit in front of each new computer for at least an hour choosing the appropriate options. The process may be repeated hundreds or even thousands of times (based on the size of the environment and the number of computers supported).

Apart from the obvious problems—risking death by boredom and allocating potentially productive time to the installation process—manual installations are plagued by inconsistent configurations. It's difficult to remember all of the options that must be configured and to carry out these processes consistently on multiple installations. Clearly, there's a need for a better solution.

Recognizing this problem, Microsoft has included *Remote Installation Services (RIS)* components with Windows 2000 Server. RIS is designed to allow client computers to boot onto a network and immediately begin installing Windows 2000 Professional over the network. This chapter looks at the various technical steps required to install, configure, manage, secure, and troubleshoot RIS. With any luck, you'll never need to sit in front of a Windows 2000 Professional installation progress bar!

Overview of RIS

 One of the dullest and most time-consuming duties of systems administrators is the process of installing and rolling out new PCs. It's a never-ending job because employees are always being added to companies and computers are often upgraded or transferred between users. Worse yet, the process is generally quite repetitive and requires hand-holding by a systems administrator. Finally, no matter how many times these installations are carried out, it seems that some aspect of the configuration is easily left behind.

Many companies use disk-duplication methods to create an image of a base workstation configuration and then to apply this image to multiple other computers. However, there are several potential problems with this method:

- It can be time consuming to create and generate disk images.

- Workstation images are hardware specific. That is, since the hardware-detection phase of a normal setup process is not carried out, two computers that have, for example, different video adapters must use two completely separate images.

- Images take up large amounts of disk space. Since each different configuration requires the storage of all data from a computer's hard disk, the size and number of the potential files can become quite large.

- Security Identifiers (SIDs) are duplicated between multiple machines. This issue is particularly troublesome in a Windows NT 4 environment. Although there are tools that can consistently change SIDs on imaged computers, this adds an extra step to the process and can be time consuming.

The purpose of RIS is to alleviate the problems and minimize the time associated with installing Windows 2000 Professional on computers, while, at the same time, preserving the benefits of performing individual operating-system installations. RIS works through the creation of images and settings for a remote installation on a RIS server. Clients then connect to the RIS server over the network and install the operating system using settings that are predefined by the systems administrator.

One of the major benefits of using RIS is that the hardware configuration does not have to be an exact match between client machines. The Windows 2000 Plug-and-Play and automatic-hardware-detection features will iron out any differences when the image is applied on client computers. Additionally, RIS is easy to install and configure.

Now that we have an idea of the problems RIS attempts to solve, let's look at the details regarding what you'll need to implement and administer RIS in a Windows 2000 environment!

Prerequisites for RIS

RIS works only with the Windows 2000 operating system platform. That means that you must be running Windows 2000 Server (which acts as the RIS server) and that you plan to install Windows 2000 Professional on client computers. Based on this information, let's drill down into the details of what's required on the server and client computers.

RIS Server Requirements

RIS relies upon several different network and operating features and services to function properly. In order to take advantage of RIS, you must have the following services installed, configured, and enabled on your network:

DNS   The Domain Name System (DNS) is used for resolving TCP/IP addresses to host names. Active Directory domain controllers and clients rely on DNS services for finding network resources.

DHCP   The Dynamic Host Configuration Protocol (DHCP) automatically assigns TCP/IP configuration information to clients. This is especially important for remote boot clients since they must be able to communicate on the network and connect to the RIS server.

Active Directory   The Active Directory hosts the Computer accounts used by RIS and allows administrators to control permissions to log on to the domain. Also, the Active Directory's Group Policies are used to specify client options. (These services are required for use by RIS clients.) Finally, security permissions related to which users and computers can be used for a remote installation are stored within the Active Directory.

For more information on DNS and DHCP, see Chapter 2, "Integrating DNS with the Active Directory."

When RIS is installed on a Windows 2000 Server computer, three services are automatically installed and configured:

Boot Information Negotiation Layer (BINL)   The *Boot Information Negotiation Layer (BINL)* service is responsible for ensuring that the correct computer is being installed and can be used to create a Computer account within an Active Directory domain.

Trivial File Transfer Protocol Daemon (TFTPD)   When a client is first connected to the RIS server computer, it only has the bare minimum information required to communicate. At this stage, the *Trivial File Transfer Protocol Daemon (TFTPD)* service is used to transfer any required files from the server to the client.

Single Instance Store (SIS)   *Single Instance Store (SIS)* technology is created to reduce the redundancy of data stored on a RIS server. One of the major problems with creating multiple boot images is that they can take up much disk space. For example, if we were to create six images (with an average size of 300MB each), this would require 1.8GB of disk space. Although this is not a huge amount of space on modern servers, there is a lot of wasted space due to the fact that most files between these images are the same. Consider, for example, that each of the 5,000+ files that reside in the I386 directory would have to be stored six times!

The SIS is designed to eliminate this type of redundant storage by finding duplicate files and then replacing them with a link to one file. For example, suppose the `MyProgram.exe` file is stored four times on the disk. The SIS notices this and replaces all but one instance of the file with links that point to the real file. Then, whenever a client attempts to access the file, the SIS automatically finds the real copy of the file.

As we'll see later in this chapter, each of these three services is important in the process of automating client installations.

Finally, you should be aware of the following minimum system requirements for a RIS server (as specified by Microsoft):

- Pentium-166 (or equivalent) processor

- 256MB RAM

- 2GB disk drive (reserved for use only by RIS)

- 10MB network adapter

- CD-ROM drive

The disk-space requirement is somewhat unique. The image files created for RIS must be stored on an NTFS volume that does not contain either the Windows 2000 system files or the boot files. The RIS process is resource intensive, especially with respect to disk input/output (I/O). Therefore, it is recommended that your RIS server computers exceed these values for better performance.

Now that we've covered the server side, let's look at the requirements for the client computers.

RIS Client Requirements

On the client side, you must use a desktop computer with a network interface card or a laptop computer with a port replicator or docking station. Windows 2000 RIS does not support the use of laptop or notebook computers that use PC Card or PCMCIA network adapters for the purpose of connecting to a RIS server.

Client computers may use one of two methods to gain network access and connect to the RIS server:

Using a PXE Boot ROM   The *Preboot eXecution Environment (PXE)* specification is designed to allow computers that do not have an operating system to access the network. The PXE Boot Read-Only Memory (ROM) chip is part of a computer's hardware. Its purpose is to allow the computer to initialize the network adapter and to then gain access to the network using DHCP.

Most recent-model computers contain network cards that include a PXE Boot ROM. Computers that meet the Net PC/PC 98 specification must include a PXE Boot ROM. In order to determine whether or not a client computer has a PXE Boot ROM, consult your computer vendor or manufacturer.

Using a Boot Floppy   For older computers that do not contain a PXE Boot ROM, there's another option: booting from a floppy diskette that contains the bare minimum information to connect to the network and communicate with the RIS server. Windows 2000 Server includes a utility that can be used to create these disks. The utility (which we'll cover in detail later in this chapter) contains drivers for several popular network cards. In order to successfully use a boot floppy for connecting to a RIS server, the client network adapter must be supported.

Regarding the hardware configuration, client computers should meet the following minimum specifications:

- Pentium-166 (or equivalent) processor
- 32MB RAM
- 1.2GB hard disk
- Network adapter
- PXE Boot ROM version .99c or later

As with the server side, it is recommended that a computer have a faster processor, more memory, and a larger hard disk than that specified. A faster network adapter also reduces the required installation time.

Implementing and Administering a RIS Server

The heart of the RIS system in Windows 2000 Server is the feature that enables it to manage images and provide remote installation shares for clients. Although there are many configuration options, the process of installing and configuring RIS is simplified through the use of various Wizards. This section looks at the exact steps that are required to install a RIS server.

Microsoft
✓ *Exam*
Objective

Deploy Windows 2000 by using Remote Installation Services (RIS)

- Configure remote installation options.
- Manage images for performing remote installations.

Configure RIS security.

- Authorize a RIS server.
- Grant computer account creation rights.
- Prestage RIS client computers for added security and load balancing.

Installing RIS

Installation of RIS is a straightforward process that involves two main steps. First, you must add the RIS service to a Windows 2000 Server and then reboot the computer. Next, you must configure the RIS server based on the options you require. Exercise 12.1 walks you through the process of installing RIS.

EXERCISE 12.1

Installing Remote Installation Services

In this exercise, you will install RIS. In order to complete the steps in this exercise, you must have access to the Windows 2000 Server CD-ROM or a network location that contains the necessary files.

1. Click Start ➢ Settings ➢ Control Panel. Double-click the Add/Remove Programs icon.

2. Click Add/Remove Windows Components.

3. To add a new item, click the Components button.

4. Place a check mark next to the Remote Installation Services item, and then click Next.

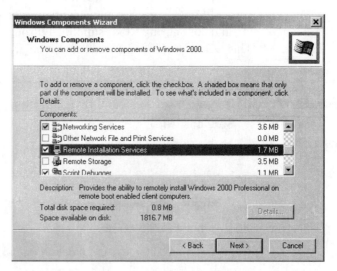

5. If you have installed any optional Windows 2000 components that require additional configuration (such as Terminal Services), you will be prompted to enter the configuration information for these items. The installation process will begin. When it has finished, you will be prompted to restart the computer. Choose Yes to restart the computer.

Configuring a RIS Server

Once RIS has been installed on the server, you need to configure the service to meet the needs of your network environment. There are two main options that can be configured for the RIS server:

Respond to all clients requesting service. This option enables the RIS server to respond to remote installation requests from clients. If this option is disabled, clients are not able to access the server for remote installation.

Do not respond to unknown client computers. If this option is checked, then a Computer object for the client requesting a remote installation must exist within the Active Directory domain. If a Computer account for the provided *Global Unique Identifier (GUID)* does not exist, the RIS server does not respond to the remote installation request.

You should choose these options carefully since using RIS in an unprotected network environment can be a potential security risk. We'll cover RIS security in detail later in this chapter. For now, let's look at the process involved in creating RIS installation images.

Creating a CD-Based Image

A RIS server can contain one or more images of operating system installation files. These images contain all of the files necessary to install and configure the Windows 2000 Professional operating system via a remote installation process. There are two main ways to create images for use with RIS. The first involves creating a standard default image through the use of the Windows 2000 Professional CD-ROM; the steps required to do this are shown in Exercise 12.2. The second method (covered in the next section) allows you to create custom images.

EXERCISE 12.2

Configuring a CD-Based Image for RIS

In this exercise, you will configure RIS to create a CD-based image of Windows 2000 Professional. In order to complete the steps in this exercise, you must have first completed Exercise 12.1 and have access to the Windows 2000 Professional installation files (located on either a CD-ROM or stored in a network location).

1. Click Start ➤ Settings Control Panel. Double-click the Add/Remove Windows Components icon.

2. Click Add/Remove Windows Components. Highlight the Configure Remote Installation Services item, and then click the Configure button.

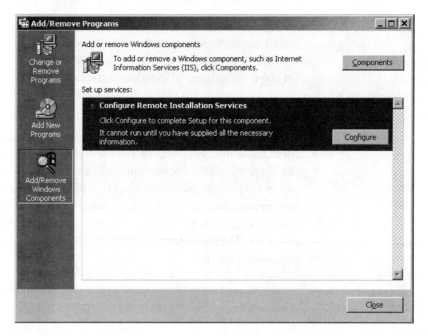

3. You will see the introductory information for the Remote Installation Services Setup Wizard. Click Next to continue.

4. Specify the folder to which the remote installation information will be written. Select a path on a local physical drive that is formatted as an NTFS 5 file system partition and that is neither the boot nor system partition. Ensure that this partition has at least 400MB free (although you will need more if you plan to store many different images). Click Next.

EXERCISE 12.2 *(continued)*

5. On the Initial Settings step, place a check mark next to the Respond to Client Computers Requesting Service option. (This will enable RIS for use by clients.) Click Next.

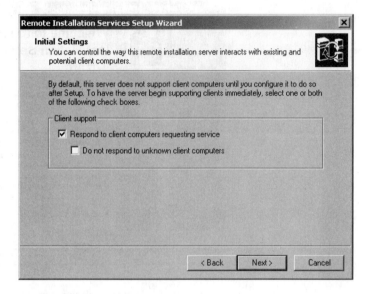

6. Specify the source file location for the Windows installation files. Insert the Windows 2000 Professional CD-ROM, and enter the path to this drive. Alternatively, you can browse for the installation files (which may be on the local system or located on a network drive) by clicking Browse. Once you have selected the appropriate path, click Next to continue.

7. Specify the name of the folder to which the installation files will be copied. The default location will be titled win2000.pro. If you are using multiple images, it is a good idea to use a clear, descriptive name for the image file. Click Next to continue.

8. Specify a friendly name and a description for this RIS image. This information will be visible to users and systems administrators that are performing remote installations. Therefore, you should make the description as meaningful as possible. Click Next to continue.

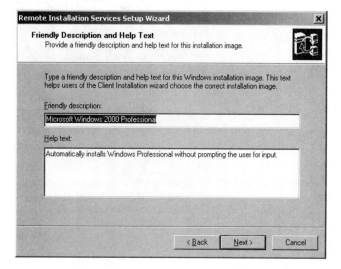

9. Finally, you are given an opportunity to review the settings you have chosen. Ensure that the correct paths have been provided. To complete the installation, click Finish.

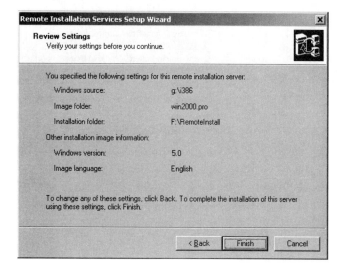

EXERCISE 12.2 *(continued)*

10. The RIS Wizard will begin copying the necessary files to the location you specified. This process is likely to take several minutes. Once it has finished, you will see a summary of all of the steps performed. To complete the operation, click Done.

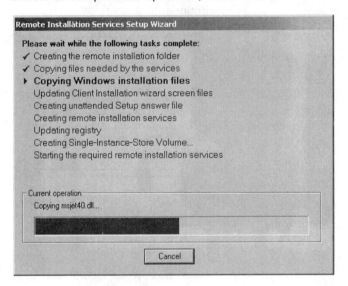

11. Close the Add/Remove Programs dialog box and the Control Panel.

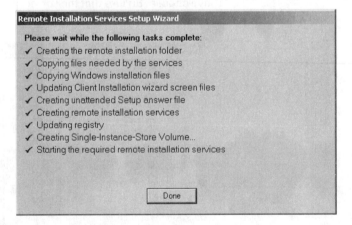

Once the Remote Installation Services Setup Wizard has completed, a new share is created on the server. This share, named REMINST, contains all of the files and settings that will be used by clients to access the CD-based image. Figure 12.1 shows the default directories that you will see.

FIGURE 12.1   Default RIS directories

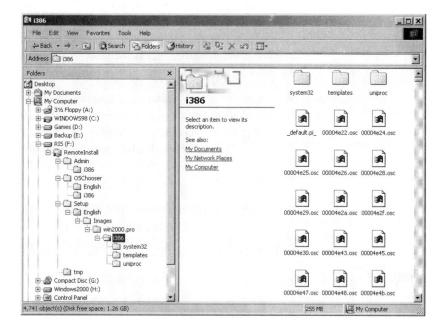

Creating a Custom Installation

There are usually two main challenges in rolling out new workstation computers. The first involves the installation of the operating system. The second challenge regards configuring the operating system and adding any additional applications that may be required by users of these computers.

Although a CD-based image is sufficient for installing the base operating system, it does not allow you to add any applications or make any other changes to the configuration. The *Remote Installation Preparation Wizard (RIPrep)* utility is designed to do just that. The process for using RIPrep is as follows:

1. Install Windows 2000 Professional. This can be done using the CD-ROM or by connecting to a network share that contains the necessary files.

2. Configure any operating system settings you want to have copied to client computers. For example, you can change desktop settings to match your company's default settings. Or you may choose to install optional Windows 2000 components such as Web services.

3. Install and configure any applications that should be installed as part of the image. (This step is mainly used for installing older applications that do not use the new Microsoft Installer technology, because newer programs can be installed automatically using software deployment. For more information on automating software deployment, see Chapter 11, "Software Deployment through Group Policy.")

4. Close any open applications and then run the RIPrep utility. You will be asked to provide information about the RIS server to which this image will be saved, along with a title and description of the image. The RIPrep utility will collect information about operating system settings and any applications that are installed on the system and then transmit the image to a RIS server.

After using the RIPrep utility, the RIS server will include a new custom image that can be used for installation. Figure 12.2 shows an example of the RIPrep utility. Figure 12.3 shows the screen that allows you to begin the process.

FIGURE 12.2 Reviewing RIPrep installation settings

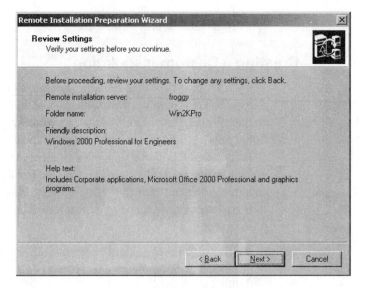

FIGURE 12.3 Beginning the image preparation process

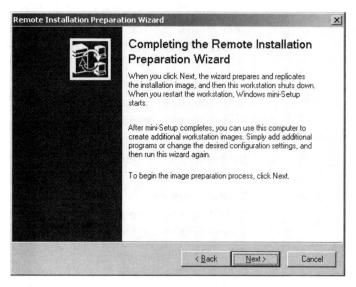

Using Setup Information Files (SIFs)

Windows 2000 Professional generally requires users or systems administrators to answer many different questions during the setup process. Although this can be done manually, it would be much better to pre-answer the questions and store the settings in a file that can be used by setup.

The specific installation options for the client are specified in a Setup Information File. These standard text files have the extension .SIF and can be edited by systems administrators to specify certain options to be used during the installation process. The following is a portion of the default `ristndrd.sif` file:

```
[data]
floppyless = "1"
msdosinitiated = "1"
OriSrc = "\\%SERVERNAME%\RemInst\
➡%INSTALLPATH%\%MACHINETYPE%"
OriTyp = "4"
LocalSourceOnCD = 1
```

```
[SetupData]
OsLoadOptions = "/noguiboot /fastdetect"
SetupSourceDevice = "\Device\LanmanRedirector\
➥%SERVERNAME%\RemInst\%INSTALLPATH%"

[Unattended]
OemPreinstall = no
NoWaitAfterTextMode = 0
FileSystem = LeaveAlone
ExtendOEMPartition = 0
ConfirmHardware = no
NtUpgrade = no
Win31Upgrade = no
TargetPath = \WINNT
OverwriteOemFilesOnUpgrade = no
OemSkipEula = yes
InstallFilesPath = "\\%SERVERNAME%\RemInst\
➥A%INSTALLPATH%\%MACHINETYPE%"

[UserData]
FullName = "%USERFULLNAME%"
OrgName = "%ORGNAME%"
ComputerName = %MACHINENAME%

[GuiUnattended]
OemSkipWelcome = 1
OemSkipRegional = 1
TimeZone = %TIMEZONE%
AdminPassword = "*"

[LicenseFilePrintData]
AutoMode = PerSeat

[Display]
ConfigureAtLogon = 0
BitsPerPel = 8
```

```
XResolution = 640
YResolution = 480
VRefresh = 60
AutoConfirm = 1

[Networking]
ProcessPageSections=Yes

[Identification]
JoinDomain = %MACHINEDOMAIN%
CreateComputerAccountInDomain = No
DoOldStyleDomainJoin = Yes

[NetProtocols]
MS_TCPIP=params.MS_TCPIP

[params.MS_TCPIP]
; transport: TC (TCP/IP Protocol)
InfID=MS_TCPIP
DHCP=Yes
```

If you have multiple images on your RIS server, you'll have multiple copies of the `*.sif` files. Each image uses its own Setup Information File, so you
can use different sets of installation options. The `*.sif` file can be modified
through the use of any standard text editor (such as Windows Notepad).

Authorizing a RIS Server

Before a RIS server is made available to clients, it must be authorized by a
systems administrator. The additional step required to authorize a server
adds a measure of security by preventing other individuals from adding new
RIS servers to the network.

The authorization process allows clients to gain the services of the DHCP
service and the RIS service. Exercise 12.3 walks you through the process of
authorizing a RIS server.

EXERCISE 12.3

Authorizing a RIS Server

In this exercise, you will authorize a DHCP server and a RIS server. In order to complete the steps in this exercise, you must have installed and configured RIS (as described in Exercises 12.1 and 12.2) and must not yet have authorized either DHCP or RIS.

1. Log in to the computer as a member of the Domain Admins or Enterprise Admins group.

2. Open the DHCP snap-in from the Administrative Tools program group.

3. Right-click the name of the local computer, and click Authorize.

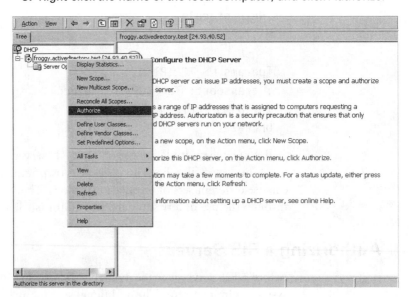

4. When you are finished authorizing the server, close the DHCP administrative tool.

Managing RIS Server Options

You can change the settings for a RIS server after the service has been configured by opening the Active Directory Users and Computer tool, right-clicking the RIS Server object, and selecting Properties. On the Remote Install tab, you can then change RIS options and settings.

By clicking the Show Clients button, you can automatically find any remote installation clients that are on the network. This is useful when you are trying to determine which computers can be used with RIS.

You can also click the Advanced button to access more options for the RIS server. Here, you'll be able to set options for automatically determining the client computer name. The default options available include the following:

- First initial, last name

- Last name, first initial

- First name, last initial

- Last initial, first name

- Username

- NP Plus MAC (two standard characters followed by the Media Access Card address of the network adapter)

- Custom

By using the Custom option, you can set several different options using variables (see Figure 12.4). This is extremely helpful if you are rolling out several computers, and your organization already has a standard naming convention for client machines.

FIGURE 12.4 Setting default client computer name settings

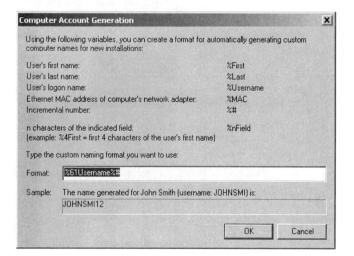

You can also set the location of the Client account within the Active Directory. Options include the following (as shown in Figure 12.5):

Default Directory Service Location   This option automatically saves the Computer object to the default location for clients. This is usually the Computers folder.

Same Location As That of the User Setting Up the Client Computer
This option saves the Computer account in the Active Directory location in which the user performing the installation process resides. For example, if the user Jane Doe resides within the RIS OU, and this user performs the remote installation, then the Computer object will also reside within the RIS OU.

The Following Directory Service Location   Using this option allows systems administrators to specify a single Active Directory location for all new Computer objects. This setting might be useful if, for example, you want to place all Computer objects in a generic container and then manually move them to the appropriate locations later.

FIGURE 12.5   Viewing RIS server and Client account location options

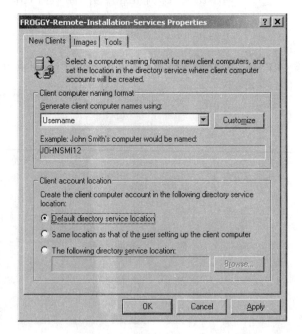

By clicking the Images tab, you will be able to view a list of images that are available on a particular RIS server (see Figure 12.6). You can also add new images, remove images (to make them unavailable for installation), and view the properties of an image (to see the title and description text).

FIGURE 12.6   Viewing a list of images on a RIS server

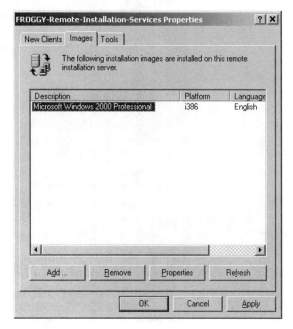

By clicking the Add button, you will access a Wizard that allows you to generate either a new answer file (also known as a Setup Information File, described earlier in this chapter) or to generate a new installation image. Figure 12.7 shows the main choices available.

FIGURE 12.7 The New Answer File or Installation Image Wizard

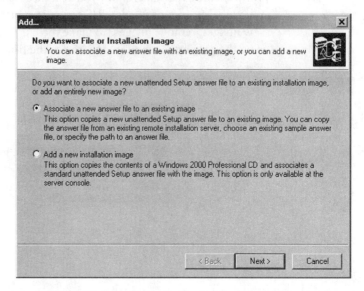

Exercise 12.4 walks you through the detailed steps that are associated with RIS server options.

EXERCISE 12.4

Managing RIS Server Options

In this exercise, you will view the various options that are available when configuring a RIS server. In order to complete the steps in this exercise, you must have first installed RIS on the local computer.

1. Open the Active Directory Users and Computers tool.

2. Find the local domain controller within the Active Directory structure. Right-click the name of this computer, and select Properties.

3. Select the Remote Install tab. Note that you have the option to verify the configuration of the current server. To see any clients that are able to use this RIS server, click Show Clients.

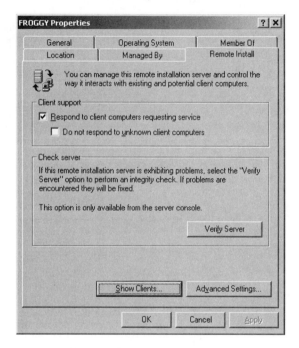

4. Click Advanced Settings to view additional options for the RIS Server.

EXERCISE 12.4 *(continued)*

5. On the New Clients tab, select Username for the Generate Client Computer Names Using selection. To see other available options, click Customize. Click OK.

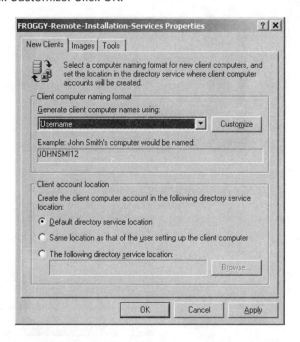

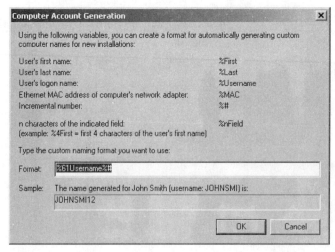

6. To manage images, click the Images tab. Note that the list includes any images that are already available for installation. You can find additional information about the images by clicking Properties.

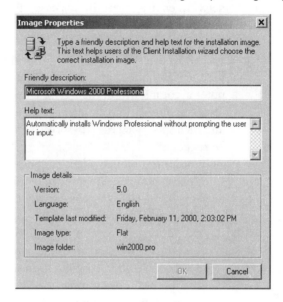

7. Finally, click the Tools tab. By default, this tab will be blank. If, however, you have installed additional Microsoft or third-party tools related to RIS, they will show up here.

8. Click OK twice to close the settings for the RIS server.

9. When finished, close the Active Directory Users and Computers tool.

By using all of these setting options, you can ensure that your RIS server will behave the way you want it to!

Prestaging Computer Accounts

Before you install a remote client, you should first create a computer account within a domain. The client computer will use this computer account during installation. When you create the computer account, you will need to set sufficient permissions to allow users to modify the account during installation.

Although you may choose to allow remote clients to request a remote installation from the RIS server, this option reduces security. This is because any valid domain account with the appropriate permissions will be able to install the image to a client computer. Furthermore, you wouldn't be able to control to *which* computer the image will be applied. Certainly, haphazardly installing images to production client machines can cause problems. Another potential problem arises when multiple RIS servers are present in the same network environment. In this case, it would be difficult to tell which RIS server responded to the client first and whether or not it contains the correct images.

So how can systems administrators control the machines that will receive remote installation images? The main method is by *prestaging* client computer accounts within the Active Directory. The process of prestaging involves the creation of a client account, supplying a GUID for the computer, and then specifying the RIS server(s) from which the remote installation can be requested.

In order to uniquely identify computers on the network, there must be some number or value that is dedicated to each machine. For computers that have them, the GUID or *Universally Unique Identifier (UUID)* can be used. This value is set by computer manufacturers and resides in the computers' Basic Input/Output System (BIOS). The BIOS code resides on a chip and is accessed during the startup of the computer. Its purpose is to provide the low-level services and configuration options necessary for system components to interact. For example, the BIOS allows your graphics adapter to use system memory and to communicate with the CPU.

On newer computers, you can find a computer's GUID on a label somewhere on the computer's case. In other cases, the GUID is written inside the computer case. Or, you may need to get this value from the system BIOS during the boot process. For specifics, contact your hardware manufacturer or reseller.

A GUID takes the form of a 32-digit hexadecimal (base-16) number. This means that the valid characters for a GUID are the digits zero through nine and the letters A through F (the value is not case sensitive). The format of the number is eight digits, followed by three sets of four digits, followed by 12 digits. For example, the following is a valid GUID:

```
{01234567-ABCD-1234-ABCD-01234567890AB}
```

RIS servers can be configured to respond to specific machine addresses. This adds security to a network environment as it prevents any user from adding a computer to the network and joining the Active Directory. Although it is recommended that this type of security be enabled, the RIS server may also be configured to allow connections from any computer on the network. When this option is chosen, a systems administrator is not required to enter in a GUID when the computer account is created.

Exercise 12.5 walks you through the steps required to prestage a computer account. Using this process, you can ensure that only authorized clients are able to join the domain via RIS, and you can balance the load of remote installations across multiple servers.

Creating a Computer Account

In this exercise, you will create a Computer object within the Active Directory and add the necessary permissions for a user to add the client computer to the Active Directory domain.

1. Open the Active Directory Users and Computers tool.

2. Create a top-level OU called RIS.

3. Within the RIS OU, create a new User object with the name Remote Admin and the logon name remadmin (choose the defaults for all other options).

4. Within the RIS OU, create a Computer object with the name RISClient. Click the Change button to specify the users and groups that will be able to add this computer to a domain. Select Remote Administrator from the list of users, and click OK. Click Next.

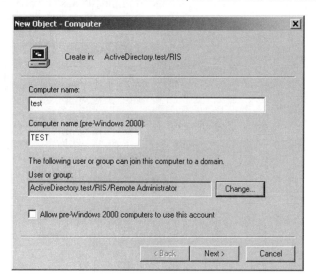

EXERCISE 12.5 *(continued)*

5. In the Managed dialog box, place a check mark next to the This Is a Managed Computer option. Enter the following (including the {brackets}) for the GUID/UUID value, then click Next:

{123FB937-ED12-11BD-BACD-076A01878937}

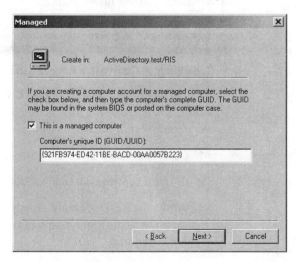

6. In the Host Server dialog box, select the Any Available Remote Installation Server option, and then click Next. Note that you could choose servers from within a specific Active Directory domain if you have multiple RIS servers on the network or if you want the RIS process to be restricted to only one machine.

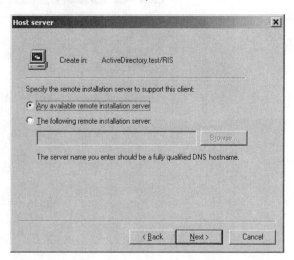

EXERCISE 12.5 *(continued)*

7. Click Finish to create the computer account.

8. When finished, close the Active Directory Users and Computers tool.

You can also change the RIS settings for an existing computer account by right-clicking a Computer object within the Active Directory and choosing Properties. By clicking the Remote Install tab (as shown in Figure 12.8), you can access the properties of the Computer object.

FIGURE 12.8   Viewing the Remote Install settings for a Computer object

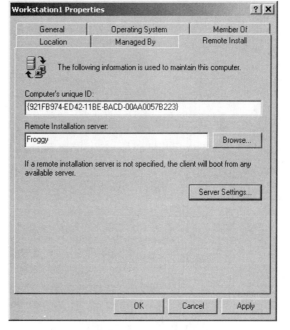

Once a Computer object has been created, you will want to designate which Groups or Users will have permissions to add this computer to the domain using RIS. This can be done by right-clicking a Computer object, choosing Properties, and selecting the Security tab (see Figure 12.9). In order to be able to view this tab, you must ensure that the Advanced Features option is checked within the View menu of the Active Directory Users and Computers console.

FIGURE 12.9 Viewing the Security settings for a Computer object

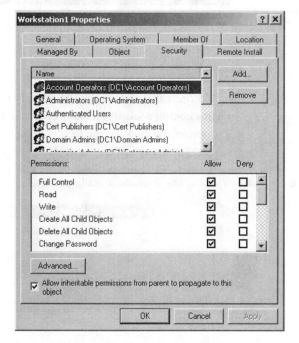

To provide a User or Group with the permissions necessary to add a Computer account to the domain, add the appropriate account(s) and then allow the following permissions:

- Read

- Write

- Reset Password

- Change Password

By clicking on Advanced, you can also set auditing permissions.

Although, in some cases, you may have the appropriate information to create Computer objects before starting the client installation process, you may also want to delegate permissions to create computer accounts within the domain.

Delegating Permissions to Create Computer Accounts

In addition to setting permissions on specific computer accounts, you can use the Delegation of Control Wizard to allow specific users to create accounts within the domain. This permission must be granted to a user in order to be able to create a new computer account.

The Delegation of Control Wizard within the Active Directory Users and Computers tool is used to assign the appropriate permissions. In the Active Directory Users and Computers tool, right-click the domain name and select Properties. Select Delegate Control. The Wizard will walk you through the steps required to select users and/or groups. As shown in Figure 12.10, you must select the Join a Computer to the Domain permission. For more information on using the Delegation of Control Wizard, see Chapter 7, "Administering the Active Directory," and Chapter 8, "Active Directory Security."

FIGURE 12.10 Delegating control to join a computer to the domain

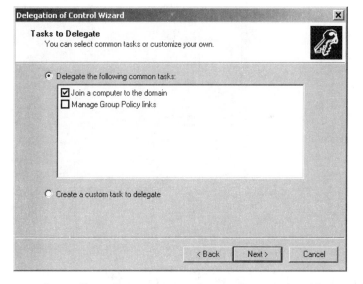

Once you have allowed certain users the permissions to add a computer to the domain, you will not be required to create Computer objects before starting the installation process. Of course, in order for these computers to have access to the RIS server, you must not have set the requirement that computer accounts exist within the domain before the process begins.

In order to allow the creation of Computer objects within an OU, you will need to modify the Group Policy object(s) that apply to the OU. The specific setting you will need to modify can be found in Computer Configuration ➢ Windows Settings ➢ Security Settings ➢ Local Policies ➢ User Rights Assignment. As shown in Figure 12.11, you can add the User and Group objects that will enable you to add computers to the domain by modifying the Add Workstations to Domain option.

FIGURE 12.11   Setting User Rights to add a computer to the domain

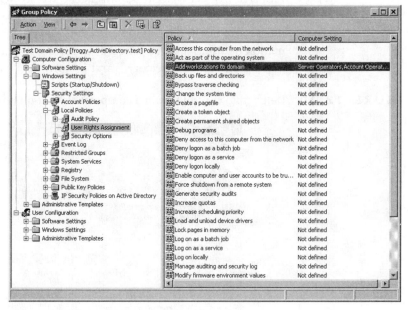

For more information on setting Group Policy, see Chapter 10, "Managing Group Policy."

Setting Up a RIS Client

So far, we have examined the steps required to set up a RIS server and to configure images. Now, it's time to put this work to use by actually using clients to connect to the server and begin the process. In this section, we'll look at the steps and processes required to install Windows 2000 Professional remotely using RIS.

WARNING   During the client installation process, all information on the hard disk of the client will be lost. Be sure that this is what you want to do before beginning the process. If not, make a backup!

RIS Installation Process Overview

When performing an automated installation of Windows 2000 using RIS, you will normally be starting with a computer that does not have an operating system installed. Because of this, there are several steps that the client must go through before beginning the actual remote installation process. The following process takes place when a RIS client computer is booted:

1. The computer gains network access through the use of a PXE Boot ROM or a RIS Boot floppy diskette.

2. The computer sends a broadcast on the network requesting an IP address; it also sends the computer's GUID.

3. A DHCP server on the computer responds with a valid IP address.

4. The client initiates a remote installation request.

5. The RIS server receives the request and looks in its database for the GUID of the client computer. If the GUID is found, it automatically begins the client installation process. If the GUID is not found, then the client is prompted to authenticate with the server using the Client Installation Wizard prompts.

6. Upon successful negotiation, the RIS server begins transferring files to the client, and the automated installation process proceeds.

All of these steps are performed automatically (with the exception of logging on to the network using the Client Network Utility).

Configuring Client Setup Options

When the remote installation process is started from the client, you may want to allow or disallow specific options. There are four main options that can be set for clients to choose during the RIS setup procedures. These include the following:

Automatic Setup   When this option is chosen, the systems administrator specifies all of the installation options, and the user is not given any choices when using the Client Installation Wizard.

Custom Setup   When this option is chosen, a user or systems administrator is able to specify various options, such as the name of the computer and the Active Directory location for the Computer object.

Restart Setup   In some cases, the setup process may terminate before it is finished. This might occur due to a loss of network connectivity or a configuration problem. When the Restart Setup option is enabled, users or systems administrators may choose to restart setup from the point at which it failed.

Tools   This option allows users or systems administrators to access various tools that are available when the Client Installation Wizard is running.

For each of these settings just listed, you can choose from among three policies:

Allow   This permits users or systems administrators to allow the particular setting during the client setup process.

Don't Care   This is the default setting. It specifies that no policy is set at this level and that settings at the parent or higher-level Active Directory objects may specify the Allow or Deny option.

Deny   This disallows users or systems administrators from choosing this particular setting during the client setup process.

Figure 12.12 shows where the options are located, and Figure 12.13 shows the various options that are available. You can access these settings by modifying the Group Policy object for an Active Directory object. The

Remote Installation Services Choice Options can be accessed by clicking
User Configuration ➢ Windows Settings ➢ Security Settings ➢ Remote
Installation Services.

FIGURE 12.12   Editing Group Policy settings for RIS

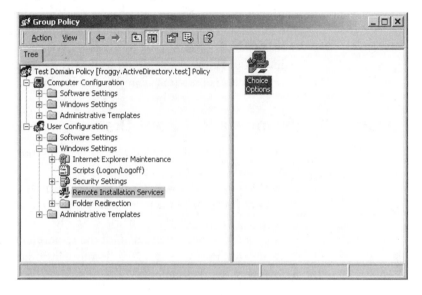

FIGURE 12.13   Setting RIS Setup Choice Options

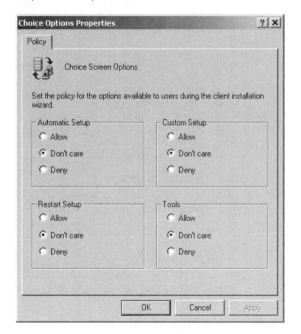

For more information on configuring Group Policy settings, see Chapter 10, "Managing Group Policy."

Using RIS through PXE-Compliant Network Adapters

In order to access the RIS server using the PXE-compliant network adapter, you must configure your computer to access the network during the boot process. This is done usually by accessing the system BIOS. The exact procedure should be available from the hardware manufacturer. The remainder of the process is the same as in the next section.

Using RIS through a RIS Boot Disk

If your computer and network adapter do not support the PXE specification, then you will need to create a boot disk. This disk can be created on a Windows 2000 server that has RIS installed. The purpose of the boot disk is the same as the purpose of the PXE Boot ROM—to load a minimal set of drivers to get the computer on the network. Once the computer has access to the network, the RIS server provides all of the required program code.

By default, the Windows 2000 Remote Installation Service supports the following network adapters:

- 3Com 3C900B-Combo
- 3Com 3C900B-FL
- 3Com 3C900B-TPC
- 3Com 3C900B-TPO
- 3Com 3C900-Combo
- 3Com 3C900-TPO
- 3Com 3C905B-Combo
- 3Com 3C905B-FX
- 3Com 3C905B-TX
- 3Com 3C905C-TX
- 3Com 3C905-T4
- 3Com 3C905-TX

- AMD PCNet Adapters

- Compaq NetFlex 100

- Compaq NetFlex 110

- Compaq NetFlex 3

- DEC DE450

- DEC DE500

- HP DeskDirect 10/100TX

- Intel Pro10+

- Intel Pro100+

- Intel Pro100B

- SMC 8432

- SMC 9332

- SMC 9432

If your network adapter is not included in this list, you will need to contact your computer manufacturer or network card manufacturer in order to obtain the appropriate driver. Note that not all vendors will support remote client installations using RIS. If you are unsure of the network adapter that is installed in the client computer, you should contact your hardware vendor or see the computer manufacturer's Web site. Exercise 12.6 walks you through the process of creating a remote boot disk.

EXERCISE 12.6

Creating a Remote Boot Disk

In this exercise, you will create a remote boot disk. In order to complete this exercise, you must have first installed and configured RIS (see Exercises 12.1 and 12.2). You will also require a single, high-density floppy diskette.

1. Using Windows Explorer, open the folder into which you placed the Remote Installation files.

2. Within this folder, open the Admin\i386 folder.

EXERCISE 12.6 *(continued)*

3. To open the Windows 2000 Remote Boot Disk Generator, double-click the rbfg program.

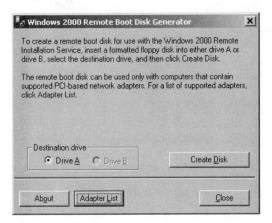

4. To specify the network adapter of the client computer, click the Adapter List button. Select the appropriate network adapter from the list. Click OK.

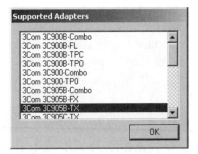

5. To create the boot diskette, click Create Disk. The Windows 2000 Remote Boot Disk Generator will begin copying the necessary file(s) to the floppy.

6. When finished, click Close to exit the Windows 2000 Remote Boot Disk Generator.

If you have chosen the wrong network adapter for the boot disk, you will see the following message on the client when you boot the computer:

```
Windows 2000 Remote Installation Boot Floppy

Error: Could not find a supported network card.  The boot
floppy currently supports a limited set of PCI based
network cards for use with the Windows 2000 Remote
Installation Service.  Ensure this system contains one of
the supported network cards and try the operation again.
For assistance, contact your systems administrator.
```

If this is the case, you will need to re-create the boot disk with the appropriate drivers and/or obtain the name of the proper drivers from your vendor. If you're having problems connecting to the RIS server or are having other problems, see the "Troubleshooting RIS" section later in this chapter.

Performing the Client Installation

Once you have booted the client (using either a PXE device or a boot floppy), you will be connected to the RIS server. At this point, the text-mode portion of setup will begin. If you chose the Deny settings for all options, then the client will not be provided with any additional choices and setup will automatically start copying files.

If, however, additional information is required (such as authentication information or a computer name), the Client Installation Wizard will appear. The Wizard will ask several questions to gather the required information. Once the information has been provided, the automated remote installation process will begin.

Optimizing RIS Performance

The actual process required to automatically install an operating system can be bandwidth-intensive. In the case of Windows 2000, the thousands of files required can lead to high network usage. If not managed properly, using RIS can reduce performance for all network users. And, the problem is greatly increased if you plan to install multiple clients at the same time!

Fortunately, there are several ways to optimize the performance of RIS in a network environment. They include the following suggestions:

Use dedicated servers. Because of the high disk I/O requirements for the automated client installation process, it is usually a good idea to use a dedicated server for RIS operations. Although using a standard file server might suffice for an occasional installation, the resource usage can add up when rolling out multiple clients.

Use fast network links. Using fast network links between RIS clients and servers can greatly increase performance. Although some of the newest and fastest networking technologies may be too expensive to roll out to every desktop, you may be able to find it in your budget to implement higher-speed networks in a computer rollout lab. The additional bandwidth will make the operation much faster.

For most companies, trying to perform a RIS operation over a WAN link should be out of the question. The high overhead and relatively low-bandwidth situation will greatly reduce performance, increase costs, and possibly prevent other users from doing their jobs!

Isolate network traffic. By placing the RIS server and clients on the same dedicated subnet within your network, you can reduce the impact on performance that results from the load on routers. Additionally, by using a separate subnet, you reduce the chances of affecting other network users.

Another method for isolating network traffic is known as *switching*. Through the use of switches, rather than routers, you can effectively reduce contention for network access. Switching is especially useful if you plan to roll out multiple client machines using RIS at the same time. It is beyond the scope of this book to discuss network design issues in depth. For more information on routing and switching, consult *MCSE: Windows 2000 Network Infrastructure Design Study Guide* (Sybex, 2000).

In general, the methods just listed will be sufficient for increasing RIS performance and minimizing the impact on users. Now that we have some optimization ideas in mind, let's move on and look at what to do when RIS isn't working the way you wanted...

Troubleshooting RIS

In most cases, the installation and configuration of RIS will be straight-forward. Through the use of the configuration Wizards and Active Directory administration tools, it is usually a simple task to set up RIS the way you want it to work. In some instances, however, you may have problems in performing a remote installation. After all, the process involves a client computer that does not have an operating system communicating with a remote server.

Microsoft ✓ *Exam* *Objective*

Deploy Windows 2000 by using Remote Installation Services (RIS).

- Troubleshoot RIS problems.

If you're having trouble performing remote installation options, there are several configuration settings you should verify. Some troubleshooting steps to attempt include the following:

Verify the server configuration.   Using the Active Directory Users and Computers tool, you can quickly and easily verify the proper functioning of a RIS server. To perform this test, open the Active Directory Users and Computers tool, right-click the name of the RIS server, and choose Properties. On the Remote Install tab, click the Verify Server button. The Check Server Wizard will perform a diagnostic test on the current RIS configuration and then provide information on the configuration in addition to other information (shown in Figure 12.14). If errors in the configuration are found, you should check the System event log for more information.

FIGURE 12.14 Verifying the configuration of a RIS server

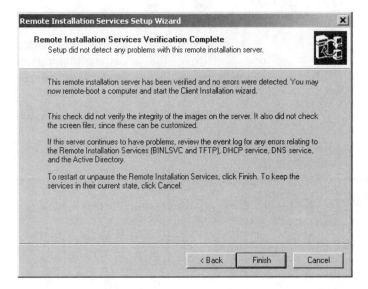

Verify the PXE Boot ROM version. In order to be compatible with Windows 2000 Remote Installation Services, the PXE Boot ROM must be version .99c or greater. You may have problems booting and connecting to the RIS server if the client is using an earlier standard.

Verify the network configuration settings. Verify the network configuration settings if the client is unable to connect to the RIS server. If the DHCP settings are incorrect, then the remote client may receive unusable TCP/IP address information. If other computers on the same network are using DHCP and are able to connect with the server, then it's likely that there is another problem.

You can ensure that the network interface card on the client is working properly by trying to connect to other resources or servers. Of course, this can only be done after you have installed an operating system (or connected to a terminal server) with this machine.

Ensure that the RIS server contains the desired images. Since there is no way for the client to specify to which RIS server it wants to connect, the client may be connecting to the wrong RIS server on the network. This RIS server may not have all of the same images that are available on others.

Although not all vendors support the use of prestaged computers, you may choose to set them up in order to ensure that only the desired RIS server responds to a client. If you want to use multiple RIS servers (for performance and fault tolerance reasons), you will need to ensure the appropriate images are available on all servers in your environment.

Verify that you are using the correct boot disk.   The Windows 2000 Remote Boot disk contains network drivers for only one type of network interface card. If you plan to install the Windows 2000 Professional operating system on multiple computers that have different network adapters, you'll need to create multiple boot disks with different drivers.

Enable clients to choose options during the RIS setup process.   If the User Configuration Group Policy settings do not allow specific options, clients and systems administrators who are performing installations will be unable to change the settings. To change these settings, simply apply the appropriate Group Policy settings for the Computer object.

Summary

In this chapter, we covered the details of working with Windows 2000 Remote Installation Services (RIS). RIS was designed to ease the headaches involved with rolling out client operating systems. It accomplishes this by allowing for centralized configuration of standard Windows 2000 Professional images. Systems administrators can specify the various setup options before installation begins. Furthermore, they can use the security features of RIS to ensure that only the appropriate client computers can perform a remote installation. Best of all, RIS is integrated with the Active Directory and makes use of Group Policy settings. All of this leads to a better experience for IT professionals and users.

If you're a systems administrator that's facing a large-scale Windows 2000 deployment, we'll bet that this was welcome news! Better yet, the automated remote installation options provided by RIS are extremely easy to configure. And, as long as you're using supported client hardware, the steps should work seamlessly. When you're planning to roll out Windows 2000 Professional computers, be sure to consider using RIS.

Key Terms

Before you take the exam, you should be familiar with the following terms and concepts:

Boot Information Negotiation Layer (BINL)

Global Unique Identifier (GUID)

Preboot eXecution Environment (PXE)

prestaging

Remote Installation Services (RIS)

Remote Installation Preparation Wizard (RIPrep)

Single Instance Store (SIS)

Trivial File Transfer Protocol Daemon (TFTPD)

Universally Unique Identifier (UUID)

Review Questions

1. Windows 2000 Remote Installation Services (RIS) can be used to install which of the following operating systems?

   A. Windows NT 4 Workstation

   B. Windows 2000 Professional

   C. Windows 2000 Server

   D. Windows 2000 Advanced Server

   E. All of the above

2. During the creation of a RIS image, which of the following must a systems administrator have in order to create a CD-based image?

   A. The Windows 2000 Server CD-ROM

   B. The Windows 2000 Advanced Server CD-ROM

   C. The Windows 2000 RIS boot disk

   D. The Windows 2000 Professional CD-ROM

   E. None of the above is required

3. The RIS root directory *cannot* be created on which of the following partitions?

   A. The boot partition

   B. The system partition

   C. A FAT partition

   D. A FAT32 partition

   E. All of the above

4. A systems administrator wants to allow a group of users to join computers to a domain. What is the easiest way to assign the appropriate permissions for the entire domain?

   A. Delegate control of a User account.

   B. Delegate control at the domain level.

   C. Delegate control of an OU.

   D. Delegate control of a Computer account.

   E. None of the above

5. Which of the following operating systems can be installed using the version of RIS that is included with Windows 2000 Server?

   A. Windows NT 4 Workstation

   B. Windows NT 4 Server

   C. Windows 2000 Professional

   D. Windows 2000 Server

   E. More than one of the above

6. All of the following are a minimum system requirement for RIS clients *except*:

   A. Pentium-166 or faster CPU

   B. 32MB RAM

   C. 800MB hard disk

   D. PXE Boot ROM-equipped network adapter

   E. None of the above

7. A systems administrator wants to make some changes to the default setup for an existing image. Which file or object should they change?

   A. OU Properties

   B. Group Policy Objects (GPOs)

   C. Domain policy

   D. Setup Information Files (*.SIF)

   E. None of the above

8. A RIS boot disk can contain network adapter drivers for up to how many network cards?

   A. 1

   B. 2

   C. 3

   D. Unlimited

9. Hardware-based Global Unique Identifiers (GUIDs) are used to uniquely identify computers. They are assigned by hardware manufacturers and are hard-coded into which of the following areas of a computer?

   A. The hard disk

   B. The smart card

   C. The BIOS

   D. None of the above

10. Which of the following is/are true regarding prestaging of RIS clients (assume that there is only one RIS server on the network)?

   A. Increases performance

   B. Decreases performance

   C. Increases security

   D. Decreases security

   E. Both A and C

11. Which of the following features of RIS increases security?

   A. Prestaged Computer accounts

   B. The use of GUIDS

   C. Assigning Active Directory permissions

   D. Delegating permissions to join a computer to the domain

   E. All of the above

12. Which of the following services must be enabled on the network in order for RIS to function properly?

   A. DNS

   B. DHCP

   C. TCP/IP

   D. RIS

   E. All of the above

13. Which of the following options can be used to increase performance of RIS when multiple clients are being configured?

   A. The use of a dedicated subnet for RIS operations

   B. Load balancing through prestaging

   C. The use of multiple RIS servers

   D. The use of high-speed networking devices

   E. All of the above

14. A systems administrator wants to create an automated installation of the Windows 2000 Server operating system. How can they do this?

   A. Create a CD-based image using the Windows 2000 Server CD-ROM.

   B. Copy a Windows 2000 Professional CD-based image, and then upgrade it to Windows 2000 Server.

   C. Modify the setup installation options to specify that the computer should be a server.

   D. None of the above

15. Which of the following services is required by RIS but may be run on a computer separate from the RIS server itself?

A. Trivial File Transfer Protocol Daemon (TFTPD)

B. Boot Information Negotiation Layer (BINL)

C. DNS

D. Single Instance Store (SIS)

E. None of the above

16. Which of the following can be used to create an image that automatically installs applications as part of the RIS process?

A. RIPrep

B. Prestaging

C. CD-based images

D. Microsoft Installation Wizard

E. All of the above

17. What is the maximum number of RIS servers that can reside on a single subnet?

A. 1

B. 2

C. 3

D. More than 3

18. A Remote Installation Boot Floppy can be created using programs that are installed on which of the following?

A. Any Windows 2000 Server computer

B. Any Windows 2000 Professional computer

C. Any Windows 2000 RIS server

D. None of the above

19. Which of the following operations allows a DHCP server to function properly in an Active Directory environment?

    A. Process

    B. Enable

    C. Authorize

    D. Prestage

    E. None of the above

20. GPOs can be used to set all of the following options for RIS clients *except*:

    A. Automatic setup

    B. Restart setup

    C. Custom setup

    D. Utilities

    E. None of the above

Answers to Review Questions

1. B. RIS supports only the automated installation of Windows 2000 Professional.

2. E. Although the Windows 2000 Professional installation files must be available, they do not have to be provided via CD-ROM. That is, the files may be available on another removable drive or on a network share.

3. E. The RIS root directory must reside on a partition that is formatted using the NTFS file system and is not a system or boot partition.

4. B. Delegating the right to join computers to the domain can most easily be performed using the Delegation of Control Wizard at the domain level.

5. C. RIS only supports the automated remote installation of Windows 2000 Professional computers.

6. D. A RIS client computer can use a boot floppy if it does not have a PXE Boot ROM-enabled network adapter.

7. D. Setup Information Files specify the basic options used during the automated installation process.

8. A. Each RIS boot disk can contain information for only one type of network adapter.

9. C. GUIDs are used to uniquely identify computers in a networked environment and are assigned by computer manufacturers.

10. C. Prestaging increases security by specifying that only certain computers can perform a remote installation from a RIS server.

11. E. All of the options listed are designed to increase the security of RIS in a networked environment.

12. E. All of the networking options listed must be functioning properly in order for RIS clients to be able to connect to a RIS server.

13. E. All of the options listed can improve performance of RIS, especially when performing multiple remote installations at the same time.

14. D. The version of RIS included with Windows 2000 Server does not support the automated remote installation of the Windows 2000 Server operating system.

15. C. DNS must be present in the network environment but does not have to be installed on the RIS server.

16. A. The Remote Installation Preparation Wizard (RIPrep) utility can be used to create a RIS image that automatically installs applications during the RIS process.

17. D. Multiple RIS servers may reside on the same subnet. When configured properly, this can be used to load balance two or more servers.

18. C. By default, only a Windows 2000 RIS server will include the `rbfg` executable file (although the file can be copied to or run from other types of computers).

19. C. A DHCP server must be *authorized* before it can function on the network.

20. D. The four options that can be set include automatic setup, restart setup, custom setup, and tools.

Appendix A

Practice Exam

Practice Exam

1. In order for a Windows 2000 Server computer to contain a copy of the Active Directory data store, it must be configured to be which of the following?

    A. A member server

    B. A domain controller

    C. A stand-alone server

    D. Both A and B

    E. None of the above

2. A systems administrator adds a domain to an existing domain tree. By default, the trust relationship between the domains in this tree will be which of the following?

    A. Transitive

    B. Two-way

    C. Sequential

    D. Both A and B

    E. None of the above

3. A systems administrator wants to change the scope of an Active Directory group for a domain that is running in native mode. Which of the following scope changes is/are *not* allowed?

    A. Universal ➢ Global

    B. Domain Local ➢ Universal

    C. Global ➢ Universal

    D. All of the above changes are allowed

4. Which of the following Active Directory objects is/are *not* considered to be a security principal?

    A. Domain Local groups

    B. Global groups

    C. Distribution groups

    D. Universal groups

    E. All of the above are security principals

5. A systems administrator wishes to configure a root directory for Remote Installation Services (RIS). On which of the following types of partitions can they create the RIS root directory?

    A. FAT

    B. FAT 32

    C. NTFS

    D. System partition

    E. Any of the above

6. A systems administrator wants to create a single Remote Installation Services (RIS) boot disk for multiple network adapters. How can they do this?

   A. Create multiple RIS boot disks, and then copy all of the files on these disks to a single disk.

   B. Modify the netboot.ini file to include multiple network adapters.

   C. Modify the boot sector of the disk to include multiple network adapters.

   D. None of the above.

7. Which of the following options prevents a lower-level Group Policy object (GPO) from changing the effective permissions placed by a higher-level Group Policy object?

   A. No inheritance

   B. No override

   C. No modifications

   D. None of the above

8. A systems administrator wants to ensure that a logon/logoff script runs regardless of the domain controller to which a user authenticates. They should place the scripts in which of the following directories?

   A. The SYSVOL share

   B. The root directory of the C: drive

   C. The WINNT directory

   D. The WINNT/System32 directory

   E. Any of the above

9. Which of the following is not a standard view in the Windows 2000 Performance tool?

    A. Chart

    B. Histogram

    C. Report

    D. Log view

    E. None of the above

10. A systems administrator is implementing a data protection plan for his Windows 2000 Server computers. Which of the following types of backups will copy all files that have changed since the last full backup and will not mark them as having been backed up?

    A. Full

    B. Incremental

    C. Differential

    D. Daily

    E. All of the above

11. Which of the following statements is *not* true regarding Global Catalog servers?

    A. All domain controllers must also be Global Catalog servers.

    B. Systems administrators can determine the types of information that are stored within the Global Catalog.

    C. The use of Global Catalog servers reduces the amount of time it takes to authenticate across domains.

    D. All of the above.

12. If Domain A is configured to trust Domain B, and Domain B trusts Domain C, then Domain A implicitly trusts Domain C. This is an example of which of the following?

    A. Transitive trusts

    B. Two-way trusts

    C. Transitive two-way trusts

    D. No trusts

    E. None of the above

13. Which of the following types of network configurations is not supported by Remote Installation Services (RIS)?

    A. A laptop attached to a docking station that contains a network adapter

    B. A laptop with a PCMCIA or PC Card network adapter

    C. A desktop computer with a nonPXE-compliant network adapter

    D. A desktop computer with a PXE-compliant network adapter

    E. All of the above configurations are supported

14. By default, the Print Operators and Server Operators groups can be found in which of the following folders displayed in the Active Directory Users and Computers tool?

    A. Foreign Security Principals

    B. NativeMode

    C. UniversalGroups

    D. Builtin

    E. None of the above

15. How can a server be configured to contain certain pieces of information from all of the domains within an Active Directory forest?

A. Rebuild the server as a forest domain controller.

B. Configure the server as a member server for all of the domains.

C. Configure the server as a domain controller and a Global Catalog server.

D. None of the above.

16. Which of the following protocols can be used to automatically assign TCP/IP information to Windows NT 4 and Windows 2000 client computers?

A. DNS

B. WINS

C. DHCP

D. IPCONFIG

E. All of the above

17. A change must be made to the types of information stored for a Group object associated with all domains within an Active Directory. This change requires access to which of the following?

A. The Relative ID Master

B. The Schema Master

C. Any domain controller

D. A computer that is a member of the domain

E. None of the above

18. Which of the following single-master operations has been created primarily for backwards-compatibility?

   A. Relative ID Master

   B. Domain Master

   C. PDC Emulator

   D. Schema Master

   E. None of the above

19. A systems administrator is trying to troubleshoot a problem in which none of the users can see a specific Printer object within the Active Directory. Which of the following are possible reasons for this?

   A. The printer was not configured to be shared with other users.

   B. None of the users have been given sufficient permissions to access the printer.

   C. The List in Directory option is not selected.

   D. The printer has not been correctly installed and configured.

   E. All of the above.

20. A systems administrator wants to configure all replication traffic between two sites to be managed by one server in each site. Which of the following should they create?

   A. Another site

   B. Additional subnets

   C. Site links

   D. Bridgehead servers

   E. All of the above

21. A systems administrator wishes to create two domains with non–contiguous namespaces. Which of the following Active Directory models supports this?

   A. Domains

   B. Trees

   C. Forests

   D. Sites

   E. None of the above

22. Which of the following types of groups can contain users from multiple domains?

   A. Domain local

   B. Global

   C. Universal

   D. All of the above

23. Which of the following types of Active Directory objects are considered to be security principals?

   A. OUs and Groups

   B. Users, Groups, and Computers

   C. OUs and Users

   D. Groups, Users, and OUs

   E. None of the above

24. A systems administrator wants to create a new DNS server within a zone in order to improve performance. However, they do not want the DNS server to act as an authority over the DNS zone. Which of the following DNS server roles meets these requirements?

A. Master server

B. Secondary server

C. Caching-only server

D. Secondary server

E. None of the above

25. A junior systems administrator accidentally deletes an entire Active Directory organizational unit (OU), including all of the objects that it contained. However, they do not realize the error until four hours later (after scheduled replication with other domain controllers has completed). What is the best way to restore the OU and all of its objects, assuming that they have access to recent backups of the System State information?

A. Perform a standard restore of the System State information.

B. Perform a standard restore of the System State, and then perform an authoritative restore using NTDSUTIL.

C. Remove the domain controller on which the change was made from the domain.

D. Shutdown the domain controller on which the change was made.

E. None of the above.

26. A systems administrator wants to make applications available to end users. Which of the following operations is/are *not* allowed through the use of the software deployment functionality of Group Policies?

    A. Assigning applications to users

    B. Assigning applications to computers

    C. Publishing applications to users

    D. Publishing applications to computers

    E. All of the above are allowed

27. All of the following are valid types of trust relationships *except*:

    A. Two-way

    B. Transitive

    C. Transitive two-way

    D. Transitive one-way

    E. None of the above

28. Which of the following tools can be used to access directory information stored in Novell Directory Services (NDS), Windows NT 4, and Windows 2000 Active Directory data stores?

    A. Shared Directory Interface

    B. Windows Script Host

    C. Active Directory Services Interface

    D. Active Directory Sites and Services

    E. None of the above

29. A systems administrator is troubleshooting a problem that they suspect is related to DNS. Which of the following tools can they use to help troubleshoot the problem?

A. The Event Viewer

B. The Performance Monitor

C. The DNS administrative tool

D. All of the above

E. None of the above

30. Which of the following protocols can be used for intersite replication?

A. WINS

B. DHCP

C. RPC over IP

D. SNMP

E. All of the above

31. A systems administrator wants to reduce the amount of time and disk space required to install a Windows Installer-based application. Which of the following options will increase performance of the installation?

A. Bypass Permissions

B. Disable Install Log

C. Always Install with Elevated Permissions

D. Disable Rollback

E. All of the above

32. Which of the following types of DNS Resource Records (RRs) are used by Active Directory clients and servers to find domain controllers?

A. A

B. PTR

C. SRV

D. MX

E. All of the above

33. Within an Active Directory domain, no two OUs can have the same
_____.

A. Parent OU

B. Distinguished name

C. Relative name

D. None of the above

E. All of the above

34. Which of the following folders seen in the Active Directory Users and Computers tool contains information about users who are located outside the Active Directory forest?

A. External Users

B. Builtin

C. Users

D. Foreign Security Principals

E. All of the above

35. A Group Policy object (GPO) linked at the Domain level sets a certain option to Disabled while a GPO at the organizational unit (OU) level sets the same option to Enabled. There are no other GPOs or GPO links for the domain. Which option can a systems administrator use to ensure that the effective setting for objects within the OU is Enabled (assuming that all other settings are configured as their defaults)?

    A. Block Policy Inheritance on the OU

    B. Set No Override on the Site

    C. Set No Override on the OU

    D. Block Policy Inheritance on the Site

    E. None of the above

36. In order to distribute administrative responsibilities, a systems administrator assigns the ability to change passwords for all users within an OU to another user. What is this process known as?

    A. Permissions granting

    B. Permissions revoking

    C. Inheritance

    D. Delegation

    E. None of the above

37. Which of the following Active Directory objects should be configured based primarily on a company's physical network structure?

    A. Domains

    B. DNS zones

    C. Sites

    D. Organizational units

    E. None of the above

38. A systems administrator wishes to establish Group Policy settings for a specific computer. However, the computer is not a member of any Active Directory domain. To which of the following should the permissions apply?

A. Domain

B. Local computer

C. Sites

D. OUs

E. None of the above—Group Policy requires the use of the Active Directory

39. Which of the following types of Active Directory objects define the physical devices that are part of an Active Directory site?

A. Site links

B. Sites

C. Subnets

D. Site components

E. All of the above

40. All of the following are valid methods for writing logon/logoff and startup/shutdown scripts *except*:

A. JScript

B. Batch files

C. Windows Script Host (WSH)-compatible languages

D. Visual Basic Scripting Edition (VBScript)

E. None of the above

41. Every domain must have one domain controller that is responsible for which of the following single master roles?

    A. Relative ID Master

    B. PDC Emulator Master

    C. Infrastructure Master

    D. All of the above

    E. None of the above

42. A systems administrator wants to create a Shared Folder Active Directory object. What is the minimum information that they must have in order to create the object?

    A. The name of the share

    B. The UNC path to the share

    C. The IP address of the server and the name of the share

    D. None of the above

43. Which of the following statements *does not* describe the relationship between Active Directory domains and DNS zones?

    A. One DNS zone can span multiple Active Directory domains.

    B. One Active Directory domain can consist of multiple DNS zones.

    C. A Windows 2000 DNS server is required for the Active Directory to operate properly.

    D. None of the above.

44. A systems administrator wishes to configure DNS to support an Active Directory environment that consists of four domains. What is the minimum number of DNS zones they can configure in order to ensure the proper functioning of the Active Directory?

    A. 0

    B. 1

    C. 4

    D. 16

    E. All of the above

45. An Active Directory domain contains objects from three branch offices that are all part of the same company. How many Active Directory sites should be created to best support this configuration?

    A. 0

    B. 1

    C. 3

    D. 4

    E. Not enough information

46. A systems administrator has created a transitive two-way trust relationship between Domain A and Domain B. By default, what permissions will users in Domain A have on resources in Domain B?

    A. Read-Only

    B. Change

    C. List

    D. Read and Write

    E. None of the above

47. A systems administrator is having problems connecting to a Windows 2000 domain controller. Which of the following tools may they use to determine the cause of the problem?

A. PING

B. NSLOOKUP

C. Performance Monitor

D. Network Monitor

E. All of the above

48. Which of the following features is supported only on NTFS 5 partition types?

A. Encryption

B. Quotas

C. Dynamic Disks

D. Remote Storage

E. All of the above

49. Which of the following command-line utilities can be used to export the contents of an Active Directory domain to a standard text file that can be read in Microsoft Notepad?

A. LDIFDE

B. WSH

C. ADSI

D. CSVDE

E. All of the above

50. In an IT department, certain systems administrators should have specific permissions over particular OUs. Which of the following features in the Active Directory Users and Computers tool can be used to most easily set the necessary permissions?

A. The OU Move command

B. The Distributed Administration Wizard

C. The Delegation of Control Wizard

D. Standard Active Directory permissions

E. None of the above

Answers to Practice Exam

1. B. Windows 2000 domain controllers store copies of the Active Directory data store. Member servers use the information stored within the Active Directory, but they do not contain a copy of the directory information. For more information, see Chapter 1.

2. D. By default, transitive two-way trusts are created between the domains in an Active Directory tree. For more information, see Chapter 5.

3. A. The scope of a Universal group cannot be changed. For more information, see Chapter 8.

4. C. Distribution groups are used primarily for creating e-mail distribution lists. They are not considered security principals. For more information, see Chapter 8.

5. C. The RIS root directory must reside on an NTFS partition that is not the boot or system partition. For more information, see Chapter 12.

6. D. Windows 2000 RIS supports only one network adapter per boot disk. Therefore, the systems administrator would not be able to add support for multiple network adapters to a single RIS boot disk. For more information, see Chapter 12.

7. B. The No Override option is used to ensure that all child objects will inherit the settings from a specific GPO, regardless of the GPO settings on the child object. For more information, see Chapter 10.

8. A. By default, the contents of the SYSVOL share are replicated to all of the domain controllers within a domain. For more information, see Chapter 10.

9. E. All the options listed are appropriate ways to view information in the Windows 2000 System Monitor. For more information, see Chapter 9.

10. C. Differential backups store all files that have been modified since the last full backup operation but do not mark them as backed up. For more information, see Chapter 9.

11. A.   Not all domain controllers must be Global Catalog servers. For more information, see Chapter 5.

12. A.   The transitivity of trust relationships allows for the implicit trusting of domains. Systems administrators, based on the security needs of an organization, can modify this behavior. For more information, see Chapter 5.

13. B.   Windows 2000 RIS cannot create a boot disk for laptop computers that have only a PCMCIA or PC Card network adapter. For more information, see Chapter 12.

14. D.   The Builtin group includes a list of all the default groups that are part of a domain. For more information, see Chapter 7.

15. C.   The Global Catalog contains information from all of the domains within an Active Directory environment. For more information, see Chapter 6.

16. C.   Although all of these tools are used in managing TCP/IP-based networks, only the Dynamic Host Configuration Protocol (DHCP) can automatically assign TCP/IP information to clients. For more information, see Chapter 3.

17. B.   The Schema Master is used for generating changes to the types of information stored for Active Directory objects and is responsible for replicating these changes to the necessary servers. For more information, see Chapter 5.

18. C.   The PDC Emulator role was created primarily for compatibility with Windows NT 4 domain controllers. For more information, see Chapter 5.

19. E.   A printer may not be visible when browsing the Active Directory for any of these reasons. For more information, see Chapter 7.

20. D.   Bridgehead servers are used to specify which machines should transmit data when routing replication traffic between sites. For more information, see Chapter 6.

21. C. Active Directory forests can include domain trees that have non-contiguous namespaces. For more information, see Chapter 5.

22. C. Universal groups can contain users from multiple domains. For more information, see Chapter 8.

23. B. Users, Groups, and Computers are the main security principals used within the Active Directory. For more information, see Chapter 4.

24. C. Caching-only servers are generally considered to primarily improve performance. They are not, however, considered to be authorities over any DNS domains. For more information, see Chapter 7.

25. B. In order to ensure that all of the domain controllers are updated with the restored portions of the Active Directory data store, the systems administrator must restore the System State from a recent backup (one that was made before the change) and then set the authoritative restore mode for this portion of the Active Directory tree. For more information, see Chapter 9.

26. D. Applications can only be published to users, whereas applications can be assigned to users and computers. For more information, see Chapter 12.

27. E. All of the types of trust relationships listed are valid. For more information, see Chapter 5.

28. C. The Active Directory Services Interface (ADSI) was created to allow developers to programmatically access information stored in various directory services. For more information, see Chapter 7.

29. D. Among the several tools that can be used to troubleshoot DNS problems are the Event Viewer, the Performance Monitor, and the DNS administrative tool. For more information, see Chapter 7.

30. C. Intersite replication can use either RPC over Internet Protocol (IP) or the Simple Mail Transfer Protocol (SMTP). For more information, see Chapter 7.

31. D.   Creating the rollback log consumes system resources and can slow the installation process. Although disabling rollback can improve performance, it prevents the rollback of transactions in the case of a failed installation. For more information, see Chapter 11.

32. C.   SRV records specify the IP addresses of domain controllers for a specific Active Directory domain. For more information, see Chapter 2.

33. B.   No two OUs can have the same distinguished name. For more information, see Chapter 4.

34. D.   The Foreign Security Principals folder contains information about users who are not part of the Active Directory forest. This information enables these users to access domain resources. For more information, see Chapter 7.

35. A.   Policy inheritance occurs when the GPO settings at a higher-level object are applied to a lower-level object. By blocking policy inheritance on the OU, you can prevent this behavior. However, this will only work if the No Override option is not set at the Site level. For more information, see Chapter 10.

36. D.   Delegation is the process by which a higher-level security authority assigns permissions to another user or group. For more information, see Chapter 4.

37. C.   Sites are used to manage replication traffic and are generally configured based on an organization's physical network constraints. For more information, see Chapter 6.

38. B.   The systems administrator should apply the settings to the local computer. This is the only option listed that does not require the use of the Active Directory. For more information, see Chapter 10.

39. C.   Subnets define the network addresses that make up an Active Directory site. For more information, see Chapter 6.

40. E. Windows 2000 offers much flexibility in creating scripts. Systems administrators can use standard batch files, or they can use JScript, VBScript, and other languages through the use of the Windows Script Host. For more information, see Chapter 10.

41. D. Every domain must contain a Relative ID Master, a PDC Emulator Master, and an Infrastructure Master. For more information, see Chapter 5.

42. B. The Universal Naming Convention (UNC) path to a share specifies the name of the server and the name of the share. This is the information required to create a Shared Folder Active Directory object. For more information, see Chapter 7.

43. C. Although the Active Directory does require the presence of a DNS server, non-Windows 2000 DNS is supported. Note, however, that certain functionalities may not be available when you do not use Windows 2000 DNS. For more information, see Chapter 7.

44. B. There is no direct relationship between the number of domains and the number of DNS zones. Since the Active Directory depends on DNS, at least one DNS zone must be configured. For more information, see Chapter 2.

45. E. The creation of sites should be based on physical network characteristics. Although it is common for remote offices not to be well-connected, this is not specifically mentioned in the question. Therefore, more information is required in order to determine the optimal site configuration. For more information, see Chapter 6.

46. E. The creation of a trust relationship allows resources to be shared between domains, but it does not automatically set permissions on resources. In order to provide access to resources in other domains, systems administrators must manually assign the appropriate permissions. For more information, see Chapter 7.

47. E.   All of the tools listed are useful for troubleshooting network connectivity problems. Although these tools may not automatically fix the issues, they will help isolate the cause of the problem. For more information, see Chapter 3.

48. E.   All of the features listed are new in Windows 2000 and NTFS 5. For more information, see Chapter 3.

49. D.   The Comma-Separated Value Directory Exchange command can be used to quickly and easily export information about Active Directory objects to a text file. Although the other methods could also be used, they require additional programming. For more information, see Chapter 7.

50. C.   The Delegation of Control Wizard has been created to allow systems administrators the ability to quickly and accurately provide other administrators with only the necessary permissions. For more information, see Chapter 7.

Appendix B

Planning the Active Directory

As you may have already realized, the Active Directory provides organizations with tremendous flexibility and power. However, the true value of the Active Directory will largely depend on the quality of its implementation. In preparing for the exam, you should be thoroughly prepared to assess the business and technical requirements of a specific company and to match those requirements with Active Directory technology.

In this appendix, we'll take an overview of the many considerations that are important when determining how best to deploy the Active Directory in a given network environment. The customizability of and configuration options available in the Active Directory make it useful for businesses ranging in size from a few employees to over a hundred thousand. Due to various factors, the Active Directory configuration will vary between (and even within) organizations. The focus of this appendix will be on applying the concepts and features of the Active Directory to real-world environments. Let's start by examining ways to evaluate the current environment.

The purpose of this appendix is to provide an overview of *all* the Active Directory features. Consequently, its coverage includes some features that are covered earlier in the book. However, while the focus of this study guide is implementation and administration, this appendix covers the same technical content from a planning standpoint. This appendix will be especially useful for readers who are not familiar with the Active Directory.

Evaluating the Current Environment

The specifics of an Active Directory deployment will largely be based on an organization's technical and business environment. Factors such as the network infrastructure, the size of the business, and its organizational layout play large roles in designing a directory services architecture.

Before diving into the technical details of installing and deploying domain controllers, you must take into account your current network and business environment. Sometimes, this is an easy task. In a small business environment, the complexity of the business may be very low. In other cases, however, several months of planning may only scratch the surface of the huge task of planning for the Active Directory. In this section, we'll take a look at several factors you should take into account when evaluating a business environment.

Number and Types of Users

The very reason to have a network in the first place is to support users by providing them with the information and resources they need. Therefore, a thorough assessment of the number of users you support is very important when planning the deployment of the Active Directory. In some cases, it will be quite easy to measure the number of users. If you're currently using a network operating system, you can simply count the accounts within it. For example, the number of accounts you have in your Windows NT security database may be a good indicator. In other cases, however, you may need to take into account the number of users the network will be supporting at some point in the future. These predictions can be made based on current human resources information as well as hiring and business growth plans. In addition to a simple count of the number of users you'll support, you should be sure to fully understand the needs of these users. Administrative staff will likely have very different requirements from Engineering, for example. Additionally, certain network-enabled applications that take advantage of the Active Directory will have additional requirements. It is important to note that gathering all of this information will require efforts from throughout your organization. For example, you may need to go to the executive managers for an estimate on company growth, while you would probably go to human resources for an accurate count of current employees.

When planning for the Active Directory, you should understand how users are distributed throughout your network environment so that you can design the optimal domain controller distribution, and information on the number and types of users you plan to support will help you to accomplish this.

Geographic Distribution

IT organizations would have a much easier job if all of their users resided in the same building. In such a scenario, you would be able to rely on fast network connections between all users and the information they need. For most medium- and larger-sized businesses, however, supporting remote sites is a common scenario. Figure B.1 provides an example of a geographically distributed organization and network.

In an ideal world, geographic distribution would not make much of a difference and all sites would enjoy the same high-speed network connectivity. While larger remote sites may be connected by faster (but more costly) connections, technological limitations and costs often require several special considerations to be taken into account when designing a distributed network.

FIGURE B.1 A geographically distributed network

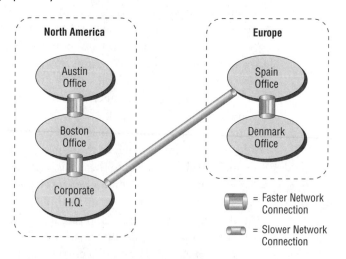

In order to deal with many of the challenges associated with remote sites, companies often implement remote access solutions. This allows telecommuters and traveling users to gain access to network resources. But whatever the case may be, a company's IT group will have to perform support and administrative functions for all of its users. To meet this need, some companies might choose to have an IT department at each location. Others, however, will have a separate IT support staff just for remote offices. In any event, remote access solutions and the means by which IT support is provided to remote access users will help to determine the optimal physical structure of an Active Directory deployment. Keeping the geographic issues in mind, let's now look at the technical issues related to evaluating your network infrastructure.

Network Infrastructure

The function of a network infrastructure is to connect users to the resources they need to effectively do their jobs. With this goal in mind, IT departments are required to purchase, implement, and manage network connections ranging in speed from analog modems to the fastest local area network (LAN) and wide area network (WAN) connections available. Because of the costs of some of these solutions, however, network administrators often have to make trade-offs. That is, few companies can afford to always invest in the fastest and most efficient network technologies available.

While planning for the deployment of the Active Directory in your organization, you must take into account your network infrastructure. If an accurate and up-to-date network map is available, this is a great place to start. If one is not available, this is a great time to start designing one. Figure B.2 provides an example of a network map that takes into account the number of servers and workstations at each site, along with the network connections between them. Of particular concern will be the bandwidth for each of the network connections and the current amount of traffic between sites.

FIGURE B.2   A high-level company network map

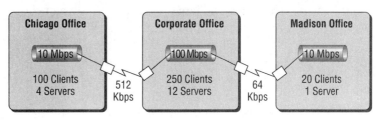

This type of high-level map will be very important when planning for Active Directory sites and domains. In some cases, you might find that upgrades to the current network infrastructure are required once you've examined the map. For example, a remote site may have a slow WAN connection, but, due to changes in the network infrastructure, more servers and other resources are required. In this case, you may choose to deploy domain controllers differently, or you may plan to purchase additional bandwidth for that site.

Also, many IT organizations are constantly upgrading their networks to keep pace with the increasing demand for file sharing, knowledge management, and Internet access. In such environments, it's just as important to take into account future plans for network performance upgrades as it is to consider the current situation. The goal of evaluating the network infrastructure is to ensure that the existing network infrastructure accommodates your organization's replication and administration traffic needs.

Centralized vs. Decentralized Administration

One of the most common and important functions of the IT department is to administer network resources. This includes planning for, evaluating, deploying, and managing server and workstation computers, as well as supporting end users. Although the fundamental goal is the same, companies might take different approaches to managing IT resources throughout the network.

One common model is that of centralized administration. In such a scenario, a single IT department is responsible for managing all of the resources on the network. This is often chosen for smaller organizations as it allows all of the IT personnel to reside in a single location. Centralized administration can also reduce a lot of redundant work as users, groups, and computers are managed in one place, through the work of a skilled group of individuals. Medium- and large-sized businesses might choose the centralized model, as well, due to economies realized by focusing IT resources in a single location.

Centralized administration may, however, present several problems. First, the need for good network communications between sites can cause problems. For example, what happens when a remote router goes down and no one is available at the other site to provide immediate support for trouble–shooting? Similarly, what if a hardware replacement is required on a client computer? These types of tasks usually require the presence of IT staff at each of an organization's locations. A decentralized administration model takes these factors into account by providing IT departments at each of the company's locations. Figure B.3 provides a comparison of centralized versus decentralized administration models.

FIGURE B.3 Centralized vs. decentralized IT administration

Centralized IT Administration

Decentralized IT Administration

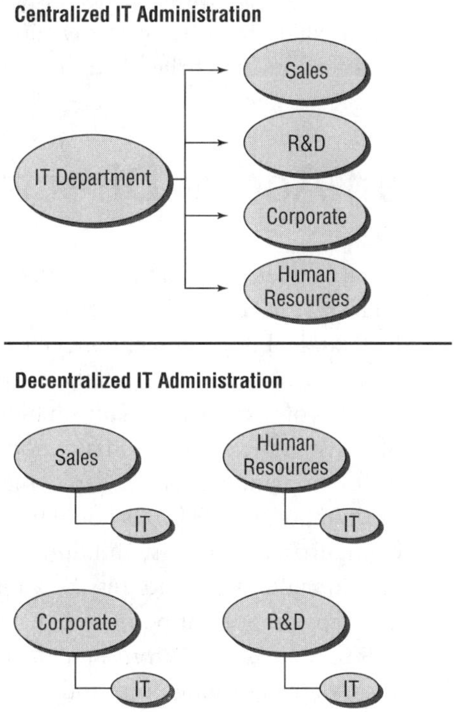

Although technical issues are one factor in determining the type of administration model to implement, political and business issues are also important. A small business might map well to a centralized model if all of the users and resources reside within one administrative unit. Centralized administration fits well in this type of environment as it simplifies the creation and management of users and resources. However, security needs and management structure may influence the creation of multiple administrative units. In some companies, departments might operate as autonomous business units. For example, the Sales department might create and manage its own user account databases and network resources, while Engineering does the same in another completely isolated environment. Each department would have its own administration staff, and the sharing of resources would be based on the cooperation of all the departments. This type of scenario is a good candidate for the decentralized model. The network administration needs of the organization will play a fundamental role in determining the best organization for the Active Directory.

So far, we have looked at several different factors that must be considered when evaluating a business environment. Now, let's take a close look at how these factors affect the planning of the Active Directory.

Choosing an Active Directory Model

In order to accommodate the various business and technical needs of your organization, Microsoft's Active Directory technology was designed to be flexible. For example, both centralized and decentralized administration models are supported. And, the Active Directory was designed to scale up to millions of users per domain—a huge improvement over the practical limits of the Windows NT 4 domain model.

When planning for the deployment of the Active Directory, one of the most important decisions you'll need to make is related to how you want to configure trees, forests, and domains. In fact, the first major decision you should make should address how many domains your organization needs. The most important point to remember about Active Directory domains is that they are *administrative* units, not technical ones. An administrative unit allows for managing users and network resources within a single shared accounts database with a separate database for security.

In most cases, it is recommended that an organization use as few domains as possible. Fewer domains are simpler to setup and maintain and result in less administrative work overall. In many situations, it is possible to work with only a single domain. This may be true regardless of the size of a business or its geographic distribution. Keeping these ideas in mind, let's look at how domains can be combined together.

Planning Trees and Forests

We have already mentioned several reasons for requiring multiple domains within a single company. What we haven't yet covered is how multiple domains can be related to each other and how their relationships can translate into domain forests and trees.

A fundamental commonality between the various domains that exist in trees and forests is that they all share the same Active Directory Global Catalog. This means that if we modify the Active Directory schema, the change must be propagated to all of the domain controllers in *all of the domains*. This is an important point because additions and modifications to the structure of information in the Global Catalog can have widespread effects on replication and network traffic.

Every domain within an Active Directory configuration will have its own unique name. For example, even though we might have a sales domain in two different trees, their complete names will be different (such as `sales.company1.com` and `sales.company2.com`). In this section, we'll look at how multiple Active Directory domains can be organized based on business requirements.

Using a Single Tree

The concept of domain trees was created to preserve the relationship between multiple domains that share a common contiguous namespace. For example, I might have the following DNS domains (based on Internet names):

- `mycompany.com`
- `sales.mycompany.com`
- `engineering.mycompany.com`
- `europe.sales.mycompany.com`

Note that all of these domains fit within a single contiguous namespace. That is, they are all direct or indirect children of the `mycompany.com` domain. In this case, `mycompany.com` is called the *root* domain. All of the direct children (such as `sales.mycompany.com` and `engineering.mycompany.com`) are called *child* domains. Finally, *parent* domains are the domains that are directly above one domain. For example, sales.mycompany.com is the parent domain of europe.sales.mycompany.com. Figure B.4 provides an example of a domain tree.

FIGURE B.4 A domain tree

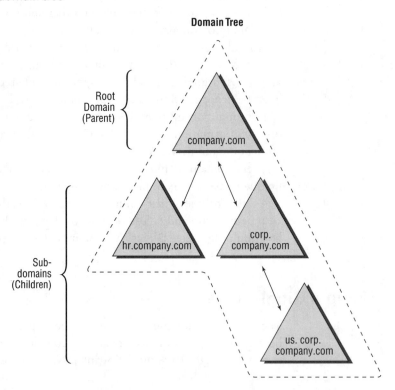

In order to establish a domain tree, the root domain for the tree must be created first. Then, child domains of this root can be added. These child domains can then serve as parents for further subdomains. Each domain must have at least one domain controller, and domain controllers can participate in only one domain at a time. However, domain controllers can be moved between domains. This is done by first demoting a domain controller to a member server and then promoting it to a domain controller in another domain.

Domains are designed to be security boundaries. The domains within a tree are automatically bound together using a two-way trust relationship. This allows users and resources to be shared between domains through the use of the appropriate groups. Since trust relationships are transitive, this means that all of the domains within the tree trust each other. Note, however, that a trust by itself does not grant any security permissions to users or objects between domains. Trusts are designed only to *allow* resources to be shared. Administrators must explicitly assign security settings to resources before users can access resources between domains.

The use of a single tree makes sense when an organization maintains only a single contiguous namespace. Regardless of the number of domains that exist within this environment and how different their security settings are, they are related by a common name. Although domain trees will make sense for many organizations, in some cases the network namespace may be considerably more complicated. Let's look at how forests address those situations next.

Using a Forest

Active Directory forests are designed to accommodate multiple noncontiguous namespaces. That is, they can combine domain trees together into logical units. An example might be the following tree and domain structure:

- Tree: `Organization1.com`

  - `Sales.Organization1.com`

  - `Marketing.Organization1.com`

  - `Engineering.Organization1.com`

  - `NorthAmerica.Engineering.Organization1.com`

- Tree: `Organization2.com`

  - `Sales.Organization2.com`

  - `Engineering.Organization2.com`

Figure B.5 provides an example of how multiple trees can fit into a single forest. Such a situation might occur in the merger of companies or if a company is logically divided into two or more completely separate and autonomous business units.

FIGURE B.5 A single forest consisting of multiple trees

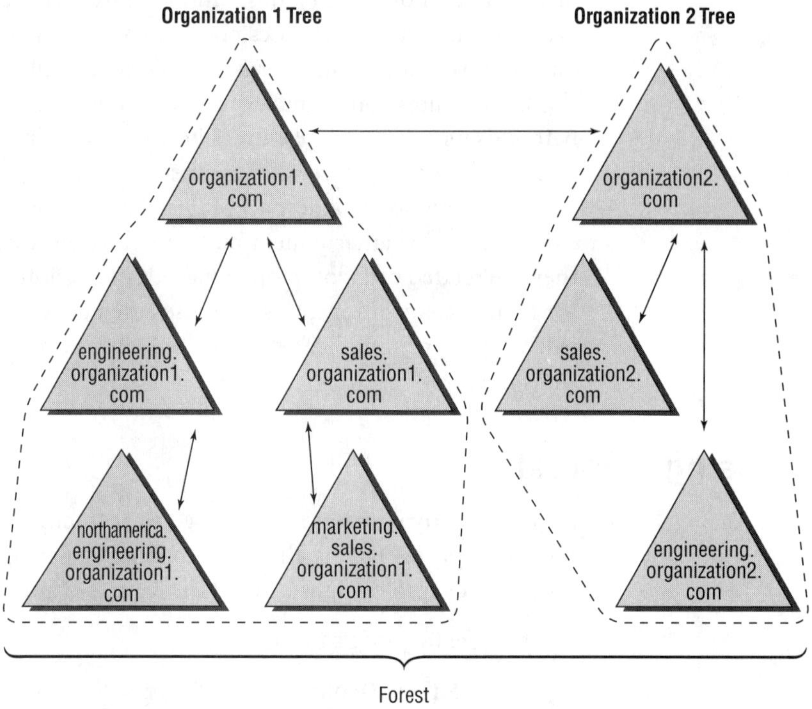

All of the trees within a forest are related through a single forest root domain. This is the first domain that is created in the Active Directory environment. The root domain in each tree creates a transitive trust with the forest root domain. The result is a configuration in which all of the trees within a domain and all of the domains within each tree trust each other. Again, as with domain trees, the presence of a trust relationship does not automatically give any permissions to users between trees and domains. It only allows objects and resources to be shared. Specific permissions must be set up by authorized network administrators.

Through the use of domain trees and forests, a company can easily manage multiple related domains in a single Active Directory configuration.

Planning Domain Structure

Thus far, we've looked at how domains can be organized within the Active Directory environment through trees and forests. Once you've determined the high-level domain topology, it's time to look into the details of the organization *within* domains themselves. This includes the location and types of servers and domain controllers that might be needed.

The same major considerations described earlier in the "Evaluating the Current Environment" section will apply to the decisions made here. That is, the business and technical requirements of an organization will play a large part in determining the overall domain configuration. In addition, if the company is currently using more than one Windows NT domain, this should be taken into account. Let's start by looking at various types of domains.

Upgrading from Windows NT 4 Domains

One of Microsoft's major goals in designing the Active Directory was to allow an easy upgrade path for users of Windows NT 4 domains. When you're planning to upgrade from Windows NT 4 domains to the Windows 2000 Active Directory, you'll need to consider the differences between the two types of structures. As we mentioned earlier in this chapter, there are several reasons that businesses might choose to have more than one domain. For reasons of performance, scalability, and administration, the added effort of implementing and managing more than one domain might be worthwhile.

The fundamental structure of Window NT 4 domains is a single flat namespace. Although the product itself does not support the concept of different *types* of domains, multiple configurations and roles for domains were created to accommodate business and technical requirements. These configurations are based on using domains for specific tasks within the network environment. These roles include:

Master Domains   In environments that support large numbers of users, one or more master domains may be established. Each master domain is primarily responsible for containing User account information.

Resource Domains   Resource domains contain the actual files, printers, and application servers to which users will require access. They generally consist of only a few administrative User accounts. Users receive security permissions in resource domains based on accounts stored in user domains.

In some cases, users and resources might be stored in the same domain. Such domain models fit well with organizations that have independent business units and prefer centralized administration. With master and resource domains, multiple configurations are possible. For example, a multiple-master domain model includes the presence of two or more user domains and any number of resource domains. Each of the resource domains trusts one or more of the master domains. The trusts are generally one-way. Users in the master domains are placed in global groups. These global groups are then given permissions on objects within the resource domains.

Another common Windows NT domain model is the complete trust model. In this system, all of the domains trust each other. Most domains generally consisted of both users and resources, but each domain is administered separately.

Although the Windows NT 4 domain models provide additional scalability and performance, administering more than a few domains can be very cumbersome. For example, since trust relationships are one-way and not transitive, the number of trusts that must be configured can be very large. Additionally, the process issues related to creating and managing users in multiple domains can lead to a less-than-optimal administration system. All of this can lead to political and technical issues that prevent the usability of network resources.

When upgrading a network to the Active Directory, the current Windows NT domain structure must be taken into account. The general practice is to upgrade master domains first and then to upgrade resource domains. Usually, the Windows NT 4 Primary Domain Controller (PDC) is migrated first. Then, other domain controllers, servers, and workstations are upgraded.

With support for backwards-compatibility, Windows 2000 domains can coexist and share resources with Windows NT 4 domains. This mode is called mixed-mode. There are, however, some trade-offs when running in a mixed-mode configuration as some of the more advanced features of Windows 2000 will not be realized until all of the servers have been upgraded to Windows 2000. Once this is done, a systems administrator can convert the domain to native mode.

Although you could translate the existing domain infrastructure into its mirror image using Active Directory domains, it is often beneficial to collapse multiple domains into fewer ones when upgrading. This is especially true for organizations that created multiple Windows NT domains for the purpose of performance and scalability. When domains are collapsed together, the user account databases from master domains and resource domains are combined together. Usually, this can be done while requiring limited re-creation of security permissions.

Overall, by combining real-world business and technical requirements, companies can find a good way to upgrade their Windows NT environments to the Active Directory. With that in mind, let's look at the how you can determine the appropriate number of domains for a given organization.

Number of Domains

The Active Directory has alleviated many of the technical issues related to working with Windows NT domains. With the Active Directory, domains can span geographic locations, take into account the network infrastructure, and contain more than one million objects. Therefore, it is recommended that, wherever possible, the fewest number of domains should be used.

The use of a single domain provides a good way to manage network resources, security permissions, and users. It also allows network administration to be distributed throughout the organization and accommodates the use of multiple domain controllers. There are, however, several reasons an organization might consider the use of multiple domains. The reasons for using multiple domains may include the following:

Retaining the Existing Domain Structure If your current environment uses multiple Windows NT domains for the purpose of sharing and administering network resources, it might make sense to retain this structure for business and technical reasons. On the other hand, several of the reasons for splitting a network into multiple domains had to do with technical limitations in the Windows NT 4 domain model. Scalability of the flat domain model was, for instance, a major reason for using multiple Windows NT domains. In such cases, it is preferable to consolidate multiple existing domains into fewer larger ones.

Using Extremely Large Numbers of Objects One of the primary design goals for the Active Directory was to support a large number of objects within a single domain database. Although testing is required to find a practical limit, you can generally count on allowing more than a million objects in one data store. The Active Directory is not without its limits, however. For very large companies, administering many users, groups, computers, and other objects may place technical limitations on scalability and performance. Additionally, replication traffic between domain controllers in very large domains may place a heavy burden on the network infrastructure. In such a scenario, it would be a good idea to break users and resources into multiple domains.

Using Multiple DNS Names   Domains are designed to accommodate only a single DNS name for all of the contained users and resources. For various reasons, however, businesses might operate under separate DNS names on the Internet. An example of such a situation is one in which we manage two different organizations, such as `sales.company1.com` and `sales.company2.com`. As the namespace for each of these domains is not contiguous, we would need to create at least two separate domains in order to accurately reflect the DNS names.

Limiting Replication Traffic   The need to replicate information between the various domain controllers that are part of a domain can use significant network bandwidth. If fast and reliable network connections are not available for certain sites, it might make sense to create a separate domain. Note, however, that you should not plan to create separate domains solely based on network or geographic distribution. The concept of sites in the Active Directory model might provide a better solution for meeting these network requirements.

Meeting Decentralized Security Needs   All of the objects within a single Active Directory domain will inherit similar security permissions. For example, if we set a requirement on the minimum password length, this same setting will apply to all of the users within the domain. If, for any reason, different security and policy information is required for different sets of users, the establishment of multiple domains might be a good solution. However, this will increase the administrative effort required to maintain the domains and might increase the possibility of inconsistencies in the configuration.

Meeting Decentralized Administration Needs   All of the information that exists between domains is stored in a single centralized database that is replicated between the domain controllers within that domain. This includes all of the user, group, and computer objects, along with security permissions. If network administration is decentralized, it might make sense to create multiple domains. Each domain would include the objects that are under the control of just one IT organization. For example, if Company A had one department for North American IT support and another for Asian IT support, two domains would allow for autonomous administration of each. However, multiple domains will require more effort to administer overall since many settings must be made independently in each domain.

Under general circumstances, a small number of domains is ideal. And many technical challenges that could hinder the decrease in the number of domains can be addressed through proper planning and use of the features of the Active Directory. However, the preceding reasons can make the use of multiple Active Directory domains the best choice. You'll need to assess the business and technical needs and limitations of your organization to decide what is the appropriate number of domains for your environment.

Planning Organizational Units

So far, we've looked at reasons why an organization might require multiple domains and ways in which these domains can be combined together to form forests and trees. Now, let's drill-down into the actual logical structure within domains themselves.

The fundamental concept used to hierarchically organize objects within the Active Directory is appropriately named the organizational unit (OU). OUs can contain other OUs (thereby creating a hierarchy), as well as the following types of objects:

- Users

- Groups

- Printers

- Shared Folders

OUs allow systems administrators to create structures that reflect their internal business environment within the domain. In this section, we'll look at several possible uses for OUs and how they can help manage and administer your network environment.

Using OUs to Manage Resources

Placing information about all of your network resources within the Active Directory allows you to easily manage users, computers, and security permissions from within a single repository. Within a domain, however, you might want to group users into various containers based on your business's organization. Let's look at an example of a hierarchical list of OUs for an

Engineering department. Within the Engineering OU, we could create levels for Engineering Managers and Software Developers. If necessary, we could even break these groups down further (Senior Software Developers could fall under the Software Developers level, for example). Figure B.6 provides an example of such a hierarchy.

FIGURE B.6   An OU hierarchy based on business needs

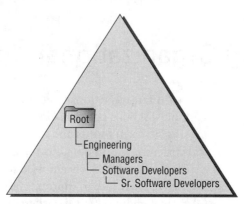

Although you could lump all of the objects within a domain into a single or a few containers, this would make it difficult to administer. If, for example, I wanted to make some settings for only members of the Sales department, I would have to choose each of the users manually. Clearly, this would be a tedious and error-prone process.

Since the concept of an OU will be new to many systems administrators, it's important to make several distinctions about these objects. First, OUs are containers that are designed specifically for administrative purposes. They do not, however, take the place of groups (which are used for administering security and applying permissions). Therefore, OUs do not technically contain members.

The general practice for administration is to place users into groups and then to place the groups into OUs. This arrangement allows for setting security permissions while at the same time making administration of such features as the Group Policy more manageable.

Depending on specific business requirements, you might be able to choose between using OUs or domains when organizing the Active Directory configuration. Earlier in this appendix, we discussed several different reasons for using multiple domains. Many of these issues can also be addressed by properly planning for OUs within a single domain.

The use of OUs instead of multiple domains offers several advantages. First, they allow for administering security and other permissions once for all of the objects within the OU. Second, they allow for flexible containers that can be moved and redesigned much more easily than domains. Finally, OUs allow all objects to use the same namespace while still reflecting the business organization. A good general practice is to use OUs where possible and domains wherever necessary.

The purpose of creating OUs is to provide a means by which to organize and manage users and other objects based on their job functions. With that in mind, let's look at the specific settings you can set with OUs.

Using OUs to Delegate Administration

When working with the Active Directory, the management and administration of objects are key concerns. *Delegation* is the process by which a systems administrator grants (or delegates) specific permissions to other systems administrators so that they, too, can assist in the management and administration. In a networked environment, you will want to ensure that you delegate administration to only the appropriate individuals.

With a flat domain model like the one used in Windows NT, it was difficult to delegate administration to specific users — either users had specific permissions within the entire domain, or they didn't. For example, if I added Jane Doe to the Print Operators group, she would automatically be able to manage all print jobs on all printers within the domain. In Windows 2000 and the Active Directory, you can still set permissions at the domain- or site-level, if that is what you truly require.

In many environments, however, much more granular security permissions are desirable. The use of OUs supports this. For example, I might want to give one systems administrator full permissions on the Sales and Marketing OU and give another full permissions on the Corporate OU. Or, I might want to give Administrator A permissions to add and delete users for the Corporate OU and Administrator B permissions to manage printers and print jobs. In this way, I can easily distribute administrator permissions while maintaining reasonable security settings.

OUs offer the additional benefit of allowing permissions to be set hierarchically. That is, child OUs and objects can inherit the permissions of parent

OUs, thereby simplifying the most common configurations. Figure B.7 provides an example of how OUs can be used to configure administration permissions.

FIGURE B.7   Using OUs to delegate administration

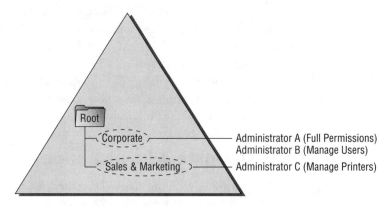

Root

Corporate —— Administrator A (Full Permissions)
Administrator B (Manage Users)

Sales & Marketing —— Administrator C (Manage Printers)

Using OUs for Group Policy

Managing permissions for systems administrators is an important concern, but maintaining appropriate settings for users and computers can prove to be a much bigger challenge. First, there are many more users and computers than systems administrators in most networked environments. Keeping track of each of these individuals and computers is a difficult task. Ensuring that each has only the required security permissions to perform their jobs makes it even more difficult.

In the past, many systems administrators chose to give all of their users many more permissions than they required. Although this gave them the rights necessary to do their jobs, it wasn't uncommon to hear stories about users accidentally deleting system files or making potentially disastrous driver changes. The main reason for the lax security was the difficulty encountered when configuring and maintaining permissions while trying to ensure that business needs were still met.

Through the use of the Active Directory, Group Policy, and OUs, however, many of these tasks are much simpler. Group Policy is a system of settings that apply to the objects contained within an OU. A Group Policy may apply to users, groups, or other objects. Examples of Group Policy settings might include:

- Logon and Logoff Scripts
- User Policy settings (such as password requirements or workstation logon restrictions)
- Application permissions
- File and printer share information

By making these settings based on OUs, you can get the full benefit of using a hierarchical system while still providing for granular security control. Figure B.8 provides an example of how Group Policies and OUs interact.

FIGURE B.8   Assigning Group Policy settings on OUs

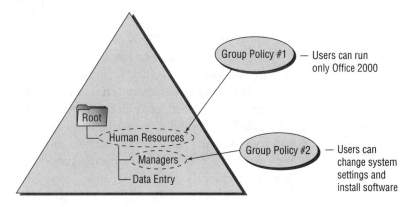

Using OUs Based on Geography

In addition to using OUs for managing permissions, you can also use them to reflect the geographic distribution of your business and its various business units. Geographically based OUs are useful when distributed administration is supported. They can make it easier to set permissions and delegate authority to specific users who reside at one or more sites within the environment.

Within the geographically based OUs, you can still reflect business structure. For example, in a highly distributed company, each business unit might have it's own Sales, Marketing, and Engineering departments. If they are administered separately, child OUs can be created for each of these administrative units.

Overall, the use of OUs provides for the hierarchical administration and management features required in organizations of almost any size. You should take care in planning OUs and should ensure that they meet your business requirements.

Planning Your Sites

Much of the challenge in designing the Active Directory is related to mapping a company's business processes to the structure of a hierarchical data store. So far, we've taken into account many of these requirements. But what about the existing network infrastructure? Clearly, when planning for and designing the structure of the Active Directory, you must take into account your LAN and WAN characteristics.

With Windows 2000 and the Active Directory, Microsoft has allowed systems administrators to deal separately with the physical and logical architecture of the Active Directory. That is, the setup of domains, trees, and forests can occur independently of the underlying network infrastructure. Through the use of Sites, systems administrators can define their network topology and limit network communications as necessary. This makes planning much easier and allows the business concerns to be dealt with separately from the technical ones. Let's see how Active Directory Sites can be used to manage replication traffic.

Planning for Replication Traffic

Synchronization of the Active Directory is extremely important. In order for security permissions and objects within the directory to remain consistent throughout the organization, replication must be used. The Active Directory data store supports multimaster replication. That is, data can be modified at any domain controller within the domain because replication, the process by which changes are transmitted between domain controllers, ensures that information remains consistent throughout the organization.

Ideally, every site within an organization has reliable, high-speed connections with one another. A much more realistic scenario, however, is one in which bandwidth is limited and connections are sometimes unavailable. The term bandwidth refers to the amount of information that can travel through a given network connection per unit of time. For example, a LAN connection might support up to 100 megabits per second (Mbps) while a WAN connection might only support 128 kilobits per second (Kbps).

Through the use of sites, network and systems administrators can define which domain controllers are located on which areas of the network. These settings can be based on the bandwidth available between the areas of the network. Additionally, subnets—logically partitioned areas of the network— can be defined between them. The Windows 2000 Active Directory services will use this information in deciding how and when to replicate data between domain controllers.

Directly replicating information between all domain controllers might be a viable solution for some companies. For others, however, this might result in a lot of traffic traveling over slow links. One way to efficiently synchronize data between sites that are connected with slow connections is to use a bridgehead server. Bridgehead servers are designed to accept traffic between two remote sites and to then forward this information to the appropriate servers. Figure B.9 provides an example of how a bridgehead server can reduce network bandwidth requirements and improve performance. Reduced network bandwidth requirements and improved performance can also be achieved by configuring replication to occur according to a pre-defined schedule if bandwidth usage statistics are available.

FIGURE B.9 Using a bridgehead server

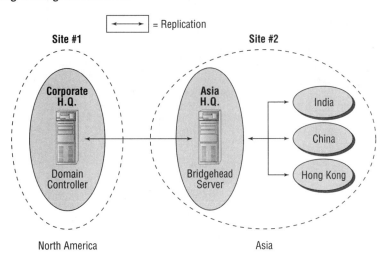

In addition to managing replication traffic, sites also offer the advantage of allowing clients to access the nearest domain controller. This prevents problems with user authentication across slow network connections and can help find the shortest and fastest path to resources such as files and printers. Therefore, it is recommended that at least one domain controller be placed at each site that contains a slow link. Preferably, this domain controller would also contain a copy of the Global Catalog so that logon attempts and resource search queries would not occur across slow links. The drawback, however, is that the deployment of more copies of the Global Catalog to servers will increase replication traffic.

Through proper planning and deployment of sites, organizations can best leverage the capabilities of the their network infrastructure while keeping the Active Directory synchronized.

Planning Naming Conventions

One of the fundamental reasons for having a directory of any type is to bring organization to your various network accounts and resources. Of course, the value of the Active Directory is only as good as the quality of the information and objects that it contains. When planning to implement the Active Directory, you should take sufficient time to plan for naming conventions. These conventions will apply throughout your network environment.

Specifically, you'll need to decide how to name the following types of resources:

- Users

- Groups

- Computers (workstations and servers)

- Domain controllers

- Printers

- File shares

- Organizational units (OUs)

- Domains

- Sites

These names should be logical and consistent with your current (or planned) business processes. They should accurately reflect the objects to which they refer and the location of these objects within the tree. For example, businesses commonly use the formula first initial + middle initial + last name for network accounts. The fully-qualified name of a user, might be akdesai@northamerica.sales.mycompany.com. Similarly, the name of a printer might be Printer-207A.northamerica.sales.mycompany.com.

Intuitive names will make it easier for users and systems administrators to find the resources they need with minimal searching. Proper planning of naming conventions can go a long way in increasing the organization and usability of your Active Directory configuration.

Summary

In this appendix, we looked at many factors that must be considered when planning for the Active Directory. We started by examining the current network environment of an organization. Based on the business and technical environments, we then examined how combinations of domains—trees and forests—could be created. Next, we examined several possible reasons for creating more than one domain. Then, we examined the structure within a domain—managing resources and permissions based on OUs. Finally, we considered the importance of proper site planning (to manage network replication traffic) and designing naming conventions (to increase organization and usability). Combined together, the result is a physical and logical structure for deploying directory services.

All of this information is absolutely essential to planning for the Active Directory—a step that will make a significant impact on the usefulness of Windows 2000, in general.

Glossary

A

access control entry (ACE) An item used by the operating system to determine resource access. Each access control list (ACL) has an associated ACE that lists the permissions that have been granted or denied to the users and groups listed in the ACL.

access control list (ACL) An item used by the operating system to determine resource access. Each object (such as a folder, network share, or printer) in Windows 2000 has an ACL. The ACL lists the security identifiers (SIDs) contained by objects. Only those identified in the list as having the appropriate permission can activate the services of that object.

access token An object containing the security identifier (SID) of a running process. A process started by another process inherits the starting process's access token. The access token is checked against each object's access control list (ACL) to determine whether or not appropriate permissions are granted to perform any requested service.

Accessibility Options Windows 2000 Professional features used to support users with limited sight, hearing, or mobility. Accessibility Options include special keyboard, sound, display, and mouse configurations.

Accessibility Wizard A Windows 2000 Professional Wizard used to configure a computer based on the user's vision, hearing, and mobility needs.

account lockout policy A Windows 2000 policy used to specify how many invalid logon attempts should be tolerated before a user account is locked out. Account lockout policies are set through account policies.

account policies Windows 2000 policies used to determine password and logon requirements. Account policies are set through the Microsoft Management Console (MMC) Local Computer Policy snap-in.

ACE See *access control entry*.

ACL See *access control list*.

Active Desktop A Windows 2000 feature that makes the Desktop look and work like a Web page.

Active Directory A directory service available with the Windows 2000 Server platform. The Active Directory stores information in a central database and allows users to have a single user account (called a domain user account or Active Directory user account) for the network.

Active Directory Installation Wizard (DCPROMO) The Windows 2000 tool that is used for promoting a Windows 2000 Server computer to a Windows 2000 domain controller. Using the Active Directory Installation Wizard, systems administrators can create trees and forests. See also *promotion*.

Active Directory replication A method by which Active Directory domain controllers synchronize information. See also *replication, intersite* and *replication, intrasite*.

Active Directory Services Interface (ADSI)   Code component that can be used for accessing information from various types of Directory Services, such as Active Directory, Windows NT, Novell Directory Services and Lightweight Directory Access Protocol (LDAP) sources. ADSI can be accessed from within various programming languages, including Java, Visual Basic and Visual C++.

Active Directory user account   A user account that is stored in the Windows 2000 Server Active Directory's central database. An Active Directory user account can provide a user with a single user account for a network. Also called a domain user account.

Active Directory Users and Computers tool   Windows 2000 administrative tool used for managing objects within the Active Directory.

adapter   Any hardware device that allows communications to occur through physically dissimilar systems. This term usually refers to peripheral cards that are permanently mounted inside computers and provide an interface from the computer's bus to another medium such as a hard disk or a network.

Add/Remove Programs   Control Panel applet that allows for installing and uninstalling software applications and components of the Windows 2000 operating system.

administrative templates   Templates that specify additional options that can be set using the Group Policy Editor tool.

Administrator account   A Windows 2000 special account that has the ultimate set of security permissions and can assign any permission to any user or group.

Administrators group   A Windows 2000 built-in group that consists of Administrator accounts.

ADSI   See *Active Directory Services Interface (ADSI)*.

alert   A system-monitoring feature that is generated when a specific counter exceeds or falls below a specified value. Through the Performance Logs and Alerts utility, administrators can configure alerts so that a message is sent, a program is run, or a more detailed log file is generated.

Anonymous Logon group   A Windows 2000 special group that includes users who access the computer through anonymous logons. Anonymous logons occur when users gain access through special accounts, such as the IUSR_computername and TsInternetUser user accounts.

answer file   An automated installation script used to respond to configuration prompts that normally occur in a Windows 2000 Professional installation. Administrators can create Windows 2000 answer files with the Setup Manager utility.

application assignment scripts   Script files that specify which applications are assigned to users of the Active Directory.

Application layer   The seventh (top) layer of the Open Systems Interconnection (OSI) model that interfaces with application programs by providing high-level network services based on lower-level network layers.

Application log   A log that tracks events that are related to applications that are running on the computer. The Application log can be viewed in the Event Viewer utility.

assigned applications   Applications installed with Windows Installer packages. Assigned applications are automatically installed when the user selects the application on the Programs menu or by document invocation (by the document extension).

assigning   The process by which applications are make available to computers and/or users.

auditing   The act of recording specific actions that are taken within a secure network operating system. Auditing is often used as a security measure to provide for accountability. Typical audited events include logon and logoff events, as well as accessing files and objects.

audit policy   A Windows 2000 policy that tracks the success or failure of specified security events. Audit policies are set through Local Computer Policy.

Authenticated Users group   A Windows 2000 special group that includes users who access the Windows 2000 operating system through a valid username and password.

authentication   The process required to log on to a computer locally. Authentication requires a valid username and a password that exists in the local accounts database. An access token will be created if the information presented matches the account in the database.

authoritative restore   See *restore, authoritative.*

automated installation   The process of installing Windows 2000 using an unattended setup method such as Remote Installation Services (RIS), unattended installation, or disk images.

B

backup   The process of writing all the data contained in online mass-storage devices to offline mass-storage devices for the purpose of safekeeping. Backups are usually performed from hard disk drives to tape drives. Also referred to as archiving.

backup, copy   A backup operation in which files are backed up but are not marked as having been backed up. A copy backup is often made for archival or redundancy purposes.

backup, daily   A backup operation in which all of the files that have changed on a certain day are backed up.

backup, differential   A backup operation in which all files that are marked as not having been backed up are copied. The files are not marked as having been backed up. In most backup plans, a differential backup includes all of the files that have changed since the last full backup.

backup, incremental A backup operation in which all files that are marked as not having been backed up are copied. The files are marked as having been backed up. In most backup plans, an incremental backup includes all of the files that have changed since the last full or incremental backup.

backup, normal A backup operation in which all of the files in a file system location are backed up and are marked as having been backed up.

Backup Operators group A Windows 2000 built-in group that includes users who can back up and restore the file system, even if the file system is NTFS and they have not been assigned permissions to the file system. The members of the Backup Operators group can only access the file system through the Windows 2000 Backup utility. To be able to directly access the file system, the user must have explicit permissions assigned.

backup type A backup choice that determines which files are backed up during a backup process. Backup types include normal backup, copy backup, incremental backup, differential backup, and daily backup.

Backup Wizard A Wizard used to perform a backup. The Backup Wizard is accessed through the Windows 2000 Backup utility.

baseline A snapshot record of a computer's current performance statistics that can be used for performance analysis and planning purposes.

Basic Input/Output System (BIOS) A set of routines in firmware that provides the most

basic software interface drivers for hardware attached to the computer. The BIOS contains the boot routine.

basic storage A disk-storage system supported by Windows 2000 that consists of primary partitions and extended partitions. Drives are configured as basic storage after an operating system has been upgraded from Windows NT.

Batch group A Windows 2000 special group that includes users who log on as a user account that is only used to run a batch job.

binding The process of linking together software components, such as network protocols and network adapters.

BIOS See *Basic Input/Output System.*

boot The process of loading a computer's operating system. Booting usually occurs in multiple phases, each successively more complex until the entire operating system and all its services are running. Also called bootstrap. The computer's BIOS must contain the first level of booting.

Boot Information Negotiation Layer (BINL) A portion of Remote Installation Services (RIS) that allows for connecting clients to a RIS server. See also *Remote Installation Services (RIS).*

BOOT.INI A file accessed during the Windows 2000 boot sequence. The BOOT.INI file is used to build the operating system menu choices that are displayed during the boot process. It is also used to specify the location of the boot partition.

Boot Normally   A Windows 2000 Advanced Options menu item used to boot Windows 2000 normally.

boot partition   The partition that contains the system files. The system files are located in C:\WINNT by default.

BOOTSECT.DOS   An optional file that is loaded if the user chooses to load an operating system other than Windows 2000. This file is only used in dual-boot or multi-boot computers.

bottleneck   A system resource that is inefficient compared with the rest of the computer system as a whole. The bottleneck can cause the rest of the system to run slowly.

bridgehead server   Used in Windows 2000 replication to coordinate the transfer of replicated information between Active Directory sites.

C

caching   A speed-optimization technique that keeps a copy of the most recently used data in a fast, high-cost, low-capacity storage device rather than in the device on which the actual data resides. Caching assumes that recently used data is likely to be used again. Fetching data from the cache is faster than fetching data from the slower, larger storage device. Most caching algorithms also copy data that is most likely to be used next and perform write-back caching to further increase speed gains.

caching-only DNS server   See *DNS server, caching-only*.

category   A grouping of applications that are available for installation by users through the Add/Remove Programs applet in the Control Panel. Categories are useful for managing large lists of available applications.

CD-based image   A type of image configured on a Remote Installation Services (RIS) server. A CD-based image contains only the Windows 2000 Professional operating system.

central processing unit (CPU)   The main processor in a computer.

Check Disk   A Windows 2000 utility that checks a hard disk for errors. Check Disk (chkdsk) attempts to fix file-system errors and scans for and attempts to recover bad sectors.

child domain   A relative term that describes a subdomain of another domain.

CIPHER   A command-line utility that can be used to encrypt files on NTFS volumes.

cipher text   Encrypted data. Encryption is the process of translating data into code that is not easily accessible. Once data has been encrypted, a user must have a password or key to decrypt the data. Unencrypted data is known as plain text.

clean install   A method of Windows 2000 Professional installation that puts the operating system into a new folder and uses its default settings the first time the operating system is loaded.

client A computer on a network that subscribes to the services provided by a server.

Comma-Separated Value Directory Exchange (CSVDE) A Windows 2000 command line utility for exchanging information between comma-separated-value files and the Active Directory.

compression The process of storing data in a form that takes less space than the uncompressed data.

Computer Management A consolidated tool for performing common Windows 2000 management tasks. The interface is organized into three main areas of management: System Tools, Storage, and Services and Applications.

computer name A NetBIOS name used to uniquely identify a computer on the network. A computer name can be from 1 to 15 characters in length.

Computer object An Active Directory object that is a security principal and that identifies a computer that is part of a domain.

connection-oriented service A type of connection service in which a connection (a path) is established and acknowledgments are sent. This type of communication is reliable but has a high overhead.

connectionless service A type of connection service that does not establish a connection (path) before transmission. This type of communication is fast, but it is not very reliable.

Contact object Active Directory objects that store contact information.

Control Panel A Windows 2000 utility that allows users to change default settings for operating system services to match their preferences. The Registry contains the Control Panel settings.

CONVERT A command-line utility used to convert a partition from FAT16 or FAT32 to the NTFS file system.

copy backup A backup type that backs up selected folders and files but does not set the archive bit.

counter A performance-measuring tool used to track specific information regarding a system resource, called a performance object. All Windows 2000 system resources are tracked as performance objects, such as Cache, Memory, Paging File, Process, and Processor. Each performance object has an associated set of counters. Counters are set through the System Monitor utility.

CPU See *central processing unit.*

Creator Group The Windows 2000 special group that created or took ownership of the object (rather than an individual user). When a regular user creates an object or takes ownership of an object, the username becomes the Creator Owner. When a member of the Administrators group creates or takes ownership of an object, the Administrators group becomes the Creator Group.

Creator Owner group The Windows 2000 special group that includes the account that created or took ownership of an object. The account, usually a user account, has the right to modify the object, but cannot modify any other objects that were not created by the user account.

D

daily backup A backup type that backs up all of the files that have been modified on the day that the daily backup is performed. The archive attribute is not set on the files that have been backed up.

data compression The process of storing data in a form that takes less space than the uncompressed data.

data encryption The process of translating data into code that is not easily accessible to increase security. Once data has been encrypted, a user must have a password or key to decrypt the data.

Data Link layer In the Open Systems Interconnection (OSI) model, the layer that provides the digital interconnection of network devices and the software that directly operates these devices, such as network adapters.

Debugging Mode A Windows 2000 Advanced Option menu item that runs the Kernel Debugger, if that utility is installed. The Kernel Debugger is an advanced troubleshooting utility.

default gateway A TCP/IP configuration option that specifies the gateway that will be used if the network contains routers.

delegation The process by which a user who has higher-level security permissions grants certain permissions over Active Directory objects to users who are lower-level security authorities. Delegation is often used to distribute administrative responsibilities in a network environment.

Delegation of Control Wizard A Windows 2000 tool used for delegating permissions over Active Directory objects. See also *delegation*.

Desktop A directory that the background of the Windows Explorer shell represents. By default, the Desktop includes objects that contain the local storage devices and available network shares. Also a key operating part of the Windows 2000 graphical interface.

device driver Software that allows a specific piece of hardware to communicate with the Windows 2000 operating system.

Device Manager A Windows 2000 utility used to provide information about the computer's configuration.

DHCP See *Dynamic Host Configuration Protocol*.

DHCP server A server configured to provide DHCP clients with all of their IP configuration information automatically.

dial-up networking A service that allows remote users to dial into the network or the Internet (such as through a telephone or an ISDN connection).

Dialup group   A Windows 2000 special group that includes users who log on to the network from a dial-up connection.

differential backup   A backup type that copies only the files that have been changed since the last normal backup (full backup) or incremental backup. A differential backup backs up only those files that have changed since the last full backup, but does not reset the archive bit.

directory replication   The process of copying a directory structure from an export computer to an import computer(s). Anytime changes are made to the export computer, the import computer(s) is automatically updated with the changes.

Directory Services Restore Mode   A special boot mode for Windows 2000 domain controllers. The Directory Services Restore mode is used to boot a domain controller without starting Active Directory services. This enables systems administrators to log on locally to restore or to troubleshoot any problems with the Active Directory.

Disk Cleanup   A Windows 2000 utility used to identify areas of disk space that can be deleted to free additional hard disk space. Disk Cleanup works by identifying temporary files, Internet cache files, and unnecessary program files.

disk defragmentation   The process of rearranging the existing files on a disk so that they are stored contiguously, which optimizes access to those files.

Disk Defragmenter   A Windows 2000 utility that performs disk defragmentation.

disk image   An exact duplicate of a hard disk, used for automated installation. The disk image is copied from a reference computer that is configured in the same manner as the computers on which Windows 2000 Professional will be installed.

Disk Management   A Windows 2000 graphical tool for managing disks and volumes.

disk partitioning   The process of creating logical partitions on the physical hard drive.

disk quotas   A Windows 2000 feature used to specify how much disk space a user is allowed to use on specific NTFS volumes. Disk quotas can be applied for all users or for specific users.

distinguished name   The fully qualified name of an object within a hierarchical system. Distinguished names are used for all Active Directory objects and in the Domain Name System (DNS). No two objects in these systems should have the same distinguished name.

Distribution group   A collection of Active Directory users that are used primarily for e-mail distribution.

distribution server   A network server that contains the Windows 2000 distribution files that have been copied from the distribution CD. Clients can connect to the distribution server and install Windows 2000 over the network.

DNS   See *Domain Name Service.*

DNS namespace A hierarchical network naming structure that is designed to resolve hostnames to IP addresses. Typical DNS names within a namespace are hierarchical, ranging from most specific on the left to least specific on the right (e.g., `server1.mycompany.com`).

DNS server A server that uses DNS to resolve domain or host names to IP addresses.

DNS server, caching-only A DNS server that is not the authority for any specific zone but can resolve DNS queries. Caching-only DNS servers are used to improve performance.

DNS server, master A DNS server that is responsible as an authority for name resolutions within a DNS zone. Each DNS zone can have only one master DNS server.

DNS server, primary A DNS server that is authoritative for a zone and that is able to receive updates of DNS information.

DNS server, secondary A DNS server that is used to resolve DNS names to TCP/IP addresses. Secondary servers contain a read-only copy of the DNS database.

domain In Microsoft networks, an arrangement of client and server computers referenced by a specific name that shares a single security permissions database. On the Internet, a domain is a named collection of hosts and subdomains, registered with a unique name by the InterNIC.

domain controller A Windows 2000 Server computer that includes a copy of the Active Directory data store. Domain controllers contain the security information required to perform services related to the Active Directory.

Domain Local group An Active Directory security or distribution group that can contain Universal groups, Global groups, or accounts from anywhere within an Active Directory forest.

domain name The textual identifier of a specific Internet host. Domain names are in the form of server organization type (`www.microsoft.com`) and are resolved to Internet addresses by DNS servers.

domain name server An Internet host dedicated to the function of translating fully qualified domain names into IP addresses.

Domain Name Service (DNS) The TCP/IP network service that translates textual Internet network addresses into numerical Internet network addresses.

Domain Naming Master The Active Directory domain controller that is responsible for handling the addition and removal of domains within the Active Directory environment.

domain user account A user account that is stored in the Windows 2000 Server Active Directory's central database. A domain user account can provide a user with a single user account for a network. Also called an Active Directory user account.

drive letter   A single letter assigned as an abbreviation to a mass-storage volume available to a computer.

driver   A program that provides a software interface to a hardware device. Drivers are written for the specific devices they control, but they present a common software interface to the computer's operating system, allowing all devices of a similar type to be controlled as if they were the same.

dynamic disk   A Windows 2000 disk-storage technique. A dynamic disk is divided into dynamic volumes. Dynamic volumes cannot contain partitions or logical drives, and they are not accessible through DOS. You can size or resize a dynamic disk without restarting Windows 2000.

Dynamic Host Configuration Protocol (DHCP)   A method of automatically assigning IP addresses to client computers on a network.

dynamic storage   A Windows 2000 disk-storage system that is configured as volumes. Windows 2000 Professional dynamic storage supports simple volumes, spanned volumes, and striped volumes.

E

effective rights   The rights that a user actually has to a file or folder. To determine a user's effective rights, add all of the permissions that have been allowed through the user's assignments based on that user's username and group associations. Then subtract any permissions that have been denied the user through the username or group associations.

Emergency Repair Disk (ERD)   A disk that stores portions of the Registry, the system files, a copy of the partition boot sector, and information that relates to the startup environment. The ERD can be used to repair problems that prevent a computer from starting.

Enable Boot Logging   A Windows 2000 Professional Advanced Options menu item that is used to create a log file that tracks the loading of drivers and services.

Enable VGA Mode   A Windows 2000 Professional Advanced Options menu item that loads a standard VGA driver without starting the computer in Safe Mode.

encryption   The process of translating data into code that is not easily accessible to increase security. Once data has been encrypted, a user must have a password or key to decrypt the data.

ERD   See *Emergency Repair Disk.*

Error event   An Event Viewer event type that indicates the occurrence of an error, such as a driver failing to load.

Ethernet   The most popular Data Link layer standard for local area networking. Ethernet implements the Carrier Sense Multiple Access with Collision Detection (CSMA/CD) method of arbitrating multiple computer access to the same network. This standard supports the use of Ethernet over any type of media, including wireless broadcast. Standard Ethernet operates as 10Mbps. Fast Ethernet operates at 100Mbps.

Event Viewer   A Windows 2000 utility that tracks information about the computer's hardware and software, as well as security events. This information is stored in three log files: the Application log, the Security log, and the System log.

Everyone   A Windows 2000 special group that includes anyone who could possibly access the computer. The Everyone group includes all of the users (including Guests) who have been defined on the computer.

extended partition   In basic storage, a logical drive that allows you to allocate the logical partitions however you wish. Extended partitions are created after the primary partition has been created.

F

Failure Audit event   An Event Viewer event that indicates the occurrence of an event that has been audited for failure, such as a failed logon when someone presents an invalid username and/or password.

FAT16   The 16-bit version of the File Allocation System (FAT) system, which was widely used by DOS and Windows 3.*x*. The file system is used to track where files are stored on a disk. Most operating systems support FAT16.

FAT32   The 32-bit version of the File Allocation System (FAT) system, which is more efficient and provides more safeguards than FAT16. Windows 9x and Windows 2000 support FAT32. Windows NT does not support FAT32.

fault tolerance   Any method that prevents system failure by tolerating single faults, usually through hardware redundancy.

file allocation table (FAT)   The file system used by MS-DOS and available to other operating systems, such as Windows (all versions), OS/2, and Macintosh. FAT (now known as FAT16) has become something of a standard for mass-storage compatibility because of its simplicity and wide availability. FAT has fewer fault-tolerance features than the NTFS file system and can become corrupted through normal use over time.

file attributes   Bits stored along with the name and location of a file in a directory entry. File attributes show the status of a file, such as archived, hidden, and read-only. Different operating systems use different file attributes to implement services such as sharing, compression, and security.

file extension   The three-letter suffix that follows the name of a standard file-system file. Using Group Policy and software management functionality, systems administration can specify which applications are associated with which file extensions.

file system   A software component that manages the storage of files on a mass-storage device by providing services that can create, read, write, and delete files. File systems impose an ordered database of files on the mass-storage device. Storage is arranged in volumes. File systems use hierarchies of directories to organize files.

File Transfer Protocol (FTP)   A simple Internet protocol that transfers complete files from an FTP server to a client running the FTP client. FTP provides a simple, no-overhead method of transferring files between computers but cannot perform browsing functions. Users must know the URL of the FTP server to which they wish to attach.

filtering   The process by which permissions on security groups are used to identify which Active Directory objects are affected by Group Policy settings. Through the use of filtering, systems administrators can maintain a fine level of control over Group Policy settings.

foreign security principals   Active Directory objects used to give permissions to other security principals that do not exist within an Active Directory domain. Generally, foreign security principals are automatically created by the services of the Active Directory.

forest   A collection of Windows 2000 domains that does not necessarily share a common namespace. All of the domains within a forest share a common schema and Global Catalog, and resources can be shared between the domains in a forest.

format   The process of preparing a mass-storage device for use with a file system. There are actually two levels of formatting. Low-level formatting writes a structure of sectors and tracks to the disk with bits used by the mass-storage controller hardware. The controller hardware requires this format, and it is independent of the file system. High-level formatting creates file system structures such as an allocation table and a root directory in a partition, thus creating a volume.

forward lookup zone   A DNS zone that is used for resolving DNS names to TCP/IP addresses.

forwarding   The process by which a DNS server sends a request for name resolution to another DNS server. Forwarding is often used to improve performance and to restrict network traffic over slow connections.

FTP   See *File Transfer Protocol.*

G

Global Catalog   A portion of the Active Directory that contains a subset of information about all of the objects within all domains of the Active Directory data store. The Global Catalog is used to improve performance of authentications and for sharing information between domains.

Global Catalog server   A Windows 2000 Active Directory domain controller that hosts a copy of the Global Catalog. See also *Global Catalog.*

Global group   An Active Directory security group that contains accounts only from its own domain.

Global Unique Identifier (GUID)   A special identifier that uniquely identifies an object within the Active Directory.

Graphical User Interface (GUI)   A computer shell program that represents mass-storage devices, directories, and files as graphical objects on a screen. A cursor driven by a pointing device such as a mouse manipulates the objects.

Group Policy   Settings that can affect the behavior of, and the functionality available to, users and computers.

Group Policy object   A collection of settings that control the behavior of users and computers.

Group Policy object link   A link between a Group Policy object and the Active Directory objects to which it applies. Group Policy objects can be linked to sites, domains, organizational units, and other Active Directory objects.

groups   Security entities to which users can be assigned membership for the purpose of applying the broad set of group permissions to the user. By managing permissions for groups and assigning users to groups, rather than assigning permissions to users, administrators can more easily manage security.

groups, distribution   Active Directory objects that are used primarily for the purpose of routing e-mail and other electronic communications. Distribution groups are not considered to be security principals.

Guest account   A Windows 2000 user account created to provide a mechanism to allow users to access the computer even if they do not have a unique username and password. This account normally has very limited privileges on the computer. This account is disabled by default.

Guests group   A Windows 2000 built-in group that has limited access to the computer. This group can access only specific areas. Most administrators do not allow Guest account access because it poses a potential security risk.

H

hard disk drive   A mass-storage device that reads and writes digital information magnetically on discs that spin under moving heads. Hard disk drives are precisely aligned and cannot normally be removed. Hard disk drives are an inexpensive way to store gigabytes of computer data permanently. Hard disk drives also store the software installed on a computer.

Hardware Compatibility List (HCL)   A list of all of the hardware devices supported by Windows 2000. Hardware on the HCL has been tested and verified as being compatible with Windows 2000.

hardware profile   A file that stores a hardware configuration for a computer. Hardware profiles are useful when a single computer (a laptop that can be docked or undocked) has multiple hardware configurations.

HCL   See *Hardware Compatibility List.*

hibernation   The storage of anything that is stored in memory on the computer's hard disk. Hibernation ensures that none of the information stored in memory is lost when the computer is shut down. When the computer is taken out of hibernation, it is returned to its previous state.

home folder   A folder where users normally store their personal files and information. A home folder can be a local folder or a network folder.

host   An Internet server. Hosts are constantly connected to the Internet.

HTML   See *Hypertext Markup Language.*

HTTP   See *Hypertext Transfer Protocol.*

hyperlink   A link within text or graphics that has a Web address embedded in it. By clicking the link, a user can jump to another Web address.

Hypertext Markup Language (HTML)   A textual data format that identifies sections of a document such as headers, lists, hypertext links, and so on. HTML is the data format used on the World Wide Web for the publication of Web pages.

Hypertext Transfer Protocol (HTTP)   An Internet protocol that transfers HTML documents over the Internet and responds to context changes that happen when a user clicks a hyperlink.

I

IIS   See *Internet Information Services.*

incremental backup   A backup type that backs up only the files that have changed since the last normal or incremental backup. It sets the archive attribute on the files that are backed up.

Indexing Service   A Windows 2000 service that creates an index based on the contents and properties of files stored on the computer's local hard drive. A user can then use the Windows 2000 Search function to search or query through the index for specific keywords.

Information event   An Event Viewer event that informs you that a specific action has occurred, such as when a system shuts down or starts.

Infrastructure Master   The Windows 2000 domain controller that is responsible for managing group memberships and transferring this information to other domain controllers within the Active Directory environment.

inheritance   The process by which settings and properties defined on a parent object implicitly apply to a child object.

inherited permissions   Parent folder permissions that are applied to (or inherited by) files and subfolders of the parent folder. In Windows 2000 Professional, the default is for parent folder permissions to be applied to any files or subfolders in that folder.

initialization files   Files used to specify parameters that are used by an application or a utility. Initialization files are often used by setup programs to determine application installation information.

initial user account   The account that uses the name of the registered user and is created only if the computer is installed as a member of a workgroup (not into the Active Directory). By default, the initial user is a member of the Administrators group.

Integrated Services Digital Network (ISDN)   A direct, digital, dial-up connection that operates at 64KB per channel over regular twisted-pair cable. ISDN provides twice the data rate of the fastest modems per channel. Up to 24 channels can be multiplexed over two twisted pairs.

Interactive group   A Windows 2000 special group that includes all the users who use the computer's resources locally.

interactive logon   A logon when the user logs on from the computer where the user account is stored on the computer's local database. Also called a local logon.

interactive user   A user who physically logs on to the computer where the user account resides (rather than over the network).

Internet connection sharing   A Windows 2000 feature that allows a small network to be connected to the Internet through a single connection. The computer that dials into the Internet provides network address translation, addressing, and name resolution services for all of the computers on the network. Through Internet connection sharing, the other computers on the network can access Internet resources and use Internet applications, such as Internet Explorer and Outlook Express.

Internet Explorer   A World Wide Web browser produced by Microsoft and included with Windows 9x, Windows NT 4, and now Windows 2000.

Internet Information Services (IIS)   Software that serves Internet higher-level protocols like HTTP and FTP to clients using Web browsers. The IIS software that is installed on a Windows 2000 Server computer is a fully functional Web server and is designed to support heavy Internet usage.

Internet Print Protocol (IPP)   A Windows 2000 protocol that allows users to print directly to a URL. Printer and job-related information are generated in HTML format.

Internet printer   A Windows 2000 feature that allows users to send documents to be printed through the Internet.

Internet Protocol (IP)   The Network layer protocol upon which the Internet is based. IP provides a simple connectionless packet exchange. Other protocols such as TCP use IP to perform their connection-oriented (or guaranteed delivery) services.

Internet service provider (ISP)   A company that provides dial-up connections to the Internet.

Internet Services Manager   A Windows 2000 utility used to configure the protocols that are used by Internet Information Services (IIS) and Personal Web Services (PWS).

internetwork   A network made up of multiple network segments that are connected with some device, such as a router. Each network segment is assigned a network address. Network layer protocols build routing tables that are used to route packets through the network in the most efficient manner.

InterNIC   The agency that is responsible for assigning IP addresses.

interprocess communications (IPC) A generic term describing any manner of client/ server communication protocol, specifically those operating in the Application layer. IPC mechanisms provide a method for the client and server to trade information.

intranet A privately owned network based on the TCP/IP protocol suite.

IP See *Internet Protocol.*

IP address A four-byte number that uniquely identifies a computer on an IP internetwork. InterNIC assigns the first bytes of Internet IP addresses and administers them in hierarchies. Huge organizations like the government or top-level ISPs have class A addresses, large organizations and most ISPs have class B addresses, and small companies have class C addresses. In a class A address, InterNIC assigns the first byte, and the owning organization assigns the remaining three bytes. In a class B address, InterNIC or the higher-level ISP assigns the first two bytes, and the organization assigns the remaining two bytes. In a class C address, InterNIC or the higher-level ISP assigns the first three bytes, and the organization assigns the remaining byte. Organizations not attached to the Internet are free to assign IP addresses as they please.

IPC See *interprocess communications.*

IPCONFIG A command used to display the computer's IP configuration.

IPP See *Internet Print Protocol.*

ISA See *Industry Standard Architecture.*

ISDN See *Integrated Services Digital Network.*

ISP See *Internet service provider.*

iteration The incremental process by which DNS names are resolved to IP addresses.

K

kernel The core process of a preemptive operating system, consisting of a multitasking scheduler and the basic security services. Depending on the operating system, other services such as virtual memory drivers may be built into the kernel. The kernel is responsible for managing the scheduling of threads and processes.

L

LAN See *local area network.*

Last Known Good Configuration A Windows 2000 Advanced Options menu item used to load the configuration that was used the last time the computer was successfully booted.

LDAP See *Lightweight Directory Access Protocol (LDAP).*

LDIFDE See *LDIF Directory Exchange (LDIFDE).*

LDIF Directory Exchange (LDIFDE) A command-line utility that is used to transfer Active Directory objects between LDIF files and the Active Directory. LDIF files can be read and modified through the use of LDIF-compatible tools.

licensing server   A Windows 2000 computer that is responsible for managing software licenses. Licensing server properties can be set using the Active Directory Sites and Services tool.

Lightweight Directory Access Protocol (LDAP)   A protocol used for querying and modifying information stored within directory services. The Active Directory can be queried and modified through the use of LDAP-compatible tools.

local area network (LAN)   A connection of well-connected computers that usually reside within a single geographic location (such as an office building). An organization typically owns all of the hardware that makes up its LAN.

Local Computer Policy   A Microsoft Management Console (MMC) snap-in used to implement account policies.

local group   A group that is stored on the local computer's accounts database. These are the groups that administrators can add users to and manage directly on a Windows 2000 Professional computer.

Local Group Policy   A Microsoft Management Console (MMC) snap-in used to implement local group policies, which include computer configuration policies and user configuration policies.

local logon   A logon when the user logs on from the computer where the user account is stored on the computer's local database. Also called an interactive logon.

local policies   Policies that allow administrators to control what a user can do after logging on. Local policies include audit policies, security option policies, and user rights policies. These policies are set through Local Computer Policy.

local printer   A printer that uses a physical port and that has not been shared. If a printer is defined as local, the only users who can use the printer are the local users of the computer that the printer is attached to.

local security   Security that governs a local or interactive user's ability to access locally stored files. Local security can be set through NTFS permissions.

local user account   A user account stored locally in the user accounts database of a computer that is running Windows 2000 Professional.

local user profile   A profile created the first time a user logs on, stored in the Documents and Settings folder. The default user profile folder's name matches the user's logon name. This folder contains a file called NTUSER.DAT and subfolders with directory links to the user's Desktop items.

Local Users and Groups   A utility that is used to create and manage local user and group accounts on Windows 2000 Professional computers and Windows 2000 member servers.

locale settings   Settings for regional items, including numbers, currency, time, date, and input locales.

logical drive   An allocation of disk space on a hard drive, using a drive letter. For example, a 5GB hard drive could be partitioned into two logical drives: a C: drive, which might be 2GB, and a D: drive, which might be 3GB.

Logical Drives   A Windows 2000 utility used to manage the logical drives on the computer.

logical port   A port that connects a device directly to the network. Logical ports are used with printers by installing a network card in the printers.

logical printer   The software interface between the physical printer (the print device) and the operating system. Also referred to as just a printer in Windows 2000 terminology.

logoff   The process of closing an open session with a Windows 2000 computer or network.

logon   The process of opening a session with a Windows 2000 computer or a network by providing a valid authentication consisting of a user account name and a password. After logon, network resources are available to the user according to the user's assigned permissions.

logon script   A command file that automates the logon process by performing utility functions such as attaching to additional server resources or automatically running different programs based on the user account that established the logon.

M

Magnifier   A Windows 2000 utility used to create a separate window to magnify a portion of the screen. This option is designed for users who have poor vision.

mandatory profile   A user profile created by an administrator and saved with a special extension (.MAN) so that the user cannot modify the profile in any way. Mandatory profiles can be assigned to a single user or a group of users.

mapped drive   A shared network folder associated with a drive letter. Mapped drives appear to users as local connections on their computers and can be accessed through a drive letter using My Computer.

master DNS server   See *DNS server, master.*

member server   A server that participates in the security of Active Directory domains but does not contain a copy of the Active Directory data store.

memory   Any device capable of storing information. This term is usually used to indicate volatile random-access memory (RAM) capable of high-speed access to any portion of the memory space, but incapable of storing information without power.

Microsoft Installer (MSI)   A standard that is used to automatically deploy applications with Windows Installer packages.

Microsoft Management Console (MMC)
The Windows 2000 console framework for management applications. The MMC provides a common environment for snap-ins.

mixed-mode Active Directory   An Active Directory mode that allows the use of Windows NT domain controllers.

MMC   See *Microsoft Management Console.*

modem   Modulator/demodulator. A device used to create an analog signal suitable for transmission over telephone lines from a digital data stream. Modern modems also include a command set for negotiating connections and data rates with remote modems and for setting their default behavior.

MSI   See *Microsoft Installer.*

multi-booting   The process of allowing a computer to boot multiple operating systems.

My Computer   The folder used to view and manage a computer. My Computer provides access to all local and network drives, as well as Control Panel.

My Documents   The default storage location for documents that are created. Each user has a unique My Documents folder.

My Network Places   The folder that provides access to shared resources, such as local network resources and Web resources.

N

native-mode Active Directory   An Active Directory mode that allows the use of only Windows 2000 domain controllers and enhances group capabilities.

NetBEUI   See *NetBIOS Extended User Interface.*

NetBIOS   See *Network Basic Input/Output System.*

NetBIOS Extended User Interface (NetBEUI)   A simple Network layer transport protocol developed to support NetBIOS installations. NetBEUI is not routable, and so it is not appropriate for larger networks. NetBEUI is the fastest transport protocol available for Windows 2000.

NET USE   A command-line utility used to map network drives.

NetWare   A popular network operating system developed by Novell in the early 1980s. NetWare is a cooperative, multitasking, highly optimized, dedicated-server network operating system that has client support for most major operating systems. Recent versions of NetWare include graphical client tools for management from client stations. At one time, NetWare accounted for more than 70 percent of the network operating system market.

network adapter   The hardware used to connect computers (or other devices) to the network. Network adapters function at the Physical layer and the Network layer of the Open System Interconnection (OSI) model.

Network Basic Input/Output System (NetBIOS)   A client/server IPC service developed by IBM in the early 1980s. NetBIOS presents a relatively primitive mechanism for communication in client/server applications, but its widespread acceptance and availability across most operating systems makes it a logical choice for simple network applications. Many of the network IPC mechanisms in Windows 2000 are implemented over NetBIOS.

Network group   A Windows 2000 special group that includes the users who access a computer's resources over a network connection.

Network Monitor   A Windows 2000 utility that can be used for monitoring and decoding packets that are transferred on the network.

network printer   A printer that is available to local and network users. A network printer can use a physical port or a logical port.

New Technology File System (NTFS)   A secure, transaction-oriented file system developed for Windows NT and Windows 2000. NTFS offers features such as local security on files and folders, data compression, disk quotas, and data encryption.

normal backup   A backup type that backs up all selected folders and files and then marks each file that has been backed up as archived.

NTFS   See *New Technology File System.*

NTFS permissions   Permissions used to control access to NTFS folders and files. Access is configured by allowing or denying NTFS permissions to users and groups.

NTUSER.DAT   The file that is created for a local user profile.

NTUSER.MAN   The file that is created for a mandatory profile.

NWLINK IPX/SPX/NetBIOS Compatible Transport   Microsoft's implementation of the Novell IPX/SPX protocol stack.

O

offline files and folders   A Windows 2000 feature that allows network folders and files to be stored on Windows 2000 clients. Users can access network files even if the network location is not available.

Open Systems Interconnection (OSI) model   A reference model for network component interoperability developed by the International Standards Organization (ISO) to promote cross-vendor compatibility of hardware and software network systems. The OSI model splits the process of networking into seven distinct services, or layers. Each layer uses the services of the layer below to provide its service to the layer above.

optimization   Any effort to reduce the workload on a hardware component by eliminating, obviating, or reducing the amount of work required of the hardware component through any means. For instance, file caching is an optimization that reduces the workload of a hard disk drive.

organizational units (OUs) Used to logically organize the Active Directory objects within a domain.

OSI model See *Open Systems Interconnection model.*

owner The user associated with an NTFS file or folder who is able to control access and grant permissions to other users.

P

packages, Windows Installer See *Windows Installer packages.*

page file Logical memory that exists on the hard drive. If a system is experiencing excessive paging (swapping between the page file and physical RAM), it needs more memory.

parent domain A relative term that describes a domain that is a parent of another domain. Parent domains may contain child domains (also called subdomains).

partition A section of a hard disk that can contain an independent file system volume. Partitions can be used to keep multiple operating systems and file systems on the same hard disk.

password policies Windows 2000 policies used to enforce security requirements on the computer. Password policies are set on a per-computer basis, and they cannot be configured for specific users. Password policies are set through account policies.

patch A Windows Installer file that updates application code. Patches can be used to ensure that new features are installed after an application has already completed installation.

PC Card A special, credit-card-sized device used to add devices to a laptop computer. Also called a PCMCIA card.

PCI See *Peripheral Connection Interface.*

PCMCIA card See *Personal Computer Memory Card International Association card.*

Peer Web Services (PWS) Software that acts as a small-scale Web server, for use with a small intranet or a small Internet site with limited traffic. Windows 2000 uses PWS to publish resources on the Internet or a private intranet. When you install Internet Information Services (IIS), on a Windows 2000 Professional computer, you are actually installing PWS.

performance log Windows 2000 performance information that is stored to a file within the file system for later analysis or for analysis using other applications.

Performance Logs and Alerts A Windows 2000 utility used to log performance-related data and generate alerts based on performance-related data.

permissions Security constructs used to regulate access to resources by username or group affiliation. Permissions can be assigned by administrators to allow any level of access, such as read-only, read/write, or delete, by controlling the ability of users to initiate object services. Security is implemented by checking the user's security identifier (SID) against each object's access control list (ACL).

Personal Computer Memory Card International Association (PCMCIA) card   A special, credit-card-sized device used to add devices to a laptop computer. Also called a PC Card.

Personal Web Manager   A Windows 2000 utility used to configure and manage Peer Web Services (PWS). This utility has options for configuring the location of the home page and stopping the Web site, and displays statistics for monitoring the Web site.

physical port   A serial (COM) or parallel (LPT) port that connects a device, such as a printer, directly to a computer.

Ping   A command used to send an Internet Control Message Protocol (ICMP) echo request and echo reply to verify that a remote computer is available.

Plug and Play   A technology that uses a combination of hardware and software to allow the operating system to automatically recognize and configure new hardware without any user intervention.

policies   General controls that enhance the security of an operating environment. In Windows 2000, policies affect restrictions on password use and rights assignments, and determine which events will be recorded in the Security log.

POST   See *Power On Self Test*.

Power On Self Test (POST)   A part of the Windows 2000 boot sequence. The POST detects the computer's processor, how much memory is present, what hardware is recognized, and whether or not the BIOS is standard or has Plug-and-Play capabilities.

Power Users group   A Windows 2000 built-in group that has fewer rights than the Administrators group, but more rights than the Users groups. Members of the Power Users group can perform tasks such as creating local users and groups and modifying the users and groups that they have created.

Preboot eXecution Environment (PXE)   A standard used to boot computers that do not have operating systems installed to connect to a network and transfer information. PXE-enabled computers are supported through the use of the Remote Installation Services (RIS). See also *Remote Installation Services (RIS)*.

Presentation layer   The layer of the Open Systems Interconnection (OSI) model that converts and translates (if necessary) information between the Session layer and Application layer.

prestaging   The process of identifying computers that are to be installed through the use of Remote Installation Services. Prestaging can increase security by only allowing specific machines to perform a remote installation. See also *Remote Installation Services (RIS)*.

primary DNS server   See *DNS server, primary*.

Primary Domain Controller (PDC) Emulator   A Windows 2000 domain controller that is used primarily for backwards compatibility with Windows NT domain controllers.

primary partition   A part of basic storage on a disk. The primary partition is the first partition created on a hard drive. The primary partition uses all of the space that is allocated to the partition. This partition is usually marked as active and is the partition that is used to boot the computer.

print device   The actual physical printer or hardware device that generates printed output.

print driver   The specific software that understands a print device. Each print device has an associated print driver.

Printer object   An Active Directory object that identifies printers that are published within domains.

print processor   The process that determines whether or not a print job needs further processing once that job has been sent to the print spooler. The processing (also called rendering) is used to format the print job so that it can print correctly at the print device.

print queue   A directory or folder on the print server that stores the print jobs until they can be printed. Also called a printer spooler.

print server   The computer on which the printer has been defined. When a user sends a print job to a network printer, it goes to the print server first.

print spooler   A directory or folder on the print server that stores the print jobs until they can be printed. Also called a print queue.

printer   In Windows 2000 terminology, the software interface between the physical printer (see *print device*) and the operating system.

printer pool   A configuration that allows one printer to be used for multiple print devices. A printer pool can be used when multiple printers use the same print driver (and are normally in the same location). With a printer pool, users can send their print jobs to the first available printer.

priority   A level of execution importance assigned to a thread. In combination with other factors, the priority level determines how often that thread will get computer time according to a scheduling algorithm.

process   A running program containing one or more threads. A process encapsulates the protected memory and environment for its threads.

processor   A circuit designed to automatically perform lists of logical and arithmetic operations. Unlike microprocessors, processors may be designed from discrete components rather than be a monolithic integrated circuit.

processor affinity   The association of a processor with specific processes that are running on the computer. Processor affinity is used to configure multiple processors.

promotion   The act of converting a Windows 2000 Server computer to a domain controller. See also *Active Directory Installation Wizard*.

protocol An established rule of communication adhered to by the parties operating under it. Protocols provide a context in which to interpret communicated information. Computer protocols are rules used by communicating devices and software services to format data in a way that all participants understand.

PXE See *Pre-Boot Execution Environment*.

published applications Applications installed with Windows Installer packages. Users can choose whether or not they will install published applications through the Control Panel Add/Remove Programs icon.

publishing Making applications available for use by users through Group Policy and Software Installation settings. Published applications can be installed on demand or when required by end users through the use of the Add/Remove Programs applet in the Control Panel.

PWS See *Peer Web Services*.

PXE See *Preboot eXecution Environment (PXE)*.

R

RAM See *random-access memory*.

random-access memory (RAM) Integrated circuits that store digital bits in massive arrays of logical gates or capacitors. RAM is the primary memory store for modern computers, storing all running software processes and contextual data.

RAS See *Remote Access Service*.

real-time application A process that must respond to external events at least as fast as those events can occur. Real-time threads must run at very high priorities to ensure their ability to respond in real time.

Recovery Console A Windows 2000 option for recovering from a failed system. The Recovery Console starts Windows 2000 without the graphical interface and allows the administrator limited capabilities, such as adding or replacing files and starting and stopping services

recursion The process by which DNS servers or clients use other DNS servers to resolve DNS names to TCP/IP address queries.

Recycle Bin A folder that holds files and folders that have been deleted. Files can be retrieved or cleared (for permanent deletion) from the Recycle Bin.

REGEDIT A Windows program used to edit the Registry. It does not support full editing, as does the REGEDT32 program, but it has better search capabilities than REGEDT32.

REGEDT32 The primary utility for editing the Windows 2000 Registry.

Regional Options A Control Panel utility used to enable and configure multilingual editing and viewing on a localized version of Windows 2000 Professional.

Registry A database of settings required and maintained by Windows 2000 and its components. The Registry contains all of the configuration information used by the computer. It is stored as a hierarchical structure and is made up of keys, hives, and value entries.

Relative ID (RID) Master The domain controller that is responsible for generating unique identifiers for each of the domains within an Active Directory environment.

Remote Access Service (RAS) A service that allows network connections to be established over a modem connection, an Integrated Services Digital Network (ISDN) connection, or a null-modem cable. The computer initiating the connection is called the RAS client; the answering computer is called the RAS server.

remote installation Installation of Windows 2000 Professional performed remotely through Remote Installation Services (RIS).

Remote Installation Preparation (RIPrep) image A type of image configured on a Remote Installation Services (RIS) server. A RIPrep image can contain the Windows 2000 operating system and applications. This type of image is based on a preconfigured computer.

Remote Installation Services (RIS) Windows 2000 service that allows for the installation of the Windows 2000 Professional operating system on remote computers.

Remote Installation Preparation (RIPrep) Wizard A remote installation tool used to create "images" of the configuration of a specific workstation. This method increases consistency in workstation rollouts and decreases the administrative effort required.

Remote Procedure Call (RPC) protocol A protocol used to allow communications between system processes on remote computers. RPC protocol is used by the Active Directory for intrasite replication. See also *instrasite replication*.

Removable Storage A Windows 2000 utility used to track information on removable storage media, which include CDs, DVDs, tapes, and jukeboxes containing optical discs.

rendering The process that determines whether or not a print job needs further processing once that job has been sent to the spooler. The processing is used to format the print job so that it can print correctly at the print device.

replication, intersite The transfer of information between domain controllers that reside in different Active Directory sites.

replication, intrasite The transfer of information between domain controllers that reside within the same Active Directory site.

Replicator group A Windows 2000 built-in group that supports directory replication, which is a feature used by domain servers. Only domain user accounts that will be used to start the replication service should be assigned to this group.

Requests for Comments (RFCs) The set of standards defining the Internet protocols as determined by the Internet Engineering Task Force and available in the public domain on the Internet. RFCs define the functions and services provided by each of the many Internet protocols. Compliance with the RFCs guarantees cross-vendor compatibility.

resource Any useful service, such as a shared folder or a printer.

resource record (RR) A DNS entry that specifies the availability of specific DNS services. For example, an MX record specifies the IP address of a mail server, and Host (A) records specify the IP addresses of workstations on the network.

restore, authoritative Specifies that the contents of a certain portion of the Active Directory on a domain controller should override any changes on other domain controllers, regardless of their sequence numbers. An authoritative restore is used to restore the contents of the Active Directory to a previous point in time.

Restore Wizard A Wizard used to restore data. The Restore Wizard is accessed through the Windows 2000 Backup utility.

reverse lookup zone A DNS zone that is used to resolve a TCP/IP address to a DNS name.

RFC See *Request For Comments.*

RIPrep image See *Remote Installation Preparation image.*

RIS See *Remote Installation Services (RIS).*

roaming profile A user profile that is stored and configured to be downloaded from a server. Roaming profiles allow users to access their profiles from any location on the network.

root domain In DNS, the name of the top of the Internet domain hierarchy. Although the root domain does not have a name, it is often referred to as ".".

router A Network layer device that moves packets between networks. Routers provide internetwork connectivity.

S

Safe Mode A Windows 2000 Advanced Options menu item that loads the absolute minimum of services and drivers that are needed to start Windows 2000. The drivers that are loaded with Safe Mode include basic files and drivers for the mouse (unless a serial mouse is attached to the computer), monitor, keyboard, hard drive, standard video driver, and default system services. Safe Mode is considered a diagnostic mode. It does not include networking capabilities.

Safe Mode with Command Prompt A Windows 2000 Advanced Options menu item that starts Windows 2000 in Safe Mode, but instead of loading the graphical interface, it loads a command prompt.

Safe Mode with Networking A Windows 2000 Advanced Options menu item that starts Windows 2000 in Safe Mode, but it adds networking features.

schema   A database structure for all of the types of objects that are supported within the Active Directory, along with the attributes for each of these objects.

Schema Master   A Windows 2000 domain controller that is responsible for maintaining the master copy of the Active Directory schema. There is only one Schema Master per Active Directory forest. See also *schema*.

Script Policy   Setting within Group Policy objects that specifies login, logoff, startup, and shutdown script settings.

SCSI   See *Small Computer Systems Interface*.

secondary DNS server   See *DNS server, secondary*.

security   The measures taken to secure a system against accidental or intentional loss, usually in the form of accountability procedures and use restriction, for example through NTFS permissions and share permissions.

Security Configuration and Analysis   A Windows 2000 utility used for creating security profiles and managing security settings across multiple machines.

Security groups   Active Directory objects that can contain users or other groups and that are used for the management and assignment of permissions. Users are placed into Security groups, and then permissions are granted to these groups. Security groups are considered to be security principals.

security identifier (SID)   A unique code that identifies a specific user or group to the Windows 2000 security system. SIDs contain a complete set of permissions for that user or group.

Security log   A log that tracks events that are related to Windows 2000 auditing. The Security log can be viewed through the Event Viewer utility.

security option policies   Policies used to configure security for the computer. Security option policies apply to computers rather than to users or groups. These policies are set through Local Computer Policy.

security principals   An Active Directory object that is used for the assignment and maintenance of security settings. The primary security principals are Users, Groups, and Computers.

security templates   Files used by the Security Configuration and Analysis tool for defining and enforcing security settings across multiple computers.

separator page   A page used at the beginning of each document to identify the user who submitted the print job. When users share a printer, separator pages can be useful for distributing print jobs.

serial   A method of communication that transfers data across a medium one bit at a time, usually adding stop, start and check bits to ensure quality transfer.

service   A process dedicated to implementing a specific function for another process. Most Windows 2000 components are services used by user-level applications.

Service group   A Windows 2000 special group that includes users who log on as a user account that is only used to run a service.

service pack   An update to the Windows 2000 operating system that includes bug fixes and enhancements.

Services   A Windows 2000 utility used to manage the services installed on the computer.

Setup Manager (SETUPMGR)   A Windows 2000 utility used to create automated installation scripts or unattended answer files.

SETUPMGR   See *Setup Manager*.

share   A resource such as a folder or printer shared over a network.

Shared Folder object   An Active Directory object that specifies the name and location of specific shared resources that are available to users of the Active Directory.

share permissions   Permissions used to control access to shared folders. Share permissions can only be applied to folders, as opposed to NTFS permissions, which are more complex and can be applied to folders and files.

shared folder   A folder on a Windows 2000 computer that network users can access.

Shared Folders   A Windows 2000 utility for managing shared folders on the computer.

shortcut   A quick link to an item that is accessible from a computer or network, such as a file, program, folder, printer, or computer. Shortcuts can exist in various locations including the Desktop, the Start menu, or within folders.

SID   See *security identifier*.

Simple Mail Transfer Protocol (SMTP)   A TCP/IP-based protocol that is primarily used for the exchange of Internet e-mail. SMTP can also be used by the Active Directory to manage intersite replication between domain controllers. See also *replication, intersite*.

simple volume   A dynamic disk volume that contains space from a single disk. The space from the single drive can be contiguous or noncontiguous. Simple volumes are used when the computer has enough disk space on a single drive to hold an entire volume.

Single Instance Store (SIS)   A feature of NTFS 5 that reduces the amount of disk space required to store files by eliminating redundancy of data. The SIS functionality is especially useful for creating images for use with Remote Installation Services (RIS). See also *Remote Installation Services (RIS)*.

Single Master Operations   Specific functions that must be managed within an Active Directory environment but are only handled by specific domain controllers. Some Single Master Operations are unique to each domain, and some are unique to the entire Active Directory forest.

SIS   See *Single Instance Store (SIS)*.

site   A collection of well-connected TCP/IP subnets. Sites are used for defining the topology of Active Directory replication.

site link   A link between two or more Active Directory sites. See also *site*.

site link bridge   A connection between two or more Active Directory site links. A site link bridge can be used to create a transitive relationship for replication between sites. See also *site* and *site link*.

Small Computer Systems Interface (SCSI)   A high-speed, parallel-bus interface that connects hard disk drives, CD-ROM drives, tape drives, and many other peripherals to a computer. SCSI is the mass-storage connection standard among all computers except IBM compatibles, which use SCSI or IDE.

SMTP   See *Simple Mail Transfer Protocol*.

snap-in   An administrative tool developed by Microsoft or a third-party vendor that can be added to the Microsoft Management Console (MMC) in Windows 2000.

spanned volume   A dynamic disk volume that consists of disk space on 2 to 32 dynamic drives. Spanned volume sets are used to dynamically increase the size of a dynamic volume. With spanned volumes, the data is written sequentially, filling space on one physical drive before writing to space on the next physical drive in the spanned volume set.

special group   A group used by the system, in which membership is automatic if certain criteria are met. Administrators cannot manage special groups.

spooler   A service that buffers output to a low-speed device such as a printer, so the software

outputting to the device is not tied up waiting for the device to be ready.

Start menu   A Windows 2000 Desktop item, located on the Taskbar. The Start menu contains a list of options and programs that can be run.

stripe set   A single volume created across multiple hard disk drives and accessed in parallel for the purpose of optimizing disk-access time. NTFS can create stripe sets.

striped volume   A dynamic disk volume that stores data in equal stripes between 2 to 32 dynamic drives. Typically, administrators use striped volumes when they want to combine the space of several physical drives into a single logical volume and increase disk performance.

subnet   A collection of TCP/IP addresses that define a particular network location. All of the computers within a subnet share the same group of TCP/IP addresses and have the same subnet mask.

subnet mask   A number mathematically applied to IP addresses to determine which IP addresses are a part of the same subnetwork as the computer applying the subnet mask.

Success Audit event   An Event Viewer event that indicates the occurrence of an event that has been audited for success, such as a successful logon.

Sysprep   See *System Preparation Tool*.

System group   A Windows 2000 special group that contains system processes that access specific functions as a user.

System Information   A Windows 2000 utility used to collect and display information about the computer's current configuration.

System log   A log that tracks events that relate to the Windows 2000 operating system. The System log can be viewed through the Event Viewer utility.

System Monitor   A Windows 2000 tool used for monitoring performance. The System Monitor includes chart, histogram, and report views.

system partition   The active partition on an Intel-based computer that contains the hardware-specific files used to load the Windows 2000 operating system.

system policies   Policies used to control what a user can do and the user's environment. System policies can be applied to all users or all computers, or to a specific user, group, or computer. System policies work by overwriting current settings in the Registry with the system policy settings. System policies are created through the System Policy Editor.

System Policy Editor   A Windows 2000 utility used to create system policies.

System Preparation Tool (Sysprep)   A Windows 2000 utility used to prepare a disk image for disk duplication.

System State   Information used to manage the configuration of a Windows 2000 operating system. For Windows 2000 domain controllers, the System State information includes a copy of the Active Directory data store. The

Windows 2000 Backup utility can be used to back up and restore the System State.

System Tools   A Computer Management utility grouping that provides access to utilities for managing common system functions. The System Tools utility includes the Event Viewer, System Information, Performance Logs and Alerts, Shared Folders, Device Manager, and Local Users and Groups utilities.

T

Task Manager   A Windows 2000 utility that can be used to quickly and easily obtain a snapshot of current system performance.

Task Scheduler   A Windows 2000 utility used to schedule tasks to occur at specified intervals.

Taskbar   A Windows 2000 Desktop item, which appears across the bottom of the screen by default. The Taskbar contains the Start menu and buttons for any programs, documents, or windows that are currently running on the computer. Users can switch between open items by clicking the item in the Taskbar.

TCP   See *Transmission Control Protocol.*

TCP/IP   See *Transmission Control Protocol/Internet Protocol.*

TCP/IP port   A logical port, used when a printer is attached to the network by installing a network card in the printer. Configuring a TCP/IP port requires the IP address of the network printer to connect to.

Terminal Server User group A Windows 2000 special group that includes users who log on through Terminal Services.

thread A list of instructions running in a computer to perform a certain task. Each thread runs in the context of a process, which embodies the protected memory space and the environment of the threads. Multithreaded processes can perform more than one task at the same time.

trace log A log file that can be created through the use of the Windows 2000 Performance tool. Trace logs record specific events and can be analyzed through the use of compatible utilities.

transformation file A type of file used by the Windows Installer to modify the behavior of the application-installation process.

transitive trust A trust relationship that allows for implicit trusts between domains. For example, if Domain A trusts Domain B and Domain B trusts Domain C, then Domain A implicitly trusts Domain C. See also *trust* and *two-way trust*.

Transmission Control Protocol (TCP) A Transport layer protocol that implements guaranteed packet delivery using the IP protocol.

Transmission Control Protocol/Internet Protocol (TCP/IP) A suite of Internet protocols upon which the global Internet is based. TCP/IP is a general term that can refer either to the TCP and IP protocols used together or to the complete set of Internet protocols. TCP/IP is the default protocol for Windows 2000.

Transport layer The Open Systems Interconnection (OSI) model layer responsible for the guaranteed serial delivery of packets between two computers over an internetwork. TCP is the Transport layer protocol in TCP/IP.

transport protocol A service that delivers discreet packets of information between any two computers in a network. Higher-level, connection-oriented services are built on transport protocols.

tree A set of Active Directory domains that share a common namespace and are connected by a transitive two-way trust. Resources can be shared between the domains in an Active Directory tree.

Trivial File Transfer Protocol Daemon (TFTPD) Used by Remote Installation Services (RIS) to transfer data to remote installation clients.

trust A relationship between domains that allows for the sharing of resources.

two-way trust A trust relationship in which two domains trust each other. For example, a two-way trust might involve Domain A trusting Domain B and Domain B trusting Domain A.

U

unattended installation A method of installing Windows 2000 Professional remotely with little or no user intervention. Unattended installation uses a distribution server to install Windows 2000 Professional on a target computer.

UNC   See *Universal Naming Convention.*

Uniform Resource Locator (URL)   An Internet standard naming convention for identifying resources available via various TCP/IP application protocols. For example, `http://www.microsoft.com` is the URL for Microsoft's World Wide Web server site, and `ftp://gateway.dec.com` is a popular FTP site. A URL allows easy hypertext references to a particular resource from within a document or mail message.

Universal group   An Active Directory Security or Distribution group that can contain members from, and be accessed from, any domain within an Active Directory forest. A domain must be running in native mode to use Universal groups.

Universally Unique Identifier (UUID)   A unique number used in newer PCs that can be used to identify a computer. The UUID can be used during the prestaging of clients for use with Remote Installation Services (RIS). See also *prestaging* and *Remote Installation Services (RIS).*

Universal Naming Convention (UNC)   A multivendor, multiplatform convention for identifying shared resources on a network. UNC names follow the naming convention `\\computername\sharename`.

upgrade   A method for installing Windows 2000 that preserves existing settings and preferences when converting to the newer operating system.

Upgrade Report   A report generated by the Setup program that summarizes any known compatibility issues that you might encounter during the upgrade. The Upgrade Report can be saved as a file or printed.

User object   An Active Directory object that is a security principal and that identifies individuals that can log on to a domain.

user profile   A profile that stores a user's Desktop configuration. A user profile can contain a user's Desktop arrangement, program items, personal program groups, network and printer connections, screen colors, mouse settings, and other personal preferences. Administrators can create mandatory profiles, which cannot be changed by the users, and roaming profiles, which users can access from any computer they log on to.

user rights policies   Policies that control the rights that users and groups have to accomplish network tasks. User rights policies are set through Local Computer Policy.

username   A user's account name in a logon-authenticated system.

Users group   A Windows 2000 built-in group that includes end users who should have very limited system access. After a clean installation of Windows 2000 Professional, the default settings for this group prohibit users from compromising the operating system or program files. By default, all users who have been created on the computer, except Guest, are members of the Users group.

Utility Manager A Windows 2000 utility used to manage the three accessibility utilities: Magnifier, Narrator, and On-Screen Keyboard.

V

video adapter The hardware device that outputs the display to the monitor.

virtual memory A kernel service that stores memory pages not currently in use on a mass-storage device to free the memory occupied for other uses. Virtual memory hides the memory-swapping process from applications and higher-level services.

virtual private network (VPN) A private network that uses links across private or public networks (such as the Internet). When data is sent over the remote link, it is encapsulated, encrypted, and requires authentication services.

volume A storage area on a Windows 2000 dynamic disk. Dynamic volumes cannot contain partitions or logical drives, and they are not accessible through DOS. Windows 2000 Professional dynamic storage supports three dynamic volume types: simple volumes, spanned volumes, and striped volumes.

VPN See *virtual private network*.

W

WAN See *wide area network*.

wide area network (WAN) A distributed network, typically connected through slow, and sometimes unreliable, links. The various sites that make up a WAN are typically connected through leased lines.

Warning event An Event Viewer event that indicates that you should be concerned with the event. The event may not be critical in nature, but it is significant and may be indicative of future errors.

Web browser An application that makes HTTP requests and formats the resultant HTML documents for the users. Most Web browsers understand all standard Internet protocols.

Win16 The set of application services provided by the 16-bit versions of Microsoft Windows: Windows 3.1 and Windows for Workgroups 3.11.

Win32 The set of application services provided by the 32-bit versions of Microsoft Windows: Windows 95, Windows 98, Windows NT, and Windows 2000.

Windows 9x The 32-bit Windows 95 and Windows 98 versions of Microsoft Windows for medium-range, Intel-based personal computers. This system includes peer networking services, Internet support, and strong support for older DOS applications and peripherals.

Windows 2000 Backup The Windows 2000 utility used to run the Backup Wizard, the Restore Wizard, and create an Emergency Repair Disk (ERD).

Windows 2000 boot disk A disk that can be used to boot to the Windows 2000 Professional operating system in the event of a Windows 2000 Professional boot failure.

Windows 2000 Multilanguage Version
The version of Windows 2000 that supports multiple-language user interfaces through a single copy of Windows 2000.

Windows 2000 Professional The current version of the Windows operating system for high-end desktop environments. Windows 2000 Professional integrates the best features of Windows 98 and Windows NT 4 Workstation, supports a wide range of hardware, makes the operating system easier to use, and reduces the cost of ownership.

Windows 2000 Professional Setup Boot Disks Floppy disks that can used to boot to the Windows 2000 operating system. With these disks, you can use the Recovery Console and the Emergency Repair Disk (ERD).

Windows Installer A Windows service that provides for the automatic installation of applications through the use of compatible installation scripts.

Windows Installer packages Special files that include the information necessary to install Windows-based applications.

Windows Internet Name Service (WINS)
A network service for Microsoft networks that provides Windows computers with Internet numbers for specified NetBIOS computer names, facilitating browsing and intercommunication over TCP/IP networks.

Windows NT The predecessor to Windows 2000 that is a 32-bit version of Microsoft Windows for powerful Intel, Alpha, PowerPC, or MIPS-based computers. This operating system includes peer networking services, server networking services, Internet client and server services, and a broad range of utilities.

Windows NT File System (NTFS) See *New Technology File System (NTFS)*.

Windows Script Host (WSH) A utility for running scripts on Windows-based computers. By default, WSH includes support for the VBScript and JScript languages. Through the use of third-party extensions, scripts can be written in other languages.

Windows Update A utility that connects the computer to Microsoft's Web site and checks the files to make sure that they are the most up-to-date versions.

WINS See *Windows Internet Name Service*.

WINS server The server that runs WINS and is used to resolve NetBIOS names to IP addresses.

WMI Control A Windows 2000 utility that provides an interface for monitoring and controlling system resources. WMI stands for Windows Management Instrumentation.

workgroup In Microsoft networks, a collection of related computers, such as those used in a department, that do not require the uniform security and coordination of a domain. Workgroups are characterized by decentralized management, as opposed to the centralized management that domains use.

write-back caching   A caching optimization wherein data written to the slow store is cached until the cache is full or until a subsequent write operation overwrites the cached data. Write-back caching can significantly reduce the write operations to a slow store because many write operations are subsequently obviated by new information. Data in the write-back cache is also available for subsequent reads. If something happens to prevent the cache from writing data to the slow store, the cache data will be lost.

write-through caching   A caching optimization wherein data written to a slow store is kept in a cache for subsequent rereading. Unlike write-back caching, write-through caching immediately writes the data to the slow store and is therefore less optimal but more secure.

Z

ZAP files   Files that can be used with Windows Installer packages instead of Microsoft Installer (MSI) format files. ZAP files are used to install applications using their native Setup program.

zone   A portion of the DNS namespace that is managed by a specific group of DNS servers.

zone, forward lookup   See *forward lookup zone*.

zone, reverse lookup   See *reverse lookup zone*.

zone transfer   The synchronization of information between DNS servers that are responsible for servicing the same DNS zone.

Index

Throughout this index **boldfaced** page numbers indicate primary discussions of a topic. *Italicized* page numbers indicate illustrations.

D

H

J

K

O

Q

R

U

V

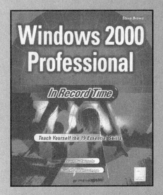

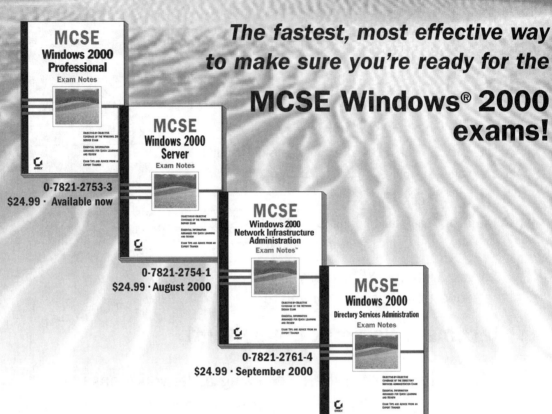

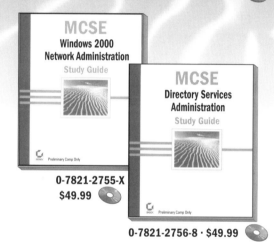
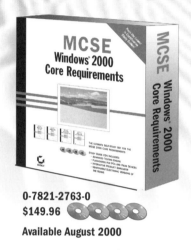

MCSE: Windows 2000 Directory Services Administration Study Guide
Exam 70-217: Objectives

SYBEX